Stoking the Fire

Stoking the Fire

Nationhood in Cherokee Writing, 1907–1970

Kirby Brown

University of Oklahoma Press : Norman

Published through the Recovering Languages and Literacies of the Americas initiative, supported by the Andrew W. Mellon Foundation

An earlier version of chapter 1 appeared as "Citizenship, Land, and Law: Constitutional Criticism in John Milton Oskison's *Black Jack Davy*," *Studies in American Indian Literatures* 23, no. 4 (2011): 27–53, published by the University of Nebraska Press. It is used here by permission.

Library of Congress Cataloging-in-Publication Data

Name: Brown, Kirby, 1974– author.
Title: Stoking the fire : nationhood in Cherokee writing, 1907–1970 / Kirby Brown.
Description: Norman : University of Oklahoma Press, 2018. | Includes bibliographical references and index.
Identifiers: LCCN 2017055609| ISBN 978-0-8061-6015-3 (hardcover : alk. paper) | ISBN 978-0-8061-6016-0 (pbk. : alk. paper)
Subjects: LCSH: American literature—Indian authors—History and criticism. | American literature—20th century—History and criticism. | Cherokee Indians—Intellectual life. | Nationalism in literature. | Cherokee Indians in literature.
Classification: LCC PS153.I52 B76 2018 | DDC 810.9/897—dc23
LC record available at https://lccn.loc.gov/2017055609

RECOVERING LANGUAGES & LITERACIES OF THE AMERICAS

Stoking the Fire: Nationhood in Cherokee Writing, 1907–1970 is published as part of the Recovering Languages and Literacies of the Americas initiative. Recovering Languages and Literacies is generously supported by the Andrew W. Mellon Foundation.

The paper in this book meets the guidelines for permanence and durability of the Committee on Production Guidelines for Book Longevity of the Council on Library Resources, Inc. ∞

1 2 3 4 5 6 7 8 9 10

For my grandfather, Henry George Starr; my mother, Sharon Starr Sneed; and generations of Cherokees past, present, and future who continue to stoke the fire

And for Katharine, who after all these years still makes me laugh, gives me strength, and loves me ferociously in spite of myself; this book would not exist without you

Contents

Illustrations

Figures

Map

Preface

In 2008 I was invited to present research on Cherokee writer, educator, activist, and intellectual Ruth Muskrat Bronson at the Sequoyah History Symposium, which was being held on the campus of Northeastern State University, the historic site of the Cherokee Female Seminary in the Cherokee capital of Tahlequah. Though I had presented work at academic conferences previously, this would be the first time that the audience would be full of Cherokee intellectual and cultural authorities, some of whom I had come to know and many of whose work had influenced my own. Because I was in the early stages of my research, I was eager to hear whether I was on the right track, asking the right questions, consulting the right texts, drawing the right conclusions. It was also an important moment for me because members of my family had returned to Tahlequah, just south of my grandfather's birthplace in Rose community, to hear my work for the first time. That former principal chief Wilma Mankiller was scheduled to speak immediately before my talk only heightened the stakes.[1]

The audience was warm and receptive, directing me to consider important questions about Bronson's family history, the place and community of her birth, her political and cultural affiliations, and other indexes by which Cherokees reckon identity and belonging. As they continued to inquire more about Bronson's life and work, it became clear that few of those in attendance were familiar with her or the other figures I was studying. Toward the end of the session, one local Cherokee woman commented on the lack of general information on the early twentieth century, referring to it as a "dark age" in contemporary Cherokee history.[2]

This formulation stuck with me, and as I got further into my research, I began to see just how accurately it captured the state of the existing scholarly archive on the period. A wealth of studies examine Cherokee life from the eighteenth century through the Removal of the 1830s and into the "golden age" of the 1850s and '60s;[3] the chaos and destruction of the Civil War and Reconstruction in the 1860s and '70s;[4] the push toward allotment and tribal dissolution in the late nineteenth and early twentieth centuries;[5] and tribal reorganization from the late 1960s through the present.[6] However, only a single published book and a few other chapters, essays, and dissertations touch on the period between Oklahoma statehood in 1907 and the political reorganization of the Nation later in the century.[7] Of these, most gloss the period as an uneventful, if not regrettable, way station on the way to the contemporary moment of sovereignty and self-determination.

In these and other studies, allotment is so devastating, statehood so catastrophic that even the possibility of Cherokees continuing to imagine themselves as a national community becomes unthinkable. The years that follow are thus left as an unqualified (and unexplored) rupture, while Cherokee nationhood languishes in the lamented "Chief for a Day" era. To be fair, not all studies draw such conclusions. Works by Circe Sturm, Virginia Carney, Daniel Justice, James Parins, and Joshua Nelson overtly work to establish continuities between Cherokee pasts and presents.[8] As crucially important as these studies are for demonstrating the longevity, continuity, and resilience of Cherokee political, intellectual, and cultural life, they nonetheless structure that continuity largely in terms of ambivalence or elision, either by situating the period within frameworks of uneasy endurance or by skipping over the first few decades of the twentieth century entirely.[9] As a result, the early twentieth century remains an understudied and often misunderstood moment in Cherokee history, producing the "dark-age" absence and neglect that were noted by the audience member above.[10]

While these dynamics largely organize the scholarly archive on early twentieth-century Cherokee life, Cherokee nationhood, I soon came to see, was all over the literary and intellectual archives I was reading. The lives and writings of two prominent Cherokees from this period—Jesse Bartley Milam and William Penn Adair "Will" Rogers—evidence precisely these commitments, though in different ways and to different ends.

As former Cherokee principal chief Ross Swimmer notes, Milam's story is in large part the story of Cherokee history from the late nineteenth through the mid-twentieth century.[11] Because of Civil War violence in Indian Territory, Milam was born outside of the Cherokee Nation in Italy, Texas, in 1884 to Sarah Ellen Couch (Cherokee) and William Guinn Milam.[12] After returning to the Cherokee Nation in 1887, he attended the Cherokee Male Seminary in Tahlequah before graduating from a Dallas area business school and launching successful petroleum and banking enterprises. In 1906, at the height of efforts to resist the dissolution of tribal governments and to forestall Oklahoma statehood, Milam married Cherokee citizen Elizabeth Peach McSpadden with whom he later had two daughters and a son. In addition to having business acumen, Milam was a voracious reader of Cherokee history, an advocate for Cherokee legal claims, and a central figure in Cherokee political reorganization throughout the early twentieth century.[13] In 1938, at a time when chiefs were unilaterally appointed by the U.S. executive in order to facilitate legal, political, and administrative actions related to land claims, he was elected principal chief by a diverse body of Cherokee people.[14] Milam was later confirmed by Presidents Roosevelt and Truman and continued to serve as principal chief until his passing in 1949.

Milam's papers and twelve hundred–volume library reflect his commitment not only to Cherokee politics and history but also to Indian affairs more broadly. Perhaps most significant is the enormous amount of material related to Cherokee political reorganization from the 1930s until Milam's death in 1949, as well as transcripts of oral accounts relating to Cherokee history and culture and newspaper clippings about Cherokee writers, artists, artisans, and others who would be recognized today as Cherokee National Treasures. As a patron, Milam privately funded Emmet Starr's extensive genealogical and historical research, which eventually became the now foundational *History of the Cherokee Indians, and Their Legends and Folklore* (1921), and he commissioned Cherokee novelist, biographer, and intellectual John Milton Oskison to write a biography of Cherokee chief John Ross (1923). His correspondence also includes periodical ephemera and reference materials on a variety of tribal nations; programs and press clippings from local Indian expositions, commencement exercises, and other gatherings; and significant exchanges with academics, politicians, and lobbyists in Indian affairs.[15]

If the balance of his correspondence reflects a man deeply committed to Cherokee and Indian issues, his library captures the sweeping intellectual contexts of the first half of the twentieth century that informed those commitments. Alongside crucial texts in Cherokee literary and political histories—including the texts by John Milton Oskison and Rachel Caroline Eaton that are examined here—sit works by Indian Territory writers such as Alexander Posey and John Joseph Mathews.[16] Also included are volumes by national Indian figures such as George Copway, Charles Eastman, Luther Standing Bear, Zitkála-Šá, and other Red Progressives, as well as tracts by non-Indian reformists and multiple works by widely read historians, sociologists, anthropologists, and folklorists of his time.[17] Coupled with drawers full of documents relating to matters of federal Indian policy and his work with the National Congress of American Indians are catalogs of items photocopied from national, regional, and local collections, which highlight the centrality of archival research to Milam's intellectual and political projects.[18]

While Milam coordinated reorganization efforts at home and Indian organization efforts nationally, William Penn Adair "Will" Rogers launched into stardom as a globetrotting entertainer, radio personality, film star, and internationally syndicated columnist.[19] A contemporary of Milam's, Rogers was born in 1879 to Clement Vann Rogers and Mary America Schrimsher Rogers on the family's ranch on the Verdigris and Caney rivers, outside the settlement of Oolagah in Cooweescoowee district in the Cherokee Nation. The Rogers family, whose members were from prominent Old Settler slave-owning families, was part of a wider class of agricultural elites, a reality which lent relative security and comfort to Will's childhood but also situated him in the complicated racial politics of nineteenth-century Cherokee life. He attended various private schools throughout the Nation and was able to get an early sense for the wider world through travels to stockyards in the Midwest with his father and to annual intertribal Indian fairs in Muskogee and from numerous tribally produced newspapers that existed throughout Indian Territory. It was through such newspapers that he likely honed his sharp yet good-natured humor and signature "aw, shucks" rhetorical style.[20]

In 1902 Rogers left the family's "White House on the Verdigris" and traveled to Argentina, hoping to continue the romantic ranching life that had defined his youth but was becoming increasingly impossible in allotment-era Indian Territory. Unsuccessful, Rogers returned to the States and began a twenty-year career as an entertainer and trick roper in Texas Jack's Wild West Show and later as a headliner for the Ziegfeld Follies. From the late 1910s through the 1930s Rogers starred in more than seventy silent films, hosted a weekly national radio broadcast, authored more than four thousand syndicated newspaper articles, and even launched a fictional presidential campaign that drew the attention (and more than a little concern) of his fellow Democrat Franklin Delano Roosevelt. At the time of his death, in a plane crash with Wiley Post at Point Barrow, Alaska, in 1935, Rogers was widely regarded as America's favorite son at home and was admired abroad for his honest wit and sharp critique of the multiple ways America failed to live up to its own ideals.

Like Milam's papers and library, the body of Rogers's writing evidences eclectic interests in social and political currents that were anchored both in the Cherokee people and places of his youth as well as in the wider world in which he moved. A dogged advocate for the average man, Rogers often targeted social, political, and economic elites—from lawyers and captains of industry to state governors, U.S. congressmen, and sitting presidents—for oppressive working conditions, self-interested hypocrisies, and failures to implement policies for the working class and the poor. He was also a tireless critic of U.S. imperialist ventures into Alaska, Puerto Rico, Hawai'i, Cuba, and the Philippines, which he often explicitly framed as extensions of the dispossession and violence embedded in U.S. federal Indian policy and ongoing issues throughout Indian Country—from appropriations of Apache lands for public works dam projects to the widespread poverty and destitution at Pine Ridge, to the lack of Indian political representation in state and federal governments.[21] In these moments, Rogers often laid waste to the unholy marriage between Christianity, American commerce, and U.S. history, pointing to the violence and dispossession that motivated America's Puritan ancestors, oft-revered Founding Fathers, and populist heroes such as "Old Andy" Jackson. As Daniel Justice, Tol Foster, and Amy Ware have documented, these and other interests were, for Rogers, deeply embedded in the historical, political, and cultural contexts of his early life in the Cherokee Nation and in Indian Territory more broadly, contexts which travelled with him and deeply informed how he understood the world and his place in it.[22]

Milam's and Rogers's lives and work present two paths that Cherokees might have followed in the wake of statehood—one *rooted* in commitments to political reorganization at home, the other *routed* through the emergent mobilities, technologies, forms, and expanding social relations attending modernity, and both *grounded* in the people, places, and histories that continued to define contemporary Cherokee life. Thus, while it might be accurate to say that the Cherokee *Nation* entered a roughly sixty-year period of political dormancy following Oklahoma statehood in 1907, Cherokee *nationhood* remained very much a part of how Cherokees from this period continued to understand themselves and the multiple worlds in and across which they moved. Milam and Rogers were hardly disconnected Cherokees wandering through the darkness of poststatehood absence and loss; rather, we might better understand them as former Cherokee citizens who, in their own ways, spent their lives stoking the fires of Cherokee nationhood across one of the most confusing and chaotic periods of Cherokee and American Indian history.

They were not alone.

Acknowledgments

Writing this book is one of the hardest and most rewarding things I have ever done, and it goes without saying that it never would have seen the light of day without the encouragement, support, and love shown to me by more people than I will ever be able to thank here.

I want to begin by extending enormous gratitude to Alessandra Tamulevich, Emily Schuster, Abby Graves, and the University of Oklahoma Press for their grace, guidance, generosity, and patience as they helped shape this project into the book it is today and marshaled its sometimes obsessive author through the ins and outs of publication. The two anonymous reviewers provided incisive readings of the original manuscript and on-point suggestions for revision. It is without question a stronger book as a result. Any errors or other mistakes are entirely my own.

Fellowships, grants, and other funding from the American Council of Learned Societies, the Harry Ransom Center for the Humanities at the University of Texas at Austin, the Oregon Humanities Center, the University of Oregon Office of the Vice President for Research and Innovation, and the University of Oregon English Department provided invaluable resources, time, and financial support, without which the project never could have gotten off the ground.

I also want to recognize the incredible research librarians who pointed me to archival materials that proved crucial to the project: Dolores Sumner, special collections librarian from Northeastern State University in Tahlequah; Kirby Tickel from Northern Oklahoma College in Tonkawa; Marc Carlson from special collections and university archives at the McFarlin Library at the University of Tulsa; Jacquelyn Slater, assistant professor of bibliography and librarian at the Western History Collection at the University of Oklahoma; Stephen Graggert from the Will Rogers Memorial in Claremore; the Claremore Museum of History (formerly the Lynn Riggs Memorial); and Victoria Helwig from the archives and special collections at Mount Holyoke College.

I have been incredibly fortunate to have the privilege of working alongside amazing mentors, colleagues, and friends who have had an enormous impact on my life. Ioannis Vassiliou and Mekonnen Haile from San Antonio Community College introduced a young, twenty-something-year-old bartender taking night classes and looking to do something more with his life to the excitement and importance of literary and cultural studies. At the University of Texas at San Antonio, Jeanne Reesman, Mark Allen, Bonnie Lyons, and the late Kenneth Hovey patiently assisted a biology undergrad in getting his bearings in the humanities while providing much-needed guidance along the way. Norma Cantú, Sonia Saldívar-Hull, Mona Narain, and Marian Aitches held my feet to fire of critical theory and exposed me to the power and passion of politically committed, community-driven research, teaching, and mentorship. Rachel Bell, Brad Adams, Patricia Trujillo, Lori Rodriguez, Marco Cervantez, Venetia Pedraza, Jeff Turpin, Larissa Mercado-Lopez, Linda Winterbottom, and Terri Pantuso provided good-humored collegiality in helping me navigate the early pressures of graduate school and kept me somewhat sane while I was trying to find my way. *¡Mil gracias por todo!*

At the University of Texas at Austin, Liz Cullingford and the late Wayne Lesser took a chance on a midyear graduate transfer and never once balked at the eclectic program of work that I proposed upon my arrival. Coursework with José Limón, John González, James Cox, and the late Barbara Harlow pushed me into ever more sophisticated critical terrain and consistently reaffirmed the stakes of the work I was doing. My dissertation committee of James Cox, John González, Domino Perez, Circe Sturm, and Daniel Justice was about as supportive a committee as I ever could have imagined. I hope that I am able to be half the mentor, teacher, advocate, and friend to my graduate students as you were for me. To my collaborators and writing partners in crime—Katherine Young Evans, Amy Ware, Amanda Moulder, Bryan Russell, Lydia French, Alberto Varón, Andrew Uzendoski, Colleen Eils, Kimberly Huyser, Kyle McGaa, and James Jenkins—I would not be here without you! For their camaraderie, friendship, and fellowship, I also want to thank everyone involved with Great Promise for American Indians and the Austin Powwow, including

Pascal Regimbeau, Lee Walters, Al Mouse, Jess Mouse, Anthony Mouse, David Hoskins, Ursula Pike, Susie Mireles, Barbara Woelk, Lois Duncan, Robbie Bass, Mario Garza, Maria Rocha, Ken McKenzie-Grant, Wilda Won, Gene Randall, Jay Hurst, Gene Nashoba Thompson, and Diane Tigges.

The English department at the University of Oregon has been incredibly supportive of my research, teaching, and programming over the past five years. Much appreciation to Courtney Thorsson, Priscilla Ovalle, Mark Quigley, Paul Peppis, Bill Rossi, Sharon Luk, Sarah Wald, Quinn Miller, Harry Wonham, Stephanie Clark, Mark Whalan, Lee Rumbarger, David Vázquez, Tres Pyle, Sangita Gopal, Mary Wood, Betsy Wheeler, Gordon Sayre, Karen Ford, and so many others for taking me in, showing me the ropes, having my back, and reminding me to breathe from time to time. Thanks also to Dan Hosang, Lynn Fujiwara, Ernesto Martínez, Michael Hames-Garcia, Cherise Cheney, Alai Reyes-Santos, Brian Klopotek, Lani Teves, Joe Lowdes, Priscilla Yamin, Loren Kajikawa, Donella Elizabeth-Alston, and everyone in Ethnic Studies, who have opened their arms and provided me another intellectual and political home on campus.

A special debt of gratitude goes out to the faculty, staff, and students of the Native Strategies Group, who volunteer time, energy, and resources that they do not often possess to make things happen for Native people and Native American initiatives on campus. For Brian Klopotek, Jennifer O'Neal, Lani Teves, Michelle Jacob, Kari Noorgard, Jan Smith, Leilani Sabzalian, Scott Pratt, Theresa May, Gordon Bettles, Kathy Lynn, Stephanie Tabibian, Cholena Wright, Chance White Eyes, Angie Morrill, Derrick Hindery, Melina Pastos, Burke Hendrix, and the students of NASU and NALSA—I can't imagine life at the U of O without you, and I am so grateful for your dedication, optimism, friendship, and fellowship. *nkena!*

From the moment I entered the field of Native American and Indigenous Studies, I have been blessed with incredible colleagues and friends whose work and friendship invigorate and sustain me. It has been particularly rewarding to get to know so many Cherokee scholars, including Jace Weaver, Daniel Justice, Chris Teuton, Sean Teuton, Jeff Corntassel, Clint Carroll, Jody Kehle, Ellen Cushman, Tom Holm, Julia Coates, Linda Dixon, Candessa Teehee, Courtney Lewis, Patti Jo King, Les Hannah, Karen Sunday, Kathryn England-Aytes, and Joshua Nelson. A special thanks goes to Richard Allen, who invited me to participate in my first conference panel, brought me to the Cherokee Nation to present my early research, and introduced me to many of the people listed here. In a very real way, many of my intellectual and personal relationships to Cherokee scholars are one-degree removed from Richard's mentorship. *Wado,* Richard!

I am also super excited and honored to have the incredible Roy Boney contribute original illustrations and cover art for the book, both of which provide an artistic complement to my own contemporary treatments of these writers and texts. A host of other colleagues have gifted me with intellectual, spiritual, and emotional medicine over the years, including Chad Allen, Susan Bernardin, Lisa Tatonetti, Beth Piatote, Craig Womack, Kyle Powys-Whyte, David Carlson, James Mackay, Dustin Tahmahkera, Joanna Hearne, Kevin Bruyneel, Circe Sturm, Leanne Howe, and Theo Van Alst. In addition to your amazing intellectual work, the casual conversations, wonderful meals, and belly laughter we have shared have meant the world to me. *Wado!*

At the end of the day, none of this would have been possible without the strength, support, and unconditional love I have received from my family. To my mom and dad, the best of what and who I am is because of you, and that is a debt I will never be able to repay. I try every day to make you proud of the son you raised. To my sisters, Andi, Ronda, and Shanna Deigh, I am a better man because of the strong, intelligent, generous, and loving women you are. I have always looked up to you and I always will. To all my beautiful nieces and nephews, being your uncle has brought more laughter, love, and joy to my life than you will ever know. I hope I have given a little of that back to you over the years in return. To my aunts, uncles, cousins, grandmothers, and grandfathers, I love all of you dearly and look forward to the next time we are all together, laughing and cutting up, whether in this life or in the next. And to Katharine . . . what can I say? You make me smile.

Stoking the Fire

INTRODUCTION

Recovering an Early Twentieth-Century Cherokee National Imaginary

After allotment, Cherokees no longer took the time to imagine a future for the Indian nation within America. That project would await later generations of Indian people in the new century.

Andrew Denson, Demanding the Cherokee Nation

Our literature is the textual testament to our endurance. . . . Cherokee literature speaks to the fact that the People are anything but "vanishing Indians." . . . With each addition to the Cherokee literary tradition, our living presence is renewed.

Daniel Justice, Our Fire Survives the Storm

It is more than metaphor to speak of our Cherokee creators as fire-bearers. Indeed, writers, thinkers, painters, weavers, sculptors as well as philosophers are in Cherokee thought the nation-bearers as well. They are those who combine their creative strengths to build and sustain the one fire that is Cherokee.

Rennard Strickland, Building One Fire

Stoking the Fire: Nationhood in Cherokee Writing, 1907–1970 critically examines how four contemporaries of J. B. Milam and Will Rogers negotiated the complicated politics of the period between Oklahoma statehood in 1907 and tribal reorganization in the early 1970s as Cherokees. In situating writings by Rachel Caroline Eaton (1869–1938), John Milton Oskison (1874–1947), Ruth Muskrat Bronson (1897–1982), and Rollie Lynn Riggs (1899–1954) explicitly within the Cherokee trans/national contexts of their emergence, this study explores the multiple and complicated ways these writers remembered, (re)imagined, and enacted Cherokee nationhood in the absence of a functioning Cherokee state. Writing in a historical moment when the idea of an Indian nation was popularly considered a contradiction in terms, Eaton, Oskison, Bronson, and Riggs turned to tribal histories and biographies; novels, short stories, and plays; and editorials and public addresses as alternative sites of negotiation, contestation, resistance, and critique. Refusing conventional narratives of assimilation and absence for those of survival and continuance, these writers variously invoke Cherokee nationhood as a sovereign literary territory, a counterhistorical site of oppositional critique, a dramatic stage on which to interrogate questions of blood and belonging, and an intellectual space of Indigenous trans/national diplomacy. Read together, these works inscribe a Cherokee national presence within academic discourses that often position Indian peoples as cultural relics *of* history rather than as political agents *in* history. *Stoking the Fire* resituates this period as a rich moment in Cherokee literary and intellectual production capable of informing critical debates over nationhood, community, identity, and belonging taking place in the Cherokee Nation and across Native Studies today.

Nationhood—defined here as the intersection of politics, peoplehood, imagination, and experience—structures this study in particular ways. Within Native Literary Studies, Indigenous nationhood has been theorized variously as the *unique legal and political status* of Indigenous peoples as preexisting extraconstitutional sovereigns possessing original and inherent rights to sovereignty and self-determination;[1] the *political expression* of the complex matrix of relations through which Native peoples reckon identity, relationality, and belonging;[2] the *rhetorical, representational, and discursive fields* through which Native peoples imagine, assert, and represent themselves in modernity as nation-peoples;[3] and a *critical practice/ethic* of responsible life and living grounded in lived relationships with and obligations to ancestral communities, territories, and traditions.[4] While each of these threads is present in various ways and to various extents throughout this study, the dissolution of the Cherokee government in 1907 necessitates that I focus mostly on the latter three. This is not to say that legal, political, and territorial questions of Cherokee state sovereignty are absent from the texts I examine. As I argue throughout the book, they are explicitly central to the narrative politics of Oskison's frontier romance and Eaton's revisionist history, and they implicitly inform Riggs's interrogation of postallotment blood politics and the trajectory of Bronson's intellectual and political life. Indeed, it is one of the claims of this study that in the absence of a state in which the legal and political status of nationhood is invested and exercised, literary, intellectual, and cultural production constitute important sites where the past, present, and future of the nation/national community might be recovered, remembered, (re)examined, (re)imagined, enacted, and critiqued.

In taking this approach, I draw on an expanding body of scholarship that explicitly situates literary and intellectual production as crucial sites for the exercise of tribal sovereignty and the ongoing expression of tribal nationhood. Acknowledging that "literature can and does successfully contribute to the politics of possession and dispossession," Elizabeth Cook-Lynn highlights "the political reality of the imagination . . . [as] a major component of nationalism" and calls on writers and critics to attend to "the body of nationalistic myths, legends, metaphors, symbols, historical persons and events" of specific tribal nations.[5] Craig Womack, in his foundational study of Creek literary nationalism *Red on Red,* similarly positions Indigenous nationhood at the "intersection of the political, imaginary, and literary." He writes, "A key component of nationhood is a people's idea of themselves, their imaginings of who they are. . . . The ongoing expression of a tribal voice, through imagination, language, and literature, contributes to keeping sovereignty alive in the citizens of a nation."[6] Daniel Justice understands Cherokee literature in analogous terms as "both a product and an extension of our nationhood; to assert oneself as a Cherokee is to locate oneself in relationship to all these complex and multidimensional discourses—stories—of community." Lisa Brooks similarly links Indigenous oral, literary, and legal traditions in a "continental tradition" of the "creative imagination of nationhood" through which Indigenous peoples continually reimagine who and what they are.[7] Drawing on Gerald Vizenor's concepts of survivance and transmotion—an active *postindian* presence that is always on the move, always imagining, always becoming—Jill Doerfler situates oral, literary, and legal traditions as central to Anishinaabe understandings of nationhood and belonging. "We create and recreate ourselves in the past, present, and future in story," Doerfler claims. "We carry the power to create a nation that honors ancestors and also envisions an everlasting future."[8] While these scholars rightly caution against conflating Indigenous *political* sovereignty with the kinds of *literary, intellectual,* and *representational* sovereignties that are mapped out here, they nonetheless acknowledge, to borrow from Jace Weaver, that while "the struggle may be land and sovereignty, . . . it is often reflected, contested, and decided in narrative."[9] As Richard Scott Lyons, Maureen Konkle, and Chris Anderson have persuasively argued, it is precisely through these public imaginings of tribal nationhood that Native peoples contest racialized colonial narratives of savagery and vanishing by staking explicitly political claims to modernity as contemporary nation-peoples.[10]

More than an imagined community constituted through discourse, Indigenous nationhood also speaks to the complex matrix of historical, cultural, geographic, and relational dynamics of Indigenous peoplehood and to the multiple ways in which Native peoples reckon identity, community, and belonging. Vine Deloria Jr. and Clifford Lytle note, for instance, that "in almost every treaty . . . the concern of the Indians was the preservation of the people" rather than the political state, an orientation which leads Lyons, following Taiaiake Alfred, to conceive of Indigenous nations less as centralized coercive states privileging individual rights and bureaucratic proceduralism and more as "nation-peoples" whose "supreme charge [is] the sovereignty of the group through a privileging of its traditions and culture and continuity."[11] Cook-Lynn similarly grounds her strident emphasis on legal and political nationhood in the geographies, histories, spiritualities, and languages of specific tribal nations, while Justice understands Cherokee nationhood as being partially rooted in "the tribal web of kinship rights *and* responsibilities that link the People, the land, and the cosmos together in an ongoing and dynamic system of mutually affecting relationships."[12] Referring to Abenaki norms of political identity and belonging, Brooks frames Indigenous nationhood as "a process of gathering from within" via "the ongoing relationship and responsibility to land and kin," an understanding that is also evident in Doerfler's work on Anishinaabe nationhood and citizenship.[13] While we might follow Justice in understanding Indigenous nationhood as "the political expression of the social rights and responsibilities of peoplehood," Clint Carroll usefully reminds us that nationhood and peoplehood represent two "distinct ideas of community," which overlap but do not map neatly onto one another.[14] Whereas nationhood is primarily legal, political, territorial, and externally directed toward other states, peoplehood is cultural, relational, spiritual, and largely internally directed toward interpersonal relations within specific Indigenous communities, a tension that Scott Lyons has discussed in detail elsewhere.[15] The utility of Carroll's observation is not in its capacity to neatly reconcile these terms but in understanding them (to borrow again from Weaver) as "bound together in a . . . stomp dance in which everyone is always an integral part of the circle."[16] As an assertion of contemporary political identity animated by tribally specific dynamics of peoplehood, Indigenous nationhood captures this at times tense interplay between the legal-political and cultural-experiential.

Bringing these threads together, *Stoking the Fire* understands Indigenous nationhood as the messy, complicated, often-contested but ultimately generative intersection where Indigenous politics, imagination, peoplehood, and experience meet, mix it up, and sometimes collide. By framing nationhood as an active site of imagination and contestation, I acknowledge the many practical and theoretical problems that nationalism and sovereignty pose for Indigenous peoples. As racialized discourses of settler-colonial power and domination, both nationalism and sovereignty have been used to deny the legitimacy of Indigenous social, cultural, and political institutions. From doctrines of discovery and conquest to legal fictions of domestic dependency and plenary power, settler states have long mobilized Eurocentric understandings of nationhood and sovereignty as instruments of dispossession and elimination, denying Indigenous political presence and domesticating Indigenous bodies, nations, and lands as internal to the U.S. state.[17] Because of the tendency of nationalism to centralize power in the bureaucratic apparatus of the state, combined with the fundamentally coercive nature of sovereignty as a norm of political authority, many rightly question the utility of such concepts to address the immediate needs of Indigenous communities or to bring about larger decolonization and liberation movements. When internalized within tribal communities, these dynamics are even more destructive. Whether in the epidemic of disenrollment, the denial of citizenship to freedmen descendants, the illegalization of same-sex marriage, the refusal to provide adequate facilities for women's health, or the overreach of repressive tribal governments, nationalism presents significant challenges for tribal communities that seek to protect their political and legal interests while avoiding the baggage of coercion, racism, heterosexism, and xenophobia that often accompanies them.

While I am intensely attuned to such issues and deal with them explicitly in the chapters that follow, I remain committed to the politics of nationhood—problematic as it is—not as an end in itself but as what Scott Lyons calls an X-mark, an accession to modernity made from within a coercive context (settler colonialism) and discourse (nationalism/sovereignty) not of our own making but in hopes that something good might come of it. Because I was reminded recently that it is always better to show than to tell, let me use the rest of the introduction to more concretely model what I am trying to get at. History is always a good place to start.

✶ ✶ ✶ ✶ ✶ ✶ ✶

Only decades removed from the Trail Where We Cried, each of the writers examined here was born as a citizen into the Cherokee Nation between 1869 and 1899, a period that was bookended on one end by the devastating aftermath of the Civil War and on the other by increasing assaults on tribal sovereignty by industrial interests, territorial advocates, and proponents of allotment and assimilation. As numerous scholars have shown, the arrival of the Civil War to Indian Territory devastated the Cherokee Nation, reigniting Removal-era animosities and exacerbating long-developing class and cultural tensions, which remain with us to this day. As Cherokees attempted to recover and rebuild, repeated crop failures, unstable revenues, and a postabolition labor shortage frustrated reconstruction programs and prevented the government from meeting basic needs of Cherokee families. The exploitation of Cherokee labor and naturalization laws, the entry of U.S. railroads into Cherokee territories, and the federal inability to police its own citizens led to spurious claims to Cherokee citizenship and increasing problems with intruders. Efforts by the Cherokee government to regulate trade and immigration and to develop its own ranching, agricultural, and industrial economies were repeatedly thwarted by competing corporate interests and the federal courts. Persistent conflicts over the citizenship status and civil rights of Cherokee freedmen, resettled Indians, and others who failed to meet the deadline of return intensified jurisdictional confusion and invited federal intervention. The rising influence of assimilationist "Friends of the Indian" reformists and a series of related court decisions and legislative actions during the waning decades of the nineteenth century further subjected tribal governments to increasing federal control.

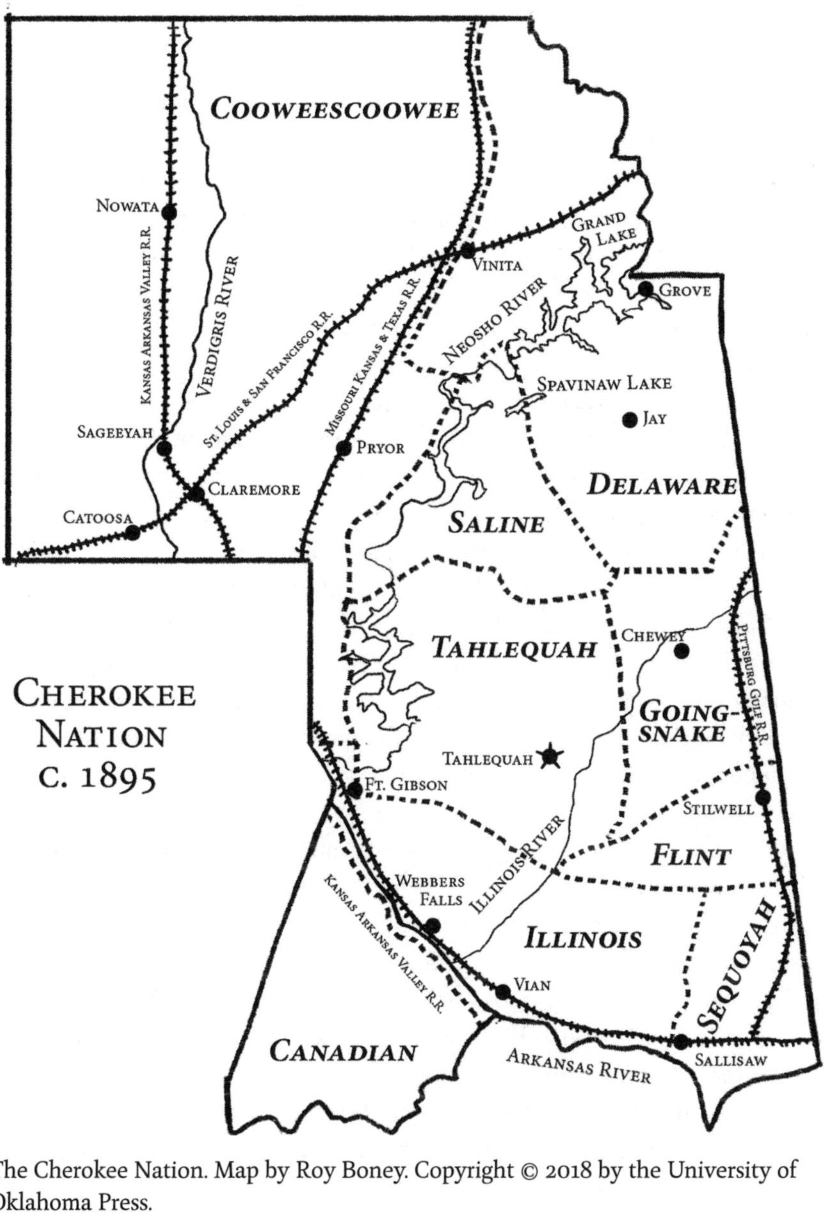

The Cherokee Nation. Map by Roy Boney. Copyright © 2018 by the University of Oklahoma Press.

Neither the Cherokee Nation nor the other Indian Territory governments took these measures lying down. Though some advocated for immediate dissolution and statehood, the vast majority of Cherokees—both conservatives and progressives alike—opposed such measures. Cherokee statesmen, journalists, and diplomats levied strong counterarguments in local newspapers, petitions to Congress, political negotiations, and legal defenses of Cherokee sovereignty, often crossing conventional political and familial lines to do so. Culturally conservative and politically resistant communities, such as the Nighthawk Keetoowah Society, the Creek "Snakes," and the intertribal Four Mothers Society, organized resistance movements that were anchored to a resurgence of tribal cultural, spiritual, and political practices and took part in active—at times militant—disruptions of allotment proceedings. As pressure intensified with the organization of Oklahoma Territory in 1890 and with the extension of allotment policies over Indian Territory governments by the Curtis Act of 1898, delegates from the Five Tribes worked intertribally to adopt a constitution and to elect representatives for a separate Indian-governed State of Sequoyah. This innovative attempt to maintain tribal control fell on deaf ears.[18] On June 16, 1906, Congress passed an enabling act to join together the Oklahoma and Indian Territories. In October of that year Roosevelt declared that Oklahoma would be the newest state in the Union, thus bringing to an end an important "third space of sovereignty" in U.S. jurisprudence.[19]

Having twice rebuilt their families, communities, and nation, Cherokees once again found themselves unprotected by their own laws, institutions, and territories. As a result, many were subject to violence, coercion, dispossession, and impoverishment in what historian Angie Debo terms "an orgy of plunder and exploitation probably unparalleled in American history."[20] Gaming of the wardship system as well as discrepancies in the twenty-year trust period that was placed on allotted lands led to the loss of more than 90 percent of Cherokee allotments by 1934. Poverty, all but absent in many parts of the Nation during the years leading up to allotment, became endemic, leaving many Cherokees vulnerable to starvation, malnutrition, and disease.

Combined with the largely assimilationist underpinnings of federal and state policies, including assimilationist education in both Oklahoma public schools and Bureau of Indian Affairs–operated residential schools such as Chilocco Indian School in Oklahoma and Sherman Institute in California, such conditions radically disrupted Cherokee cultural and familial structures. This led more than half of the Nation's forty thousand citizens to seek educational and economic opportunities elsewhere in what Cherokee novelist and historian Robert Conley dubs "a second Trail of Tears."[21] Depression-era outmigrations, appropriations of restricted Cherokee lands for military expansion and public-works dam projects in the 1920s and '30s, and the passage of termination and relocation programs in the 1950s and '60s initiated what Wilma Mankiller characterizes as yet another forced removal of Cherokees into an increasingly urban diaspora away from their families, communities, and lands in northeastern Oklahoma.[22] The implications of these histories are evident today: of the more than 320,000 enrolled Cherokee citizens, at least two-thirds live outside the political boundaries of the Cherokee Nation, and it is estimated that fewer than eight thousand speak the language fluently. As the late Cherokee National Treasure and deputy principal chief Hastings Shade noted, such conditions constitute one understanding of this period as a "dark age" in Cherokee history.[23]

As children of mixed-race multicultural families, the writers studied here span the gamut of Cherokee culture, class, and politics across this period—from Old Settlers and Removal survivors to Southern sympathizers and antislavery nationalists, from subsistence farmers and large-scale industrialists to cultural resisters and allotment advocates, and from Texas Confederates and Missouri Unionists to English and Irish immigrants. Children of both native Cherokees by blood and intermarried white citizens who were naturalized under Cherokee constitutional law, they lived or held relations in both tightly knit, rural, Cherokee-speaking communities of extended families and in more nuclear-oriented families in the railroad boomtowns of Claremore and Vinita. Raised in and around both traditional and acculturated Cherokee households, they were also reared in both Cherokee- and English-speaking churches, educated in Cherokee and Oklahoma public and private schools, and exposed to a vibrant social, political, and intellectual life that was articulated primarily, though not exclusively, through Cherokee institutions. With the imposition of allotment policies on Indian Territory governments, which were stipulated in the Curtis Act of 1898, their families were enrolled and received allotments according to the terms set out by the Dawes Commission. This was a contentious moment in which some—like Bronson's father, James—found themselves at political odds with their friends and relations. While some of these lands remained in their families well into the twentieth century, others were mortgaged or sold in order to finance educational and economic opportunities elsewhere.

Whereas many Cherokees worked locally to hold their families and communities together in the wake of allotment, these writers followed Will Rogers's path and pursued educational and professional opportunities, which took them increasingly away from their tribal national home. Eaton leveraged a liberal education from the Cherokee Female Seminary and graduate degrees in history from the University of Chicago into a twenty-year career as a respected historian, educator, and administrator in a variety of institutions and school districts in Oklahoma, in Texas, and across the Midwest. Overcoming a disjointed early education that was interrupted by the backbreaking demands of agricultural life, Oskison capitalized on relationships he formed at Willie Halsell College, Stanford, and Harvard to launch a forty-year publishing career in some of the most prestigious literary and intellectual venues in the country, writing about everything from Oklahoma and national Indian issues, to technological development and international relations as well as numerous novels, short stories, and fictional biographies about life in Indian Territory. After stints at the Universities of Oklahoma and Kansas that were financed by the mortgage of her allotment, Bronson graduated from Mount Holyoke College in 1923 and began a five-decade career as an educator and public servant, which took her from the classrooms of Haskell and the halls of Congress to Alaskan courtrooms and kitchen tables throughout Indian Country. Riggs similarly leveraged his allotment to pay for his education at the University of Oklahoma before embarking on a career as a widely acknowledged poet, dramatist, and screenwriter, equally as comfortable in the modernist salons of Santa Fe and bright lights of Broadway as in the glitz and glamour of Hollywood and what was for him the cultural refuge of Mexico.

These movements and migrations connected these writers to the wider intellectual and political circles that informed Oklahoma Indian experience, and American Indian experience more broadly, during the first half of the twentieth century. Eaton was instrumental in founding historical societies in Tahlequah, Tulsa, and her hometown of Claremore, each of which was dedicated to historic and cultural preservation as well as to contesting erroneous images of Indian people in American popular culture. In recognition of this work, she was named "one of Oklahoma's outstanding women" and was posthumously honored as an inaugural member of the Oklahoma Hall of Fame by the Oklahoma Memorial Association.[24] Spending most of his life in the publishing mecca of New York City, Oskison became involved in national progressive and American Indian politics, first as a tenant and volunteer organizer for the University Settlement in Manhattan's East-Side Jewish ghetto and later as a founding member and executive secretary of the Society of American Indians, where he worked alongside other Red Progressives such as Arthur Parker, Charles Eastman, Laura Cornelius, Carlos Montezuma, Zitkála-Šá, and Henry Roe Cloud through the early 1920s. As an educator at Haskell Institute, a scholarship coordinator for the Bureau of Indian Affairs (BIA), and a founding member of the National Congress of American Indians, Bronson worked alongside other Indian scholar-educators, such as Ella Deloria, Henry Roe Cloud, and D'Arcy McNickle as well as fellow Cherokees J. B. Milam and N. B. Johnson, on a variety of projects ranging from education reform and Indian legal claims to economic development and lobbying efforts.[25] Arguably the most cosmopolitan of the bunch, Riggs moved in some of the most influential artistic and intellectual circles of the period, including Mable Dodge Luhan's Santa Fe literary salon and experimental theater companies like the Provincetown Players and the American Laboratory Theatre; he also ran with some of Hollywood's biggest stars, including Bette Davis, Joan Crawford, Gary Cooper, and Clark Gable to name but a few.[26]

While such trajectories might well have struck popular American audiences of the time as "anomalous" or "unexpected" expressions of contemporary Indian life, they are actually deeply embedded in Cherokee history.[27] Versions of the Cherokee *Elohi* narrative and accounts of popular rebellion against an oppressive priestly class, for instance, situate migration, movement, and social transformation as central to Cherokee oral histories.[28] Political and cultural migrations that took place in response to increasing pressures for assimilation and demands on Cherokee lands are documented in eighteenth-century transoceanic detachments to England; diplomatic engagements to colonial centers to the east and south in the United States, Texas, and Mexico; forays into eastern institutions of higher education; and the series of coercive removals throughout the nineteenth century. War service abroad, repeated economic crises, and relocation policies in the early twentieth century bring these narratives of movement and migration into the contemporary moment, further embedding Cherokees in the developing transnational political economies of an increasingly urbanizing and globalizing modernity. The reach of

Cherokee entertainers, artists, and writers—such as Will Rogers in print, radio, and cinema; Riggs in drama and film; Oskison in print; and Yvonne Chouteau in ballet—also locates Cherokees in the broader American cultural and consumer-driven milieu that was exploding in the early decades of the twentieth century.[29]

Of such movements Christopher Teuton writes, "We separate from our homelands, our communities, our kin and friends, and, of course, from our best selves. And we return home, reunite with each other, and reestablish connections with our communities and homeland. We learn something about the world, about diversity, and about each other in the process."[30] While I do not claim that the lives Oskison, Eaton, Bronson, and Riggs were able to carve out for themselves in the wake of statehood are representative of Cherokee experience during this period, they do mark familiar paths of departure and return that are grounded every bit as strongly in Cherokee history and experience as their emergences and origins in the Cherokee Nation and in northeastern Oklahoma.

By attending to the ways that these contexts inform the writers and texts examined here, *Stoking the Fire* amplifies recent work in Cherokee studies—much of it by Cherokee scholars—which has begun to present a much more energetic picture of life on the ground in the poststatehood era. As Rose Stremlau has shown, Cherokee families adapted customary kinship relations and commitments to community well-being, reciprocity, and hospitality in order meet the needs of their extended kin and to provide mutual aid to their communities throughout the allotment era and across numerous economic crises.[31] At the same time, Joshua Nelson highlights how cultural conservatives affiliated with the Keetoowah Society continued to mobilize dispositions toward inclusivity, flexibility, and innovation in order to revitalize Cherokee cultural and spiritual traditions at stomp grounds and to explore options for development, mutual aid, and self-sufficiency outside of BIA or Oklahoma state structures.[32] Ellen Cushman's work on the Cherokee language shows that while declining in speakers, the use of the Cherokee syllabary in family histories, church worship, personal communication, and local governance continued to function as an instrument of collective identity and political activism in many communities.[33] Clint Carroll similarly documents how Cherokees worked in a variety of venues on issues of environmental governance to contest federal and state land management practices that ignored treaty rights to land and resources.[34] Various Cherokee interest groups also came together during the 1920s to form the Cherokee Executive Council, which reestablished a council form of governance, elected a principal chief for the first time since before allotment, and began laying the groundwork for cultural revitalization and political reorganization later in the century.[35] Daniel Justice's, James Parins's, and Amy Ware's work on Cherokee intellectual production, along with Gregory Smithers's study of Cherokee diasporic experiences, remind us of a long and ongoing history of exiles, migrations, and returns—both physical and imaginative—across Cherokee tribal-national boundaries.[36] Although scholars rightly note that such efforts were not without significant tensions around race, class, culture, place, and politics—indeed, they are front and center in the texts studied here—they nonetheless reflect Mankiller's sense of the "tenacity" of Cherokee nationhood across the poststatehood period and into tribal reorganization in the 1970s.[37]

Stoking the Fire extends and amplifies these efforts by recovering an active Cherokee national imaginary at work in the public arena that runs parallel to and often overlaps these more localized efforts. Throughout his corpus Oskison focuses on subjects such as the backbreaking labor of agricultural life, debates over allotment and the threat of intruders and corporate interests to post–Civil War Cherokee sovereignty, and the complicated intersections of citizenship, land, and law. Explored in chapter 1, these themes are deeply resonant with late nineteenth- and early twentieth-century Cherokee experience as he lived it and later remembered and (re)presented it. Similarly, Eaton's strong critique of U.S. duplicity, graft, and corruption is grounded in a complex oppositional discourse and a long tradition of self-determined representation extending from late eighteenth-century treaty negotiations to nineteenth-century developments of Cherokee literacy and constitutional law to an extensive array of public speeches and writing that extends into the contemporary moment. Bronson's dedication to Indian education and youth leadership development reflects longstanding commitments to literacy and formal education in her own family, and in Cherokee history more broadly, while her forays into politics and activism are situated within a long, if neglected, tradition of Cherokee women's political and diplomatic influence. We might also do worse than read the complex, and at times devastating, social relations captured in many of Riggs's Indian Territory dramas—and especially in *The Cherokee Night*, which is examined here—less as endorsements of Indian bloodlust or pessimistic resignation than one Cherokee's attempt to contend with the chaotic aftermath of allotment and statehood during the early decades of the twentieth century. Cherokee nationhood exists in these texts as both a concrete literary presence and a conceptual framework through which the past, present, and future of the Nation is recollected, remembered, represented, and reimagined.

A central component of this reimagining, in the texts examined here and in the study as a whole, is the (re)centering of Cherokee women as central figures in Cherokee literary, intellectual, and political histories. While a great deal of ground has been made up to recover Native women more broadly since Rayna Green's and Paula Gunn Allen's early critiques of misrepresentation, erasure, and absence in the 1970s and '80s,[38] there still exists a surprising lack of attention to Cherokee women, an absence that reflects an explicitly gendered version of the "dark ages" discussed in the preface.[39] As numerous scholars have noted, the political shift from semiautonomous towns governed by matrilineal clan relations toward a more centralized constitutional government predicated in large part on Euro-American social and gender norms in the early nineteenth century increasingly marginalized Cherokee women from the political life of the Cherokee Nation.[40] While Theda Perdue and Joshua Nelson have importantly qualified these claims, pointing, for instance, to the ways Cherokee women continued to exert authority and influence through spirituality, agricultural practice, domestic economies, and familial social relations, one consequence of these shifts, as Virginia Carney discusses, has been the marginalization, and at times complete erasure, of Cherokee women from Cherokee literary and intellectual landscapes.[41] What work exists is typically restricted to late eighteenth- and early nineteenth-century petitions by Cherokee women, Catherine Brown's Christian conversion narrative, and scattered mentions of Cherokee Female Seminary students and individual writers such as Lucy Lowery Hoyt Keyes (1831–1912), Narcissa Owen (1831–1911), Mabel Washbourne Anderson (1863–1949), and Ora Eddleman Reed (1880–1968).[42] With the exception of Sarah Hill's analysis of Cherokee women's basketry, Carney's recovery of Eastern Band Cherokee women's writing, and Stremlau's gendered analysis of Cherokee family relations, Cherokee women are all but absent from the early twentieth century, even in texts authored by Cherokee scholars.[43]

My close reading of Eaton's *John Ross and the Cherokee Indians* and my recovery of many of Bronson's essays, speeches, and political tracts (re)affirm the central place of Cherokee women in Cherokee literary and intellectual traditions in particular ways. For instance, Eaton's use of Cherokee oral histories, family records, and local archives held by fireside storytellers like her grandmother elevates these sources as legitimate repositories of historical knowledge and (re)positions Cherokee women—including herself—as authoritative, explicitly public voices in those conversations. Bronson's extensive work with Indian and non-Indian communities as both a negotiator of change and an oppositional voice of resistance and critique situates her in a long tradition of Cherokee states(wo)manship, connecting her forward to Principal Chief Wilma Mankiller and backward to eighteenth- and nineteenth-century Beloved Women such as Nanye'hi (Nancy Ward) who doggedly cultivated diplomatic relations while also remaining committed to the long-term well-being of their families, communities, and nations.[44] *Stoking the Fire* explicitly situates Eaton and Bronson within this tradition as keepers and producers of knowledge, insightful social critics, and accomplished stateswomen in their own right. In this way, I model a tribally specific reading practice that is attentive to Indigenous feminist critiques voiced by Shari Huhndorf, Cheryl Suzack, and others of the gendered dynamics of erasure, elision, and male/masculine privilege that have largely organized tribal nationalist approaches to Native literary studies.[45] By devoting more than half the book to two Cherokee women and by attending to questions of gender representation in Oskison's and Riggs's work, I begin to reconstruct a better sense of the centrality and scope of Cherokee women's intellectual, political, and cultural contributions to early twentieth-century Cherokee history and experience. My own work in the archives has revealed that we have only begun to scratch the surface.

More than a project of historical recovery and critical revisionism, *Stoking the Fire* also looks to these writers and texts for how their lives and work might speak forward to contemporary questions about identity, family, community, nation, and belonging. As Justice, Nelson, Parins, and others have demonstrated, Cherokee histories structured around intractable tensions between conservatives and progressives, traditionalists and assimilationists, or nationalist patriots and self-interested traitors force Cherokees into reductive paradigms that elide the rich diversity of opinions, experiences, and contexts that informed late nineteenth- and early twentieth-century Cherokee life.[46] These writers' lives and works provide case studies in the limitations of such frameworks. For instance, though on opposite sides of bitter divisions between the Treaty Party and the Ross Party that emerged during the Removal crisis and persisted through the Civil War, Bronson's paternal grandfather, Jacob Muskrat, a survivor of the Trail of Tears, and her paternal grandmother, Martha Fields, an Old Settler, fell in love and built a large family. Decades later, as pressure for allotment and statehood intensified, their son, James, a member of the culturally traditional and politically conservative Keetoowah Society, reluctantly came to endorse the policy, a decision which put him at odds with his extended relations as well as other resistant groups throughout Indian Territory. Conversely, the more acculturated Oskisons, Eatons, and Riggses seem to have opposed it, at least until it became a foregone conclusion.

These writers' respective class backgrounds and family relations also indicate a wide cross section of Cherokee experience throughout this period. Both Oskison and Bronson were born to working-class farm families in the more culturally and politically conservative Delaware district while Eaton and Riggs hailed from prominent ranching and banking families in and around the more acculturated agricultural and financial district of Cooweescoowee. While the Muskrats and Oskison's maternal relatives, the Buzzards, maintained subsistence farms in rural Cherokee-speaking communities on the Neosho River and Pawpaw Creek, the Eatons, Riggses, and Oskisons managed larger agricultural and real estate operations near the railroad boomtowns of Vinita and Claremore. And whereas during allotment the Eaton and Oskison families enrolled in nuclear family arrangements centered on paternal relations, the Riggs and Muskrat households enrolled according to both bilateral and matrilocal extended family relations. As Rose Stremlau, Julia Coates, and others have argued, such stories capture more than family genealogies and property records. Rather, they suggest a diverse array of relations and understandings of belonging, which often transcend the racial, cultural, political, class, and historical boundaries through which Cherokee history is often understood.[47]

As the chapters that follow demonstrate, this nexus of history, family, politics, place, culture, race, and nation deeply informs how these writers continued to understand themselves as Cherokees in the twentieth century and how they variously imagined and represented Cherokee nationhood in their work. To acknowledge this reality is not to say that very real tensions do not exist; nor is it an attempt to downplay their significance. Ongoing attempts by Cherokee freedmen to secure full citizenship (a concern of chapter 3), pressing efforts to address language loss and cultural revitalization, contentious questions over residency and at-large citizenship, and interventions by the federal courts into the most intimate of Cherokee relations—the family—remind us of the ongoing and immediate stakes of these differences. However, we might gain insight into understanding and imagining affirmative solutions to the complexities of our own historical moment if we acknowledge that Cherokees have long formed intimate and political relationships over and above the internal divisions that typically organize Cherokee history and if we pay attention to how those relations are variously represented in Cherokee writing. Whether speaking of a multicultural (though not always multiracial) citizenry grounded in Cherokee land and law, recovering a nationalist ethic of self-sacrifice and a commitment to Cherokee relations, interrogating the devastating impacts of blood politics on Cherokee families, or drawing on Cherokee experiences as a foundation for tribal-international work, these writers present diverse meditations of nationhood that are at once celebratory and critical, grounded and always on the move, anchored equally to the people and places that informed their early lives and to the movements and migrations that came to influence their later work.

✶ ✶ ✶ ✶ ✶ ✶ ✶

Because each of these writers explicitly chose to reopen and reexamine histories that many considered closed, and did so at a moment when the widespread condemnation of allotment policies and BIA oversight was gaining momentum in both local and national venues, we must resituate them more explicitly within the larger currents that informed American Indian life during the early twentieth century. Thus, while I make sure to embed these writers and texts in the Cherokee contexts of northeastern Oklahoma, I also explore the influence of their movements and migrations outside their tribal national home. In this I follow a host of scholars who have convincingly argued that texts that are grounded first and foremost in tribal specificities amplify a writer's more expansive aesthetic and political projects.

For instance, speaking of Joy Harjo's intertribal, pan-Indian, and trans-Indigenous poetry, Craig Womack and Mishuana Goeman argue that it is precisely Harjo's Creek-centricity that lends substance and weight to her more expansive projects. "Harjo's vision of pan-tribalism does not endorse Indian genericism, writing that obscures concrete tribal and land relationships,"

Womack writes, "but rather engenders a type of Creek specificity that takes on larger meaning for all tribal peoples because of its very grounding in the poet's own culture, a rootedness that comes out of her willingness to imagine and learn about her own tribe."[48] Where Womack turns to Creek culture, Goeman links Harjo's Creek specificity to place, specifically to the concrete and conceptual space of Creek stomp grounds. "The literal stomp grounds are found in a particular, tangible space, Oklahoma, and are a place where Creek dances and ceremonies continue to be held," Goeman observes. "However, that space is not fixed in time or landscape and has many meanings." Noting that stomp grounds can signal both specific *places* of origin and more conceptual *spaces* that Harjo carries with her, Goeman states, "The stomp grounds are a particularly apt vehicle for Harjo's scalar approaches: the local is already in relation to these larger global forces."[49]

Indeed, as Womack notes in his defense of an "ethical" literary nationalism, these radiating relations from the local to the global are embedded in the very idea of tribal nationhood itself: "Since sovereignty, by definition, has to do with government-to-government relations, it has everything to do with intersections and exchanges between inside and outside worlds." If attentive to these relations, tribal literary nationalism "can do local work with global implications" by focusing on "the way a microcosmic view of the world can lead to macrocosmic understandings and relations."[50] As a methodology, tribal specificity here signals not the ghettoization or parochialization of Native literary studies, for which it has been critiqued on theoretical grounds, but rather the grounding required to fully appreciate the significance of intertribal or Indigenous transnational literary and intellectual work.

If tribal specificity lends local substance to more global concerns, attending to the extratribal can also amplify tribal nationhood in important ways. For Mvscogee/Creek critic Tol Foster, this involves balancing tribal specificity with what he terms a "relational regionalism" that is capable of accounting for exchanges between the "world 'out there'" and its "influence upon [tribal communities] 'in here.'" Understanding this dynamic as part and parcel of "knowing ourselves in the world," Foster argues that a tribally specific framework is incomplete if it cannot account for the "multiple perspectives and voices" that are fundamental to such exchanges.[51] Lisa Brooks also picks up on questions of relationality and exchange in her comparative study of early Native writing of the Northeast. Expanding on Robert Warrior's metaphor of "intellectual trade routes," Brooks points to the vast "trade networks, shared histories, and specific relationships between nations that have been so much of a party of our common experience within this land" as another model of comparative study.[52]

Attentive to tribal specificity and the complicated dynamics of cultural exchange, Jill Doerfler and Scott Lyons similarly root Anishinaabe notions of identity and community in longstanding traditions of migration, mobility, adaptation, innovation, and exchange. Doerfler understands Anishinaabe nationhood as being a "nexus of relationships . . . [that is] constantly being (re)defined and (re)created" in the community's attempts "to create a rewarding, ethical, and nourishing life," a process which, according to Lyons, fundamentally places "the tribe and the world in close proximity to and intimate relationship with each other."[53] It is precisely through an analysis of political, social, cultural, and diplomatic exchanges that Joseph Bauerkemper and Heidi Kiiwetinepinesiik Stark theorize an Indigenous transnationalism that situates "the sophisticated boundaries that differentiate indigenous nations as discrete polities" and "the legacies of indigenous diplomacies" within "the transnational flows of intellectual, cultural, economic, social, and political traditions between and across these [permeable] boundaries."[54] The point here is not simply to reconcile what appear at times to be competing frameworks, but to recover Indigenous understandings and practices of nationhood, grounded not in independence *from* or power *over* other communities but in "collective [trans/national] responsibilities" *with* and commitments *to* one another and the wider non-Indigenous world.[55]

As with Womack and Goeman above, these moves—whether understood in regional, intertribal, relational, or trans/national terms—are less about leveling tribal nations' differences and distinctions into transnational sameness than recovering and (re)situating Indigenous understandings of identity, community, and nationhood as being "shaped not only by a nuanced and realist understanding of one's own group, but of the many relations"—economic, legal, political, cultural, spiritual, familial, geographic—"it has with groups outside of it."[56] Part and parcel of this reframing is coming to more productive terms with "the intensely relational nature of sovereignty" and with the multiple visions of tribal nationhood that are produced by those relations.[57] Though these methodological trajectories are often positioned as mutually exclusive projects—one local and nationalist, the other global and pan-Indian or pan-Indigenous—*Stoking the Fire* claims both as complimentary components of

Cherokee nationhood, anchored at once to the peoples, places, relations, and geographies of northeastern Oklahoma and to the larger networks and relations that these writers formed outside their tribal national home.

By taking this approach, *Stoking the Fire* advances gains in recent scholarship that have begun to productively complicate how we understand American Indian writing across this period and its relationship to our own contemporary moment. By engaging with popular and political thought alongside academic and legal discourses, and by grounding my readings in the complex intellectual, political, and personal contexts that informed these writers' lives and work, I respond to calls by other Native scholars to expand our historical scope and objects of study. As Robert Warrior, Jace Weaver, Craig Womack, Daniel Justice, Lisa Brooks, and others have written, exclusive attention to the literary ignores the multiple mediums and forms through which Native peoples have exercised intellectual sovereignty and self-determination directed at Native and non-Native audiences alike.[58] In his expansive study of Native American literature and community, Weaver understands "literature" as including "all written output by a people" regardless of aesthetic judgment or disciplinary distinctions.[59] Womack and Justice similarly situate poetry, drama, and fiction alongside everything from oral traditions, constitutions, petitions, and histories to essays, radio addresses, newspaper articles, and biographies. Attention to constitutional criticism, treaty discourses, and alternative sites of cultural and intellectual production by Elizabeth Cook-Lynn, Craig Womack, Robert Warrior, Lisa Brooks, Jill Doerfler, David Carlson, and others highlights the expansive archive that emerges when scholars cast ever-wider nets, to borrow Warrior's turn of phrase. Doing so increases not only our sense of scale but also the historical scope of Indigenous literary and intellectual production. For instance, Jace Weaver, Robert Dale Parker, James Cox, Lisa Brooks, and Christopher Teuton have drawn attention to how continued study of the post-1968 "Renaissance," while important, risks obfuscating longer Indigenous literary histories in the Americas dating back to Samson Occom in English, El Inca Garcilaso de la Vega in Spanish, the Mayan *Popal Vuh,* and countless examples of Indigenous literary expressions in everything from Aztec codices, Anishinaabe birchbark scrolls, and Haudenosaunee wampum belts to Lakota winter counts, Cherokee basketry, Navajo weavings, and a host of other expressive forms.[60]

To a great degree, the complicated representational politics in the literature that I examine hinges on my attention to such materials and contexts.

For instance, if restricted to the handful of poems and short stories that Bronson wrote as a young woman (even if we tracked them down in the various archives where they are held) or to her only widely accessible text, *Indians Are People, Too* (1944), we would miss entirely her five-decade-long contribution to Native intellectual and political thought. Similarly, reading Riggs's complicated and at times devastating explorations of race, family, and community in his Indian Territory dramas without considering his neglected theoretical writings on the transformative potential of socially conscious theater misses the significance of the politics of dramatic form that is evident throughout his work. The subversive politics of Eaton's and Oskison's respective appropriations and (re)visionings of academic historiography and of the American western novel become legible if read through Cherokee constitutional law and against the dominant, racialized discourses of progress and civilization that organized federal policy, popular writing, and academic conventions of their time. In similar terms, understanding the shift in Bronson's political thought—from a bootstrap ethic of individual self-reliance to a politics of self-determination—is largely dependent on contextualizing her work through the lenses of federal Indian education policy reform and the personal and political relationships that informed her extensive travels across Indian Country. Though this text is not the exhaustive study of early twentieth-century Cherokee writing that I initially set out to write, its close attention to the diverse forms and venues through which these writers were working suggests the expansive range of those efforts as well as the scope of scholarship yet to be done.

This more expansive sense of the archive also allows us to refigure the politics and possibilities of Native writing from this period. Beginning with Hazel Hertzberg's foundational study of the Society of American Indians and the Native American Church, Native writing from this period has been largely understood by scholars as occupying a spectrum bookended by the assimilationist, integrationist politics of the first three decades of the twentieth century on one side and the broadly accommodationist politics that defined the years between the Indian Reorganization Act in 1934 and Termination in the early 1950s on the other.[61] Faced not with militant Indians openly resisting settler authority but with middle-class, relatively acculturated, formally educated ministers, professionals, and bureaucrats who were more interested in negotiating with the dominant culture than dismantling it, many early scholars looking back from the 1970s conceded that while these writers might technically be Indian, their acculturated lives, problematic politics, and overdetermined writings left much to be desired.[62] The pivot toward nationhood and sovereignty during the mid-1990s by Cook-Lynn, Warrior, Weaver, Womack, Justice, and others usefully recentered attention on the historical contexts, intellectual networks, and complex political commitments that informed Native literary and intellectual production from this period.[63] However, as James Cox notes, even this work is ambivalent, and the period remains largely characterized by the absence of tribal nationalism, leaving the generational paradigm mostly intact.[64] While such frameworks provide useful models to *broadly* situate the politics of Native writing in relation to the ever-shifting tides of federal Indian policy, they are less useful in coming to grips with the political and intellectual complexities at work *within* a specific period or in capturing how an individual's politics shift *across* historical moments.

The broadly historical, tribal transnational approach to four Cherokee writers that I employ here, attentive to both historical context and literary form, complicates one-size-fits-all genealogies of Native intellectual and political history and attunes us to the nuanced and at times conflicting and contradictory ways a writer's politics and representational strategies shift in response to changing circumstances. What emerge are four Cherokee figures whose lives and work occupied the full spectrum between what Daniel Justice terms the "beloved path of accommodation" and the "Chickamauga consciousness of resistance," sometimes in the space of a single text.[65] In recognizing this fact, I seek neither to represent these figures as heroic freedom fighters of Cherokee sovereignty and tradition (they were not) nor to recover them somehow into a critical model that privileges a particular political orientation (resistance, sovereignty) over others (accommodation, assimilation). Rather, my goal here is to examine how their historically and socially situated experiences as citizens of a sovereign Indigenous nation persisted in their intellectual and creative work, and in so doing come to some understanding of the degree to which Cherokee nationhood remained central to how they perceived the past, evaluated the present, and imagined various paths into the future.

Tied closely to the generational paradigm, many scholars have also understood Native writing from this period primarily in terms of mediation, subversion, or resistance, directed largely at U.S. settler audiences and discourses. Led by a series of important studies by Frederick Hoxie, Chadwick Allen, Malea Powell, and Lucy Maddox, scholars have begun to identify the multiple rhetorical and performative strategies through which early twentieth-century Native intellectuals, artists, and performers disrupted stereotypes, influenced public opinion, and turned assimilationist reform policies explicitly toward Native interests.[66] Focused primarily on "pan-Indian issues . . . arising from the wardship status of Indians," these Red Progressives attempted to "put the best face on the oppressive policies of allotment and assimilation" while also locating a gradualist path into modernity that did not require abject assimilation or vanishing.[67] Operating within a wide range of discursive, rhetorical, and political contexts, they often as not "talked back to civilization" in support of tribal claims against the federal government, critiques of BIA inefficiency and graft, citizenship protections for all Indians, and gradual rather than rapid integration of Native peoples into mainstream U.S. life.

While this scholarship has greatly enriched how I understand the ways that early twentieth-century Cherokee and Native writers navigated the postallotment, poststatehood period, I am concerned that we should not understand these acts exclusively in terms of subversion and resistance (the "writing back" model) or cultural exchange and contestation (the mediation model) and in so doing elide the tribal national contexts at work in each. In expressing this hesitation, I want to be clear that I am not rejecting these approaches outright. Simon Pokagon's *Red Man's Rebuke* delivered at the Chicago World's Fair, Pauline Johnson's disruptive performances of civilization and savagery on stages throughout the United States and Canada, or essays by Arthur Parker, Laura Cornelius, and Thomas Sloan in the Society of American Indians' *Quarterly Journal* were explicitly written for Native and non-Native audiences alike within venues and discursive paradigms largely targeting progressive-oriented settler audiences. The same holds for Zitkála-Šá's indictment of federal Indian school policies that was serialized in *Atlantic Monthly*, John Joseph Mathews's *Wah-Kon-Tah* that was distributed as a book-of-the-month club selection, and Todd Downing's pulp mysteries that were translated into multiple languages. Whether in romances and fictional biographies, popular defenses of Native lifeways, or across silent films, radio addresses, and syndicated newspaper columns, Cherokee writers like Oskison, Bronson, and Will Rogers are also pretty clearly operating in many ways as what Maddox terms "citizen Indians."

That said, while we might well acknowledge writing and performance as thoroughly colonized spaces mediated by grossly inequitable power relations that necessitate concessions not of our own choosing, Native peoples nonetheless engage in writing not simply to "talk back" but also to articulate our own visions of ourselves, the worlds we inhabit, and our aspirations for the future.[68] To riff on Joy Harjo and Gloria Bird's apt phrase, this understanding of "reinventing the enemy's language" necessarily presupposes a multidirectionality of exchange in which Native peoples produce counternarratives and claim presences not only by translating Native experience into a Euro-American imaginary but also by indigenizing Euro-American histories, genres, and expressive forms through Native social and cultural frameworks.[69] Explorations of unexpected presences and globetrotting mobilities in Wild West shows, the cinema, vaudeville, and popular music by Philip Deloria, Amy Ware, Christine Bold, and John Troutman have drawn attention to the diverse venues through which Native peoples navigated the postallotment era and to the continued importance of both tribal-national and trans-Indigenous familial, intellectual, and artistic networks across those travels.[70] More recent studies on the transnational politics of Indigenous culture, revolutionary imaginings of Indigenous Mexico, literary interrogations of U.S. and Canadian settler law, and revisionist treatments of the Society of American Indians by Shari Huhndorf, James Cox, Beth Piatote, Chadwick Allen, and others have begun to reveal a much more subversive, inter/transnational politics at work than was previously thought.[71] Combined with primary-text anthologies by David Martínez and Daniel Cobb,[72] this work highlights the ways many Native peoples not only negotiated but actively embraced the circumstances and technologies of modernity as they attempted to put their own "X-marks" on a rapidly changing, thoroughly modern, but still Indigenous world.[73]

Using these arguments as points of departure, *Stoking the Fire* shifts the emphasis of mediation a bit from a predominantly U.S.-settler perspective to a Cherokee transnational perspective. My readings of Oskison's western novel, Eaton's history, Riggs's drama, and Bronson's nonfiction privilege the Cherokee contexts that inform their work while also exploring the ways they leverage those contexts as sites to critique settler power and imagine decidedly modern alternatives to Cherokee pasts and Cherokee futures. As I demonstrate throughout, these writers were not simply translating or "talking back to civilization" from an Indian subject position; they were not just mediating Indian interests or Indian difference for a non-Indian audience. Rather, as Konkle has argued in another context, they were also appropriating, interpreting, and refiguring the circumstances, technologies, discourses, and forms of settler modernity *into* and *out of* an explicitly Cherokee frame of reference, grounded at once in the people, places, and experiences of their births as well as in the larger contexts and relations that came to influence their lives and work.[74] Modernity, for these writers, is not just a series of forces acting on them from the outside that they are forced to mediate. It is also a richly creative site where they actively contest the assimilationist mandates of manifest manners; refuse exclusive associations of civilization, progress, and modernity with settler whiteness; and reimagine Cherokee presences at once embedded in Cherokee pasts and directed toward Cherokee futures.

Attending to the Cherokee contexts that informed their work as well as the influence of their lived experiences outside the Nation on how they remembered, (re)imagined, and enacted Cherokee nationhood not only captures a more robust and complex picture of Cherokee nationhood in the first half of the twentieth century. It also presents a vision of nationhood and a tribally specific reading practice that is both grounded and always on the move, anchored both to origins and to migrations, capable of speaking both to the immediate experiences of northeastern Oklahoma and to the tribal transnational geographies that have always informed Indigenous imaginings and understandings of nationhood. By resituating mediation from the perspective of a Cherokee transnational imaginary as well as from my own position as a transnational Cherokee citizen in the twenty-first century, *Stoking the Fire* recovers an imagined community of Cherokee readers for whom Oskison's novels, Eaton's histories, Riggs's dramas, and Bronson's writings would likely resonate in particularly Cherokee ways—readers like Milam and Rogers, the Cherokees in an auditorium on a summer afternoon in Tahlequah, my grandfather, and myself.

✶ ✶ ✶ ✶ ✶ ✶ ✶

The recovery of these writers and texts from the dark ages is important in its capacity not only to *recover* voices and texts long silenced by colonial violence but also to put that recovered archive to work in order to *revisit, revise,* and *reinvigorate* our understandings of the politics and possibilities of Native intellectual and artistic production as it continues to speak across time to our own historical moment. To these ends, I read these texts as much for what they have to tell us about Cherokee futures as for how they recollect/re-collect and remember/re-member Cherokee pasts.

Chapter 1, "Citizenship, Land, and Law in John Oskison's *Black Jack Davy*," draws upon Cherokee constitutional traditions to revise understandings of the politics of popular forms—in this case, the frontier romance—from a tribally specific framework. Though superficially conventional, conflicts over land tenure, citizenship, and Cherokee legal authority eventually eclipse the conventional romantic plot, suggesting an alternative political unconscious at work in the novel. By reopening a history that many considered closed, *Black Jack Davy* transforms the manifest manners of the frontier romance from an alibi for U.S. settler-colonial violence into a dark-age declaration of Cherokee independence and a popular case for Indian sovereignty.

Chapter 2, "Oppositional Discourse and Revisionist Historiography in Rachel Caroline Eaton's *John Ross and the Cherokee Indians*," emphasizes recovery over revision, as Eaton's life and work have garnered little critical notice. Though fraught by its complicated negotiations with racialized settler discourses of civilization and progress, the text—which privileges local archives, family collections, and oral histories; subverts generic and narrative conventions of Indian life writing; and sees the legal, political, and diplomatic relationships between the Cherokee Nation and the United States as a conflict between national sovereigns—offers a potent counterhistory to settler historiography while also modeling what I read as a Cherokee ethic of self-sacrifice and communitism through the life of its most recognizable historical figure.

Chapter 3, "Blood, Belonging, and Modernist Form in Lynn Riggs's *The Cherokee Night*," shifts the book's considerations of genre from romance and historiography to drama, resituating Riggs's 1936 modernist drama through the lens of his neglected commentaries on the transformative potential of revolutionary realism and leftist experimental theater of the 1920s and '30s. Focusing on its self-conscious disruption of linear, national time and its devastating interrogation of postallotment blood politics, I argue that the play refuses teleologies of settler progress and Native declension, turning instead toward alternative modes of recognition and belonging that are anchored to flexible understandings of kinship and shared historical experience.

Chapter 4, "Cherokee Trans/National Stateswomanship in the Nonfiction Writings of Ruth Muskrat Bronson," recovers Bronson as a central figure of early twentieth-century American Indian activism and situates her in a long tradition of Cherokee women's diplomacy. Drawing on a wide array of nonfiction, touching on everything from education policy and leadership development to economic empowerment and trust responsibilities over a roughly forty-year period, I reframe what many have read as a concessionary position of accommodation in her work to an ever-developing diplomatic strategy of negotiation and intellectual practice that is born of, informed by, and responsive to the families, communities, and geographies in which she moved.

Drawing on relationships between family, place, and nationhood in Oskison's 1935 realist epic *The Brothers Three*, the afterword brings these discussions into the contemporary moment and argues that historically nuanced, politically engaged literary and cultural scholarship can and should inform urgent debates over nationhood, citizenship, sovereignty, and the politics of belonging.

By examining how Cherokees from earlier generations attempted to escape the victimizing narratives of dark-age dissolution and loss by imagining alternative futures, Cherokees—to paraphrase one of Riggs's dramatic characters—not only actively engage how we got here, but also assume responsibility for where we're going, how we're going to get there, and what that's going to look like in the process. In a Cherokee Nation exceeding 320,000 citizens, most of whom reside outside the traditional fourteen-county area in an ever-increasing Cherokee diaspora, openly wrestling with these questions is perhaps more urgent now than ever. Participating in some small way in these discussions is, for me, the most significant potential contribution of this study.

ONE

Citizenship, Land, and Law in John Milton Oskison's *Black Jack Davy*

We, the Representatives of the people of the Cherokee Nation, in Convention assembled, in order to establish justice, ensure tranquility, promote our common welfare, and secure to ourselves and our posterity the blessings of liberty; acknowledging with humility and gratitude the goodness of the sovereign Ruler of the Universe, in offering us an opportunity so favorable to the design, and imploring His aid and direction in its accomplishment, do ordain and establish this Constitution for the Government of the Cherokee Nation.

Preamble, Constitution of the Cherokee Nation, 1827

It's important for all of us to have all people know that when Native American people fought, they were fighting for their land and for their way of life. They were, in fact, fighting invaders. It's also important for people to know just how those Native people felt about what was happening around them. Tribal historical fiction, historical fiction written from a specific tribal point of view, can go a long way toward providing that kind of knowledge to a large number of people. In addition, it lets Native people know that their literary traditions are alive and well and vital and still evolving.

Robert Conley, Cherokee Thoughts

As the preamble to the Cherokee Constitution of 1827 attests, Cherokees have exercised rhetorical sovereignty and represented themselves as a nation-people through discourses of nationhood and constitutional citizenship for almost two hundred years. Though officially recognized as a sovereign nation in international treaties as far back as the mid-1730s and declaring itself a republic as early as 1817, the Cherokee Nation authored its first self-determined legal and political articulation as a contemporary national community in the Cherokee Constitution of 1827. As Rennard Strickland reminds us, to read this move toward nationhood as a decisive break from Cherokee tradition would be to ignore the systematic and often contentious efforts Cherokees made during the previous three decades to maintain control over Cherokee homelands and to hold the nascent national community together in the face of radical change.[1] Emerging in the context of intense settler-colonial conflict and persistent threat of expulsion from their southeastern homelands, Cherokee constitutionalism survived the factional violence and trauma that were engendered by the Removal crisis and intensified by the Civil War; endured innumerable late nineteenth-century assaults on Cherokee autonomy by railroad interests, land speculators, and territorial advocates; and persisted across genocidal policies of allotment and termination.[2] Though the tribal government was unilaterally dissolved in 1907, ushering in the infamous "Chief for a Day" era, a shift in federal policy toward self-determination in the early 1970s opened the door for Cherokees to reorganize under a new constitutional government in 1976.[3] Twenty-three years later Cherokees voted to replace the federal subjection clause with a statement of tribal sovereignty, to reaffirm the political boundaries of the Nation, and to exchange the language of "tribes" and "membership" for that of "nations" and "citizenship."[4] Recent referendums to address contentious issues of citizenship and belonging show evidence of continued commitments to constitutional self-determination. At times fraught with violence, bitter factionalism, and emotionally charged debate, Cherokee constitutionalism—from the first written law in 1808, through the 2003 referendum, and into the present—stands firmly as a significant component of Cherokee nationhood and national identity.[5] Understood as a dynamic collectively authored vision of Cherokee nation-peoplehood, Cherokee constitutionalism also exists within the "vital and still evolving" Cherokee literary tradition of which Conley speaks.

John Milton Oskison lived through and wrote about many of the singular events that comprise this history. He was born on September 21, 1874, on a small farm outside the Cherokee capital of Tahlequah, Indian Territory, to Rachel Buzzard Crittenden and John Oskison.[6] His mother was a Cherokee citizen

John Milton Oskison, Cherokee novelist, essayist, and biographer. Illustration by Roy Boney.

and a descendant of Old Settler families who relocated from the southeast to Arkansas Territory sometime between 1817 and 1819. During the Removal crisis of the 1830s, they eventually settled in a Cherokee-speaking community along Pawpaw Creek, north of the Cherokee capital of Tahlequah. Oskison's father was an Englishman who had come to live with extended family in Illinois after being orphaned as a child. After working as a farmhand and gold miner in California, the elder Oskison arrived in the Cherokee Nation in 1870 on a work visa issued by the Cherokee government as part of a Reconstruction program following the Civil War.[7] Shortly after his arrival, he and Rachel were married and quickly set up a small family farm just north of Tahlequah. Due to drought and failing crops, they relocated to Oregon between 1875 and 1876. However, because of Rachel's declining health and her desire to return to her family and the place of her birth, the Oskisons returned to the Cherokee Nation. Upon Rachel's death, the elder Oskison remarried and relocated the family again, this time to what would eventually become the family homestead west of Vinita in the Delaware district of the Cherokee Nation. After brief sojourns to California and northeast Texas, the Oskisons returned permanently to their Vinita farm and transformed it into one of the more successful Cherokee ranching enterprises in that part of the Nation. By the late 1880s it provided enough income to finance full-time education for the Oskison children, first at Cherokee subscription schools and later at Willie Halsell College, a private preparatory institution just outside of Vinita, which was also attended by Will Rogers, with whom Oskison maintained a lifelong friendship.[8]

After graduating from Willie Halsell, Oskison was accepted for undergraduate study at Stanford University in 1894, where he was a frequent contributor to and eventual editor of the campus magazine. The first American Indian graduate in the school's history—now memorialized through the John Oskison Scholarship for Native Students—Oskison took his BA in law and moved to the East Coast in 1898, doing graduate work in English language and literature at Harvard. Encouraged by the national recognition he received for his short story "Only the Master Shall Praise" in *Century Magazine*, Oskison relocated to New York in 1903 to concentrate on writing and publishing. Over the next decade and a half, he established himself as a successful journalist, short story writer, and editor for such publications as *McClure's* magazine, the *New York Evening Post*, *Century* magazine, the *North American Review*, the *Saturday Evening Post*, the *Southern Workman*, and *Collier's Weekly*. During this time Oskison also became involved in progressivist politics. As a tenant and volunteer organizer for the University Settlement, a tenement in Manhattan's East-Side Jewish community, Oskison helped to provide services and social support for immigrant and low-income families in the city's poorest neighborhoods. In 1912 he joined Charles Eastman, Arthur Parker, Henry Roe Cloud, Carlos Montezuma, Zitkála-Šá, Laura Kellogg, and other Red Progressives to form the Society of American Indians (SAI). The first national all-Indian organization of its kind, the SAI sought to ameliorate popular attitudes toward American Indian history and culture while also advocating for the integration of American Indians into mainstream American life, a dual project which informs much of Oskison's own work.[9] Oskison continued to publish extensively in nonfiction throughout this period in a variety of periodicals, boarding school magazines, and regional newspapers on everything from Oklahoma Indian issues and federal Indian policy to economic development, technological innovation, and international relations. After returning home from service in World War I at the age of forty-four, he married Hildegarde Hawthorne, Nathaniel Hawthorne's granddaughter, and was seriously considered for the post of commissioner of Indian affairs under the Wilson and Harding administrations.[10]

In the mid-1920s Oskison stepped away from public political life and refocused his energies on creative writing. From 1925 to 1941 he wrote six novels, three fictionalized historical biographies, and a series of historical and cultural essays about Oklahoma that he coedited with Oklahoma historian Angie Debo.[11] Though Oskison located much of his earlier short fiction in Indian Territory—what he affectionately referred to as the "Old I.T."—this final chapter of his creative life demonstrates a decided shift away from popular fiction and toward a more critical orientation to Native American subjects beginning with his last two published works, *The Brothers Three* (1935) and *Tecumseh and His Times: The Story of a Great Indian* (1938). The former tells the story of a mixed-race Cherokee family's efforts to hold on to the family farm, from just prior to allotment through the economic booms and busts of the 1920s and '30s. The latter is an unabashed celebration of the Shawnee diplomat and military strategist, replete with scathing critiques of British military incompetence, U.S. duplicity, and federal Indian policies recalling those levied by Eaton twenty years earlier, which are documented in the next chapter. An unpublished biography of Cherokee principal chief John Ross, *Unconquerable: The Story of John Ross, Chief of the Cherokees, 1828–1866,* shares this more critical take on federal power and reflects Oskison's continued interest in Cherokee history. Its commission by Oskison's contemporary—and later principal chief—J. B. Milam in 1943 also situates him in close proximity to tribal reorganization efforts that were taking place across Cherokee country during this time.[12] At the time of his passing, which occurred on his brother's farm outside of Vinita in 1954, Oskison was still working on manuscripts for *The Singing Bird,* a dual-plot multicultural frontier romance chronicling the successful survival and reestablishment of the Cherokee Nation in Indian Territory following the Removal, and an unfinished memoir entitled *A Tale of the Old I.T.*[13] An obituary notice captures Oskison's relationship to Cherokee country and its influence on his writing: "It was significant that John Oskison, despite his wide travels in this country and abroad, never left—in spirit—the old I. T. . . . He came home to Vinita to write his best books."[14] Indeed, from his early short stories to his later novels, historical biographies, and autobiography, Oskison's creative oeuvre provides a rich literary take on nineteenth- and early twentieth-century Cherokee life as he experienced and remembered it.

Despite his prolific output across one of the most chaotic and unstable periods in American Indian history, and though lauded by the late Robert Conley as a groundbreaker in Cherokee literature, Oskison remains a marginal figure in American Indian letters.[15] In the earliest and most influential treatment of his life and work, Charles Larson points to Oskison's mixed-race background, the assimilationist era in which he wrote, an absence of identifiably Indian protagonists in his novels, and a decided lack of artistic merit as evidence of his "limited concern with the social issues confronting Native Americans" as anything other than "a kind of backdrop of authenticity" in their "Indian Territory setting."[16] These basic sentiments have been expressed to one degree or another by Arny Strickland, Bernd Peyer, Priscilla Oaks, Andrew Widget, Kathleen Whitson, and others, though they moderate Larson's dismissive estimation of Oskison's work in significant ways.[17] A. LaVonne Brown Ruoff and Paula Gunn Allen have similarly noted Oskison's attention to Oklahoma's social and economic history in favor of things Indian, though both observe a critical attitude toward colonialism and racial prejudice in his later writings.[18] Robert Warrior draws upon Ruoff's assessment in *Tribal Secrets*, while Craig Womack—speaking through his alter ego, Jim Chibbo, in *Red on Red*—writes off Oskison's work as "mostly about white cowboys and cattle ranching."[19] Acknowledging that Oskison's politics are more complex than critics had previously given him credit for, Jace Weaver nonetheless cites Oskison's involvement in "aggressively assimilationist" organizations such as the SAI and the American Indian Association and the absence of Indian protagonists and plotlines in his novels as evidence of "an overall assimilationist trajectory" throughout his work.[20]

As Joshua Nelson surmises in a recent analysis of *The Brothers Three*, such evaluations often have less to do with the work itself than with critical paradigms and reader expectations that are ill-equipped to account "for the realistic diversity of Indian identity" presented in Indian-authored texts from this period.[21] Armed with tribally specific methodologies and a revisionist understanding of the early twentieth century, scholars have recently begun to reappraise the literary and political merit of Oskison's writing. Gretchen Ronnow, for instance, identifies a number of ideological ambiguities, rhetorical subversions, and "echoes of irony, satire, and perhaps even despair" structuring his short fiction and novels.[22] Timothy Powell and Melinda Smith Mullikin point to similar dynamics in his novel *The Singing Bird*, noting its attention to Cherokee history and oral traditions and its satirical take on the conversion narrative as Oskison's "first real venture into writing a counternarrative that explicitly argues for a distinctly Native American view of history."[23] Preceding Powell and Mullikin's edition by a year, Daniel Justice's landmark literary history *Our Fire Survives the Storm* was the first text to locate Oskison explicitly within a Cherokee literary tradition, identifying an ambivalent optimism for Cherokee futures across Oskison's work.[24] Expanding on Justice's tribally specific methodology, recent essays by James H. Cox, Joshua Nelson, Jenna Hunnef, and Brian K. Hudson have brought questions of hemispheric indigeneity, audience and genre, and animal and gender studies to bear on Oskison's work.[25] Such scholarship has begun to recover what Daniel Littlefield and James Parins identified back in 1982 and what Conley would point out two decades later: the very content that critics understood as non-Indian and even as assimilationist—mixed-bloodedness, farming, ranching, banking, railroads, formal schooling, Christianity, modern economic and business practices, constitutional law—were actually deeply embedded in Cherokee life.[26]

This chapter extends these efforts by turning to Cherokee constitutional understandings of citizenship, land, and law as a lens through which to read Oskison's frontier romance *Black Jack Davy*. In adopting this methodology, I draw on recent work on tribal constitutionalism within American Indian literary studies, which is situated within ongoing traditions of Indigenous self-governance and self-representation. In his foundational statement on Creek literary nationalism, Craig Womack anchors the development of Creek constitutionalism within customary Creek social relations, ceremonial practices, political structures, and a long history of Creek self-governance. "At the core of modern Creek national life," Womack observes, "is a continuation of adapted forms of Muskogean traditionalism" such that "Creek government might be characterized as 'ever changing, ever remaining the same.'"[27] Robert Warrior similarly understands the development of the Osage Constitution of 1881 as "not only a record of history, but an expression of the modern intellectual aspirations of a people confronting the need to transform themselves on their own terms."[28] Written on the heels of decades of loss amid massive social change, Osage constitutionalism emerged "as a vehicle for asserting not just political independence, but for retaining their sense of peoplehood and its distinctive features in the midst of a changing world."[29] Neither a rejection of Indigenous cultural pasts nor a romantic retreat from modernity into a rigid traditionalism, tribal constitutions exist alongside oral traditions, ancestral memories, family histories, ceremonial practices, and other expressive forms in what Lisa Brooks terms "a living tradition" of Indigenous self-determination with "a deep and extensive genealogy on this continent."[30] As aspirational documents, tribal constitutions function not simply as legal and political bulwarks against settler states, but also, as Richard Scott Lyons and Jill Doerfler have variously argued, as an attempt to continually articulate and (re)imagine the collective histories, identities, relationships, and futures of the nation-peoples they call into being.[31]

Published in 1926—twenty years after the dissolution of the Cherokee Nation, two years after the Indian Citizenship Act, and less than a decade before the Indian Reorganization Act of 1934—Oskison's novel performs just such a reimagining. It chronicles the romantic trials of two Anglo teens whose families have legally settled in the eastern portion of the Cherokee Nation during the latter half of the nineteenth century, leasing land from a Cherokee citizen named Ned Warrior. On the surface, it closely follows the conventions of a typical western frontier romance, replete with gunfights, drunken brawls, femmes fatales, frenetic horseback rides, and villainous plots, all culminating with the successful union of the young lovers and the restoration of law, order, and futurity to the novel's frontier community. Because of these rather conventional dynamics, even those critics who have begun to reevaluate Oskison's more serious fiction have continued to frame the novel as popular entertainment having little to do with Cherokee or Indian concerns. In doing so, they have largely ignored the complex conflict over land tenure, citizenship, and legal authority that runs parallel to and eventually eclipses the romantic plot. Set in Indian Territory at a historical moment when U.S. authority and allotment policies were still vigorously contested by tribal nations, Oskison positions *Cherokee* citizenship, land, and law as the legal and political contexts in which both plotlines ultimately play out.

These geographic and political contexts have profound consequences on the story Oskison spins. Whereas conventional frontier romances go to great lengths to appropriate Indians into, or write them out of, a U.S. national narrative, Oskison's novel presents a fully functioning, multicultural, and politically autonomous Cherokee state. Rather than Native political and cultural spaces giving way to civilization and settlement by the Anglo frontier family, the imagined spaces in which Oskison resolves the plot's conflicts are identifiably sovereign Cherokee territories. Though violence and criminality exist in the narrative, they are aligned not with the inherent savagery of the frontier or the intractable lawlessness of Indian Territory but with self-interested white intruders who are bent on undermining Cherokee law and order for their own personal gain. What situates characters as heroes or villains is less a consequence of race, religion, or American exceptionalism than their situated relationships with Cherokee peoples and their commitments to Cherokee sovereignty. Put differently, *Black Jack Davy* models a constitutional ethic of Cherokee nation-peoplehood grounded not simply in legal *rights* but also in *responsibilities* and *relationships*. By situating the conventions of the frontier romance explicitly within the contexts of Cherokee citizenship, land, and law, Oskison repurposes the genre from a settler-colonial alibi for dispossession and violence to a dark-age declaration of Cherokee sovereignty.

Romancing the Nation

In the edited collection *Nation and Narration*, Timothy Brennan and Ernst Renan, writing decades apart, both highlight the construction of "the nation" as a dual process of creative imagination and historical forgetting. Extending Benedict Anderson's emphasis on the role of print capitalism on the construction of nations as "imagined communities" to literary production, Brennan points to an "apparatus of cultural fictions," including "imaginative literature," which works to constitute and consolidate national subjects and the idea of the nation itself.[32] This project is no easy task, however, since, according to Renan, national unity "is always effected by means of brutality." In order to elide these "constituting" moments of violence and residual conflicts that remain, collective forgetting becomes a necessary precondition for national unity: "The essence of a nation is that all individuals have many things in common, and also that they have forgotten many things. . . . It is good for everyone to know how to forget."[33] The cultural and political work of national narratives is not so much the revelation of commonality, but the erasure of difference, which is brought about through an insistent forgetting of the violence and trauma that mark the nation's origins. Less collective amnesia and more what Kevin Bruyneel describes as an excess of habituated memory predicated on disavowal, Brennan's "apparatus of cultural fictions" works in a U.S. settler-colonial context to construct memories, histories, and cultural narratives that affirm U.S. settler nationalism while at the same time appropriating, containing, or repressing alternative experiences and claims to representative truth.[34]

No cultural fiction has been taken up and put to work by so many and for such disparate purposes as the American frontier romance.[35] Governed by a dialectical binary that orders the world according to easily discernible moral polarities, the frontier romance attempts to resolve or flatten social contradictions through quasi-epic conflicts between representative forces of good and evil, generally within an identifiable and familiar setting, which itself takes on mythic significance. Most often deployed during moments of profound civil unrest or social transformation, the frontier romance articulates and institutionalizes a given set of values and beliefs, reorganizes emergent social relations around existing power dynamics, and legitimizes a specific idea of national identity acting on the present but refracted though the lens of a usable imagined historical past.[36] The effect of this process is the displacement of historical contingency and political contestation into the ideological realms of mythic inevitability and common sense.[37]

One of the ways in which historical romances pull off this bait and switch is by recasting historically situated geopolitical locations into ideologically invested national spaces.[38] No imagined geographies have been used so widely and been so influential on the progressivist narrative of U.S. settler history and national identity as the frontier and the American West. As others have chronicled this development in detail, I do not wish to duplicate their work.[39] What is important to note, however, is the rapidity with which the unambiguously nonnational wilderness was refigured in the late eighteenth century and throughout the nineteenth century into the iconic Western frontier, a mythic site where, according to Frederick Jackson Turner, American identity and ideals were to be fully realized.[40] What was, in the journals and sermons of Puritan fathers, an irredeemable den of demonic heathenism to be avoided at all costs became, in the Cooperian and western traditions of American frontier romance and discourses of Manifest Destiny, "a place where afflicted humanity raises her drooping head; where conscience ceases to be a slave, and laws are no more than the security of happiness."[41] Reflecting the contradictions embedded in the promise of regeneration through violence that underwrites U.S. settler-colonial history, the West is imagined as both "a border zone that harbored mystery and danger" and "a plentiful, inviting space where the desires of common citizens, if they were diligent and brave, might be richly fulfilled."[42] By the early 1830s and into the late 1840s, the spatial antithesis of civilization and progress—the savage wilderness—became *the* mythic symbol of what would later be seen as America's Manifest Destiny.

Together with early policy decisions, Supreme Court rulings, and an increasingly nationalistic rhetoric of expansion, frontier romances went a long way in naturalizing claims of American exceptionalism through the creation of "a set of spatial and representational conventions that normalized the United States' expansionist project," often with violent repercussions for those deemed foreign to that narrative.[43] As Kevin Bruyneel, Mark Rifkin, and Mishuana Goeman have demonstrated, this normalization and naturalization of U.S. settler claims to political legitimacy and jurisdictional authority functioned to domesticate Indigenous social, political, and sacred lands as U.S. national territories.[44] Maureen Konkle argues that for American Indians, this meant a mass denial of even the possibility of a modern Indigenous nation. Operating within an "epistemology of ignorance," which locks Native peoples in the mists of a romantic cultural past by denying their place as political actors in the present, the very idea of Indigenous nationhood becomes a contradiction in terms.[45] By displacing the political components of social history into the realm of fantasy wish fulfillment, frontier romances sanitize their imagined pasts, rendering them "'safe' for the reader because they are 'closed off,' 'finished.'"[46] As James Cox argues, such practices perpetuate "the colonial effort by obscuring violence committed against Native people, disguising the motives for that violence, [and] relieving their readers of responsibility for that violence and domination."[47] From the late eighteenth century into the early twentieth century, a great deal of labor was spent rendering as natural and inevitable what in reality were ongoing political contestations over land, law, and territory.

Read as a literary vehicle thoroughly complicit with settler-colonial power, one might expect that American Indians such as Oskison would have avoided the frontier romance like the plague. This has decidedly not been the case. John Rollin Ridge's 1854 racial revenge fantasy *The Life and Adventures of Joaquin Murieta: The Celebrated California Bandit* mobilizes the moral weight of the frontier romance to critique the illegal dispossession of aristocratic Californios following the Treaty of Guadalupe of 1848 and the criminalization of legitimate moral and political resistance to racial violence and terror. The novella also operates on another register as an allegory for the forced removal of Ridge's own Cherokee relations from their southeastern homelands a decade earlier; the internecine violence that took the lives of his grandfather, father, and uncle; and his own lifelong exile from his tribal-national home.

Creek novelist Alice Callahan's *Wynema: A Child of the Forest* (1898) similarly repurposes the genre's anxieties over miscegenation and acculturation as existential threats to the racial project of Manifest Destiny into a narrative of mutual acculturation and respect, uniting Indians and whites in amity and peace. Though often read as a politically naïve endorsement of assimilation, the novel's scathing account of the 1890 Wounded Knee massacre and the existential crisis it produces in its protagonists render any vision of racial reconciliation ambivalent. This hesitancy, as Justice notes, also informs Oskison's *The Singing Bird* and many of his short stories.

In Mourning Dove's 1927 novel *Cogewea, the Half-Blood: A Depiction of the Great Montana Cattle Range*, which is more explicitly set in the iconic imagined geography of the American West, the mixed-race Indigenous characters are rescued from tragic narratives of disappearance and death in what becomes a comedic affirmation of tribal relations, Salish cultural survivance, and Indigenous futurity. The text explicitly critiques reductive representations of Native peoples and of Native women in sensationalist romances such as Theresa Broderick's *The Brand: A Tale of the Flathead Reservation* (1909), and it attends to federal Indian policies and historical contexts, marking two additional narrative strategies that are shared across these and other novels written during this period. They also inform the narrative dynamics of the prison-authored autobiography *Thrilling Events: The Life of Henry Starr* (1914), written by one of Oskison's Cherokee contemporaries, as well as Robert Conley's The Real People series and other novels set along the Cherokee-Anglo frontier. Oskison's novels *Wild Harvest* (1925) and *Black Jack Davy* thus exist within Cherokee and American Indian traditions of the genre from the beginnings of American Indian creative writing to the present.

Highly self-conscious of how the frontier romance works to normalize and naturalize racialized discourses of Indian savagery, primitivism, and Manifest Destiny, American Indian engagements with the genre reflect what Stephanie LeMenager terms "a species of counter-site . . . that challenge[s] hegemonic spatial representations and praxes like Manifest Destiny and, in so doing, inspire[s] revisionist historiography."[48] Drawing on Richard White's idea of the "middle ground" in colonial America, LeMenager argues that by remembering, returning to, and reinscribing contested literary geographies, writers make visible the remaining "inconsistencies, reversals and doubts" that are embedded in the seemingly inexorable and inevitable vision of U.S. imperial expansion.[49] In refusing "to naturalize the westward course of empire," such texts "reveal the fissures in that symbolism" and reopen "the nineteenth century to counter-narratives that are now more readily associated with colonial and early national contexts."[50] Taking such observations as jumping-off points, I suggest that despite efforts by romantic nationalists to domesticate Indian Territory and the Cherokee Nation as distinctly American national spaces—from Emerson, Child, and Cooper to O'Sullivan, Whitman, and Longfellow, to London, Roosevelt, and Wister—Oskison's romance (re)imagines an alternative to that totalizing project. By reappropriating American romantic-nationalist spaces as Cherokee geopolitical territories governed by Cherokee constitutional law, Oskison refigures the genre from a narrative vehicle of Indigenous vanishing and settler-colonial presence into an instrument of Cherokee national memory, re-memberment, and (re)imagination.

(Re)Writing the Nation

Black Jack Davy presents, on one level, a familiar sentimental romance on the open ranges of the western frontier. More specifically, it tells the story of young love between two Anglo youths whose families have settled as farmers in the Indian Territory with the permission of the Cherokee Nation. The eponymous hero, Davy Dawes, is an orphan taken in by Jim and Mirabelle Dawes, farmers who lease a farm from Cherokee citizen Ned Warrior. Davy soon develops a romantic interest in his adopted cousin, Mary "May" Keene, whose family also leases land from Warrior. The main plotline centers on this romance and complications that arise due to Davy's exotic interracial attraction to Warrior's Cherokee wife, Rose, and the machinations of Jerry Boyd, an intermarried white citizen who exploits the jurisdictional chaos of the late nineteenth century in order to amass vast tracks of Cherokee land for his own private interests. After a failed effort to have Ned Warrior arrested and an unsuccessful attempt on Warrior's life, Boyd shifts tactics and attempts to turn Warrior against his lessees by informing him of a forbidden romance between Davy and Rose. Consumed with jealousy, Warrior plots Davy's murder but is persuaded not to act when he finds out that it is not Davy but Boyd who is the source of conflict. In the interim, Boyd solicits the help of the notorious Indian Territory outlaw Jack Kitchin to help him force the Dawes and Keene families from their lands so that he can assume possession of them. During the ensuing firefight, Mary escapes on horseback to seek reinforcements and returns just in time to witness Warrior enacting his revenge on Boyd and putting down the attempted takeover of their—and his—lands. Though Davy's foster father is fatally wounded in the fight, the narrative ends in an apotheosis to his pioneer spirit, the reunification of Ned and Rose, the marriage of Davy and Mary, and the restoration of law and order to the frontier community.

The sensationalist plot structure and heroic portrayal of the pioneer ethos are exactly what one would expect in a novel chronicling the settlement of the American frontier. But *Black Jack Davy* is a novel not about settlement on the *American* frontier but of the complicated politics of Indian Territory and the sovereignty of the Cherokee Nation. Oskison carefully locates the text in such terms. The novel opens by narrating the Dawes family's movement from working an Arkansas farm as U.S. citizens to entering the Cherokee Nation as foreign nationals on a labor permit. Focalized through Davy's perspective, the narrator conveys, "Early that morning, they had crossed the border from Arkansas to the Indian Territory, but it was only when Selim stepped into the broad stream that Davy felt quite cut off from the old life. . . . 'Aht-dog, nearly home!' It was an impulsive blare of triumph, as well as a defiance of the doubts that had crept into his active brain and stirred his imagination."[51] As James Cox notes, "This border crossing on the novel's opening page moves US readers into a foreign territory" as it documents the movement from U.S. to Cherokee legal and political jurisdictions.[52] It also places readers in foreign narrative territory as the Dawes family's relocation west does not move from the comforts of civilization into the dangerous promise of the frontier but rather from one civilized nation to another. This would likely prove disruptive for readers reared on the sensationalist accounts of Indian Territory lawlessness and violence that were propagated in pulp westerns and popular discourse, as Littlefield and Parins explain:

> During the last two decades of the nineteenth century, especially during the 1890s, the popular magazines published unflattering descriptions of the Indian Territory as a place where whiskey flowed freely, lawlessness and violence were the rule, tribal officials were incapable of ruling and enriched themselves with tribal funds and white inhabitants (though there illegally) were virtually without protection of the law. This image was reinforced by public statements and reports of federal officials and bureaucrats . . . who were urging the Indians to give up their tribal status. If not in concert with the land speculators and others who, for selfish reasons,

> wanted the Indian Territory opened, these writers and officials contributed to the cause, for their reports added credence to congressional attempts to dissolve the Indian Territory for the "good" of the population there.[53]

Davy's conflicted feelings of being "cut off from the old life," his triumphant declaration of arrival at a new home, and "the doubts that had crept into his active brain and stirred his imagination" are no doubt informed by such stories and anxieties produced at this moment of political, legal, social, and cultural crossover. Though it leverages generic expectations for Indian Territory lawlessness and violence, *Black Jack Davy* never quite delivers on them, or at least not in the way that readers of these popular accounts might expect.

Aside from this image of political and narrative border crossing, the narrator also goes to great lengths to identify numerous geographic markers that are recognizable to anyone familiar with the topography of northeast Oklahoma. For instance, the first chapter of the book, which opens as described above, is entitled "West of Six Bulls River," a framing reference to a specific landmark that readers soon find out is located within the Delaware district of the Cherokee Nation. Where other chapter titles emphasize elements of character or plot—"Cale Boyd's Measure," "The Power of the Press," "Rose and Davy," "Attack," etc.—this first chapter explicitly situates the narrative on its opening page at a major waterway within a Cherokee political district. Having established the Neosho (or Six Bulls) River as the spatial anchor of the novel—it is Ned Warrior's and the Keenes' land on the east side of the river that Boyd desires—Oskison builds out the rest of the narrative's geography.

The Keene farm, we are told, lies just west of the town of Big Grove and east of Horsepen Creek. Big Grove, the narrator notes, is a new settlement east of the larger town of Vinita. Aside from these landmarks, Oskison mentions the Verdigris and Arkansas Rivers, which run on either side of the Cherokee capital of Tahlequah before linking up outside of Muskogee. If conventional frontier romances operate largely to empty Indigenous political geographies of their historical content and refigure them as ideologically invested, romantic-national spaces, Oskison reclaims those spaces in the first pages of the novel as identifiably Cherokee territories. For those familiar with northeast Oklahoma, such references would undoubtedly resonate. For those not educated in the region's geography, however, this attention to detail frustrates any attempt to too easily incorporate the novel's explicitly Cherokee settings into conventional ahistorical frontier spaces evacuated of their historical or political content. The Dawes family is not simply "striking out for the Territory"; rather, the family is entering into a legal contract with a Cherokee citizen who resides in a specific Cherokee voting district that is outlined by natural and political boundaries evident to all involved.

While Oskison's penchant for such geographic specificity no doubt functions to provide realist verisimilitude and a regional grounding to his sensationalist narrative (he has often been both praised and derided as a regionalist), it is a decidedly Cherokee, or more broadly, Indian Territory, regionalism. If the novel is read within the context of Cherokee treaty and constitutional history, we might also see an Indigenous territorial politics at work, explicitly focused on maintaining Cherokee control over the tribal estate.[54] From the earliest treaties with colonial officials in the mid to late eighteenth century, Cherokees placed a high value on clearly articulating territorial boundaries both to demarcate the sovereign borders of their own lands and to identify the geopolitical limits of colonial authority. As pressure for their lands increased and as U.S. officials played one town against another in order to secure cessions, Cherokees began the slow process of centralizing political authority in the National Council. At the Council of Ustanali in 1810 they made cessions of land by individuals an illegal offense punishable by death. The subsequent constitutions of 1827 and 1839 refer to the boundaries identified in treaties with the United States as a basis for determining the extent of their national domain and defining the use of national common lands.[55] Article 1 of the 1827 document asserts:

> *Sec. 1.*—The boundaries of this Nation, embracing the lands solemnly guaranteed and reserved forever to the Cherokee Nation in treaties concluded with the United States, are as follows, and shall forever hereafter remain unalterably the same, to wit . . . [extended, detailed descriptions of national boundaries]
> *Sec. 2.*—The sovereignty and Jurisdiction of this Government shall extend over the country within the boundaries above described, and the lands therein are, and shall remain, the common property of the nation.[56]

The detailed descriptions of the specific rivers, mountains, valleys, meadows, town sites, and other recognizable landmarks between these two sections concretely demarcate the political boundaries of the Nation and legally codify national lands as common property. Writing twenty years after the territorial integrity of his own nation had been dissolved, in a climate when Indian nationhood and common property were being reconsidered as integral to Indian policy reform, Oskison's attention to geographic specificity in the Cherokee Nation can be read as part of a Cherokee constitutional tradition linking nationhood and territory within a matrix of Cherokee legal jurisdiction. From within the arrested geopolitical frame of the frontier romance—a narrative moment just before the West is won via the imposition of Anglo law, order, and civilization on the frontier wilderness but before settler civilization has fully established its hegemony—Oskison's detailed descriptions of recognizably Cherokee places lay claim to those spaces as sovereign Cherokee territories under the Cherokee legal and political jurisdiction.

Constitutionally defined territorial boundaries also establish citizenship requirements and a citizen ethic of collective responsibility to the land and the people. In addition to defining national lands as common property, section 2 (of both the 1827 and 1839 constitutions) defines common land use rights, limits the sale of improvements to noncitizens, and restricts citizenship to a function of residence within territorial boundaries. Though the Cherokee Nation claims collective title to all land,

> the improvements made thereon, and in the possession of the citizens of the Nation, are the exclusive and indefeasible property of the citizens respectively who made, or may rightly be in possession of them; provided that the citizens of the Nation possessing exclusive and indefeasable [*sic*] right to their respective improvements, as expressed in this article, shall possess no right nor power to dispose of their improvements in any manner whatever to the United States, individual states, nor to individual Citizens thereof; and that whenever any such citizen or citizens shall remove with their effects out of the limits of this Nation and become citizens of any other Government, all their rights and privileges as citizens of this Nation cease.[57]

This conflation of national citizenship, common territory, and residence signaled a fundamental shift in Cherokee understandings of cultural and political identity. As William McLoughlin notes, while Cherokee belonging had previously been dependent on matrilineal clan relations, shared language, and regional town affiliation, in the constitution it also became subject to legal residence within the boundaries of the Cherokee nation-state and accession to Cherokee national law: "The Cherokee Nation was not simply a people; it was a place. To leave that place 'without the consent of the nation,' knowing that the federal government might unilaterally use that action to expropriate land from the nation, was traitorous, a betrayal of one's duties as a citizen and patriot and an act that merited deprivation of citizenship."[58] Just as the maintenance of Cherokee territory became inextricably intertwined with Cherokee national sovereignty, the relationship between sovereignty, territory, and national identity as citizenship was legally cemented by the constitution.[59] Consequently, "failure to observe the emerging tribal laws came to be considered as treason in the context of the fight for tribal lands."[60]

This emphasis on the treasonous implications of undermining Cherokee land and property laws is reflected in the novel's shift in emphasis less than halfway through the narrative from the romantic plot to the struggle over land. Law-abiding Anglo and Cherokee farmers, ranchers, and merchants battle with a consortium of Anglo commercial interests and annexation advocates bent on amassing vast tracts of land as a means of encouraging U.S. settlement and economic development. Oskison highlights this conflict from the beginning by explaining that on one side of the struggle is the relationship between Cherokee national lands and Anglo residence in the Nation and on the other are the machinations by commercial interests and advocates for U.S. territorialization of Indian Territory who are trying to undermine that relationship. We learn, for instance, that Anglos are encouraged under certain legal circumstances to enter the Cherokee Nation and improve its land provided that they find a Cherokee lessor and work out the legal terms of the lease with them. This is, in fact, how J. A., Bess, and Mary Keene—Mirabelle's brother's family—arrived in the Nation five years before the novel's opening. "Filled with enthusiasm over the promise of fortune in the Indian country," J. A. obtained a permit to farm on land occupied by Ned Warrior, and he extended the invitation, ostensibly with Warrior's blessing, to his brother Jim.[61] Since all land was constitutionally held as the collective property of the Cherokee Nation, Anglo settlers such as the Keenes would not have officially held title, though they would be entitled, as legal residents, to all improvements, equipment, and livestock produced in this "land of Canaan" during their tenure.[62]

This representation is consistent with Cherokee immigration and labor policies during the mid to late nineteenth century. In order to rebuild infrastructure and wealth following the Civil War and to cultivate political relationships as a means of staving off pressure to absorb Indian Territory into the U.S. territorial structure, the Cherokee Nation aggressively courted immigrants from neighboring states to fill a dramatic labor shortage. It was precisely these conditions that led to the entrance of Oskison's, Eaton's, Riggs's, and Bronson's Anglo relations into the Nation during the 1860s and '70s. Exactly what conditions would be mutually beneficial to all parties involved was a matter of great debate, however. Between 1819 and 1892 the National Council addressed these and other issues at least nine times. Incorporating permit and fee requirements from earlier resolutions, the legal code of 1867 restricts permits to mechanics and laborers and requires Cherokee employers to vouch for the character of their employees.[63] The code of 1881 includes artisans as acceptable laborers, requires U.S. citizens to take oaths of their good standing and of their intent to leave within ten days of permit expiration (generally one year), prevents permit employees from hiring other noncitizen employees, and makes provisions for rescinding permits in cases of abandonment.[64] By 1892 the law mandated that employment be useful and continuous, rescinded the oath requirement, collapsed the categories of labor and artisan into "agriculture," and explicitly forbade the employment of noncitizens in the cattle industry.[65] As the details of Cherokee labor law suggest, regulating labor in a way that addressed Cherokee needs while also protecting Cherokee political and economic interests was a complicated and often contentious affair made infinitely more so by the arrival of the railroads in the 1870s and by the intensification of the ranching industry during the next two decades. The Keene and Dawes families' peaceful tenures on Warrior's lands and their respect for Cherokee immigration, labor, and property law, function as an endorsement of Cherokee sovereignty and territorial legal authority as well as their voluntary and willful submission to its laws and jurisdiction.[66] It is thus not only the fact that their presence on Warrior's land complicates Boyd's plan to take it for himself, it is also that their commitments to the promise of a better life under Cherokee law undermines the racist logic of Boyd's motivations.

Indeed, the text juxtaposes this mutually beneficial relationship outlined between Warrior and his Anglo lessees with Jerry Boyd's self-interested machinations and utter disregard for Cherokee property law. We are first introduced to Boyd as he approaches the Dawes family's wagon, still on its way to their Six Bulls lease. Though at first cordial and welcoming, Boyd quickly begins slandering their Cherokee landowner, whom we later come to know as the politically astute and strategic Ned Warrior. Mobilizing racist assumptions of Indigenous criminality and popular views of a lawless and ungovernable Indian Territory, Boyd informs the newly arrived immigrants, "This Ned Warrior you folks're rentin' from is a bad Indian. . . . Facts are, Warrior's a boot-legger and an' a killer! He's wanted by the United States court at Tarko for peddlin' whiskey an' shootin' a white man, a deputy marshal of Big Grove that tried to arrest him. . . . Warrior shot him all to pieces."[67] Knowing Warrior to be otherwise via her brother's productive five-year relationship with him, Mirabelle sarcastically wonders why others have "jest let him along now" if Warrior is such a bad man.[68] Caught in a bind, Boyd admits that Warrior has many friends but claims that that is precisely the problem—they protect him from arrest and the wheels of justice. "Maybe," Mirabelle replies, "he's a good neighbor even if he is a God-a'mighty bad man."[69] At this, Boyd loses his temper and rides away from his new neighbors.

After arriving at their lease, the Dawes family receives a very different story of Boyd from others familiar with the area and its politics. Warrior himself identifies Boyd as "a big fat snake" who married an Indian woman and has become a naturalized non-land-owning citizen of the Nation.[70] From James Keene, Davy's uncle, we find out that Boyd showed up in Big Grove twenty years earlier as a stranded medicine show proprietor. After marrying the daughter of Soggy Roberts, "a second chief," Boyd was given a stake and some land, which he quickly populated with a large cattle herd under suspicious circumstances.[71] What Keene only implies, his daughter, Mary, confirms, stating bluntly, "Mr. Boyd wants to get hold of all this land between the river and Horsepen creek—more than three thousand acres. He got mad when Ned came in and he and papa made their bargain."[72] In a later conversation with Davy, Tom Winger—a white rancher in business with a Cherokee citizen named Bill Ridge and the hero of Oskison's earlier novel *Wild Harvest*—similarly situates Boyd with other "two-legged wolves" who have exploited Cherokee law and upset the peace of the countryside.[73] Soon after this exchange and following another contentious encounter with Boyd, Davy, who is by now established as the romantic hero and moral barometer of the narrative, thinks to himself, "Boyd was a type new to Davy—the deliberately scheming, merciless and powerful enemy who fought with weapons you could not meet with your hands."[74] Through representative discourse the text confirms such suspicions, as Boyd thinks through "the moves he meant to make" to force the Warrior, Keene, and Dawes families from the land:

> First, he must get rid of Ned Warrior; and he believed that he could accomplish the Indian's removal soon and with no peril to himself. Next, he must make life so hard for Keene and the Dawes family that they would be willing to sell out. . . . He would give Ned Warrior one more chance to sell. . . . Then, if Ned refused, he would bring pressure on Cap. Black, compel the deputy to go after Warrior and serve that long outstanding warrant for his arrest. Black would act, and the result? Capture? No, Warrior would not be taken alive, so strong was his dread of the white man's prison. . . . The Indian dead, he would deal with Rose; he believed he knew how to remove her from the scene. Keene was a lessee of Warrior's, and Jim Dawes his renter. "Once I get hold of that Indian's own place, I'll have them fellows out of there in short order!"[75]

As James Cox has shown, Boyd's plan for violent dispossession, targeting both Indian and white parties, "includes many of the strategies for dispossession long used against American Indians by non-Natives and the US government," ranging from bribery and coercion to criminalization, forcible removal, and murder.[76] Angie Debo chronicles many such schemes in her indictment of corruption, collusion, dispossession, and violence during the allotment era—which she characterizes as "an orgy of plunder and exploitation probably unparalleled in American history"—in *And Still the Waters Run: The Betrayal of the Five Civilized Tribes*.[77] While Boyd's statement would likely have resonated with these contexts for Indian Territory and Oklahoma readers, it also would have struck a chord with readers familiar with the more recent exposé of the Osage oil murders, the dynamics of which read like one of Oskison's own romances. Whether in fiction or history, machinations like Boyd's were not only about individual relationships and private property, but were also fundamentally about undermining tribal treaty rights and constitutional authority.

Hardly an anomaly, Boyd is, as Oskison makes plain, representative of an opportunistic, self-interested type that was infiltrating Indian nations from the United States. He communicates the seriousness of the threat to Cherokee sovereignty by placing some of the stronger critiques of men like Boyd in the words of officials charged with upholding U.S. and Cherokee constitutional law. After rejecting Boyd's demand to arrest Warrior for his altercation with a Deputy Burke five years earlier and his subsequent attempt to discredit the families on Horsepen Creek, the local sheriff, Cap. Black, escorts Boyd from his office, and as Boyd walks away, he says to himself, "There's the biggest liar west of the Mississippi!"[78] Later, when a newspaper editor asks the deputy to respond to Boyd's public accusations, Black identifies Boyd's motivations: "Why's he so anxious to get Warrior run in? So's he can jump his place! Why'd him an' Stannard cook up that horse-stealin' plot agin J. A. Keene an' Honey Wade? To break Keene an' run him off the creek! Why's he circulatin' stories about the Dawes family, that young Davy in pa'ticular? To get 'em into trouble, get 'em out. Just plain, devourin' greed, the kind that don't stop at anything, is what's eatin' Jerry Boy!"[79]

The aptly named Judge Pease (modeled on the real-life "hanging judge," Isaac C. Parker) situates Boyd in similar company when speaking to the Dawes family at their farm following Boyd's first aborted attempt to turn them off he land.[80] "It seems that bad men from the whole United States are flocking into the Indian country," Pease says, "we must stand up straight for law and order. Men like you—and this youngster . . . will be militant missionaries of peace, and security of life and property."[81] Embedded in these statements is an implicit indictment of the U.S. government's categorical failure to live up to its treaty responsibilities to regulate white incursions into Cherokee lands and to remove squatters when notified of their presence.[82]

As Mary considers these dynamics following her father's arrest by Stannard—one of Boyd's lackeys—she recalls how extensive Boyd's influence runs: "Hadn't her father said that Commissioner Hall was under obligations to the fat man, that the fine saddle horse he rode was Boyd's gift? Stannard, going forth after midnight on the man's dirty business, was perhaps only one of his tools. Judge Pease had called this a land of violence. The law was weak, men like Boyd held it in contempt."[83] Such observations point to a failure of U.S. sovereignty often leveled at Indian nations; whether through a self-conscious abrogation of treaty provisions or as the result of a fundamental inability to discipline its own citizens, the federal government consistently failed to secure the Cherokee Nation's borders with neighboring states and to regulate the actions of its citizens. Though Pease's naïve confidence in the rule of law is later rendered absurd in light of Boyd's easy manipulation of jurisdictional issues, the likes of which were endemic to Indian Territory by the late nineteenth century, Pease nonetheless expresses an anxiety that many Cherokee citizens, legal residents, and U.S. officials felt at the time—that legal and political control of the territory were being eroded at the hands of unscrupulous characters like Boyd.

The challenges to Cherokee political authority that Boyd's character presents in the narrative are writ large in the history of the Nation from at least the early nineteenth century. Similar to their efforts to arrive at pragmatic immigration and labor policies, Cherokees also had to decide whether or not to admit as citizens white men who married Cherokee women, whether to set restrictions on marriage, how to determine the citizenship status of mixed-race offspring, and how to codify the rights of spouses and children in cases of death, abandonment, or remarriage.[84] The earliest such law from 1819 required any white man who intended to marry a Cherokee woman to announce his intent and to secure a license from the National Council; it also mandated the consent of Cherokee women to alienate their property and rescinded citizenship immediately upon divorce, abandonment, or in cases of polygamy.[85] Six years later, in an attempt to account for an increasing number of unions between Cherokee men and white women, a law was passed extending full rights and privileges of citizenship to children of such marriages, effectively reducing the legal influence of both clans and matrilineal authority with respect to political identity.[86] After 1843 Cherokees required all intermarried whites to take an oath of allegiance in which they repudiated citizenship in and protection from all other nations and pledged to "honor, defend, and submit to the constitution and laws of the Cherokee Nation." Such efforts were more than simple matters of politics; they also carried economic implications. For instance, though adopted citizens by marriage were accorded political and civil rights, they never received per capita payments from land sales and were denied claims to the national lands during allotment. This issue became intensely contentious during allotment, and the Cherokee courts ultimately ruled that intermarried whites, Cherokee freedmen, and adopted Delawares and Shawnees were ineligible for per capita payments and allotments.[87] Though later laws allowed white widows and widowers to retain their citizenship, provided they remain in and remarry within the Nation, citizenship was stripped from any intermarried white who brought a suit against any Cherokee under the Trade and Intercourse Act of 1834.[88]

Intermarriage in Cherokee history is often (and rightly) read as a significant cultural disruption, but details of laws passed over a period of seventy years, such as those highlighted above, emphasize the potential for political and legal disruption that intermarriage posed as well. When combined with the self-interested actions of whites and Cherokees alike, this potential was quickly translated into a reality. "In many cases white traders and business-people were an asset to the nation," McLoughlin writes, "since they provided capital, services, and jobs, but most of the whites who sought their fortunes in Indian nations were motivated by the thought that they would have easy pickings among people they considered ignorant."[89] In addition to peddling whiskey, many whites married Cherokee women strictly to gain access to common lands, became silent business partners (reaping significant profits), squatted on Cherokee lands, or simply stole Cherokee natural resources such as timber, salt, and coal. Though Cherokees had the legal right to expel intruders or to demand their expulsion by U.S. agents, such provisions were difficult to effect in practice in such open and often unpopulated spaces, with unpoliced borders between the Nation and other territories and states. Measures such as these clearly point to the jurisdictional complications that emerged after Removal and that continued to intensify throughout the rest of the century.

As the narrator of *Black Jack Davy* observes, Indian Territory in the early 1890s "was a chaos of disputed authority—Indian tribal courts, the courts of neighboring states, and the federal courts in many cases each claiming jurisdiction—and outlawry flourished."[90] As a result of easily manipulated jurisdictional quandaries, the system was beset by corruption and abuse by interested parties on all sides. Despite Cherokee legal maneuvers designed to prevent the consolidation of wealth and of large areas of contiguous land in the hands of the few, many wealthy Cherokees used the system to lay claim to thousands of acres of Cherokee lands for agricultural production, ranching enterprises, and resource extraction.[91]

Because Boyd exploits his marriage to his Cherokee wife in order to gain access to vast tracks of land under Cherokee law and openly flouts his allegiance to the Nation by aggressively encouraging the subversion of the social order, he is clearly positioned as the primary threat to the safety and security of the Cherokee national community and as the villain of Oskison's narrative. Within the generic conventions of the frontier romance, such struggles over land and the ensuing conflicts between the established order and external threats are standard tropes. Henry Nash Smith argues that most frontier romances explicitly turn on the conflicts and tensions between "the old forest freedom versus the new needs of a community that must establish the power of law over the individual."[92] These conflicts often play out as a struggle between "the primitive free access to the bounty of nature" and "individual appropriation and the whole notion of inviolable property rights."[93] Also at play is the debate over the presumed equality of man in the state of nature versus the social stratification and class division that organize modern civil relationships.

While, as James Cox and Scott Lyons have shown, such readings may explain the ideological underpinnings of American romantic nationalist novels by James Fennimore Cooper, Lydia Maria Child, and Catherine Sedgewick, they fail to explain the politics of Oskison's text.[94] In *Black Jack Davy* the community under assault by Boyd represents neither the "old forest freedom" of the frontier nor the "primitive savagery" through which Indian communities are conventionally represented in the genre. Rather, Boyd's machinations threaten the safety of a fully functioning civilized (by the genre's own standards) Cherokee political community, the security of which rests not on a commitment to individual land rights but on the delicate constitutional balance between common lands, individual property, and interpersonal relationships. Though the conflict in Oskison's text at least partially revolves around this tension between common and private property, the narrative reverses the arc of that struggle: resolution takes place not with the institution of allotment in severalty as U.S. lawmakers would have it but with the restoration of Cherokee common property law.[95]

Re-Membering the Nation

Reading the novel as I have from within the contexts of Cherokee constitutional history and law encourages us to consider what happens to the politics of the frontier romance when the threatened community is no longer what Mary Lawlor identifies as "the most powerful icon of the civilization of the wilderness: the settlement family," but a Cherokee political community.[96] Since the imagined resolution of contradictions is where romantic narratives advance their most powerful statements about the emergent moral and political order, it is important to examine closely how Oskison resolves his Cherokee frontier romance and to consider how a contextualized constitutional reading reveals the Cherokee nationalist politics at work in the text.

The conflict comes to a head as Boyd's consortium of hoodlums and grafters sneak up on the Dawes homestead in the cover of night and engage the family in a firefight designed to literally eliminate them as a threat. Most of the tension in the final scene is created by the failure of some of their allies to show up in time due to misinformation as well as by Mary's Paul Revere–like ride through the night to secure their aid. Alone and outnumbered, only the Keene and Dawes families are ready for battle. J. A., Jim, and Davy are the only men present, but in good frontier fashion, the women take up arms, and a gunfight ensues that would make Butch Cassidy and the Sundance Kid envious. As the fire draws to a close, Mary returns with the cavalry and, punctuated by the martyrdom of Jim Dawes, the marriage of Davy and Mary, and the desire of Warrior to retire with Rose into "a life of quiet happiness," everything ends as readers of conventional frontier narratives might expect.

While such events create a certain degree of suspense by teasing generic expectations, they are ultimately irrelevant to the way in which Oskison actually draws the conflict to a close. Instead we find out as the battle reaches a fevered pitch that Warrior—the Cherokee lessor to both Anglo families and the one-time revenge-seeking husband of Rose—has previously infiltrated the battlefield and set up an elaborate series of explosions disguised in hay bales to short-circuit Boyd's planned siege. In fact, it is Warrior's strategic mind and patriotic heroism rather than that of his Anglo tenants or their allies—including, significantly, the romantic protagonist, Davy—that effectively brings the conflict to an end, wounding Boyd, killing his son Cale, and disabling their accomplices until the legal authorities arrive. Almost comically, the cavalry, sought so valiantly by Mary, very nearly misses the entire exchange, arriving just in time to get a few shots in, apprehend what is left of Boyd's gang, and commemorate Jim's heroic sacrifice. In Oskison's frontier romance, then, it is not the heroic frontiersman, the rough mountain man, or even the handsome cowboy—much less the frontier militia or Anglo cavalry—who comes to the rescue, but rather the only Cherokee principal character in the text, on whose common lands the struggle takes place and who, as a consequence, has the most to lose and gain by the outcome.

Such a plot contrivance in the hands of Cooper, Child, or Sedgwick would generally suggest Native complicity, if not endorsement, of white settlement and the imposition of civilization on the frontier. By acceding to the arrival of civilization and assisting their white counterparts by either advocating their position or voluntarily retreating into the wilderness, Native characters in conventional frontier narratives legitimize the conventions of the genre and in doing so depoliticize, close off, and sanitize the violent extratextual consequences of the actual history of settler-colonial conflict.[97] As Cox points out, this absencing convention "is the storytelling equivalent of conquest, . . . a basic colonial desire for a landscape emptied of its Indigenous population. . . . Either there has been a conquest, there will be conquest, or the conquest is always-already completed because it has been foreordained by the Christian God."[98] In Oskison's frontier romance centered on the struggle over Cherokee national lands and the territorial authority of the Cherokee Nation, however, Warrior's quiet recession at the end of the narrative signals neither a concession to disappearance nor the inevitable dispossession of Cherokee lands. Rather, in protecting his lessees, Warrior guarantees not only continued revenue from their arrangement but also his constitutional claim to those lands *as a Cherokee citizen*. Because Warrior's efforts lead ultimately to Boyd's imprisonment, the forfeiture and redistribution of his vast farmlands, and the sale of his improvements—the profits for which would legally go to Boyd's Cherokee wife, Jennie—political and social stability are restored to that region of the Nation.

More than a restoration of peace to the families on Horsepen and a neat resolution to the novel's two main conflicts, Warrior's centrality to a plotline of Cherokee land and law amplifies the novel's protonationalist politics. As Robert Conley, James Cox, and Jenna Hunnef have each outlined in detail, Oskison modeled Ned Warrior on another Cherokee nationalist—Ned Christie—who also found himself on the wrong side of federal authorities in the jurisdictional no-man's-land of nineteenth-century Indian Territory.[99] A blacksmith and gunsmith, Keetoowah ceremonialist, Cherokee council member, and adviser to Principal Chief Dennis Bushyhead, Christie was popularly accused of a variety of shenanigans ranging from whiskey running and brawling to the alleged murder of a federal deputy marshal in Arkansas. The year of the alleged shooting, 1887, was also the year that Congress passed the General Allotment Act amid a tide of illegal squatters pouring into Cherokee territories and the increasing influence of men like Boyd in Indian Territory politics. Though opposed by the majority of Cherokee citizens, the strongest opposition to any imposition into Cherokee self-governance came from conservative communities and Keetoowah ceremonialists with whom Christie held strong familial, cultural, and political ties. Though staunchly opposed to federal intervention of any kind, Christie was a strong advocate of Cherokee law and order and decided to turn himself over to authorities in the hope of securing bail and proving his innocence. When the hanging judge Isaac C. Parker (Judge Pease in Oskison's novel) refused to grant bail, Christie, rightfully fearing the treatment he would receive from a non-Indian jury in federal court, retreated to his stronghold in the hills of present-day Adair County. It was there where, with more than a little assistance from his conservative family members and allies, Christie waged a five-year standoff with U.S. officials. Christie was finally killed at his home in 1892 after a twenty-four-hour assault that was punctuated by canon fire, dynamite, and more than four thousand rounds of ammunition. One account from the March 18, 1906, edition of the *Daily Oklahoman* remembered the altercation in these terms: "Thus end[ed] a period of seven years of outlawry and crime by a man who had fought a greater number of battles with the officers of the government than any other outlaw known to civilization."[100] Twenty-six years later Christie was cleared of all wrongdoing, reinforcing many Cherokees' belief that his death had been a politically motivated assassination rather than a legal execution.

Indeed, as Conley has documented, Christie was one of a number of Cherokee outlaws who emerged in the four decades between the end of the Civil War in Indian Territory in 1866 and Oklahoma statehood in 1907.[101] While he acknowledges that some were genuinely unlikable figures, Conley notes that many of those who were most feared and celebrated by non-Indians—Zeke Proctor, Mose Miller, Wili Woyi, Charlie Wycliffe, Ned Christie—were all full-blooded Keetoowahs and outspoken opponents of allotment and Oklahoma statehood and thus of federal interventions of any kind into Cherokee jurisdiction.[102] Read in this context and also in light of the vague lack of specificity in any accounts of their alleged crimes, Conley wonders:

> Is it not possible, or even probable, that the same government that had created within the borders of the Cherokee Nation a lawless territory by denying that nation the right to police its own lands, then used that very lawlessness as an excuse for imposing its own jurisdiction in that territory and was carrying that process even further by passing laws to dissolve the Cherokee nation and deny the tribal existence of the Cherokee people—is it not possible and even probable that same government would find a way to destroy its opposition's most vocal and influential leaders? I believe that to be the case.... I believe they were Cherokee patriots dedicated

> to the preservation of the Cherokee Nation. I further believe they were victims—singled out, labeled as outlaws, and pursued as outlaws in order to silence their political interference with the process of fulfilling what the US government viewed as its manifest destiny.[103]

While Oskison does not *explicitly* situate Warrior as a Keetoowah nationalist, Warrior's centrality to the plot over Cherokee land and law and the consistent threats to his life and family at the hands of unscrupulous ranchers, politicians, and law enforcement officials *implicitly* encourage similar questions and conclusions.

Like Christie, Ned Warrior has been wanted for five years for the shooting of a federal marshal, a story which is sensationalized in the local press and leveraged by Boyd and others in their agitation for Warrior's arrest and dispossession. In addition to the initial yarn of Indian outlawry and violence that Boyd spins upon first meeting the Dawes family, he also repeats and amplifies the narrative of Warrior's imminent threat to the community in letters to the local newspaper and in arguments to local and federal authorities for Warrior's arrest.[104] Also like Christie's story, events come to a head at Warrior's fortified cabin where, against enormous odds, canon fire, and explosions, he faces down the reluctant posse led by Cap. Black.[105] As Cox importantly notes, however, this is where the parallels end. Rather than die at the hands of the posse as a symbol of Anglo frontier justice, Warrior is only injured and lives to fight another day. Rather than fulfill the narrative expectation of Indian masculine violence, jealously, and revenge, which Oskison teases earlier in the novel, Warrior comes to recognize Boyd as the engine of violence and redirects his rage toward stopping Boyd's designs on his life and land as well as those of his neighbors and friends. Perhaps most significant, rather than fulfilling the demands of absence and vanishing that the genre often places on Indian male characters—Child's Hobomok, Cooper's Chingachgook, and Longfellow's Hiawatha come immediately to mind—Warrior reunites with his estranged wife, Rose, and commits to writing "a story of quiet happiness" for himself, his family, and his community on the novel's closing pages.[106]

More than relating it as an individual act of heroism or a restoration of peace to the families on Horsepen Creek, however, the novel explicitly situates Warrior's action within a much longer history of Cherokee national survivance. In an earlier part of the novel, following an address by the Cherokee chief encouraging citizens to rise above the crime and chaos precipitated by the opening of the Cherokee Outlet for white settlement, the narrator condemns the land run as "a riotous jumble of sound and color," a "cheap jack show" in "the final scene of an epic drama that had begun two-thirds of a century before with the wholesale removal of the tribe from lands in Georgia and Tennessee coveted by the whites."[107] In a rare extended editorialization, the narrator angrily goes on to connect the graft, violence, and corruption of Removal to similar dynamics following the Civil War and continuing through to allotment and to the arrival of sooners and too-lates to the territory: "In sixty years what a change! Land which then, in the judgment of those wise men at Washington who had ridden to the Capital in stage coaches, would remain unsettled forever, was now looked upon as a rich prize by covetous homesteaders. For years Congress had been negotiating with the tribe to recover that 'Strip' for clamorous whites. Last year the bargain had been concluded and the 'Strip' thrown open to settlement."[108] As he contemplates enacting his plan for revenge separate from, though in solidarity with, his white tenants, Warrior arrives at a similar conclusion:

> Ned had his own private war to wage to-night. If his friends wondered, and worried, over his apparent desertion he couldn't help it; it was a matter that to his Indian mind, could not be explained or advertised.
>
> Shaken by a silent, passionate rage, not merely against Cale [Boyd], but all such scum from the white man's world as were riding this night against his friends, Ned understood better than ever before why old Running Rabbit and his fellow full-bloods of the hill country met in secret councils and planned to drive out the aliens and close the border to them. If they only could! Of course, there were many honest whites, good friends of the Indians and good neighbors. . . . But they appeared, sometimes, to be a helpless minority. They seemed to count for so little compared with the horde of lawless invaders, the whiskey peddlers, cattle thieves, store thieves, train robbers, greed-crazed land grabbers like Jerry Boyd.[109]

As Hunnef explains, Oskison here refers to the sale of the Cherokee Outlet, a massive tract of land west of the Cherokee Nation that was negotiated during Removal to ensure safe access to the rich hunting prairies of the Great Plains.[110] From almost the moment of their arrival, however, Cherokees were pressured to sell the outlet back to the government. Following the Civil War, efforts intensified as Cherokees dealt with massive budget shortfalls and were continually thwarted in court in their attempts generate income through agricultural partnerships with non-Indians. Facing the inevitability of allotment and statehood and unable to leverage the land for revenue, Cherokee leaders were forced to sell the Outlet, leading to the largest land run in U.S. history.

By derisively connecting late nineteenth-century contexts of allotment and the land runs to those of Removal perpetrated earlier in the century, Oskison reframes ostensibly heroic moments of white settlement and expansion as an extended history of Indian dispossession and white American greed. Framed in this way, Hunnef rightly argues that Warrior's "criminality is only the natural response to a much more rampant and insidious threat: the appropriation of Indian lands by the US government and its citizens, whether by 'legitimate' or illegitimate means."[111] If read from within these legal and political contexts as a Cherokee national allegory, Warrior's *individual* defense of Cherokee lands, the Anglo residents living on them, and the community constituted by those relationships stands as a profoundly symbolic assertion—and within the narrative arc of the text, a restoration—of the *collective* sovereignty of the Cherokee Nation.[112]

As is evident in Cherokee law and many of the political conflicts in the Nation from the period in which the novel is set, issues such as these were of persistent concern to the Cherokee government. Measures to restrict white employment, to levy heavy taxes on non-Cherokee industrial interests, and to limit white, black, and non-Cherokee Indian access to per capita payments from land sales point to the intensity of disagreement between progressives and traditionalists, capitalists and populists, and defenders of common lands and advocates of allotment. Though Warrior attempts to work for reform within the Cherokee legal framework, even at times exercising his right to civil disobedience in protest of tribal authority—he acknowledges that he "himself was no tabby cat" and "had walked his own path in defiance of tribal law"—he is also sympathetic with conservative Cherokee traditionalists who have opted out of contemporary politics in protest of what they view as a crisis of immigration and acculturation.[113] Recognizing that the closing of national borders and the removal of all non-Cherokees is impossible on one hand and that opening them up freely to white settlement and allotment is undesirable on the other, Warrior adopts a pragmatic political approach of alliance with sympathetic white residents who are committed to the Nation's authority, safety, and security. Rejecting neither traditionalists nor progressives, capitalists nor populists, Indians nor non-Indians, the full-blooded, Cherokee-speaking Warrior attempts to walk the fine line between resistance and accommodation, a complicated position variously articulated by Daniel Justice, Christopher Teuton, and Joshua Nelson as a "beloved path," "middle way," or "progressive tradition" of Cherokee life.[114] As the only principal character with ties to each of these communities, Warrior stands as a kind of diplomatic intermediary and political broker between political factions (a position not dissimilar to that occupied by Ruth Muskrat Bronson, discussed in chapter 4). In this sense, the idea of citizenship that emerges in the text becomes a question not of *being* but of *doing*, not a question of who or what one *is* but of what and for whom one *does*, and is thus not strictly an issue of rights and the law but also of responsibilities and relationships.[115] In *Black Jack Davy*, whatever future exists for the Cherokee Nation after the narrative ends is firmly and significantly in the hands of Cherokee citizens and legal residents who are committed to the security and sovereignty of the Nation.

While the forces that win out in the end very well may be those of progress and civilization, the victory does not depend on the displacement of Cherokee peoples from their lands or the political dissolution of the Cherokee government. In contrast to Konkle's "epistemology of ignorance" in which a constitutionally defined, territorially autonomous, civilized Indian nation is a contradiction in terms when situated within the racialized discourses of savagery and civilization, in *Black Jack Davy* such discourses exist in the narrative as co-constitutive elements of Cherokee sovereignty. Such an argument for cultural and political coexistence emerged in the nineteenth century as a central component of Cherokees' understanding of their relationship with the federal government and of what it meant (and means) to be a sovereign nation. McLoughlin writes:

> Sovereignty for Ross and most Cherokees meant the right to govern themselves in their own way under their own leaders and to expect the federal government to honor their treaties as it would honor treaty stipulations with any foreign nation. . . . The Cherokee constitution, though modeled on that of the United States, *was its own supreme law*. Total sovereignty was limited only by treaty negotiations *mutually beneficial and voluntarily signed*, and treaties were permanently binding on both the Cherokee Nation and the United States.[116]

As Justice observes in a reading of Oskison's *The Singing Bird*, a similar assumption is at work about Indian Territory: "Indian Territory isn't just about

Indians. . . . The growing White population was already alarming Indian leaders, and that growing population threat brought with it many challenges for the People. Yet it is still *Indian* Territory; it is still the land under the political jurisdiction and authority of the Real People; and it is still the place where they exercise their rights of self-determination and sovereignty, where they fight to determine their own way in the world without interference from the United States and its citizens."[117] Replace "Indian Territory" with "the Cherokee Nation" within the context of *Black Jack Davy*, and we have a useful statement of the vision of Cherokee nationhood that the novel puts forward. Read in this light, the text's depiction of Jim Dawes's death as a tragic though heroic martyrdom for "the cause of law and order," and its immediate apotheosis of his sacrifice as guaranteeing "the safe structure of civilization for which the best men of the Territory worked, and the women prayed" takes on an entirely different significance, especially when considered against another Dawes familiar to students of American Indian history.[118]

Henry Laurens Dawes, the architect of the General Allotment Act, which led to the dissolution of Indian governments in the early twentieth century, entered Indian Territory in the late nineteenth century on the assumption that Indian nations were inimical to progress and that Indian peoples must either assimilate or disappear from the earth. Oskison's Dawes family immigrates to the Cherokee Nation assuming its survival, and they are optimistic about a prosperous future as legal residents if not at some point as naturalized citizens. Whereas the historical Dawes believed that Indian survival necessitated the breakup of the tribal estate, Jim Dawes and his family take up arms to defend the Nation's common properties as central to the future they envision. And whereas men like Senator Dawes looked at Indian nations and saw violence, lawlessness, and savagery, Jim and Mirabelle Dawes see for their family a hopeful future of prosperity, safety, and security in the Cherokee Nation, a national vision for which Jim pays the ultimate price. By depicting the frontier community as a distinctly Cherokee political entity and by defining the threat not as savage Indians or overcivilized eastern socialites but as self-interested Anglo capitalists who willfully disregard Cherokee constitutional authority (and thus internationally recognized norms of sovereignty), *Black Jack Davy* disarticulates civilization with the West and with whiteness, claiming both the genre and the debate over progress as distinctly Cherokee nationalist endeavors.

Tribal Literature and the Limits of the Nation

Speaking from a Cherokee center at the margins of U.S. romantic-nationalism, *Black Jack Davy* identifies what Homi Bhabha characterizes as "the mark of the ambivalence of the nation as a narrative strategy—and an apparatus of power," which attempts to collapse the irreducible plurality of a community into the essentialist categories of "nation" and "people." Neither the beginning nor the end of national narratives, such categories signify "a problem of knowledge that haunts the symbolic formation of social authority, . . . the cutting edge between the totalizing powers of the social and the forces that signify the more specific address to contentious, unequal interests and identities within the population."[119] It is precisely in these margins of contention and inequality between the imagined idea of the nation and one's often disjunctive lived experience of it where the "discursive ambivalence" of the nation-as-narration becomes visible.[120] By exposing the historicity of Indian dispossession and the dissolution of tribal nations not as the inevitable climax of a grand moral drama of white racial triumphalism but as the result of self-interested human action, *Black Jack Davy* imagines alternative possibilities of Indigenous nationhood that are rendered impossible in the totalizing discourses of U.S. settler exceptionalism.

Arguably, it is in this move toward reopening an Indigenous national history that many considered closed that the text performs its most important political work, for at the time when Oskison was writing, the disastrous policies of allotment and assimilation were being seriously reconsidered. For the first time in a generation, tribal nationhood, collective ownership of tribal lands, and the foundations for what would become a reinvigorated principle of tribal sovereignty were back on the table, and Indians like Ned Warrior were themselves asserting their place in the process. As Oskison would have known well from his own experiences in federal Indian policy activism with the Society of American Indians, any hope for Indian law reform would emerge as the result of cooperative alliances between Indian activists and sympathetic Anglo lawmakers. Perhaps the text's ironic treatment of the Dawes family's name is an invitation to a new generation of federal lawmakers to forge a different path than their predecessors chose, one that would work with Indian people rather than against them, that would value their philosophies of governance rather than dismiss them. Together with its insistence on Cherokee territorial authority, law, and citizenship, the novel's portrait of the Cherokee Nation as a functioning, sovereign, and multicultural state presents a powerful argument for the reinvestment of land and sovereignty in whatever form of Indian nationhood might potentially emerge out of those reform efforts.

Though the promise of Indian policy reform was never fully realized, and though it would take the Cherokee Nation another fifty years to officially reorganize as a sovereign nation-people, in looking back, *Black Jack Davy* imagines the possibility and promise of what a renewed Cherokee Nation might look like. Make no mistake, it is not a perfect vision. Its restrictive positioning of women as either idealized subjects of Christian virtue or racially coded objects of male sexual desire and its almost total erasure of significant characters and communities of African descent present significant problems for any contemporary reading of the novel. Though the text ostensibly imagines a Cherokee Nation that is open to anyone committed to the political autonomy and legal integrity of the Cherokee state, it clearly conceives of its ideal citizen in strictly racialized and gendered terms.[121] There are no Nanye'his on the Neosho, no models from which a future Ruth Muskrat Bronson or Wilma Mankiller might emerge to lead the Nation. Similarly, there appears to be no place for citizens of African descent outside of domestic service or agricultural labor much less on national councils or judicial benches.[122] In the national narrative of land, law, and citizenship that I have been arguing for here, both blacks and women are troublingly relegated to Oskison's narrative margins.

As unappealing as such dynamics are to contemporary readers, they capture the complexities of Cherokee constitutionalism and its effects on how some Cherokees understood, experienced, and imagined nationhood and citizenship even after the dissolution of the tribal state. Such contradictions beckon further scholarly attention not only to the content of Cherokee nationhood evident in such texts but also to the historical, social, legal, and political processes through which such concepts, ideas, and practices emerge and continually shift in response to specific historical circumstances. If we buy into the idea that nations are constituted in moments of violence, which must then perpetually be disavowed through an "apparatus of cultural fictions," then the place of constitutions and legal codes as part and parcel of that apparatus, that tribal-specific literary tradition, must be critically considered. Doing so reminds us that the rule of law is a legal construct that is continually in the process of articulation and revision and focuses critical attention on the complicated ways that Indigenous-authored texts can at once speak back to settler discourses from the colonial margins even as they silence those that are similarly marginalized within their own national borders. If the Cherokee Nation that Oskison recalled and the national imaginary that he drew upon were at least partially the product of the constitutional history I have attempted to recount here, the text's marginalization of women and black people might fruitfully be interrogated as a narrative translation of their similar exclusion from full-participant citizenship in a thoroughly racialized and gendered Cherokee constitutional tradition.

Indeed, shifting the lens from questions of nationality—the law—to nationhood—that discursive and experiential space where politics, history, culture, kinship, and imagination overlap—forces a consideration of the ways in which narratives of tribal nationhood, resistant as they may be to dominant nationalist discourses, reproduce many of their excesses, ambiguities, and ambivalences. If, in looking back, *Black Jack Davy* reimagines the possibility and promise of a renewed Cherokee Nation, the question now becomes one of the content of nationhood that the text imagines, the ways in which it defines the character and integrity of Cherokee national identity, and what kind of ideal citizen such discourses ultimately produce. To the extent that a constitutional framework can contribute significantly to studies of Native literatures and other cultural productions, it will probably rest on engaging internal issues such as these as a means of informing and historicizing contemporary discussions of nationhood, citizenship, and belonging within and among Indian nations themselves. Read within the long and continuous tradition of Cherokee constitutionalism, *Black Jack Davy* is a significant text of both Cherokee and American Indian letters not only for its intervention into American romantic nationalist discourses but also for its imaginative, hopeful, and at times complicated engagement with Indigenous nationhood itself.

TWO

Oppositional Discourse and Revisionist Historiography in Rachel Caroline Eaton's *John Ross and the Cherokee Indians*

Coming to know the past has been part of the critical pedagogy of decolonization. To hold alternative histories is to hold alternative knowledges. The pedagogical implication of this access to alternative knowledges is that they can form the basis of alternative ways of doing things. Transforming our colonized views of our own history (as written by the West), however, requires us to revisit, site by site, our history under Western eyes.

Linda Tuhiwai Smith, Decolonizing Methodologies

Each generation has created and re-created the Cherokee in the image of that age. . . . This mythical Cherokee looms so large today that the real one is in danger of being forgotten by many Indians and much of white society that has come to believe many of these often-contradictory myths.

Rennard Strickland, "In Search of Cherokee History"

In the written records of America the place accorded the aboriginal peoples who once ruled over the whole western world can scarcely be considered a reputable one. . . . That he has ever cherished any but sinister sentiments for those who dispossessed him of his birthright or that he has exercised any but destructive influences upon the history of the country has been too often ignored. It is even denied that he is capable of Anglo-Saxon civilization.

Rachel Caroline Eaton, John Ross and the Cherokee Indians

There is a well-known need in Indian Country to contest and revise the massive archive produced *about* Native peoples via the production of counter-histories *from* Indian communities themselves, which the quotes above by Smith, Strickland, and Eaton make plain. As Philip Deloria, Shari Huhndorf, Ned Blackhawk, Jeanne O'Brien, and others have written, such projects require Native historians to identify bias and correct historical inaccuracies as well as listen to the silences and attend to the gaps that structure how colonialist narratives erase Indigenous views of history, community, and nation.[1] In doing so, historians often draw on the vast, largely untapped archive of personal recollections, family histories, and community-centered narratives of experience and the collective historical memory of Indigenous national communities—all of which constitute crucial components of Indigenous nation-peoplehood.[2] Such work provides more complex or comprehensive accounts of the historical dynamics of contact, conflict, collision, adaptation, and exchange while also making claims to humanity, nationhood, sovereignty, and universal human rights within discourses that have historically reserved such privileges as the special purview of Euro-American subjects and states.[3] To enter the historical archive as an Indigenous scholar is, to paraphrase Linda Tuhiwai Smith, to engage in a dual process of re*writing* history in order to re*right* the place of Indian people in it.[4]

The importance of such work and the challenges that remain to decolonize Indigenous historiography were on display at a keynote panel during the 2010 Sequoyah Symposium on the campus of Northeastern State University, the former home of the Cherokee Female Seminary in the heart of the Cherokee capital of Tahlequah.[5] The panel assembled Cherokee and other Indian contributors to the "Trail of Tears" installment of PBS's *We Shall Remain* series, a five-part historical docudrama depicting significant—and, for popular audiences, familiar—events in Native and U.S. history from Indian cultural and political perspectives.[6] Consisting of director Chris Eyre (Cheyenne and Arapaho), principal actor Wes Studi (Cherokee Nation), scholar and commentator Jace Weaver (Cherokee descent), and Cherokee genealogist and tribal councilman Jack Baker (Cherokee Nation), the panel sought to re-present Cherokees as historical agents rather than as the tragic victims of federal policy and white racism, and to resist reductive narratives positioning patriotic antiremoval heroes against duplicitous proremoval villains. While acknowledging the horrific consequences of Removal, the panelists also wished to honor the profound triumph of survival and reconstruction in Indian Territory and to reposition the Removal as one significant moment in a much longer and continuing history of Cherokee nation-peoplehood.

By and large, audience reaction to the film was enthusiastic. Like the filmmakers, most recognized that by focusing on the tragedy of Removal and on the cultural and political schisms that emerged as a consequence, popular and academic histories reinforced narratives of vanishing and disappearance belied by the actual survival of those who walked the trail and by the contemporary presence of the Cherokee Nation. Other respondents spoke to the ways in which scientific theories of evolutionary social progress and heroic narratives of Anglo-triumphalism work to depoliticize legitimate political contestation; naturalize and sanitize conquest; and alleviate any moral, ethical, or reparative responsibilities from settler-colonial audiences. As the discussion turned to the film's representation of specific Cherokee historical figures, however, the dynamics of the conversation turned. Where some criticized what they viewed as an overly sympathetic depiction of the Ridge/Treaty Party faction, others cited the film's failure to critically evaluate the Ross/National Party's opposition to removal and the traumatic consequences of those decisions. Breaking along political lines shot through with decades-old familial, cultural, class, and racial tensions, the discussion quickly transformed into emotionally charged arguments between Nationalist, Treaty Party, and Old Settler descendants, each indicting the others for the trauma suffered, the lives lost, and the chaos that followed the Trail Where They Cried. Though occurring more than 170 years ago, the Removal remains both a powerful memory and an immediate experience for many Cherokee families as well as a central narrative component of Cherokee national identity in the West.

Writing almost one hundred years before the symposium, and only seven years after the dissolution of the Cherokee Nation into which she was born a citizen, Rachel Caroline Eaton entered the archive and penned a counterhistory of Cherokee nationhood as told through the life of its most recognizable leader. Written in both a historical moment and a discipline still dominated by ethnocentric narratives of Anglo racial triumphalism and social evolutionary paradigms of human history, *John Ross and the Cherokee Indians* (1914) remarkably anticipates many of the contemporary scholarly concerns highlighted above. Its use of local archives, family collections, and oral histories as a supplement to conventional authoritative sources locates the narrative firmly within Cherokee historical contexts and privileges forms of knowledge typically excluded from conventional histories. The text also recenters the narrative explicitly within Cherokee geopolitical territories and in important locations within the Cherokee Nation. Further, its subversion of generic and narrative conventions of Indian historiography and life writing refuse tragic vanishing narratives of Native absence, recovering both Ross and the Cherokee Nation as historical agents in a narrative of Indian nation-peoplehood in the Americas. Combined with its attention to political and diplomatic relationships between the Cherokee Nation and the United States, such strategies reframe that history not as a clash between savagery and civilization but as a political contest between national sovereigns.

This chapter examines Eaton's complex navigation of settler historiography and considers both the subversive potential and the critical limitations of the interventions into Cherokee historiography and Indian life writing that she attempted. After situating Eaton within the Cherokee and the larger contexts that informed her life and work, I historicize her negotiation with the discourses of civilization, progress, and modernity that structured not only Cherokee historiography but also federal Indian policy and popular attitudes toward Indian peoples. Embedded in both Cherokee and broader Native rhetorical traditions of appropriation, inversion, indictment, and critique, Eaton's text works to dissociate civilization, progress, and modernity from their exclusive racial and political associations with whiteness and U.S. settler statehood. With this larger discursive framework as context, I then survey the archival authorities with and against which Eaton writes and consider the radical disciplinary and narrative interventions that she makes in conventional historiographic practices and in the narrative conventions structuring Indian life writing. By way of conclusion, I explore both the potentialities and the limitations of Eaton's project and reflect on how such issues might inform contemporary historiographic work that is taking place at all levels of Cherokee community, not least of which in personal and public interactions such as those that opened the chapter.

The Makings of a Cherokee Historian: Family, History, Education

The first of four children to Nancy "Nannie" Elizabeth Ward Williams (1851–1896) and George Washington Eaton (1845–1929), Rachel Caroline "Callie"

Rachel Caroline Eaton, Cherokee historian, educator, and administrator. Illustration by Roy Boney.

Eaton was born July 7, 1869, in the far eastern section of the Delaware district of Cherokee Nation, just west of Siloam Springs, Arkansas, and east of Jay community.[7] Her mother was a Cherokee citizen and a descendant of a prominent Old Settler family, the Wards, with ancestral ties to the Cherokee Beloved Woman Nanye'hi (a.k.a. Nancy Ward) and other important figures in Cherokee history such as Granny Hopper, Old Hop, and Moytoy. Her great-grandfather, James Ward, relocated with other Old Settler families who moved to Arkansas Territory after 1817–19 in order to put more distance between themselves and an increasingly hostile Georgia government. Shortly before the Treaty of New Echota in 1835 and ahead of the larger Removal that occurred four years later, the family moved once again to the newly established Cherokee Nation in Indian Territory, settling in the Goingsnake district in what is Adair County today. It was here that Eaton's mother, Nancy, would attend Dwight Mission before the outbreak of the Civil War in the early 1860s.

Eaton's father was a native Texan who enlisted at the age of sixteen in Company B, Morgan's Battalion, a Texas cavalry unit out of Rusk County, Texas, that was stationed primarily at Arkansas Post just outside of Indian Territory during the Civil War.[8] Though he no doubt spent some time in the Cherokee Nation throughout the conflict, George was also likely familiar with the large contingent of Cherokee families with ties to the Treaty Party who had relocated to Rusk County in the 1840s to escape factional violence after Removal. Settling in and around Nacogdoches, these families included the Adairs, Mays, Bells, Starrs, and Waties among others.[9] After the war George returned to the Cherokee Nation, perhaps accompanying these families, who had received amnesty from the Ross government, and he and Nancy were married there on May 17, 1868. In 1874 the family relocated to Sahgeeyah community in Cooweescoowee district, just outside of present-day Claremore in Rogers County. It was in Claremore that George Eaton would establish himself as a prominent cattle rancher, real estate developer, and oil man alongside the likes of Clem Rogers and Lynn Riggs's father, William.[10]

Educated in Cherokee public schools, Eaton attended the original Cherokee Female Seminary in Park Hill from 1883 until April 10, 1887, when the school was destroyed by fire while students were away for Easter weekend. She, along with the rest of her class, continued her studies at the male seminary and graduated on June 30 of that year.[11] After an absence of five years, probably during a stint as a teacher at Prairie Grove School in the Goingsnake district, she returned to the seminary as first assistant principal under the legendary A. Florence Wilson, a position she held for the next six years.[12] Described as "forthright in her approach," "precise in her speech," and "always the 'Educator,'" Eaton was also remembered by her students for her "quiet sense of humor" and "impeccable manners," which were always on display, whether during meals in the Seminary dining hall, while chaperoning students about Tahlequah, or when exercising her biting humor to bring prideful students back down to earth.[13] A proud and devout Presbyterian who at one time considered a life of missionary service, Eaton, along with another Cherokee assistant principal, Blue Adair, cofounded a branch of the Young Women's Christian Association at the seminary. The organization offered a Sunday prayer meeting as an addition to the required morning Sunday school and afternoon service.[14]

Eaton left the seminary to continue her studies at Drury College in Springfield, Missouri, graduating cum laude with a BS in 1895. In 1901, a few years after returning to the Cherokee seminary, she married James Alexander Burns, a graduate of the Cherokee Male Seminary and a fellow educator. The couple moved to Chicago in 1905 where Eaton enrolled in graduate work in history at the University of Chicago. After receiving her AM (the equivalent of a masters degree) in 1911 upon the completion of her fifty-three-page thesis, "John Ross,"

Eaton significantly expanded the thesis into a 212-page manuscript, which situates Ross in the longer history of the Cherokee Nation up to his death in 1866. This text was published in 1914, and remains a pivotal text on the Cherokee statesman today. She condensed and revised this publication into her dissertation, "John Ross and the Cherokees," and took her PhD in 1919; she privately published the dissertation two years later.[15] Her PhD is thought to be the first of its kind for a woman from Indian Territory.[16] Eaton followed these publications with a handful of articles for the *Chronicles of Oklahoma*, all of which dealt with actors and events prominent in Cherokee and Oklahoma history and with the landscapes and geographies that she called home.

In addition to her scholarly pursuits, Eaton kept up an active professional and public life, holding a variety of appointments from Ohio and Missouri to Oklahoma and Texas. She served as professor of history at Lake Erie College in Painesville, Ohio, and as chair of the departments of history at State College for Women in Columbia, Missouri, and at Trinity University in Waxahachie, Texas, where she also served as dean of women. In 1920 Eaton was elected the supervisor of schools for Rogers County, the first woman so honored, and served two consecutive terms over the next six years.[17] She was also instrumental in founding and supporting a number of local historical organizations for the purposes of preserving Cherokee history, challenging erroneous stereotypes, and building community. The Sequoyah Historical Society in Tahlequah, composed entirely of members of Indian descent (at one time listing more than seventy on the roster, including fellow Cherokee historian Emmet Starr), was organized explicitly "for the purposes of preserving Indian history and relics," which we might infer means protecting Indian artifacts from destruction, development, theft, or expatriation.[18] Eaton was also a central figure in the founding of the Tulsa Historical Society—the inaugural chapter of which bears her name as "one of Oklahoma's outstanding historians"—as well as the Indian Women's Pocahontas Club, which was originally organized in Claremore and for which Eaton is alleged to have composed the club motto: "Speak kind words and you will receive kind echoes, Sky Father and I bless you."[19] Will Rogers, a fellow Cherokee and product of Claremore, was inducted as an honorary member.

In recognition of her intellectual achievements, public service, and social activity, Eaton was profiled in J. G. Sanders's *Who's Who among Oklahoma Indians* and in Lyle H. Boren and Dale Boren's *Who Is Who in Oklahoma: A Biographical History of Men and Women in Oklahoma Life Today* eight years later. On July 7, 1936, the Oklahoma Memorial Association praised Eaton "as one of Oklahoma's outstanding women, because of her great and good service to humanity and the State of Oklahoma" and honored her as one twelve figures inducted into the Oklahoma Hall of Fame in the state capital building.[20] In 1935 Eaton returned to her childhood home of Claremore to research and work on what would be her final manuscript, *The History of the Cherokees,* which she completed only months before she died of breast cancer on September 21, 1938, and which remains unpublished to this day.[21] In December of that year, Choctaw historian and colleague Muriel Wright memorialized Eaton as "the first woman of Indian descent to achieve distinction as an educator and writer of history" and credited her as "one of the outstanding personalities reared under the regime of the old Cherokee Nation as an Indian republic."[22] Only seven years after the dissolution of her own tribal nation, it was precisely the story "of the old Cherokee Nation as an Indian republic" to which Eaton turned as the first Cherokee professional historian—male or female—to tell the story of her people.

"Civilization" and Cherokee Rhetorics of Sovereignty and Survivance

Writing from within the discursive and disciplinary restrictions of early twentieth-century academic history, and without the benefit of decolonization theory, a reaffirmed notion of tribal sovereignty, or the institutional apparatuses of Native Studies and New Indian History, Eaton situates her narrative of Cherokee nationhood within the racialized, decidedly U.S.-nationalistic discourses of civilization and progress. Considering the dominant intellectual paradigms of the moment, this is perhaps not surprising.

Nineteenth-century writings on American Indians, whether in ethnological accounts or amateur histories, had long been ruled by racial developmental theories that were advocated by figures such as Francis Parkman, George Bancroft, Henry Roe Schoolcraft, Lewis Henry Morgan, and others.[23] As it is outlined in *Ancient Society,* Morgan's theory holds that all human societies progressed differentially through distinct stages of social organization, from savagery and barbarism into civilization and modernity, with private property and agricultural-industrial modes of production as defining characteristics. Understood by many as a Darwinist juggernaut consuming everything in its path, this seemingly unstoppable social force often positioned American

Indians either as natural casualties or tragic victims or as ideal candidates for salvation and uplift.[24] Whether articulated by amateur ethnologists and historians, assimilationist "Friends of the Indian" organizations, or an emerging class of professional anthropologists, these attitudes, as Frederick Hoxie observes, resulted in a conflicted ambivalence between sympathy and resignation toward American Indians. Whereas professional ethnologists sought to salvage Indian cultural forms before they vanished entirely, reformers hoped to avoid their complete destruction by raising Indians to a higher level of progress while attempting to minimize the trauma that this rapid advancement might induce.

Preprofessional historians of American Indian history were no different. As John Rhea has recently documented, the lines between ethnology and history, when it came to American Indians, were fuzzy well into the late 1890s as historians sought to adopt a more objective, scientific methodology anchored to documentary research.[25] Until this shift, American Indians were often situated in pan-Indian frameworks, which leveled tribal distinctions, ignored politics, and presented the colonial interaction—from Removal and warfare to assimilation and allotment—as regrettable but "unavoidable steps along the road to progress."[26] Though professional academic historiography had begun to reject racial developmentalism, it still largely ignored tribal-specific legal, political, and social histories. In order to tell an academic history of Cherokee nationhood and sovereignty that refused the comfortable rhetorics of inevitability, progress, and assimilation, Eaton necessarily had to battle with the legacies of this historiographic archive.

Considering her position as a mixed-race Cherokee citizen educated in Cherokee public schools who had graduated from the Cherokee Female Seminary, Eaton's reliance on discourses of civilization and progress is also firmly embedded in Cherokee and American Indian histories and rhetorical traditions. As a fundamental provision of treaty relationships with the federal government and as a central component in the move toward Cherokee nationalization in the late 1810s, Cherokees had long adopted a strategic relationship with the federal government's civilization program and its attempts to transform Indian savagery into a civilized reflection of itself. Early efforts to abolish blood law and to centralize political authority over Cherokee communities, for instance, reflected as much a pragmatic need to mitigate internal tensions and regulate external conflict with frontier communities as it did a rejection of Cherokee social and political conventions. Similarly, though signaling a more "civilized" division of gendered labor around settler notions of masculine agriculture and feminine domesticity, Cherokee women continued to farm and used money earned from spinning and weaving to forward their own material interests, while men stocked the range with cattle, sheep, goats and pigs as an adaptation of conventional hunting practices. Christianity and Western education were similarly adopted by many Cherokees not as strategies to eradicate traditional spiritual practices or to alienate children from their families as civilization advocates intended, but to arm a generation of Cherokees with the knowledge and skills necessary to defend the political and economic interests of the Nation in the post-Revolutionary period. While the adoption of a constitutional government and a written code of law concentrated political and legal authority in the hands of a relative few, it also incorporated Cherokee understandings of common land tenure, matrilineal property and maternal rights, and religious practice that differed significantly from its U.S. counterpart. As is suggested by petitions from Cherokee women protesting land cessions, demands by clan relations to attain citizenship for Afro-descent kin, and provisions for naturalization based on local relations and affirmations of character, traditional forms of gendered influence and authority persisted, if often behind closed doors and in a more restricted way. To be sure, such accommodations resulted in significant changes to Cherokee lifeways, and important differences existed over the conditions, extent, and rapidity by which acculturation should (or should not) proceed. Despite these differences, many Cherokees viewed a *qualified* adoption of Euro-American norms as a preservation of national autonomy and a guarantee against military conflict. The question, then as now, focused not on the merits of white civilization versus Indian savagery, but on the extent to which certain elements of "civilized life"—formal education, English literacy, industrial development, Western agricultural practices, written codes of law, constitutional democracy, etc.—might productively contribute to and advance Cherokee political and cultural aspirations.[27]

As part of this project, Cherokees developed a distinct rhetoric of civilization that links Cherokee understandings of land, kinship, and community to Euro-American rhetorics of republicanism, democracy, and Christian charity.[28] In a 1777 address to the Continental Congress, Old Tassel invoked the language of "free will and equality" to indict his white "brothers" for arbitrary demands for more land "by right of conquest" and for attempts to impose settler law over

Cherokee domestic matters.[29] Similarly, in a series of addresses to both U.S. and Cherokee officials from the late eighteenth through the mid-nineteenth centuries, Cherokee women, including Eaton's own ancestor Nancy Ward, combined matrilineal kinship relations with American notions of Christian virtue and republican womanhood in order to broker peace not simply as a *legal* condition of treaty provisions but also as an *ethical responsibility* of "civilized" familial relations.[30] Decades later, John Ross, John Ridge, and Elias Boudinot would juxtapose Cherokee advances in civilization against the savage violence of Georgia militias and federal authorities in a series of impassioned defenses of Cherokee sovereignty at the height of the Removal crisis.[31] Reflecting his own bitterness and anger engendered by the traumatic consequences of the Removal and its aftermath on his family, John Rollin Ridge's *The Life and Times of Joaquin Murieta, the Celebrated California Bandit* turns the frontier romance on its head to deliver a scathing indictment of U.S. imperial violence and dispossession—a tradition that John Oskison and Robert Conley would continue to draw on on in the twentieth and twenty-first centuries. Later in the nineteenth century, Narcissa Owen and Lucy Lowrey Hoyt Keys would look to Cherokee historical traditions, family narratives, personal experiences, and collective memories in order to compose highly localized histories of Cherokee nation-peoplehood not as a break from tradition or cultural authenticity, as many ethnologists and historians would frame it, but as the continuation of Cherokee identity and tradition into the modern age.[32] As Denson and Parins extensively document, Cherokee statesmen throughout the late nineteenth century also leveraged rhetorics of civilization and progress as a defense of Cherokee sovereignty against foreign corporate and industrial interests and territorial and allotment advocates alike.[33] Daniel Justice's literary history shows how this rhetorical tradition carries over well into the twentieth century across a variety of narrative and literary forms, perhaps most popularly through the syndicated editorials and radio broadcasts of Will Rogers.[34] Throughout this genealogy of Cherokee intellectual and political thought, Cherokees consistently detach civilization, progress, nationhood, and modernity from their exclusive associations with whiteness and the U.S. settler state. Their commitments to discourses of civilization function less to celebrate the idea itself and more as a strategic rhetorical device—an "X-mark" or "progressive tradition," to use Lyons's and Nelson's terms—through which to advance their political demands to "be, still, a nation."[35] In doing so, Cherokees consistently reframe the "Indian problem" not as a choice between assimilation or vanishing, wardship or citizenship, but as "the defense of Indian nationhood" itself.[36]

These tribally specific defenses of sovereignty are also tied to long-standing rhetorics of survivance that have been practiced by Native peoples from the moment they began to write in colonialist languages.[37] From Samson Occom's thinly veiled critique of Christian hypocrisy in his "Sermon on the Execution of Moses Paul" (1772) to William Apess's indictment of Euro-American ethnocentrism and colonial violence in "Eulogy on King Philip" (1836); from Ridge's denunciation of U.S. imperial violence to Sarah Winnemucca's exposé of federal duplicity, graft, violence, and oppression in *Life Among the Paiutes* (1883); and from Simon Pokagon's refusal to celebrate the Columbian Exchange in "A Red Man's Rebuke" (1892) to Zitkála-Šá's attack on the boarding school apparatus in *American Indian Stories* (1921), American Indian writers have long held up a looking glass to U.S. audiences in order to make visible the wide gulf between American ideals and American practice.[38]

Additionally, national political organizations like the Society of American Indians focused their energies on questions of Indian civic integration and citizenship, access to education and economic opportunities, tolerance for Indian cultural and religious practices, and reform of the Bureau of Indian Affairs. In essays, policy statements, and autobiographical narratives, Red Progressives such as Arthur Parker, Charles Eastman, Carlos Montezuma, Luther Standing Bear, and others drew on and disrupted conventional performances of Indianness in order to present alternative images of Indian identity that were at once traditional and modern, both tribal and American. Figures like Laura Cornelius Kellogg, Zitkála-Šá, Ruth Muskrat Bronson, and D'Arcy McNickle engaged in individual economic, cultural, and educational development work outside their own communities as well as under the auspices of the SAI and the BIA. Though such figures variously subscribed to what they understood to be universal ideals of enlightenment and progress, they consistently refused attempts to frame those discussions in terms of Indian racial character or biological fitness. Whether utilized in tribally specific defenses of nationhood or in popular debates over policy and representation, Cherokee and American Indian writers throughout the nineteenth and early twentieth centuries turned to civilization as a recognizable shared discourse through which they could leverage popular sentiments to their own ends.[39]

Well versed in these overlapping rhetorical and historiographic traditions, Eaton appropriates and subverts dominant discourses of civilization in order to undermine its Anglocentric underpinnings and to levy strong critiques against the United States' hypocrisy, exploitation, violence, and arbitrary abuses of power. That her project is different from those that came before is already evident in the differences in tone between the foreword that that opens the book, written by University of Chicago professor William E. Dodd, and Eaton's own preface, which immediately follows. Reflecting an imperialist nostalgia of the regrettable though inevitable demise of tribal peoples in the face of Euro-American expansion that dominated popular understandings of Cherokee history, Dodd writes, "There is no more tragic history than that of the Cherokee Indians."[40] After noting the "growth and development of this group of aborigines" toward "building a culture of their own," Dodd understands the impact of Eaton's text primarily in terms of how it speaks to students of American history: "What would the people of Georgia do if the United States refused to guarantee the integrity of her boundaries? What would the Federal Supreme Court answer to a petition under the treaties with the national government for local authority and self-government inside the bounds of one of the thirteen original states? And if the Georgians and the Indians came to blows, what would be the effect of federal intervention? Thus we see that the history of the Cherokee Nation offers a good opportunity to any student who has sympathy for the natives and a proper sense for the realities of American national development."[41] For Dodd the tragedy of the Cherokee story lies not in the dissolution of a tribal nation and the ethnic cleansing of a people from the Southeast but in the stain such events have wrought upon American history and the failure of its institutions to prevent such atrocities. Readers "sympathetic" to such a narrative, Dodd writes, will appreciate Eaton's attempt to answer these questions and reflect on this miscarriage of justice. That part of the tragedy, and thus the sympathy with which readers should lend the subject, rests on the Cherokees' development of culture (i.e., Euro-American markers of civilization such as property, written language, and legal and political institutions) suggests the developmentalist teleology, however sympathetic, that continued to organize professional academic historiography of the day.

Though noting that the purpose of her text is to provide a "sympathetic" account of "the evolution from barbarism to civilization of one of the most progressive tribes of North American Indians," the opening lines of Eaton's preface seem to take this logic to task and suggest that she might be interested in pursuing different questions to different ends. Whereas Dodd's indictment of U.S. duplicity is left implicit, Eaton explicitly situates her story within a long history of continental dispossession and violence against Indigenous peoples for which contemporary historiography has failed to account. "In the written records of America," she opens, "the place accorded the aboriginal peoples who once ruled over the whole western world can scarcely be considered a reputable one. The very name Indian is a misnomer due to a geographical error of the fifteenth century which enlightened knowledge has failed to correct."[42] She goes on to link that record and its effects on "aboriginal peoples" to the reductive manner in which Euro-American histories position Indigenous peoples in those stories: "On the pages of United States history the Indian usually appears seated at the council fire grimly plotting the destruction of his enemy, or formidable in feathers and war paint, tomahawk in hand, he lurks darkly on the outskirts of civilization awaiting an opportunity to fall on defenseless pioneers whose scalp he can display as proof of his prowess. That he has ever cherished any but sinister sentiments for those who dispossessed him of his birthright or that he has exercised any but destructive influences upon the history of the country has been too often ignored. It is even denied that he is capable of Anglo-Saxon civilization."[43]

In contrast to these portrayals, Eaton mentions the number of "eminent physicians, eloquent preachers, prominent authors, astute financiers, and constructive statesmen" who hail from these seemingly primitive peoples.[44] No doubt drawing on her own tribal experience and especially on the subject of her research, Eaton is also likely thinking of contemporaries such as Seneca anthropologist Arthur Parker, Oneida economist Laura Cornelius Kellogg, Ho-Chunk minister and philosopher Henry Roe Cloud, and writers ranging from Charles Eastman (Dakota) and Zitkála-Šá (Dakota) to her own Cherokee contemporaries John Oskison and Emmet Starr. Though betraying more than a little of the Cherokee chauvinism common to her peers—Oskison, Riggs, Rogers, Bronson, and others often distinguished Cherokees from less "civilized" tribes and other racial minorities—Eaton also alludes to a diverse array of American Indians living thoroughly modern contemporary lives.[45] Like the previous generation of Cherokees about which she writes, contemporary Indians also work "to maintain their tribal identity and ancestral domains against the overwhelming tide of economic development."[46] Just as William Apess, decades earlier, turned to the colonial history of ethnic cleansing of Indigenous people from New England in order to draw attention to the ongoing history of dispossession in the Americas during the Removal era, Eaton similarly revisits Cherokee history as a context in which to contest early twentieth-century attitudes, which at the time of her writing still largely understood "American," "Indian," "civilization," and "progress" as mutually exclusive terms. If Oskison's attention in the opening pages of *Black Jack Davy* embeds his frontier romance in Cherokee geographies, places, and jurisdictions, Eaton's preface similarly begins to refigure the assumptions and conventions of academic historiography away from narratives of tragedy and toward other ends.

To be sure, Eaton's use of discourses of savagery/civilization and primitivism/progress fall hard on contemporary ears. Framed in the discourse of race ("aboriginal stock"), environmentalist and evolutionary models of human development and progress (from "barbarism into civilization"), and spatial assumptions of savagery/civilization ("wilderness"/"nation"), Eaton's narrative of Ross's rise to power and influence parallels the conventional emphasis on Cherokee advancement and civilization highlighted by Dodd. After introducing Ross's early years and moving quickly through a sketch of early Cherokee history, Eaton notes the nascent national community's moves toward nationalization via acculturation: "Except in remote mountain regions, the hunting shirt, leggings and moccasins, along with old customs and religion, were fast disappearing under the influence of commerce, education, and missionary zeal."[47] These moves parallel the emergence of a tripartite constitutional government. Just as Ross was the product of a bicultural marriage, mercantile and agricultural economies, and Western formal education, so was the emergence of the Cherokee Nation a product of Cherokee acculturation to white ways via education; Christianity; literacy; mercantile and plantation economics; log, brick, and mortar architecture; written law; and tripartite constitutional government. Together, such moves demonstrate for Eaton and her audience the efforts of "an aboriginal tribe groping towards the light of a civilized form of government."[48] The national narrative that parallels and informs the personal narrative, then, traces the movement of both Ross and his people out of an ahistorical aboriginal past and into civilization, history, and modernity.

Though Eaton no doubt subscribed to these frameworks to some extent, she qualifies how she understands civilization from within a Cherokee historical context in important ways. She notes, for instance, that Cherokees had long "gradually adopted such civilized arts" not out of intellectual inferiority or as a consequence of conflict but as an acculturative mechanism to better meet their own needs.[49] "That they so long remained conservative to European ideas and appeared to disdain anything alien," she writes, "was due to the fact that there was so little in civilization that appealed to people in the barbarous stage, and not to their lack of intellectual vigor."[50] Cherokee adoptions of metal tools, spinning wheels for cloth, firearms, and the practice of raising stock signified less a desire to move away from whom and what they had been and more what Joshua Nelson describes as a "progressive tradition" designed to help them continue on that path in innovative and perhaps more responsive ways.[51]

Eaton frames the arrival of missionaries and the adoption of Christianity in similarly pragmatic terms. Noting "considerable opposition" in debates about whether to allow missionaries into the Nation, the National Council at Tellico ultimately agreed provided that prospective missionaries first build schools and institute a formal education system for Cherokee children. When two Moravian ministers began hosting religious lessons in the home of David Vann prior to building and establishing the promised school, the council promptly informed them "that the Cherokee Nation wanted educators, not theologians, and unless the missionaries could open a school within six months they should leave the Nation."[52] It was out of these pragmatic dynamics that the missions at Spring Place and Brainard emerged as sites not only of proselytization but, more importantly, of education in and exposure to Western social, political, economic, and intellectual norms. Indeed, as Eaton makes clear, Cherokees were less interested in religious conversion—"up to this time there were remarkably few conversions to the Christian religion"—than in the practical benefits that Western education might provide their children and, by extension, their communities.[53] Many of the figures who would later fight for Cherokee legal, political, and territorial rights—Charles Hicks, John Ross, Elias Boudinot, and John Ridge—had ties to these and other institutions, which signifies the wisdom of this accommodation. Although, as Scott Lyons has observed, decisions such as these were always informed by the contexts of colonial violence and coercion, Cherokees in Eaton's narrative nonetheless choose to pursue these and other avenues—domestic agriculture, literacy, constitutional organization—of their own volition.[54]

We might also understand Eaton's reliance on discourses of civilization and the assertion of Cherokee nationhood in similarly strategic terms. As

Maureen Konkle has argued, Cherokee claims to political autonomy, territory, and sovereignty necessarily had to be made through dominant racial and cultural discourses in order to be legible within Euro-American systems of thought.[55] Dating from Columbus's diaries and sixteenth-century Spanish juridical debates and extending through European travel and captivity narratives, colonial histories, and popular romances and drama, Native peoples had never been taken on their own tribally specific terms. Rather, as Roy Harvey Pearce and Robert Berkhofer extensively document, they were collapsed into a singular image of Indianness—a simulation, to use Vizenor's term—which signified not the presence of Native peoples but their absence.[56] Locked into a series of racial binaries and what Audra Simpson terms "ethnographic entrapments"—savage/civilized, primitive/modern, tribe/nation, oral/written, custom/law, occupancy/sovereignty—Cherokee *cultural* difference was refigured as an absolute and irrevocable Indian *racial* difference, always and forever defined as *pre*political, *pre*historic, *pre*national, and *pre*modern.[57] The result is that culture, and specifically a racialized understanding of cultural *difference*, becomes the only site of agency for Native peoples, the only thing they can claim as truly and fundamentally their own within a settler system that attempts to domesticate them at every turn. But it is a limited agency, one which forecloses adaptation and change or which, as Joshua Nelson frames it, positions adaptation, change, and continuity as fundamentally antithetical to an Indian authenticity that is located forever in the past.[58] If, as Jodi Byrd argues, Indianness functions as an adaptable, exportable image against which settler states leverage claims to moral authority and political legitimacy, whiteness, as Aileen Moreton-Robinson points out, becomes the property through which such claims become the exclusive possessions of Euro-American settler states.[59] In much the same way that Cherokees claimed nationhood, sovereignty, and civilization to align themselves in closer proximity to the social and political cachet of whiteness and to distance themselves from settler norms of radical Indian racial difference, Eaton's use of these discourses does similar work in a discipline that equated civilization with history and modernity in contrast to a distant and vanishing aboriginal traditionalism. By situating Cherokees definitively on one side of that spectrum in this, the first Cherokee-authored academic history, Eaton claims both history and modernity for Cherokee people. Indeed, embedded in this developmentalist political *bildung* of John Ross is a narrative of Cherokee nationalism and resistance centered on "strengthening the government and wielding the Cherokees into a strong, united nation in order that they might present a solid front of resistance to any further project of removal."[60] Hardly the tragic narrative of loss and dissolution that Dodd suggests, Eaton's narrative from this point forward works against any sense of tragic inevitability.

In fact, Eaton insists throughout the text that the central conflicts that played out over and over again in Cherokee history were not the inevitable by-products of a clash of civilizations but the abject failure of the English and U.S. governments to deal fairly and equitably with Cherokee people. After chronicling the multiple failures of a series of pre-Revolutionary treaties with the colonies of South Carolina, North Carolina, and Virginia between 1721 and 1777, Eaton ascribes the resulting conflict to a function of colonial duplicity, deception, and ineptitude and to the inability of both sides to enforce restrictions on their respective communities:

> The mother country and her colonies by failing at the outset to adopt a definite systematic policy of justice and humanity towards the Indians established the precedent for all subsequent dealings with them. Charters and patents granted by England to the Colonies neglected to give due consideration to the prior claims of the aboriginal tribes. The colonies left their course with the Indians to be directed by circumstances. Agents and commissioners were given a free hand in securing land cessions and arranging treaties. Bribes were used without scruple and chiefs and headmen corrupted by every available means. That any advantage which might be taken of the ignorance and misunderstanding of natives unfamiliar with the English language was considered legitimate is evident to any one familiar with the history of Indian treaties. Neither governments nor individuals considered it dishonest to cheat an Indian, criminal to rob him nor murder to kill him.[61]

In a perceptive analysis of ethnocentric bias and systematic policy failures that parallels contemporary arguments by Carolos Montezuma and anticipates the basic thrust of the Miriam Report and New Deal reform two decades later, Eaton highlights the predictable failure of any platform that operates as a function of prejudice and self-interest and that fails to give due consideration to Indigenous land claims, social customs, and principles of consent. In such circumstances, Eaton suggests, violence was all but guaranteed, not because of some fundamental racial or cultural irreconcilability but because of white ineptitude, duplicity, and greed. In a moment of particular frustration at the dynamics leading up to Removal and its aftermath, she writes, "Not for a moment does [the federal government] seem to have recognized its own responsibility for the state of affairs in the Cherokee Nation, where its secret agents by dark and devious methods had started a train of events which threatened to blot a nation out of existence."[62] Only seven years removed from the dissolution of her own tribal government, Eaton's words about the Removal speak forward to her own generation. Whether referencing post-Revolutionary frontier violence of the late eighteenth century or the factional violence engendered by Removal and the Civil War, Eaton consistently reframes conflict and violence within the Cherokee Nation not as the result of tragic inevitability but as the consequence of policy failures and the willful and unjustifiable destruction of one people by another.

Having reframed Cherokee-U.S. history in such terms, Eaton explores the ways in which U.S. treaty and constitutional law not only failed to protect Cherokee people but also were instrumental in their dispossession. When discussing eighteenth-century treaties with the colonies of South Carolina, North Carolina, and Virginia, Eaton emphasizes the ethnocentricity of the colonial negotiators and the inability of colonial governments to enforce the provisions of the agreements. Unable or unwilling to prevent settlers from continually encroaching on Cherokee lands, colonists repeatedly sought cessions for more and more land, conditions which eventually led to the Anglo-Cherokee conflict of 1754–60. Eaton documents how subsequent failures to secure borders following the Treaty of Hopewell in 1785 produced more violence, this time from the lower Chickamauga towns that had most acutely experienced the blunt end of such invasions. Yet another treaty in 1790 at Holston finally brought an end the violence but only at the expense of more Cherokee lands. Looking back on what she characterizes as a "humiliating" history of violence and land loss, Eaton identifies these early exchanges as "but the beginning of land cessions [in] which, year after year, from this time on, under one pretext or another, the aborigines were shorn of their ancestral domains and found themselves powerless to prevent it."[63] Eaton's subsequent discussions of legal machinations to get at Cherokee lands throughout the text—from Washington's civilization policy and Jefferson's vision of Removal (chapter 2) to the Treaty of Fort Jackson following the Battle of Horseshoe Bend in 1814 and the first removal treaty of 1817 (chapter 3), to the Georgia laws in the 1820s (chapters 4 and 5)—deliver on this observation.[64] Though on the surface it is a political biography of John Ross, his individual story in many ways provides the context for Eaton's larger, and in my estimation more important, indictment of colonial dispossession and its aftermath.

For Eaton these dynamics are nowhere more evident than in the breakdown of constitutional authority following the Supreme Court's ruling in *Worcester v. Georgia* in 1832. Building upon a previous ruling in *Cherokee Nation v. Georgia* a year earlier, which had framed tribal nations as "domestic dependents" of the federal government, the 1832 decision upheld a clear yet limited form of Cherokee sovereignty and national status and denied any state the right to extend its jurisdiction over Indian lands.[65] Quoting Cherokee statesman Elijah Hicks, Eaton writes, "News of the decision reaching the Cherokee Nation in March was like 'a shower of rain on thirsty vegetation.'"[66] Noting that "depression and uncertainty vanished like the mists before the sun," Eaton writes that Cherokees "celebrated by dances and feasts" now that "the Cherokees seemed standing upon a solid [legal] foundation."[67] Eaton quickly contrasts these scenes of jubilation with the reality of Andrew Jackson's refusal to enforce the ruling, repeating his now-infamous statement, "John Marshall has made his decision, now let him enforce it."[68]

To be sure, Eaton understood that Jackson was in no uncertain terms an Indian-hater. An earlier chapter in *John Ross* on the central role that Cherokees played in securing Jackson's victory over resistant Creeks in the Battle of Horseshoe Bend documents how he immediately turned on his Creek and Cherokee allies by attempting to force land cessions from them in a subsequent treaty negotiation. Led by John Ross, Cherokees exposed Jackson's plans to federal officials and had the treaty nullified. In light of this humiliation, Eaton depicts a self-interested Jackson who is more dedicated than ever to Indian removal: "He was naturally no friend to the Indians, though he did not hesitate to accept favors from them when occasion arose, and his determination to rid the Southern states of them was strengthened by his temporary embarrassment and humiliation. From this time forward he and his friends managed to secure more and more of the Indian patronage and their influence on the War department tended steadily and persistently toward the ultimate aim, removal."[69] Informed by prior experience with Jackson's duplicity—he was swept into office at least partially due to a policy of Indian removal—Cherokees were right to be concerned about his accession to the presidency. Eaton writes that these concerns were partly allayed by Jackson's promise in his inaugural address that it was "his sincere and honest and constant desire to observe towards the Indians a just and liberal policy, and to give that humane and considerate attention to their rights and their wants which was 'consistent with the habits of our government and the feelings of the people.'"[70] In one of many editorial intrusions related to Jackson, Eaton observes, "The last clause [Cherokees] were not yet prepared to interpret and appreciate. The Georgia contingent in Congress knew better."[71] Over the next few pages, Eaton documents Jackson's rapid, merciless, and often duplicitous efforts to push through removal legislation despite significant public and political opposition, which was often in opposition to his own stated political commitments.

Rather than villainize Jackson as an abject Indian hater, Eaton points instead to the political and moral hypocrisies embedded in his advocacy of removal. In an earlier conflict over federal annulment in South Carolina, Jackson upheld a Supreme Court ruling on federal preemption of state authority, warning the state, "Those who told you that you might peaceably prevent [the execution of federal laws] have deceived you. Their object is disunion, and disunion by armed force is treason."[72] As the executive responsible for enforcing federal law, Jackson's support of the court here bode well for Cherokees, and "there was every reason to believe that he would ultimately enforce the treaties and intercourse acts for their protection."[73] Eaton's attention here to questions of reason, logic, and principle informs her larger treatment of Jackson's character and credibility. Against one historian's retrospective lionization of Jackson as a man committed to "the idea of union, and the supremacy of the constitution," Eaton suggests, "It was the supremacy of the constitution as President Jackson chose to interpret it . . . that the doughty general would defend so gallantly, and not as the Supreme Court interpreted it."[74] In upholding commitments to federal preemption in one instance but refusing to do so in the case of Indian removal, Jackson's major sin, as Eaton sees it, is not simply his racial antipathy toward Native peoples, though that is definitely in play, but his self-interested situational application of political principles and constitutional commitments. By appropriating the judicial authority of interpretation and abrogating the executive responsibility of enforcement, Jackson undermined the constitution itself. Eaton's observation that "consistency is not a jewel that adorns Andrew Jackson's crown, if perchance he wears one" captures at once the fragility of constitutional authority and republican government under an autocratic regime as well as the impotence of a legal system that depends on self-interested human beings to issue and enforce its rulings.[75] Anticipating contemporary critiques of settler-colonial law and Indigenous peoples, Eaton's focus on the long-standing political relations between the United States and the Cherokee Nation, and specifically her account of the legal and legislative mechanisms by which the federal government systematically undermined Cherokee sovereignty, exposes the colonialist roots of concepts such as discovery and conquest. In doing so, Eaton denaturalizes U.S. claims to sovereignty and plenary power that were asserted over Native lives.[76] In this, as John Rhea argues, Eaton's text was one of the first documentary-driven academic histories to draw explicit attention to the colonialist workings of U.S. law that were directed at the dispossession of Native peoples.[77]

Lest readers understand Jackson's position strictly as a disagreement of legal philosophy, however, Eaton also highlights the moral failure of U.S. officials to realize the full potential of their own values. Pointing to the graft, corruption, political favoritism, and financial benefit that Jackson's supporters received as a consequence of Cherokee dispossession, Eaton writes, "Many a political debt was paid with the capital furnished by the sale of the Cherokee Nation, east."[78] That such actions were perpetrated "at the hands of a government established less than three quarters of a century before upon the principle of justice and the rights of men" suggests not simply a failure of policy but also an abject moral failure on the part of the federal government to live up to its own enlightened ideals, a fact that Eaton emphasizes repeatedly.[79]

Eaton's analysis of the civilization program similarly suggests a critical understanding of the gulf between rhetoric and practice when applied to Indian people and Indian lands. She frames accusations of savagery, obstinate refusals to recognize Cherokee acculturation, removal arguments rooted in states' rights, and coercive treaty negotiations as the hypocritical rationalizations of those "who coveted Indian lands" in order to fulfill their own political and economic ambitions.[80] Referring explicitly to citizens of Georgia, Eaton writes, "The fact that Indians were becoming civilized and showed evidence of the ability to develop into good American citizens, thereby adding strength to the whole American nation, did not appeal to politicians who coveted Indian lands. In truth this class of men opposed any policy for civilizing the Indians, since it would tend to attach them more firmly to the soil. And to many a white man just over the border the Indian country was the promised land of wealth and plenty which he hoped someday to possess."[81] Although ostensibly sympathetic politicians and reformists—from Washington, Jefferson, and Emerson through Pratt, Dawes, Helen Hunt Jackson, and Theodore Roosevelt—might well frame policies of civilization and acculturation as a necessary benevolence, Eaton understands those policies as so many rationalizations for the acquisition of Indian land. When adopted explicitly for the purposes of strengthening *tribal* sovereignty and *Cherokee* claims to territory, benevolence and principle conveniently drop out of the conversation. As Eaton makes clear, whereas the Cherokees' rapid acculturation to Anglo-American norms firmly located them as "exemplary" or "good" Indians in the eyes of assimilation advocates, their adamant refusal to abandon their homelands and national identity placed this privileged position in political peril. The moment Cherokees refused to accede defeat or yield "even one foot of ground," they were disparaged as "bad," "ungrateful," or otherwise "ignorant" savages regardless of how philosophically sound or legally unassailable their claims.[82] Such is the slippery slope of discourses of civilization, progress, and nationhood for Indians, a conundrum of which Eaton is clearly well aware.

Eaton's repeated juxtapositions of the ignorance, duplicity, ineptitude, and brutality of civilized Americans with enlightened, honorable, and enormously capable Cherokees further highlights the instability of savage and civilized representational categories, a rhetorical move that aligns her with the Cherokee statesmen about which she writes as well as Indian public intellectuals such as William Apess, Sarah Winnemucca, and many of those associated with the SAI, including John Oskison. Those associated with the Removal are, not surprisingly, rendered in particularly derogatory terms. In addition to painting Andrew Jackson as a manipulative and duplicitous egomaniac, Eaton describes Georgia boomers, gold diggers, and other frontier opportunists as "lawless rabble," "petty tyrants," and "intruders" who flouted both Cherokee and U.S. federal laws.[83] Speaking specifically of prospectors who descended on Cherokee country after gold was discovered in May 1829, Eaton writes: "These gold diggers were intruders operating unlawfully under an enactment of the Cherokee Nation prohibiting anyone to settle or trade on their land without a permit from Cherokee officials, and under a Federal intercourse law which prohibiting nyone frm [*sic*] selling or trading in Indian territory without a special license from United States authorities."[84] Absent a respect for the rule of law, which is every liberal democracy's raison d'être, a "period of lawlessness prevailed in which the Cherokees who had joined eagerly in prospecting got the worst of the bargain."[85]

The violence and chaos of the Removal era was further exacerbated by the series of coercive measures that Georgia attempted to extend over Cherokee people. From the opening up of Cherokee lands for white mining and settlement to the denial of fee simple title on Cherokee reservations, to the exclusion of anyone of Indian blood from bringing suit or testifying against the state, to the abrogation of contractual obligations to Indian parties, the Georgia laws worked systematically to prevent Cherokees from having access to all mechanisms of justice, protection, and redress. As with Jackson, Eaton penetrates Georgia's abstract arguments for states' rights and identifies the true stakes at play. "The purposes of these laws was not far to seek," Eaton concludes. "Georgia was 'building fires around the Cherokees' to force them to remove," a tactic which she immediately links to the increase in theft, dispossession, violence, and other "atrocities perpetrated by the Georgians."[86] Reading in concert with a long series of legislative failures to fund annuities, executive ambivalence and inaction, and exploitative treaty negotiations, Eaton consistently sees U.S. law as applied to Native peoples as neither blind nor just, an astonishingly prescient observation that historians would begin to explore in earnest decades later.

More than simply drawing a correlation between the workings of U.S. settler law and Cherokee dispossession, Eaton also targets the brutality and embodied violence visited on Cherokee lands and bodies as a consequence of the legislation. As with some of her contemporaries such as Alice Callahan, Charles Eastman, Zitkála-Šá, and others, she makes her outrage and anger most evident in these moments. In one example, Eaton documents how white winners of Georgia's lottery of Cherokee lands freely took possession of Cherokee property and forcibly evicted Cherokees—affluent and nonaffluent, conservative and progressive—from their homes, all under the protection of Georgia law.[87] "One Georgia lottery gambler," Eaton recounts, "whose sole possessions consisted of the clothes he wore and two or three pistols, drew the lot belonging to an industrious Indian boy who had improved his premises until they were of considerable value. . . . [He] went into Cherokee country, entered the house of the Indian, [and] took possession of the comfortable buildings and cultivated fields."[88] In another example, two Georgia men leveraged a legal technicality that prevented Cherokees from contracting with white laborers in order to lay claim to Joseph Vann's extensive plantation at Spring Place. While Vann's appeals played out in Georgia courts, two white men took possession of opposing halves of the estate and commenced a violent struggle over ownership, which claimed the lives of some of the participants and laid waste to many of the estate's improvements. "After the smoke of battle cleared away," Eaton writes, the Vanns "were driven out and forced to make their way over the snow-covered fields into the limits of Tennessee. Here they found shelter in an open log cabin with a dirt floor."[89]

The same held true for other prominent Cherokees. While he was away at negotiations, John Ross's estate was confiscated and his family turned away from their home at Ross's Landing. Second principal chief Charles Hicks was similarly deposed from his home "in the dead of winter," and his family was forced to find "shelter in an old sugar camp."[90] In order to emphasize the pervasiveness of such stories, Eaton acknowledges that she cannot hope to capture all occurrences. "Hundreds of other cases might be added," she concludes, "but it is useless to multiply examples to show that in her determination to cleanse her soil of the aborigines the state and her citizens were prepared to go to any length, though all the while strenuously disavowing any selfish or sinister motives toward the Indians."[91] Eaton documents in painstaking detail the legal means by which Georgia citizens increased their own social and economic status through policies of ethnic cleansing and the "legal theft" of property and wealth, regardless of political or social status.

Eaton reserves her most stringent critiques of settler-colonial violence for the months leading up to the Removal. Drawing particular attention to conditions in the internment camps directed by Winfield Scott, Eaton highlights the horrors perpetrated by state militia and federal troops on "disarmed and starving natives."[92] Describing this period of Removal as a "Reign of Terror"—invoking the postrevolutionary hysteria of the French Revolution and anticipating the Osage oil murders just on the horizon—Eaton relates accounts documented by James Mooney of the armed removal of families from their homes even as their stock and possessions were being raided by white Georgians; the shooting of a deaf adolescent who, in fear, attempted to escape capture; the neglect of elderly or starving Cherokees left to die in their cabins; and armed manhunts in which Cherokee men, women, and children were hunted down "like wild beasts."[93] Upon capture, she continues, Cherokees were often confined to disease-infested and famine-ridden stockades, offered rotten meat and infested cornmeal when offered food at all, and subjected to all forms of physical and sexual violation.[94]

Lest she be accused of bias (which, in fact, she was in a later rejection letter by the University of Oklahoma Press),[95] Eaton presents Anglo-American recollections of events that depict similarly bleak conditions. On orders from the government to keep recalcitrant Cherokees in line, a General Wool informs Washington of the "heartrending," deplorable conditions that Cherokees lived in and of the white men who were "hovering like vultures watching to pounce upon their prey and strip them of everything they had."[96] General Dunlap from Tennessee, who was also called in to quell violence among the Cherokees, "soon found that the Indians, not the whites, needed protection . . . from the lawless rabble of Georgia who, he declared, had long played the part of petty tyrants."[97] Eaton cites a Colonel Z. A. Giles, a Georgia militiaman and Civil War veteran, who delivers the most damning assessment. "I fought through the Civil War and have seen men shot to pieces and slaughtered by the thousands," he remembered, "but the Cherokee removal was the cruelest work I ever knew."[98] By situating such voices as authoritative non-Indian commentaries on the horrific circumstances that she relates, Eaton not only draws attention to the brutality of colonization but also provides to potentially sympathetic readers figures with whom they might better identify.

Driving home the horrific consequences of Removal, Eaton pays a great deal of attention to the brutal conditions that defined the forced march west, contrasting the systematic order, discipline, and concern for human life of the Cherokee-directed efforts with the chaos, disorganization, violence, and utter lack of sympathy that characterized federal projects. She similarly situates the deplorable violence and destruction of the Civil War, to which both Cherokees and white Americans contributed, as a function of Union and Confederate military ineptitude and as a "petty game of personal ambition and state politics."[99]

Eaton is careful to also document and critique instances of Cherokee violence and lawlessness, for instance the criminal activities of disaffected members of the Ridge faction and the scorched-earth tactics employed by Stand Watie and his Confederate Cherokees.[100] But she often as not understands them as regrettable by-products of Removal and the Civil War, economic crises resulting from delayed federal annuity payments, and a repeated pattern of the federal government's moral and legal failure to honor its international political commitments to Cherokee people. Situated on the right side of the savage/civilized binary and possessing the full support of U.S. political, legal, and military authority, white Americans in Eaton's narrative are offered no moral avenue through which to escape this history of civilized savagery. As in Corntassel's address, Apess's "Eulogy," and Zitkála-Šá's treatment of boarding school experience, there is no space in Eaton's text in which to mourn the tragic passing of the vanishing American, no "settler move to innocence" from which readers might escape their own complicity in the history she tells.[101]

As such, Eaton's history reflects what Daniel Justice, in another context, terms a "*consciousness of Removal,* the full embrace of history, pain, and continuing existence."[102] Justice's emphasis on continuance in the face of colonial trauma speaks back to Eaton's text in important ways as she seeks not only to cultivate empathy and provoke outrage over historical actors and events but also to intervene in contemporary debates about Indian people. Like other Indian writers of her time, Eaton leverages history in order to appeal to the progressive sensibilities of a white liberal readership capable of connecting the dots between the violence and chaos of the *historical* narrative she tells and the horrific conditions generated by allotment and assimilation policies experienced by *contemporary* Cherokees. In a particularly revealing moment, Eaton expresses fear that Americans had become desensitized to this tragic yet familiar story of dispossession. She claims that "with few exceptions the world read the story unmoved."[103] Eaton intends to give a "sympathetic interpretation to their struggle" but does not wish to cultivate a general sense of colonialist nostalgia in white Americans—that is, the nostalgic sentimental mourning of the passing of Indigenous communities by settler-colonists and the appropriation of that loss as their own.[104] Rather, she means to mobilize reader empathy, pathos, and pity on behalf of *contemporary* Cherokee communities: "If, peradventure, it comes not too late, like tears and flowers for the dead, who in life would have been made happier and better for the sympathetic word we had not sense to say, and the helping hand we had no time to extend, then a recreant nation may awake to the enormity of its injustice and inhumanity toward a valiant aboriginal people, and hasten to make what amends it may to their crushed and decadent descendants crowded back into remote corners of a country where once they were kings and emperors."[105]

Through the romantic language of Indian nobility and the sentimentalist language of Native suffering and American dishonor, Eaton connects sympathy for a "valiant aboriginal people" who have been mistreated by a "recreant nation" to contemporary circumstances facing many of their descendants. Just two decades earlier Cherokees had been citizens of sovereign tribal nations governed by laws and national institutions of their own making. They had access to as much of the more than four million acres of tribal estate as they could cultivate so long as they did not intrude on another citizen's improvements. Additionally, the Nation provided free access to elementary and higher education, institutions for the care of orphans and the sick, a national bilingual press, and health care. Their two-million-dollar federal trust was supplemented with agriculture, cattle ranching, coal mining, forestry, and other industries. Despite the fact that a relative few tribal citizens monopolized large portions of the tribal estate, abject poverty, by all accounts, was utterly absent.[106] Within decades of the imposition of allotment and Oklahoma statehood, and absent access to common lands, educational and other institutions, and the civil protections of Cherokee law, many Cherokees, especially those in rural areas, became impoverished landless wards of the state. Though often understood to be the consequence of an inherent failing of Indianness itself, a problem to be solved by ethnographic study or assimilationist social engineering, Eaton recovers the human element of Cherokee history by reframing contemporary circumstances as a function of an incompetent, overreaching, and at times brutal federal government.

In this way, the story of *John Ross and the Cherokee Indians*, framed as a movement from savagery into civilization, is also for Eaton a story of white America sacrificing its own democratic ideals and historical legacy on the altar of self-interest not at the expense of a vanishing race but of another contemporary human community.[107] It is the story of Cherokee struggle, survival, persistence, and moral right against a backdrop of broken promises, self-interest, hypocrisy, and federal inaction—a "century of dishonor," to use Helen Hunt Jackson's phrase—perpetrated by Great White Fathers who continually failed to live up to their own enlightened ideals and manipulated hugely inequitable power relations to "blot a nation out of existence."[108] By appealing to her audience's reformist sense of common decency for an exploited class, Eaton strategically ties her revisionist history to progressivist moral outrage at the abuse of power by large governmental bureaucracies and industrial interests.

Like her Cherokee compatriots and Red Progressive peers, she endeavored not so much to undermine the fundamental premises of civilization, but to challenge its anti-Indian bias and revise its Anglo-exclusivist assumptions.[109] As in *Black Jack Davy*, *John Ross and the Cherokee Indians* situates both past and contemporary conditions not as the inevitable conclusion to the cosmic moral drama of civilization triumphing over savagery, of whiteness over Indianness, but as the historically situated consequences of willful human action. In doing so, Eaton leaves open the possibility for a "recreant," regretful, and presumably less cynical American nation to "make amends," distribute reparations, and right historical wrongs on behalf of contemporary Cherokees and other Indian communities.

Disciplinary Interventions and Narrative Subversions

Just as Eaton challenges the anti-Indianist assumptions at the heart of popular discourses of civilization and progress, she similarly pushes back against historiographic practices and narrative paradigms that deny the legitimacy of alternative sources of historical authority and position Indian peoples in an antithetical relationship to modernity. As a document-driven professional academic history, Eaton's counternarrative of Cherokee nationhood is necessarily situated against a series of texts that had come to constitute a vast, interreferential archive of textual authority—a kind of canon—organizing both popular and academic engagements with Cherokee historiography.[110] These include widely read colonial travel narratives, historical sketches produced under the aegis of the Bureau of Ethnology, formal academic and popular histories, and a wide array of materials from the United States Indian Office and other state and federal archives.[111] Many of these sources are predictably racist if not explicitly anti-Indian. George Bancroft's *History of the United States* (1834) is an unapologetic celebration of U.S. Anglo racial triumphalism over Indigenous savagery, while former Georgia governor Wilson Lumpkin's history of the Removal presents a decidedly anti-Cherokee version of events. Though less egregious, Samuel Drake's *Biography and History of the Indians of North America* (1857) and *Early History of Georgia* (1872) display similar biases with respect to the Removal and U.S. expansion. Though Thomas McKenney and James Hall's *History of the Indian Tribes of North America* (1855–70) presents a more romantic picture of Indian nobility, it is an image that is inevitably corrupted, if not overwhelmed, by the march of civilization and progress. As Daniel Justice has written with respect to Cherokee historiography, such frameworks force Indigenous histories into "the assumptions of Eurowestern progressivism" in which "indigenous primitivism fades away before the inevitable cultural superiority of the White American empire." In such narratives, tribal presence "becomes nothing more than quaint ethnic pride assimilated into the body politic of the United States."[112] Conscious of such biases, Eaton draws on these sources only sparingly, generally as a source for basic historical content and strategically useful quotations, but never as interpretive authorities.

It is significant, then, that the sources that Eaton repeatedly draws on to frame her narrative are more sympathetic to Cherokee peoples. These include James Adair's *History of the American Indians* (1775); William Bartram's *Travels through North and South Carolina, Georgia, East and West Florida* (1791); John Howard Payne's papers held in the Newberry Library; Charles Royce's *Cherokee Nation of Indians* (1884); and James Mooney's *Myths of the Cherokees* (1897–98). Whereas both Royce's and Mooney's texts are more identifiably historicist—they are extensively sourced and cited—Adair's and Bartram's are more ethnological in nature, a non-Indian's tour through and interpretation of the origins, languages, social structures, and cultural practices of Indigenous peoples of the Southeast. As a journalist and dramatist by trade, Payne captures in his papers an outsider's firsthand experience of the Removal crisis from within the Cherokee Nation, offering important counterarguments for Cherokee nationhood to those advanced by the Jackson and Van Buren administrations as well as by Georgia state officials.

Though sympathetic to Cherokee history, racialized binaries of savagery/civilization and primitivism/progress also constrain each of these texts. Both Adair's and Bartram's narratives variously exoticize Indigenous social and cultural practices and serve colonialist ends by mapping Indigenous geopolitical space for colonial audiences. However, they also advance cases for the essential humanity of Native peoples,[113] and valorize the nobility, simplicity, and natural reason of Native life against the morally bankrupt and vice-ridden condition of civilized British and Spanish colonies.[114] Payne's papers—assembled while he was a guest of John Ross's during the height of Georgia aggression and dispossession in the 1820s and '30s—celebrate Cherokee advances in civilization and nationalization while also documenting the violence, trauma, and factionalism that resulted from increasing incursions into Cherokee territories by Georgia officials and disinterest on the part of the federal executive.[115] Written at the end of the nineteenth century amid enormous pressure to allot tribal estates and dissolve tribal governments and responding to white progressive anxieties about the presumably inevitable vanishing of Native peoples, both Royce's and Mooney's texts leverage Cherokee advances in civilization as the basis for legitimizing claims to Cherokee national identity, though to different ends. For Royce, Cherokee civilization substantiates both legal and moral claims to Cherokee national identity while also holding the U.S. government ethically responsible for upholding its treaty and trust relations with the Cherokee Nation.[116] In Mooney, civilization also marks Cherokees as a national community, but no longer an authentically Indian one. This position speaks less about Cherokee cultural and political life and more about the social evolutionist thinking underpinning Mooney's ethnographic imaginary.[117]

Despite these contradictions, each of these texts presents arguments for Cherokee humanity and national status that Cherokees themselves would draw on throughout the nineteenth and early twentieth centuries. It is primarily these ethnohistorical sources—rather than the more celebrationist literary-historical works of Bancroft and others—to which Eaton turns for documentary information related to Cherokee history and culture and as support for her strongest critiques of U.S. settler-colonial violence. If one of Eaton's primary tasks as a Cherokee professional historian was to challenge anti-Indian bias within historiography itself, then her alignment with more sympathetic sources and her exclusion of long-held authorities such as Francis Parkman, Henry Roe Schoolcraft, and Lewis Henry Morgan might be seen as a disciplinary strategy to stack the deck, so to speak.

In addition to privileging selective historical accounts over others, Eaton also refuses historiographic practices that dismiss local historical knowledge as unreliable and that confine Indians to tragic plots that deny them historical agency and full humanity. As a professional academic history grounded in documentary sources, one of the text's most significant interventions is its affirmation of oral histories and local archives as legitimate sources of authority. Eaton supplements the decidedly U.S.-settler archive of congressional documents, Supreme Court decisions, and records from the Indian Office and committees on Indian affairs with materials from the Sequoyah Historical Society in Claremore, Oklahoma (of which she was a founding member), Cherokee National Records in Tahlequah, documents on Cherokee education from a local Tahlequah historian, and "rare collections of letters and documents" from the Ross family archives. Of the latter, Eaton informs readers (and other historians) of the significance of these largely untapped local collections for Cherokee historiography, asserting that they "consist of a mass of unorganized material very valuable to those interested in the subject of Cherokee history."[118]

Eaton amplifies this implicit critique of the lack of Cherokee voices in conventional historiography by turning to other Cherokee writers and intellectual traditions as primary documentary sources. Eaton repeatedly draws on Elijah Hicks's journal from 1837—which was held at the time in the Sequoyah Historical Society archives and which Eaton was actively working to compile and expand—as a crucial source on Cherokee experiences of and reactions to Removal. Similarly, when commenting on the development of Cherokee law and the origins of specific provisions in the Cherokee legal code, Eaton draws directly on the *Laws of the Cherokee Nation*, the texts and contexts of specific Cherokee treaties, and manuscripts from the Cherokee National Records held in Tahlequah rather than rely on previous accounts from secondary sources. Additionally, Eaton draws on previous writings by fellow Cherokees. For material on post-Removal and post–Civil War Cherokee life, she turns to an 1893 biography of Cherokee intellectual and newspaper editor, Principal Chief W. P. Ross, which was authored by his wife, Mary Jane. She also relies heavily on fellow Cherokee historian and Sequoyah Historical Society member Emmet Starr's *The Cherokee "West," 1794–1839* (1910) for historical and genealogical data about the families and communities who relocated from the eastern Cherokee Nation during the decades prior to Removal. If, as James Parins writes, we can view Cherokee writing in one sense as "a series of Cherokee intellectual endeavors that served to unify what was perceived as a fragmenting society" and "hold individuals together" through the creative "expression of Cherokee intellectual life," we might read Eaton's commitments to local, familial, and literary archives in this, the first professional academic history authored by a Cherokee historian, as performing similar work.[119] Indeed, at least until Starr's complete *History of the Cherokee Nation* was published in 1921, Eaton's text was, in terms of source material and perspective, the most locally sourced history of Cherokee people. Her hometown newspaper agreed, noting that the text "gives the history of the Cherokee people as drawn from numerous authentic records" and characterizing it as "the first [book] covering in a thorough manner the period mentioned from strictly authentic sources."[120]

Eaton's was also one of only three histories to acknowledge the influence of oral histories and personal narratives on the work.[121] In the final paragraph of the preface, Eaton acknowledges her debt to local Cherokee knowledge keepers and specifically recognizes her grandmother: "Lastly, if the background of the story adds anything to the merit of the book the credit is due to Mrs. Lucy Ward Williams, one of the last of the fireside historians of her race, whose vital interest in her people constrained her to repeat their story in season and out of season until it was rooted and grounded in my memory from earliest childhood."[122] Though Eaton does not explicitly mention it, Lucy Ward Williams was in fact her maternal grandmother and a descendant of Cherokee Beloved Woman, Nanye'hi (Nancy Ward). Aside from this notation, neither Eaton nor Dodd (the author of the foreword) explicitly identifies Eaton as a Cherokee. Considering that Eaton openly identified as both Cherokee and Indian in other situations throughout her life, this omission probably reflects more a disciplinary prejudice in favor of disinterested objectivity than any willful attempt to cover up her national or ethnic identity.

This connection that she makes from her own history to her grandmother, through to Nanye'hi, is more than a nostalgic nod to Cherokee oral history, however. By acknowledging her grandmother's knowledge and "vital interest in her people" as central influences on her own historical imagination, Eaton situates her study within a long history of Cherokee women as keepers and producers of knowledge and as insightful social critics. This is an important move because while it was likely acknowledged and affirmed at "firesides" throughout Cherokee country, contributions of Cherokee women to Cherokee intellectual and political history were largely absent from the official archives that Eaton navigated. The reasons for this are multiple. The political shift from semiautonomous towns governed by matrilineal clan relations into a more centralized, constitutional government, predicated in large part on Euro-American social and gender norms, increasingly marginalized Cherokee women from the public political life of the Cherokee Nation.[123] As a result, their voices and influence were either minimized or erased entirely in histories relying exclusively on a gendered documentary archive that was inherently biased toward a male-dominated public political discourse.[124] Consequently, Cherokee women exist as concerned maternal figures and supportive wives, but rarely as active participants in and producers of Cherokee history. While more recent historiographic and scholarly work has begun to address this erasure, the lion's share is still largely directed at Cherokee men. By anchoring her own authority as a professional historian to that of her grandmother and other women "fireside historians" from whose knowledge she undoubtedly drew, Eaton recovers this gendered history of Cherokee women's intellectual work, extending from Selu's gift of corn and community to Cherokee people through to Eaton's own academic history.[125]

While we can explicitly track the influence of the Cherokee written sources that Eaton draws on through her use of footnotes, it is more difficult to determine whether and to what extent oral histories influence the text. Though neither cited nor listed in the bibliography, it would be surprising if Eaton's work not only *in* local archives but also *with* local archivists, historians, family members, and others yielded details that did not find their way into the scholarly apparatus of the text. A number of vignettes providing intimate details of Ross's early experiences, fanciful accounts of frontier trials and warfare, and personal drama and conflict, which are absent in other official sources on which she drew, suggest at least the likelihood of such possibilities.

One early passage, for instance, recounts the Ross family's participation in a Green Corn ceremony at Hillstown for which Ross's mother, Mollie, had outfitted him in "his first suit of nankeen brand new made after the white man's style." Eaton goes on to document how the future chief's playmates assailed him with "shouts of derision and taunts of 'Unaka!'" Though the young Ross "stood staunchly by his suit until bedtime," Eaton informs readers that when dressing in the same suit the next morning, "he burst into tears and after much coaxing told [his grandmother] of his humiliation of the day before. She comforted him as grandmothers are wont to do the world over. Promptly the nankeen suit came off, the hunting shirt, leggings and moccasins went on, and the small boy ran shouting to his play happy and 'at home' again."[126] Like other historians, Eaton draws on such scenes to comment on Ross's bicultural, biracial identity and the challenges and advantages it presented him throughout his life. Unlike other texts, however, Eaton captures the emotional and affective context of such moments, between Ross and his playmates, between mother and son, and between grandmother and grandson. Moments like these remind readers that before he was a major political figure in Cherokee history, Ross was an average, ordinary boy beloved by his mother and grandmother, but other instances evidence an insider perspective of historical events.

Another story relates Ross's first assignment as a representative of the Cherokee Nation, involving an expedition to western Cherokees, which was intended to prevent them from entering into Tecumseh's alliance against the United States. Noting that from "start to finish the story of the expedition fairly bristles with stirring adventures and hairbreadth escapes," Eaton not only explicates what happened on the expedition but also verges on free indirect discourse to narrate the immediacy of Ross's experience: "After sixty days upon the rivers in dead of winter, chased by warlike Indians who thought they were whites, and suspicious settlers who thought they were an Indian party on mischief bent, they wrecked their boat, lost the greater part of their baggage and were compelled to finish the way on foot. Often up to their knees in mud and water and with only such game as they could kill for food, they covered the remaining two hundred miles in eighty days."[127] This, too, is a well-known and much-recounted episode in Ross's life. Most stop short, however, from narrating—as opposed to documenting—the harrowing circumstances and experiential details of the journey. Eaton's version reads like a correspondence from Ross's own pen or from a story passed down through the family from whose archives she was working.

The fact that this and similar episodes are lacking a scholarly apparatus that clearly identifies source material lends the text an insider fireside authority. While these vignettes might well have emerged from Eaton's own imagination or from local archives, they might just as well have come from oral histories, family narratives, or personal memories to which she was "rooted and grounded" from childhood. The point, of course, is not to concretely identify the orality of the text but to acknowledge the influence that local place- and family-based histories had on Eaton's life and her work as an academic historian, an influence that Eaton herself explicitly honors and acknowledges. Considering that contemporary Indigenous historians are still arguing for the acceptance of local histories as legitimate sources of historical knowledge, we have to consider Eaton's nod to such traditions, in the same preface where she indicts a history of settler-colonial misrepresentation and ignorance about Native peoples, as both a pointed disciplinary intervention to "write from home" and a political statement of presence and local authority.[128]

In addition to its localized production, *John Ross and the Cherokee Indians* also refuses historiographic conventions that position civilization and progress as antithetical to Indian nationhood and modernity. In much the same way that

Oskison appropriates and subverts the conventions of the frontier romance to advance a narrative of Cherokee national sovereignty, Eaton similarly disrupts disciplinary conventions to tell a history of Cherokee nationhood that is at once "civilized" and distinctly modern. One such convention denies historical agency to Native actors by relegating them to the margins of dominant national narratives. The canonical histories surveyed above provide useful examples. While documenting their interactions with specific tribal communities, both Adair's and Bartram's travel narratives largely speak of Indian peoples either in collective terms as "Cherokees," "Indians," "aborigines," and "savages" or according to exoticizing and largely erroneous social and political categories such as "chief," "shaman," "princess," or "king." Though both Royce's and Mooney's historical sketches identify individual military, political, and historical figures, the extent to which these authors depict them as legitimate historical agents capable of effecting change is restricted by the overwhelming sense of determinism embedded in their developmentalist frameworks and the colonial centers from which their narratives proceed. In all four accounts, history—like civilization and progress—functions as a disembodied, fatalistic force forever acting on Cherokee peoples, moving evolutionarily from savagery to civilization, temporally from past to present, and geographically from east to west. Claims to both history and agency are thus zero-sum games in which hard-won settler gains are exactly balanced by—indeed, predicated upon—inevitable Native losses.[129]

Eaton's nationalist biography positions Ross and other Cherokee statesmen, military leaders, intellectuals, and entrepreneurs as central agents in their own history. In contrast, U.S. officials, Indian agents, military officers, and other familiar historical figures are largely situated on the narrative's identifiably Cherokee national margins. The text chronicles Ross's travels through the explicitly *Cherokee* frontier on diplomatic engagements with federal officials, other Indian nations, and later, Old Settler communities in the Arkansas territory. Drawing attention to the central role that Indian military alliances and resistances played throughout the southeast, Eaton notes both the might of Tecumseh's confederacy and the Creek resistance and the crucial contributions of Cherokee military detachments in putting down those movements.

The text's treatment of the origins and implementation of the civilization program as part of a well thought out and carefully implemented Cherokee strategy of adaptation subverts the program's colonialist intentions. Mission education, Christianity, English literacy, plantation agriculture, and written law are presented not as signs of assimilation and cultural loss, as Mooney would have it, but as tactical adaptations through which Cherokee peoples might better negotiate their changing relationship to the United States and assert their own claims to political autonomy. To this point, Eaton repeatedly highlights Ross's and other Cherokee leaders' facilities with diplomacy and public debate, emphasizing time and again the very real gains they were able to make despite the generally coercive nature of those negotiations. She celebrates Sequoyah's development of the Cherokee syllabary, the composition of the Cherokee Constitution, and the opening of the national press as evidence not of European cultural superiority but of the adaptive "national genius" of Cherokee people. Eaton's recovery of historical agency and her depiction of the qualified adaptation of civilized institutions into Cherokee society rip both from their exclusivist Euro-American associations, relocating them firmly within a Cherokee national context.

Eaton similarly disrupts the geographic directionality embedded in civilized discourse by shifting the narrative center from Adair's eastern colonial seaboard to important locations within the Cherokee Nation. While familiar sites of Euro-American political and economic power such as Savannah, Charleston, Philadelphia, and Washington, D.C., are certainly present in the text, they exist on the periphery as foreign locations with respect to the Cherokee cultural and political centers of Chota, Hiwasee, Ustanali, New Echota, Red Clay, and Tahlequah. From the narrative's opening scenes of Ross's childhood on the Coosa River to its conclusion with his burial at Park Hill, the great majority of Eaton's history takes place within the territorial boundaries of the Cherokee Nation. Considering the ways in which colonial and settler narratives about Indigenous others use space to delimit narrative and political possibilities for Native peoples, Eaton's geographic reorientation within the Cherokee Nation is politically significant. As Philip Deloria writes, by "mapping space and human difference together in ways that [use] the past to naturalize colonial dominance," settler-colonial geographies delimit narrative and epistemological conditions of possibility for Native peoples.[130] Divested of their historical, cultural, and political content, Indigenous territories are transformed into empty wildernesses (terra nullius), savage frontiers, and lawless—because Indian—territories where Indian savages are prevented from doing anything but reveling in their savagery for all eternity regardless of how well they meet—or in Eaton's text, exceed—markers of and claims to Euro-American civilization.

As Kevin Bruyneel, Mark Rifkin, Mishuana Goeman, and others have pointed out, the implications of these settler mappings for Indigenous peoples are enormous. The racialization of Indigenous polities and territories into conquered peoples within settler spaces—whether in historical romances, legal decisions, legislative actions, or other venues—transforms Indigenous nations into domestic minority populations subject to the legal, political, and territorial authority of settler states.[131] Put differently, by domesticating and absorbing (that is, eliminating) Native life and land, settler claims to legal and political authority are legitimized and naturalized within settler law. Rendered as aesthetic categories of knowledge, Indigenous geopolitical territories become "not just the place[s] where civilization and wilderness made American democracy" but "the ragged edge of history itself, where historical and nonhistorical defied and defined each other."[132] When translated into popular and academic narratives, these territorial and geographic domestications reinforce the domestication/annihilation imperatives that structure dominant popular narratives and academic histories of Native peoples.[133]

If, as Kerwin Lee Klein observes, we can learn more about history by "exploring its edges and mapping its contraries, complements and cognates," we might do well to read Eaton's remapping of the American wilderness as Cherokee national territory—inhabited not by ignorant savages but by intelligent, sophisticated citizens—as a narrative refusal of settler appropriations and attempted domestications of Cherokee political spaces.[134] The text's self-conscious remapping of Cherokee history and of U.S.-Cherokee geopolitical space evidences a critical understanding of how space structures social and political relations and resituates Cherokee lands within a U.S. national territory in what Clint Carrol understands "as cornerstones of American Indian political and cultural continuance."[135] In doing so, *John Ross and the Cherokee Indians* recovers what Bruyneel describes as a "third space of sovereignty," a supplementary inassimilable claim to Cherokee nationhood "that resides neither simply inside nor outside the American political system but rather exists on these very boundaries . . . where competing notions of political time, political space, and political identity shape the U.S.-indigenous relationship."[136] As an academic history of the Cherokee Nation that looks east from Cherokee country, Eaton's text carves out its own historiographic third space, which contests the authority of settler archives, exposes the artifice of colonialist binaries, and subverts the disciplinary conventions through which Cherokee history was often told.

Refusing Convention, Rejecting Tragedy

Complementing these subversions of historiographic rules and disciplinary regulations, Eaton's text also refuses the conventions and assumptions of Indian biography and life writing traditions through which Native histories are still often told. That she chose to write about a historical Indian figure from the nineteenth century is not surprising. As Arnold Krupat has argued, Indians had long been biographical and autobiographical subjects for American writers and publishers. Whether demonized as murderous savages (Metacomet, Pontiac), mourned as tragic victims of civilization's onslaught (Black Hawk, Chief Joseph, Black Elk), ennobled as primitive warriors, orators, and statesman (Tecumseh, Crazy Horse, Sitting Bull, Geronimo), or held as exemplars of the virtues of assimilation and civilization (Eastman, Standing Bear, Crashing Thunder), Native biographies and autobiographies are almost always framed as the tragic precondition to the comedic narrative of American conquest, progress, and expansion. Though speaking specifically of early and mid-nineteenth-century autobiographies, Krupat's schema applies just as well to biographical and fictional treatments of Native peoples. "Whereas victory is the enabling condition of western autobiography," Krupat explains, "defeat is the enabling condition of Indian autobiography. . . . For it is only when the Indian subject . . . acknowledges his defeat, when he becomes what Patterson calls a 'State-prisoner,' that he can appear as a 'hero.' . . . Native American decline is the necessary condition for the comic ascent of Euramerican civilization and it is by means of this particular structure—the apparent tragedy as actual comedy—that the silent, absent editor speaks his acceptance of progressivist ideology, confirming the inevitability of Indian defeat."[137] The same might well be said of the silent, absent biographer, historian, or statesman.

In much the same way that Adair, Jefferson, and generations of reformists presumed a civilize-or-perish attitude toward Cherokee peoples, and as Royce consigned the survival of the Cherokee Nation to hands of fate, Indian heroes as narrative objects all meet their tragic end through death on battlefields, defeat on reservations, or humiliation in Wild West Shows or are tragicomic successes in boarding school classrooms. Where survival is an option, it is invariably predicated on the erasure of identifiable markers of Indian cultural or political identity. In historiographic and narrative paradigms based on discovery, conquest, civilization, and progress, Indian national figures must necessarily yield, disappear, or die in order that enlightened revolutionary fathers, heroic frontier fighters, and sacrificial Civil War veterans might assume their place as U.S. national heroes. The defeat of Native protagonists, as exemplary representatives of their communities, stands discursively for the defeat of their cultures, peoples, and nations. The definition of Indigenous heroism in a Euro-American tradition is thus predicated on the assumption of Indigenous death, which ensures—indeed, authorizes—the emergence and futurity of the settler-colonial nation.[138] To allow Indigenous heroes to live *as heroes* would be, to borrow from Taiaiake Alfred, an intrusion on settler-state mythologies that are predicated on the inevitable disappearance of Indigenous peoples.[139]

Eaton's history performs such an intrusion by taking as its subject a heroic Cherokee national figure whose life's work culminated in his own lifetime not in the dissolution of his national community but in its survival and continuance. To be sure, Ross plays a central role in historical accounts by other writers. Both Royce and Mooney, for instance, situate him as a primary actor in their narratives of events from the Removal crisis in the 1830s through his death thirty years later. Looking back at Ross's life, what strikes Royce as "remarkable" is not Ross's dogged defense of Cherokee national autonomy or the intellectual and philosophical arguments that he and his contemporaries advanced about nationhood and sovereignty. Rather, Royce is struck by Ross's inexplicable dedication to "the full-blood as against the mixed-blood members of the nation" despite his own mixed-blood "Scotch-Indian parentage."[140] Misapprehending racial identification for political commitment, Royce misreads Ross's dedication, which was not so much to full-blooded Cherokees as a racial group as it was to their staunch political position against removal and insistence on their right to exist as a self-determined nation in their homelands. Royce's collapse of political disagreement into a racialized conflict between mixed-blooded and full-blooded Cherokees also ignores the fact that, as Joshua Nelson, Rose Stremlau, and others remind us, while cultural orientation, parentage, class, and politics often converged to produce factionalism, each party counted allies from a range of racial, cultural, and economic backgrounds.[141] Eaton's celebration of Ross's life despite her own personal connections to Old

Settler, Treaty Party, and Southern Confederate Cherokees against whom he often struggled is a testament to such complexities.

While Eaton also documents the schisms that emerged between conservative and progressive Cherokees, and while her civilized frame privileges acculturated actors and political positions over those of conservatives and traditionalists, Eaton understands internal conflicts over removal as being less a consequence of racial antagonisms and more about fundamental political differences over national policy.[142] Believing that their legal, moral, and philosophical arguments to nationhood were unassailable, Ross and the majority of the Nation cautioned patience and resistance. Despairing that they would ever receive a fair hearing in U.S. courts and legislative chambers, Ridge allies encouraged removal as a means to avoid the complete dispossession and impoverishment of the Nation. While Eaton acknowledges self-interest as a partial motivation for both groups—she emphasizes this more with respect to earlier removal advocates and to a lesser extent to the Ridge/Treaty Party—she ultimately situates both groups as being committed nationalists who were acting on what they respectively felt was in the best interest of the Nation.[143] As men of "honor and patriotism" who were concerned with the increasing concentration of power in the Ross government, and who were genuinely afraid of the implications of further refusing removal, Eaton writes that many in the Treaty Party "were undoubtedly high-minded, far-sighted men who, honestly convinced that their people could never be restored to peace and happiness in the east, and seeing the futility of further resisting the Federal Government, took what appealed to them as the only way out of the difficulty."[144] Though she later castigates the treaty that they ultimately signed as fraudulent and duplicitous, Eaton renders the actors themselves not as romantic villains or tragic victims but as patriotic Cherokees who were caught in an impossible situation.[145]

Similarly, though she expresses horror at the "brutal and savage" reprisal killings that took the lives of Major and John Ridge, Elias Boudinot, James Starr, and others in the immediate aftermath of Removal, Eaton frames them not as simple acts of revenge or as the "good savage ethics" of an anachronistic blood law, but as the consequence of violating Cherokee constitutional provisions forbidding land cessions that they themselves authored: "The blow, long deferred, had fallen with a heavy, a brutal hand," which no doubt came as "a shock to the whole nation" and was seen as "an act greatly to be deplored from all points of view." The chapter, entitled "Triple Tragedy," explores the traumatic fallout from these acts in the new territory. However, "it could not possibly have been a complete surprise to the friends of the victims. For, as has been suggested before, they were but paying the penalty of a law which the Ridges, both father and son, had been instrumental in placing on the statute books ten years before and which Boudinot had been the first to put into print."[146] Eaton's focus on this explicitly political component of factional strife reveals the mixed-blooded Ross's defense of Cherokee sovereignty alongside conservative full-blooded Cherokees as being less "remarkable." In this sense, Ross's action mirrors Ned Warrior's alliance in Oskison's novel with non-Indians against threats to Cherokee sovereignty and his rights as a citizen. It also refuses the determinism and fatalism embedded in intractable racialized antagonisms, a problem which Lynn Riggs would examine twenty years later in his play *The Cherokee Night* and which formed at least part of the context behind the arguments over the PBS series discussed in the opening of this chapter.

Whereas Royce reads Ross's life as an anomaly, James Mooney more explicitly situates it as an allegory for the history of the Cherokee Nation. For Mooney, Ross's education in Cherokee lifeways, social norms, and politics, complemented with his English literacy, Christianity, and familiarity with mercantile economics that he gained from his father, situated him perfectly to emerge as leader and mediator for his national community. His dedication to the more conservative traditional element of Cherokee society and his commitment to remaining on the lands of his ancestors further ingratiated him with the ethnologist. Like Ross, the Cherokee Nation itself had greatly acculturated to Western social and political norms, the apogee of which for Mooney is the adoption of a representative constitutional government. However, the Cherokees' continued residence in the land of their ancestors combined with the persistence of cultural conservatism positioned them as both an authentically Indian and a civilized nation. Aligned with the "Great Man" theory of history—that is, the belief that great figures make history rather than vice versa—Mooney's conclusion—"In this long period, comprising the momentous episodes of the Removal and the War of the Rebellion [the Civil War], it may be truly said that his history is the history of the Nation"—seems to confirm Ross's place as a Cherokee national hero.[147]

Yet, as with Royce's confounding relegation of Cherokee national history to the hands of fate, Mooney's work embeds both Ross and the Cherokee Nation within a tragic paradigm in which the very idea of a modern *Indian* nation is an epistemological impossibility.[148] For, what is important for Mooney is not the *national* history of the Cherokee Nation but the *aboriginal* history of the Cherokee people. Shortly after relaying the events leading up the Removal, Mooney writes, "With the final removal of the Cherokee from their native country and their reunion and reorganization under new conditions in Indian Territory in 1840 their aboriginal period properly comes to a close *and the rest may be dismissed in a few paragraphs as of concern rather to the local historian than to the ethnologist*."[149] Arguing that the cultural trauma and political disorganization effected by the Removal completed and finalized the movement from "hunter and warrior" to "farmer and mechanic"—and thus the settler-colonial project itself—Mooney laments that those in the West exchanged ball play, age-old ceremonial cycles, and traditional political councils for railroad contracts and cattle leases dominated by "shrewd mixed-blood politicians, bearing white men's names and speaking the white man's language, and frequently with hardly enough Indian blood to show itself in the features."[150] Conflating cultural conservatism and residence in traditional lands with tribal authenticity and reinforcing the racialized rhetoric of mixed-blood corruption and degeneracy that was propagated by self-interested territorial advocates and Christian reformers, Mooney's narrative suggests an irrevocable schism between what he considered the truly aboriginal Cherokees remaining in the East and those in Indian Territory who are Cherokee in name and political status only. Mooney's history thus locks both Ross and the Cherokee Nation into a colonialist-oriented plot of nationhood predicated on the tragic loss of aboriginal authenticity.

Against the rhetorical and political efforts of Cherokee writers and politicians from Eaton's generation, the idea of an Indian nation was a contradiction in terms for Mooney, as it was for the white progressive reformers of his time. It is no wonder that Eaton brackets questions of authenticity and cultural loss; in discourses that set tribalism and nationhood in irrevocable opposition, Cherokee claims to modernity and sovereignty must necessarily come at the expense of tribal identity. In order to avoid this conundrum, Eaton claims Ross unequivocally as a Cherokee national hero, based not on his relationship to some stagnant, externally defined notion of tradition or authenticity, but on his commitment to Cherokee sovereignty, his willingness to perform "the duties of a citizen of the Cherokee Nation," and his vision "of a greater

Cherokee Nation, a republic of civilized Indians that should be the wonder and admiration of the world."[151] For Eaton, Ross's patriotic citizen ethic reflects a larger national commitment to "strengthening the government and welding the Cherokees into a strong, united nation in order that they might present a solid front of resistance to any further project for removal."[152] Though problematically framed as a chronicle of "the evolution from barbarism to civilization of one of the most progressive tribes of North American Indians," Eaton's story is also one of national struggle by Cherokee citizens "to maintain their tribal identity and ancestral domains against the overwhelming tide of economic development" that was advancing from the East.[153] Like Mooney, Eaton positions Ross's biography as a Cherokee national allegory. Unlike Mooney, she reads it not as a story of the tragic loss of tribal identity but as the adaptive emergence of an explicitly modern tribal nation.[154]

Since the death of the Indian hero and his accession to his own defeat/vanishing are fundamental components of fictional narratives of Native absence as well as Indian biographies and autobiographies, and since Eaton's biography ends with the death and burial of her national hero, the manner in which the text treats Ross's death deserves some comment.[155] The book's final chapter, "Reconstruction of the Cherokee Nation," documents the coercive processes by which Cherokees and other Confederate-allied nations were forced into massive land cessions and legal provisions that restricted tribal sovereignty as a condition of resuming the trust relationship with the federal government following the Civil War. Critiquing the ways in which settler accounts frame treaty negotiations as equitable exchanges, Eaton highlights the fundamentally exploitative conditions they imposed on tribal governments. As with her critique of the graft, political favoritism, and self-interest that defined the Removal, Eaton similarly characterizes the post–Civil War treaties as thinly veiled assaults on tribal sovereignty, systematic attempts to reduce the tribal estate "to mere reserves," and efforts to open up Indian lands to white settlement and eventually to U.S. territorial status. Under threats of tribal division, the National Party, led by Ross, concluded the Treaty of 1866 on July 17. Described by Eaton as "at best . . . a three-cornered compromise which pleased nobody," the treaty mandated land cessions, amnesty for war crimes, the repeal of Cherokee confiscation laws, guarantees of citizenship and property for freedmen, future promises to cede railroad rights of way, and provisions to establish federal courts in the territory.[156] Eaton wryly notes that the "federal government, as usual, came out the greatest gainer."[157] Though seriously ill at the time, Ross led the delegation, which concluded on July 19. A month later he passed away in Washington, DC, away from his beloved Park Hill and the Nation he fought his entire life to protect.

Just as Oskison immortalizes the sacrificial death of Jim Dawes as a selfless and heroic act of Cherokee patriotism, Eaton situates Ross as a heroic man who consistently held the admiration, respect, and confidence of his people and whose commitment to Cherokee sovereignty remains unparalleled in history. "When news of his death reached the Cherokee Nation," Eaton writes, "there was sincere mourning among a large portion of his people, both full-bloods and the mixed element who realized they had lost in their venerable chief a warm friend and an able champion."[158] Though acknowledging in retrospect Ross's political miscalculations as well as his personal flaws, Eaton, on the whole, dismisses accusations of despotism, corruption, and embezzlement as the biased opinions of political opponents and other "prejudiced persons not competent to judge the man fairly."[159] Rather, she elevates Ross as a paradigm of moral virtue and an exemplar of Cherokee national character: "To understand him it must not be forgotten that he was first, last and always a Cherokee Indian, a citizen of the Cherokee Nation which was to him a sovereign, independent nation. His consuming desire and purpose were to serve and protect to the best of his ability this nation at whose head he stood so proudly and staunchly for many years. He had no other patriotism, a fact which can be understood and appreciated fully, perhaps, only by those who have lived under conditions similar to those under which he lived and have possessed sentiments and attachments akin to his."[160] Such passages strongly suggest that Eaton considers herself and others of her generation to be among those who share the "sentiments and attachments" that defined Ross's patriotism and nationalist commitment to his people. After all, she elected to write a highly localized heroic biography of a Cherokee figure as an allegory of Cherokee national history within a discipline and genre that largely confined Native historical figures to the past in decidedly nonnational plots of death and decline. What is evident is that Ross's death at the end of the text is in no way meant to signal the death—tragic or otherwise—of the Cherokee Nation. As a matter of both historical fact and narrative design, Ross's life, as Eaton presents it, not only guarantees national preservation and survival but also provides a model of moral courage and political commitment through which the expression of Cherokee national character might live on into subsequent generations.

If, as Robert Sayre argues, historical biographies and autobiographies at some fundamental level express the values, beliefs, ideals, and commitments of a national community, then Eaton's apotheosis of Ross's life as an exemplary model of Cherokee national character must be read in similar terms. The biographical and autobiographical subject "is not only a 'who,' he is also a 'what'—what he lived for, what he believed in and worked for."[161] Eaton's text leaves no room for ambiguity with respect to such questions; Ross lived for the Cherokee Nation, believed profoundly in the moral right and legal authority of Cherokee peoples to exist as a modern nation according to their own designs and worked his entire life toward that goal. Like those noble deaths given to Founding Fathers in settler hagiographies, Eaton elevates Ross's life and death not as an allegory of tragic vanishing but as an exemplary legacy of Cherokee survivance, an active presence that refuses settler mandates of vanishing, assimilation, and erasure. Such reframing absorbs the *tragic* elements of Removal, factionalism, and the Civil War into a *comedic* narrative of Cherokee tribal-national survivance through the continued expression of Cherokee national character modeled on one of its own founding fathers.

Writing from Home, Telling New Stories

Contemporary Indigenous historians have long argued that Native historiography will remain woefully incomplete until historians begin to privilege Native archives, experiences, and the collective historical memory of tribal-national communities. Doing so not only shifts the historiographic focus from a settler to an Indigenous center, it also better accounts for the complex dynamics of conflict and exchange between Indians and non-Indians; understands Indian peoples as actors and agents in history as well as producers of historical knowledge; and refuses the linear teleology, historical inevitability, and moral resignation inherent to paradigms of conquest, civilization, progress, and settler-exceptionalism that have conventionally organized Indian histories.[162] Correcting historical inaccuracies, combating stereotypes, recovering historical agency, and identifying sites of subversion and resistance are not sufficient ends in themselves but are tactics within a much larger strategy of decolonization. On one hand, as both Taiaiake Alfred and Audra Simpson have argued, refusing historical and legal fictions of settler-state sovereignty predicated on the principle of conquest recovers the plural histories of Indigenous nationhood and continued political contestation that settler histories explicitly deny.[163] At the same time, contemporary histories will, as Devon Mihesuah and Philip Deloria argue, attend to historical circumstances that produced and continue to produce conflict, oppression, and violence within and among tribal communities.[164] To "write from home," as Donald Fixico argues, is thus to approach Native history from the inside, within the context of tribal traditions and experiences and with an eye toward the larger implications of knowledge production for Indian communities.[165] It is to identify the ways in which historical archives authored by non-Indians have constructed historical time and space and positioned Native peoples ambivalently as central to their own narrative designs yet consigned to their historical, legal, and political margins.[166] And it is the process of challenging those histories, writing oneself out of the discursive and epistemological binds of settler-state narratives, and levying claims not just to historical agency and nation-peoplehood but to humanity itself.

Written in a historical moment and a discipline still dominated by ethnocentric narratives of Anglo racial triumphalism and social evolutionary paradigms of human history, *John Ross and the Cherokee Indians* remarkably anticipates many of these concerns. From privileging local archives as authoritative sources to remapping Cherokee history within Cherokee geopolitical contexts and from refusing historiographic practices and generic conventions to recovering Cherokees as actors and agents in a story of Indian nation-peoplehood in the Americas, Eaton's text effectively reframes this history not as a clash between savagery and civilization but as a political contest between national sovereigns. In doing so, the text recovers a history of *multiple sovereignties* in the Americas that state-national narratives explicitly deny.[167] Negotiating the discursive restrictions of the discourse of civilization, the disciplinary practices of conventional historiography, and the generic conventions of Indian biography and Indian history, Eaton tells a story that is at once a critique of exploitation and graft, a celebration of Cherokee survival and continuance, and a profoundly human story of a people's self-determined struggle to be "still, a nation."

At the same time, her reliance on the fundamental value of civilization and progress—though not civilized discourse—and her use of the "Great Man" theory of history limit her narrative in important ways. Considering Eaton's own precarious position as a Cherokee female historian and her affirmation of Cherokee women's knowledge, her elision of Cherokee women from her own history is striking. Eaton's text is absent any significant female protagonists, and she mentions the historical centrality of matrilineality and the pervasive influence of the Cherokee clan structure only in passing. Though Eaton acknowledges that Ross's mother was profoundly committed to Cherokee traditions and that she was adamant about passing that knowledge down to her son, she receives only one paragraph of substantive commentary: "She was a woman of strong character and unusual intelligence, and her influence upon her children was one of the dominant factors of their lives. Herself intensely loyal to the traditions of her ancestors, she lost no opportunity of instilling these sentiments in the minds of her children. For her son John, who was the pride of her heart, she had cherished the greatest love and ambition. He was heartbroken and almost prostrated with grief at her loss and never, throughout his long life, ceased to cherish her memory."[168] After this celebratory passage of Mollie's crucial place in Ross's life and biography, Eaton never mentions her again. It is enough that she provided him with the cultural grounding necessary to be a good leader to his people. One wishes that Eaton would have provided—or felt authorized to provide—a Cherokee-specific context for this maternal influence and authority within the matrilineal clan relations that were still powerfully operative in Ross's youth. The same might be said for Ross's first wife, Quatie, who perished on the Trail of Tears. As with Ross's mother, Eaton describes Quatie as "a full-blood Cherokee . . . of much intelligence and native ability, possessing race prejudice and considerable influence within the tribe."[169] We are not told to what extent she leveraged that influence for Ross's benefit or to what extent he relied on her to ingratiate him with conservative communities (subsequent historians have suggested that they did both extensively). Instead, she disappears from the text only to reappear seventy pages later in a sentimental reference to her death, as one of among "more than four thousand [that] had perished along the way."[170] The only other Cherokee woman mentioned in the text is Catherine Brown, whom Eaton praises in passing as a laudatory example of mission education and Christian acculturation.[171] And despite being a central figure in the early nineteenth-century history that Eaton recounts in chapter 2, her own ancestor, Nanye'hi, who was at the forefront of Cherokee women's efforts to resist land cessions and the erosion of Cherokee women's authority in the emerging national government, is not mentioned at all. Indeed, Eaton's chronicle of Cherokee national emergence completely ignores the impact of nationalization on gender relationships within the Nation, never considering the ways in which Cherokee women lost public political, economic, and diplomatic power to the increasingly affluent, mixed-race men at the center of her narrative. Her treatment of the civilization program under Jefferson is similarly superficial, depicting the gendered reorganization of labor and political influence embedded in the program as historical givens. In perpetuating such elisions, the text reinforces the idea, as Theda Perdue has argued, that the story of history as change over time signaled by cultural and material innovation and adaptation was understood largely to be the domain of great men like Ross rather than Cherokee women—such as Eaton's grandmother or her ancestor, Nanye'hi—who birthed, raised, educated, initiated, supported, and accounted for them.[172]

Eaton's understanding of Cherokee national emergence as a decidedly modern and masculinist project that was driven primarily by acculturated Cherokee diplomats and political figures also minimizes the significance of cultural traditionalism and marginalizes the influence of political conservatism in Cherokee national development.[173] Though Eaton mentions a conservative rebellion against centralized authority in the 1820s—identified today as White Path's Rebellion—she fails to document the extensive political, cultural, and social resistance to Christianity, acculturation, and political centralization, which has been documented by others such as Royce and Mooney. Consequently, conservative-traditionalist figures, while at times alluded to in the narrative, function more as oppositional indexes for the ideas, motivations, and actions of the dominant mixed-blooded leaders. Against the progressive, civilized ideas of the mixed-blooded population, she positions the "good savage ethics" of conservative full-bloods, or the "wild beasts and wilder men" that populated the pre-Removal Indian Territory and points west.[174] Thus, while Eaton at one point acknowledges that many of the gains made following Removal were at least partially due to the efforts of "a number of strong and able men in some whose veins ran no drop of white blood," the rest of the narrative makes clear that the story situates national struggle and persistence as a decidedly mixed-blooded affair.[175] As with Oskison's frontier romance, Eaton's text exhibits its own national ambivalence about cultural and political conservatives: she admires their connection to tradition while also lamenting their backwardness, celebrates their physical prowess and connections to land while also condescending to their lack of manners and civility, and holds them up as candidates for acculturation while also defending them against exploitation and oppression. Cultural tradition and political conservatism for Eaton, as for Bartram, Mooney, and a host of non-Indian biographers, function as touchstones to a primitive tribal past, which confirms the noble Indian heritage of the acculturated, mixed-blooded protagonists while also acting as an evolutionary barometer for their road on the path to civilization.

As Devon Mihesuah observes, such narratives perpetuate the privilege of "mixed-blood, Christianized, 'white Cherokees' who support colonialism, giving the impression to the modern U.S. public that all Cherokees look and act like their colonizers and they are an acceptable enough tribe to claim as part of their exotic, yet civilized, heritage."[176] While Mihesuah's implication of all mixed-race Cherokees as abject colonial sympathizers and collaborators is overstated (Ross was a "mixed-blood," after all), her overall point suggests one of the central limitations of Eaton's discursive frame. Though rejecting the racialized associations of civilization, progress, modernity, and nationhood with whiteness, the text's investment in the savage/civilized distinction reinforces the equation of civilization—and thus Cherokee nationhood—with history and modernity. Echoing similar rhetorics that are evident across nineteenth-century Cherokee writing, Eaton denies a legitimate place for traditional practices, relations, and beliefs except as cultural curiosities, markers of authenticity, or anachronistic ties to primitive practices and institutions. From this perspective, Eaton's history does not advance historical, moral, and legal claims to nationhood for the Cherokee people as Indigenous First Nations, but as aboriginal peoples who had more than proven their capacity to acculturate to Euro-American cultural and social norms.

Despite these limitations, what Eaton accomplished is still quite extraordinary. Just as nineteenth-century Cherokee politicians mobilized the rhetoric of civilization in service of Cherokee national interests, Eaton appropriates civilization discourse in order to tell a story of Cherokee nationhood and political leadership that is both Indian and civilized, both tribal and thoroughly modern. Staking claims to humanity, history, modernity, and nationhood, Eaton's subversions of historiographic and biographical conventions effectively resituate Ross's life and the story of the Cherokee Nation as legitimate subjects of historical inquiry that are every bit as significant as celebrationist biographies of Revolutionary fathers and patriotic epics of the winning of the West. In Eaton's narrative, Cherokee national history, exemplified in the life and political commitments of its most recognizable leader, is a story of Cherokee tribal innovation, adaptation, resistance, survival, and resilience. Written in an intellectual and political climate that still conflated Euro-American social, cultural, and political norms with enlightened subjectivity, historical agency, modernity, and nationhood, Eaton's positioning of the Cherokee Nation as an acculturated civilized nation alongside England, France, and the United States is also an implicit argument for the right of Indian peoples to exist as modern nation-peoples in a historical moment that was still very much ruled by the racist policies of allotment and assimilation. Both in terms of its successes and limitations, and situated in the context of ongoing debates over the structure and significance of the events it relates, Eaton's history deserves consideration as an early, important, forward-looking critical intervention in Cherokee historiography and as an example of the very real challenges that such projects entail for Indigenous historians and for Native peoples more broadly.

THREE

Blood, Belonging, and Modernist Form in Lynn Riggs's *The Cherokee Night*

> Citizens of the Cherokee Nation shall be only those originally enrolled on, or descendants of those enrolled on, the Final Dawes Rolls of the Cherokee Nation, commonly referred to as the Dawes Rolls, for those listed as Cherokees by Blood.
>
> *Amendment to the Cherokee Constitution, March 3, 2007*

> Theater is an excellent medium through which to attack or embrace the world. Any play which makes no attempt to realize this function is bad. It is intellectually shoddy to use the theater for entertainment alone.
>
> *Lynn Riggs,* San Francisco Chronicle, *1937*

> The blood. . . . Stop the blood. . . . Lost so much blood. Feel my life runnin' out of me, slow. White blood, Indian—it don't matter. It spills out, runs out of me like water. Don't try to stop it any more.
>
> *Lynn Riggs,* The Cherokee Night

On March 3, 2007, Cherokee Nation voters amended the 1997 constitution to define citizenship strictly as a function of direct lineal descent from an ancestor on the final "by blood" Dawes Rolls of 1906. On the surface, the amendment emerged as a political response by some in the Nation to intensified claims to citizenship by descendants of Cherokee freedmen and to a ruling by the Cherokee Supreme Court that supported those claims. Freedmen and their descendants had long fought for recognition as full participant citizens of the Cherokee Nation per a provision in the post–Civil War Treaty of 1866 that stipulated that freedmen would enjoy "all the rights and privileges of Native Cherokees." It was not until their explicit disenfranchisement in a 1983 Cherokee statute, which tied citizenship to an ancestor of Cherokee blood, that they began to mobilize politically and openly challenge the antiblack undertones of such policies. Some viewed the amendment's passage in political terms as an exercise of Indigenous sovereignty and self-determination. Others viewed the amendment's articulation of direct lineal descent to an Indian ancestor as an affirmation of family relations and matrilineal and bilateral kinship to existing Cherokee families and communities. Still others read it as a cynical manipulation of Cherokee law that was motivated by political self-interest and was anchored to an unfortunate holdover of racialized understandings of Cherokee identity and belonging dating back to the nineteenth century. In the context of such disparate views, this move to bring the amendment to a referendum hit a nerve that reverberated out of the Nation, across Indian Country, and into legislative chambers and federal courts. The contentious debate over the place of Cherokee freedmen in Cherokee history and contemporary Cherokee society brings into stark relief the long, complicated legacy of settler-colonial discourses of race, blood, and belonging within Cherokee communities.[1] At stake in such arguments and in the histories that inform them is not simply the legacy of slavery or the place of freedmen descendants in contemporary Cherokee social and political life, but the very substance of Cherokee identity and nationhood itself.

Conceived in 1930 and published in 1936, Lynn Riggs's *The Cherokee Night* centers itself on exactly these relationships within the contexts of postallotment, poststatehood Cherokee life. Presented nonlinearly in seven episodic vignettes set variously between 1895 and 1931, the play dramatizes the disruption of Cherokee social and political life in the wake of allotment, with specific emphasis on the disintegration of Cherokee families and communities. The play opens in 1915 with a scene of intergenerational conflict and cultural disconnection at a historical site of intertribal violence that culminates in a full-blooded elder's denunciation of a "Good fer nothin'" generation of mixed-race Cherokee youth and the romantic announcement that night has set on the people.[2] The next five scenes dramatize a series of intersecting, dysfunctional social, familial, and intertribal/interracial relations between 1906 (the year before Oklahoma statehood) and 1931 (three years before federal Indian reform). The final scene, set in 1895, presents a devastating image of violence, death, and loss on the precipice of allotment and statehood. As the curtain falls, generations are at an impasse; youths are lost, alienated, and confused; friends have fatally betrayed friends; families are torn apart; and violence and trauma are pervasive components of everyday life.

Due to the overwhelming sense of racial determinism that structures all the conflicts in the play, critics understandably have been at odds over precisely what to make of it. Less generous readings argue that the play uncritically draws upon the violence and dispossession embedded in conventional declension narratives of Native absence ultimately reinforcing a settler status quo that leaves little room for productive Cherokee futures. Juliette Little Thunder, for instance, condemns what she reads as the play's perpetuation of stereotype and Indian blood lust, going so far as to recommend that it not be taught or included in anthologies of Indigenous theater.[3] Though he notes its significance for Native American letters, the play's strong critique of the dislocations that allotment wrought on Cherokee communities, and its engagements with an encoded queer politics, Craig Womack ultimately reads the play as a conflicted deferral to a heteronormative and settler-colonial status quo.[4] More sympathetic readers acknowledge the play's significance to Native artistic and intellectual traditions, but disagree widely over its critical stance toward blood discourse and the visions of Cherokee futures that it does or does not imagine. Whereas Jaye Darby, Qwo-Li Driskill, and Christy Stanlake read the play as a decolonizing reclamation of place and traditional cultural practices and beliefs, others such as Jace Weaver and Daniel Justice share Womack's ambivalence about its politics.[5] Weaver argues, for instance, that the play's inexorable movement toward destruction and its nostalgic longing for a prestatehood Cherokee past undermine any communist intentions and commitments that it might possess.[6] "Only before statehood," Weaver writes, "before the loss of political, territorial sovereignty, was there any hope for wholeness. Now the hope rests in memory, in not forgetting one's Indianness and in moving ahead along an uncertain path."[7] Justice largely agrees, noting that the play's preoccupations with cultural purity and individual psychological trauma subsume political questions regarding Cherokee social and political autonomy.[8] "Riggs's romantic nostalgia allows only for a redemptive self-sacrifice outside of the cruel realities of this world," Justice concludes, "not a healing change in circumstances in *this* life."[9] In his study of midcentury Native American writers and Indigenous Mexico, James Cox resituates *The Cherokee Night* within a larger anticolonial politics that is evident throughout Riggs's dramatic oeuvre. According to Cox, Riggs's work moves from the romantic nostalgia and regretful lament identified by Weaver, Womack, and Justice in his early plays such as *Big Lake* (1927), *Green Grow the Lilacs* (1931), and *The Cherokee Night* (1936) toward more militant imaginings of Indigenous revolution, U.S. imperial critique, and Cherokee survivance found in *The World Elsewhere, The Year of Pilar, Dark Encounter,* and *The Cream in the Well* (1947).[10] "With remarkable consistency," Cox concludes, "Riggs dramatizes the lives of impoverished Indian Territory families and communities in the midst of struggles" brought about by the massive social and political changes attending allotment and statehood.[11]

Ultimately, each of these readings expresses critical anxieties concerning Riggs's relationship to dominant discourses of blood and belonging and the social, cultural, and political vision of Indigenous futures that his plays offer in the contexts of their own production and in our contemporary moment as well. This chapter expands on these discussions by offering another entry point into the play that Riggs considered his best and most important work. Like most of these critics, I am in interested in what the play has to say about Cherokee identity, community, and nationhood in the early twentieth century, and I work hard to embed my reading of the play within those contexts. Where my reading departs from others is in its attention to two contexts that have largely gone unexamined in the scholarship: Riggs's theoretical commitments to formally innovative, politically committed theater, and the play's explicitly modernist, self-conscious disruption of linear time.[12] As the epigraph above suggests, and as I show in detail below, Riggs was intimately concerned with the politics of modern dramatic form and its capacity to bring about transformative social change. By situating both Riggs and the play within Cherokee and modernist American dramatic contexts, I explore how Riggs appropriates and refashions modernist dramatic techniques in order to interrogate the post-statehood politics of Cherokee blood and belonging. Within these contexts, I argue that the play's modernist disruption of linear time undermines and in significant ways refuses the inevitability and overwhelming sense of doom that run as a thread throughout. Framed by a brief biographical sketch in which I situate Riggs within Cherokee history and early twentieth-century American drama, I consider Riggs's critical commentaries on the theater as a site for social critique and transformation. From there, I offer formalist readings of five scenes in *The Cherokee Night* as one Cherokee's distinctly modern(ist) vision of

Rollie Lynn Riggs, Cherokee dramatist, theorist, screenwriter, and poet. Illustration by Roy Boney.

poststatehood Cherokee nationhood, anchored in common experience, shared histories, and an expansive and adaptive understanding of kinship, extricated from the destructive discourse of blood politics.[13]

Cherokee Roots, Modernist Migrations, and the Theater as Site of Social Transformation

The third of five children, Rollie Lynn Riggs was born into the Cherokee Nation on August 31, 1899, to Rose Ella Buster Gillis and William Grant Riggs in the small community of Sahgeeyah, just outside Claremore, in the Cooweescoowee district of the Cherokee Nation. His mother was a Cherokee citizen through her mother, while his father, the son of a Union soldier, was a prominent cattle rancher, banker, and businessman who had been naturalized into the Nation as an intermarried white citizen. Like Oskison, Riggs lost his mother at a young age; three months after Riggs's second birthday, Rose died of typhoid fever but not before enrolling herself and each of her three children as "Cherokees by blood" on the Dawes rolls under the auspices of the Curtis Act of 1898. Soon after Rose's death, Riggs's father married another Cherokee woman with whom Riggs had a contentious relationship, straining an already complicated dynamic between the bookish Lynn and his father. William's disdain for Lynn's "feminine" interests and belief in a masculinist, bootstrap ethic of self-reliance forced Lynn to finance his own intellectual and creative pursuits. In this, Rose's decision to enroll herself and her children would prove crucial for in addition to monies earned as a cowpuncher, delivery boy, journalist, and copyeditor in cities like Chicago, New York, and Los Angeles, Riggs would later use the mortgage of his eighty-acre allotment to fund his education. After graduating from the Oklahoma Military Academy (now Rogers State University) in Claremore, Riggs enrolled in the English department at the University of Oklahoma in 1920 where he would gain notoriety as poetry editor of the *University of Oklahoma Magazine*, a member of the Blue Pencil literary club (which also included Osage writer John Joseph Mathews), a tenor in the Sooner Singers, a member of Pi Kappa Alpha fraternity, and a frequent contributor to local theatrical productions as both a writer and an actor.

Struggling with poor health and depression, Riggs relocated to Santa Fe, New Mexico, in 1923 where he became acquainted with an avant-garde literary and artistic circle, which included D. H. and Frieda Lawrence, Alice Corbin Henderson, Carl Sandburg, Sinclair Lewis, Mary Hunter Austin, Georgia O'Keefe, and Mabel Dodge Luhan among others. Riggs left Santa Fe for Chicago before settling in New York in 1927. It was while on a Guggenheim fellowship in France between 1928 and 1929 that he conceived and penned *Green Grow the Lilacs* and *The Cherokee Night*, companion plays about Oklahoma statehood, which would bring Riggs widespread acclaim.[14] *Green Grow the Lilacs* narrowly missed winning the 1931 Pulitzer Prize for drama, finishing second to Susan Glaspell's *Allison's House*. Riggs's 1936 satire on romantic settler-colonial attitudes toward Indigenous New Mexicans, *Russet Mantle*, also narrowly missed the Pulitzer, which went to Robert Sherwood's *Idiot's Delight*. In addition to drama, Riggs also developed a reputation as a respected scriptwriter and Hollywood socialite, often running with a group that included Bette Davis, Joan Crawford, Jean Muir, Douglas Fairbanks, Gary Cooper, Henry Fonda, and Barbara Stanwyck. Over the next fifteen years, splitting time between New York, Hollywood, Santa Fe, and Mexico, Riggs produced sixteen full-length plays, two one-acts, a number of film scripts and television vehicles, and a collection of published poetry.[15]

His dramatic prospects on Broadway declined by 1941, and Riggs accepted an appointment as Rockefeller Professor at Baylor University in Waco, Texas, where he directed a production of *Macbeth* and his own play *Borned in Texas* (a.k.a. *Roadside*).[16] When his semester was up, he was drafted into the army, serving the majority of his term in the 846th Signal Service Photo Battalion. Upon completing his service commitment, Riggs continued to work for the Office of War Information during which time he wrote a thinly veiled theatrical critique of U.S. imperialism entitled *Dark Encounter.* With royalties from the huge success of Rogers and Hammerstein's adaptation of *Green Grow the Lilacs* as *Oklahoma!,* Riggs finally achieved the financial security he desired. In 1947 he purchased a farm on the tip of Long Island, where he remained for the rest of his life and penned the last of his great Oklahoma plays, *All the Way Home* and *Out of Dust.* He completed his final play in 1951, a historical pageant celebrating the 125th anniversary of Western Reserve University, which emphasizes the school's history of support for abolition. Like Oskison and Eaton, Riggs spent the final years of his life revising work for publication, composing an unpublished novel, and assembling another collection of poetry, which was also unpublished at the time of his death. Eventually succumbing to a long-term battle with stomach cancer, Riggs passed away at Memorial Hospital in New York City on June 30, 1954, just shy of his fifty-fifth birthday. Though all but forgotten until the publication of Phyllis Cole Braunlich's 1988 biography and the recovery efforts of Weaver, Womack, Justice, and others, Riggs was widely admired in his own time as one of the era's most well-respected poets and dramatists.[17]

Riggs's professional theatrical career (1929–54) spanned what many theater historians consider one of the most artistically innovative and politically active eras in American drama. Viewed by one critic as "an aesthetic response to the very real fears and anxieties attending historical modernity," American dramatic modernism was marked by an intense exploration of the relationship between aesthetic innovation and social engagement.[18] As a central figure in this milieu, Riggs possessed extensive relationships with many of these individuals and groups. He was a close friend of Ida Raugh Eastman and Susan Glaspell from the Provincetown Players, the former often staying in his apartment in Greenwich Village. In 1923 Riggs was a featured speaker, along with Paul Green, at a conference held at the University of Iowa sponsored by the National Drama Conference and National Theater Council designed to promote nonprofessional university and community theaters. The founder of the Hedgerow Theatre, Jasper Deeter, who was with the Provincetown Players from 1919 to 1922, staged many of Riggs's plays. In 1927–28 Riggs's play *Rancor* shared the season's billing at the Hedgerow with Henrik Ibsen's *A Doll's House*, George Bernard Shaw's *The Devil's Disciple*, Susan Glaspell's *Inheritors*, and Eugene O'Neill's *Emperor Jones.* The Hedgerow would go on to produce *A Lantern to See By* and *Roadside* in 1932. A year later, five of Riggs's plays shared the season's bill with six by O'Neill and four by Glaspell. According to John Wentz, *Roadside* was one of the company's most performed dramas between 1926 and 1932 and Riggs one of its most popular playwrights.[19] Riggs was also close with George Auerbach, director of the American Laboratory Theatre, which produced Riggs's 1927 drama *Big Lake* with a young Stella Adler in a starring role. Riggs's sometimes companion Ramon Naya was a writer in residence with the Group Theatre in the early 1930s, some of the founders of which were also involved in launching the Hedgerow. Riggs also maintained lifelong friendships and correspondence with Group Theatre associate and Pulitzer Prize winner Paul Green as well as major figures in American literary modernism such as Witter Bynner, Barrett Clark, Alice Corbin (Henderson), Yvor Winters, and Spud Johnson. Riggs was particularly close with Corbin and Johnson, sending each a number of inscribed copies of his published works and referring affectionately to the latter as "Spudito," "Spoodle," and "Spuddest."[20]

In addition to these personal and professional relationships, Riggs was also directly involved in the foundation of the Theatre Union, a nonprofit consortium of leftist writers, actors, directors, and producers that included Jon Dos Passos, Maxwell Anderson, Sherwood Anderson, and Stephen Vincent Benet. Formed in 1933, the Union sought to produce affordable, accessible theater for proletarian (and later, liberal and leftist bourgeois) audiences that might speak to their experiences, expose exploitative social conditions, and agitate revolutionary foment and social change.[21] Influenced by Marxist theory and agitprop socialist theater, those at the Theatre Union rejected what they understood to be the bourgeois politics of conventional realism and advanced instead an explicitly leftist artistic and political program called revolutionary realism.[22] As Ira Levine writes, "Revolutionary realism depicted [common] characters who, through the application of their reason and their collective will to the environment, actively changed their destiny. The new drama . . . portrayed man not as the world's victim, his will enervated, but as the proud possessor of an active and potent will that could transform society."[23] Rather than seeing social circumstances as a rigid, nihilistic status quo acting on unwitting human subjects-as-victims, the Theatre Union understood them as historically situated social relations that were subject to human action by characters with whom audiences could sympathize and for whom they would translate emotional investment—revolutionary catharsis—into direct political action.

Though the Theatre Union never developed the kind of influence it set out to achieve, its existence expresses anxieties about the continued significance of theater and the ethical responsibility of the arts to critically engage social conditions. Speaking specifically of the Provincetown Players, J. Ellen Gainor describes 1920s and '30s American drama as being engaged in "an active critical discourse on the development" of the form, specifically with respect to dramaturgical innovation and experimentation, debates over the relationship between commercialized theater and socially engaged art, and questions about conservative morality, community, and national identity.[24] Of leftist dramatists emerging from the free experimentalism of the '20s into the more politically charged '30s, Levine writes that they "shared a sense of the writer's social responsibility and a common emphasis on practical reform," and they agreed that "artistic work, and especially literary and dramatic activity . . . were to be less a matter of personal expression than a testament of belief and an exercise of political participation. In the process, art would be remolded into an instrument of social expression."[25] Often at the center of these conversations as a dramatist, critic, and theorist, Lynn Riggs developed over the course of his life a theory of theater that attempted to balance a commitment to artistic innovation and intellectual rigor with the ethical responsibility to use the form as a medium for social critique and a vehicle for social change.

Responding to a query from the *Southwest Review* in March 1929 concerning his focus on Oklahoma subject matter, Riggs admits that much of his writing is influenced by the peoples and scenes of his youth. In a profound commentary on the intersections of race, class, and privilege, Riggs writes, "But it so happens that I knew mostly the dark ones, the unprivileged ones, the ones with the most desolate fields, the most dismal skies. And so it isn't surprising that my plays concern themselves with poor farmers, forlorn wives, tortured youth, plow hands, peddlers, criminals, slaves—with all the range of folk victimized by brutality, ignorance, superstition, and dread. And will it sound like an affectation (it most surely is not) if I say that *I wanted to give voice and a dignified existence to people who found themselves, most pitiably, without a voice, when there was so much be cried out against?*"[26] Riggs expands on this early vision of the theater as a medium through which to give voice to the voiceless in a 1932 radio interview. "American stage must become a platform for fervor, for eloquence, for a blinding revelation of man," Riggs argues. "It must be more than entertainment, more than life, more than ritual, more than color and glamour. It must touch and illumine the spirit of striving man. It must believe in the word—which is God. That's the theatre I believe in. That's the theatre I intend to spend my life in."[27] For Riggs, the central purpose of drama is not to serve as a vehicle for escape or as popular entertainment but rather to "make people examine the world we are living in now."[28] He further claims, "Unless the drama does something for the soul of man it isn't justifying itself."[29] Like his experimentalist colleagues, Riggs decried what he viewed as contemporary theater's failure to speak out against jingoistic nationalism, patriotic fervor, and other forms of social oppression.

While Riggs viewed the theater as a vehicle through which to present society with an honest critical reflection of itself, he also mandated that it not stop at critique. Good theater, socially responsible theater, must also challenge audiences intellectually and motivate them politically to become agents of change. Believing that the theater's formal characteristics made it especially suited to fulfill such responsibilities, Riggs indicted the theatrical realism that drove much commercial theater of his time for its failure of imagination and for refusing to adequately engage social conditions truthfully. In an essay, "When People Say 'Folk Drama'" in the *Little Theatre Dallas* magazine from March 1932, Riggs argues, "Too much realism gets in the way of a play. That is, too much photographic realism. Nearly all my plays, by intention, have a slight edge beyond realism. In other words, the little lying thing beyond realism makes them important to me. Perhaps that's what Art is—a subtle lie, for the sake of telling the truth."[30] Noting a distinction between the "facts" of events themselves and the "truth" that emerges by dramatizing those events onstage, Riggs contends, "Realistic truth is not real enough, certainly not good enough. A realer truth has to be uncovered. I don't think I should like a play if at some time the drama didn't just walk right out of realism on to a more illuminating and wiser plane."[31] The point for Riggs was not simply to give voice to the voiceless but to provide his audiences with an uncompromisingly raw image of the lives, experiences, and conditions of those living on America's social and economic margins.

Riggs sharpened this position in a 1937 *San Francisco Chronicle* commentary on the ethical and social responsibilities of theater, writing that the "theater is an excellent medium through which to attack or embrace the world. Any play which makes no attempt to realize this function is bad. *It is intellectually shoddy to use the theater for entertainment alone.*"[32] Speaking specifically of playwrights' relationships with their audiences in an address to the San Diego Community Theatre three years later, Riggs charges that playwrights "certainly have no right to ask anyone to sit through one of your productions and to go out without being in some way *changed.*"[33] If social theater has done its job, "we [will] have had an experience that has reached us, and we are never quite the same again. *Even more so—and more often, we should see those moments on the stage.* We—as theatre people—*should make those moments happen,* or consider ourselves failing in our craft."[34] Riggs connects personal revelation to social action in order to drive his final point home: "The more we seek to know and to comprehend, then *to add what we can to make it more bearable for ourselves and others to live*—the more revelation we can stumble on, and the more we have in our hands the power to change that world."[35] Rejecting any notion that what happens in the auditorium should stay in the auditorium, Riggs desired that audiences would translate individual revelation into efforts toward social justice.[36]

These commitments are perhaps nowhere better expressed than in a letter Riggs penned to his friend and colleague Paul Green about a visionary new theatrical project that Riggs hoped Green would support.[37] Similarly political, but with a more optimistic critical focus than the Theatre Union, the Vine Theatre sought to create drama that was at once artistically innovative and intellectually complex yet capable of reaching working-class audiences. Conceived by Riggs and Riggs's long-time romantic partner Enrique Gasque (a.k.a. Ramon Naya), the Vine was to be the antithesis of Broadway overproduction and banal Hollywood escapism. In the letter to Green, Riggs and Naya outline a thirty-five-point manifesto for the project, which envisions the Vine as a freely creative revolutionary space in which all involved would contribute to a transformative theatrical experience. Formal innovation and nonrealist representation would organize the Vine's creative process. "Our theatre, by its very nature, will produce new forms," Riggs and Naya announce, utilizing "all the exciting manifestations of theatre art now current in theatrical usage," including modern music, dance, movement, and expressionist theatrical techniques.[38] Against the "theatre of entertainment" and the superficiality of "the movies," the Vine "must change the cells of the people who come within its doors. . . . The person who goes away from of a play of ours should not be the same person who came in. He must have had as vital an experience as life itself can give him."[39] Rejecting sectarian and confrontational paradigms of social realism and agitprop drama, the Vine sought instead to intervene in the world through a creative rather than destructive process. "Our theatre will attack nothing," Riggs and Naya write. "It will expose the state of our world, of course, but it will lean, by its very nature, to the affirmative principles of goodness and truth. . . . Having looked at the world, we shall aim our attempt to fix and comprehend that world right back at the forces that brought it into being."[40] Reflecting the leftist intellectual climate of the day, Riggs and Naya affirm that the Vine is "not to be a theatre of ideas" but a "lyric . . . theatre of feeling," which seeks to "remind human beings of the dignity of man." Short of awakening such sensibilities, they write, the Vine would be "a failure from the first."[41] In addition to Green's enthusiastic reception, Riggs and Naya's project also attracted the support of contemporaries Mary Hunter (Wolf) and Russian actor and playwright Andrius Jilinsky, who studied with Boleskawski at the Moscow Art Theatre and eventually directed Riggs's *Sump'n Like Wings* for the American Actor's Company. Together they envisioned a "more free theatre" capable of resisting the restrictive commodifying forces of the Broadway establishment that Riggs believed stifled creativity and innovation.[42]

Though often read by Womack and others as politically disconnected from the more radical politics of the interwar period, it might be more accurate to say that Riggs understood art itself as possessing radical political possibilities.[43] Indeed, Riggs's reflections on theater reveal a profound faith in and commitment to the power of the arts to effect positive change in the world. Whether in individual plays or in his larger theory of socially committed theater, Riggs viewed the mission of drama as neither entirely pedagogical nor exclusively pleasurable; its mission was not simply to teach and delight. Rather, the kind of politically committed, socially engaged theater that Riggs theorized and wrote was pedagogy-as-praxis, its mission to teach, delight, *and transform.* This was the kind of drama that Riggs spent his entire theatrical life trying to compose, and it is within this critical framework that I turn to *The Cherokee Night*, the play that Riggs long considered his most important artistic and intellectual achievement.

Blood, (De)Generation, Declension, and Kinship

The Cherokee Night opens with a group of Cherokee young adults picnicking on a landing below Claremore Mound in the summer dusk of 1915, nine years after the unilateral dissolution of tribal governments in 1906 and eight years after Oklahoma statehood in 1907. The year 1915 also marks one year since hostilities had erupted in Europe, initiating what would erroneously be termed the war to end all wars. The juxtaposition of the two events, which is made explicit in the relationship between returning Cherokee and Osage veterans Hutch Moree and Clabe Whiteturkey in scene 6, suggests a correlation: just as the Great War was devastating to Western nations, so were federal Indian policies of extermination, assimilation, and allotment catastrophic for Indian peoples. In much the same way that American GIs, including an unprecedented number of Native soldiers, defended U.S. interests by responding to acts of war on foreign soils, American Indians, the play suggests, have also defended their own homelands against acts of aggression perpetrated by the very body charged with their trust and protection: the federal government. In the dramaturgical political economy of *The Cherokee Night*, Oklahoma statehood was as much an act of war and an assault on the basic principles of nationhood and sovereignty as the German invasion of France was.

While these larger contexts operate on each of the major characters in the play, Riggs localizes the social conflicts that result from imperial histories of violence through the symbolic presence of Claremore Mound—a haunting, ghostlike apparition that is present throughout the play. Home to an Osage community with roots antedating the arrivals of southeastern Native peoples to the region between the 1810s and 1840s, the mound was the site of a brutal massacre perpetrated by Old Settler Cherokees against Osage women, children, and elders. The conflict, largely the result of Removal policies of the nineteenth century that forced Indian peoples into territorial conflicts over ever-shrinking lands and resources, serves as the central historical mooring of the play, pointing at once to the event, the site on which it took place, and the historical forces that were ultimately responsible for engendering the conflict in the first place. Claremore Mound stands in the play as an incisive reminder of the white-on-Indian violence that was perpetrated through federal Indian policy and the Indian-on-Indian violence that so often emerged as a consequence.

In order to demonstrate the effects of such intersecting histories on the Cherokee Nation, Riggs presents a set of characters divided by race, class, nation, cultural heritage, and attitudes toward modernity, all of which are thoroughly mediated through complex racially coded discourses of blood and belonging.[44] Where blood signifies an ideology of cultural authenticity and racial purity that sets older and younger generations of Cherokees in irrevocable opposition in scene 1 (set in 1915), in scene 2 (1927) it stands as a biological determinant of mixed-blood deviance that erodes productive gender relationships between Cherokee men and women. In contrast, in scene 3 (1931) blood functions as a code for Indian poverty and cultural backwardness that undermines the matrilineal relations between Cherokee sisters and, by extension, between an aunt and a niece. Scenes 4 (1906), 5 (1913), and 6 (1919) examine how blood discourse frustrates interracial and intertribal relationships with other outcasts from prevailing U.S. social and political orders—African Americans, Osages, and white religious separatists—in terms of a debilitating suspicion, paranoia, and fear of racial otherness. Combined with the pervasive sense of declension, death, and doom with which the play ends—confirmed in the final scene with the violent death of a Cherokee man, the fracturing of multiple families, and the nihilistic pronouncements of a Cherokee elder—reading the play as anything but another deterministic story of Native absence becomes difficult. As the final curtain falls on the play, it would appear that night has indeed fallen on the Cherokee people.

Had Riggs written a linear drama, such readings would hold merit. The story would proceed from an elder Cherokee traditionalist's cabin on the eve of allotment and statehood in 1895 through the next forty years, providing audiences and readers with glimpses into the gradual erosion of Cherokee communities. But Riggs did not write a linear narrative of Cherokee decline. As the schematic below demonstrates, *The Cherokee Night* dispenses with the linearity of historical time for a dramatic experience that moves back and forth through time:

Scene 1. Sixty-seven Arrowheads: Claremore Mound. Dusk, summer. (1915)
Scene 2. The Hatchet: Rogers County Jail. A spring night. (1927)
Scene 3. Liniment: A room. A winter morning. (1931)

Scene 4. The Place Where the Nigger Was Found: The woods near Claremore. A summer afternoon. (1906)
Scene 5. The High Mountain: A church near Tahlequah. Noon, summer. (1913)
Scene 6. The White Turkey: A farmhouse. An autumn morning. (1919)
Scene 7. The Cherokee Night: A log cabin. A winter night. (1895)

If, as James Cox argues, one identifying attribute of colonialist narratives of Native absence is an inexorable drive toward the inevitable vanishing of Native peoples, then we must account for Riggs's rejection of the linear temporality on which such narratives depend as an inadequate paradigm through which to dramatize his critical exploration of contemporary Cherokee relationships.[45] *The Cherokee Night* is not a story that moves linearly from Cherokee autonomy toward a preordained moment of tribal dissolution and cultural decline via the juggernaut of blood politics. Rather, it is a story about the power of discourse itself to undo families, destroy communities, and undermine reconciliation and renewal. By disrupting the linear determinism of settler-national time, the play recasts the familial conflicts and social ruptures that it dramatizes as historically situated social phenomena that are amenable to revision and change.

Key to making this relationship explicit are the numerous yet fleeting instances that Riggs opens up for Cherokee characters to recognize and claim one another outside of blood discourse. The first such opportunity occurs in the opening scene with the appearance of Old Man Talbert, a Cherokee elder who holds blood quantum as a romantic signifier of Cherokee cultural authenticity. Often hostile to younger generations, Talbert is variously characterized by younger Cherokees as "that Old Indian—kinda crazy," a "Pore old man. Crazy's a loon," and a "half-witted old ghoul."[46] Viewing the old man as a potentially murderous threat—not unjustified considering the hateful invective he levies against them from the moment he walks onstage—most of the kids categorically reject the man and his message as threatening, if not insane. In a particularly violent response, Art Osburn—a character who, years later in scene 2, is charged with murdering his Indian wife—threatens to "crack his head open" with a rock if Talbert makes a threatening move, an assault which the others gradually begin to endorse as tension between the young adults and Talbert reaches a crescendo.[47] Only Gar and Bee, half-siblings and the characters with the most Cherokee blood, attempt to establish a respectful connection with the old man:

> GAR: (*Interfering.*) Let him alone, Art. (*He turns to the* OLD MAN.) Mr. Talbert. Mr. Talbert, don't you know me?
> TALBERT: (*Fiercely.*) Git on away from here!
> GAR: I'm Gar Breeden. You ort to recollect me.
> TALBERT: Never seen you before!
> GAR: Why, I've come on up on picnics here at Claremore Mound ever since I was knee-high. Gar Breeden. You know *me.* Once I ask at yore house for water, and you give me a drink from the well, years ago. And you give me sump'n else, too. (*He pauses, as if at a troubled ecstatic memory.*) You give me a eagle feather. Don't you remember? . . . I kep' it.[48]

Gar's attempt to claim Talbert as a member of his community contrasts dramatically with Art's violent rejection of the experiential authority of elders. Influenced by his past experiences and interactions with Talbert on this very spot, Gar sees the old man not as a menace but as an elder who affirmed significant kinship obligations by providing Gar with physical and spiritual nourishment. In doing so, Talbert legitimized Gar's place in Cherokee community in ways that circumvented and subverted legal articulations of legitimacy and belonging. Gar is, after all, an orphan child of the murderous, mixed-race Cherokee outlaw, Edgar Spench. Consistent with the values of reciprocity on which kinship obligations depend, Gar attempts to act in kind. Unfortunately, Talbert is unable to accept Gar's offering. Though he admits recognition—"I know you all! Everyone of you. Knowed you all yer lives, the whole goddamn crew of you!"—Talbert sees not fellow Cherokees but a useless, lost, and corrupt generation of mixed-blooded miscreants: "I seen too much of you, anyway! Clutter up the world—all of you—that's whut you do! Good fer nothin'. . . . You're no use to anybody. You're lost. *You might as well be dead.*"[49]

Talbert's notions of racial purity and cultural authenticity, interpreted and articulated as they are through the romanticized conflation of blood quantum and culture, are most evident in his apocalyptic message of Cherokee degradation and loss. Ten years earlier, while napping at Claremore Mound, Talbert experienced a vision of the Cherokee-Osage massacre: "The Cherokees! Painted for war! A-stealin' up on the Osages asleep up there by their campfires! (*Savagely, with frightful passion.*) Fall on 'em, cut their th'oats, bury their tomahawks in their thick skulls, let yer muskets thunder! At every Cherokee belt a row of Osage scalps—with long black hair swishin' and drippin'! I seen it—all of it—*my people!* I heared the Osage groans!"[50] Talbert's observation of the violence and bloodshed of the event is both vivid and, by most accounts, accurate. With federal consent, ostensibly in order to counteract unprovoked hostilities by the "savage" Osages against peaceful, "civilized" Cherokee settlers, Cherokees launched a series of attacks against Osage settlements between 1817 and 1818. In one of the more violent encounters, Cherokees and their allies descended on the settlement below Claremore Mound. Within minutes they massacred anywhere from thirty-eight to eighty-four men and women, many of them elderly, and took more than one hundred Osage children as captives and as payment for allies in the attack. After a series of retaliations and reprisals over the next year, both parties agreed to peace in the Treaty of 1818 in which Osages were forced to cede a vast section of land between the Neosho and Verdigris Rivers and to guarantee Cherokees an outlet to the rich Kansas hunting grounds to the north. Plagued by hunger, dwindling territory, decreasing access to game, demographic pressures with the arrival of thousands more southeastern Indians, and intensified internal dissension, the Osages were forced into the Treaty of 1839 in which they ceded the remainder of their lands in Indian Territory and were forcibly removed to a small reservation in Kansas.[51]

This conflict was popularly depicted by Removal and civilization advocates, as well as some Old Settler Cherokees, as an epic struggle between the "civilized" Cherokees and "savage" Osages. Though highly attuned to the racial politics of federal policies and the extent to which they often intentionally encouraged conflict between Indian peoples, either to facilitate Removal or to gain access to Indian lands, both Cherokees and Osages were forced to negotiate the savage/civilized discourse through which such policies were articulated. Possessing a greater familiarity and longer history with U.S. cultural mores and legalese, Cherokees often positioned themselves as helpless victims of Osage savagery rather than as unwelcome arrivants into Osage territory who had their own political interests in gaining access to rich Osage lands. Playing on the cultural chauvinism of civilized Americans and their fear and disdain of Indian savages, Cherokees parlayed their reputation as a civilized tribe in order to gain support for the expulsion of their Osage antagonists and to consolidate their own hegemony in the region.[52]

It is precisely Talbert's ignorance of the policy decisions and historical events that placed Osages and Cherokees into violent conflict over territory and resources that prevents him from reading the event as anything but a romantic epic of Cherokee heroism, the last great gasp of a Cherokee warrior ethic: "Now you've saw, you've been showed. *Us*—The Cherokees—in our full pride, our last glory! This is the way we are, the way we was meant to be."[53] Taking these passionate sentiments of the bloody warrior at face value, Talbert uncritically adopts the frustrating contradictions embedded in the Noble Savage and holds them up as an exclusive paradigm for an authentic Cherokee identity. Talbert's romantic ideal of Cherokee warrior nobility forecloses the possibility of bringing his apocalyptic vision into the present and of making it relevant for any kind of model articulating a viable Cherokee future.[54] In Talbert's racial logic, both racial purity and cultural authenticity are impossible to attain.

Talbert's vision intersects with a long history of Native prophecies that advocate the rejection of white ways and a return to Indigenous cultural practices and beliefs in response to moments of drastic social and cultural upheaval.[55] In fact, as William McLoughlin has documented, a Cherokee Ghost Dance movement, known as the Rocky Mountain Vision, emerged as a response to a series of catastrophic events between 1811 and 1812, which included the collapse of the fur and pelt trade, famine and natural disasters, U.S. intrusion, and the rising influence of a secular, mixed-race political and economic elite.[56] The prophesy, which was rooted in many of the conventions that are apparent in Talbert's own vision—the mysterious appearance of Cherokee elders, a qualified rejection of white ways, an admonition to return to traditional practices, and the evocation of the supernatural—differed dramatically from Talbert's in its ultimate goals. Though it "looked backward to a better age when much game was present, old ways were followed, and the Cherokees practiced their dances and rituals in the sacred towns," it also advanced a vision of cultural syncretism that advocated Western education and English literacy, a codified system of law, and political alliance with sympathetic whites, even as it admonished Cherokees to make no further land cessions and mandated a respectful cultural and political separatism for all peoples.[57] Whether effected through a peaceful spiritual revival, a return to cultural traditions, an apocalyptic military resistance, or a combination of the three, Indigenous millenarian movements were more often than not practical, pragmatic efforts to secure order and stability in the present, often by reconciling contemporary circumstances with a people's long-held understandings of culture, identity, and belonging.

Talbert's vision diverges dramatically in its foreclosure of transformative possibilities and its failure to provide a coherent hopeful vision of the future for the people. While castigating the kids for having "forgot" their ancestors and characterizing them as "withered leaves," Talbert's own romanticized notions of Cherokee authenticity and his vexed understanding of history implicate him in his own indictment. The absurdity of this situation is rendered even more apparent in Talbert's conclusion that the only way to reclaim this presumed birthright is to dig up arrowheads—artifacts that ostensibly stand as symbolic proof of Cherokee warrior nobility—and distribute them to the community in the hope of reawakening a romanticized heroic idea of themselves.[58] While it is perhaps lost on both Talbert and the others, the ironic pageant of a Cherokee elder searching for "Indian" artifacts as a means of reclaiming an essentialized, idealized birthright from the past all the while rejecting contemporary Cherokee youths who represent the potential future of the Nation amplifies the misguidedness of his vision. Seeing the problem of cultural discontinuity as one inherent to this "lost," "dead" generation of mixed-blooded Cherokees, Talbert's vision can only assume the form of an absolute repudiation of the young rather than a potentially nourishing act of intergenerational healing and cultural transformation.[59] Thus he becomes the quintessentially self-loathing, internally colonized Indigenous person, a psychological state of being which, in the political economy of *The Cherokee Night*, renders him insane and a social outcast.

The vision of Cherokee identity, authenticity, and history that Talbert presents in this opening scene, then, is not Riggs's vision; nor does Talbert speak for the larger blood politics that the play examines. Rather, when combined with the alternative image of intergenerational kinship modeled in the final scene, Riggs explicitly positions Talbert on the play's moral and ethical margins. That his vision provokes fear in the younger generation says more about the racial logic that organizes his romantic imaginary than it does about the rightness, or righteousness, of his ideas. Unequipped with a nuanced historical understanding of the material histories that brought them to this site of settler-colonial and inter-Indigenous violence, neither Talbert nor the children are able to see through the discursive haze of blood discourse and its attendant concepts of racial purity and cultural authenticity that set them in irrevocable opposition. In exchanging the rights, responsibilities, and obligations of kinship for the absolutist binaries of racialized authenticity, Talbert reproduces the very generational divide that he laments. Put simply, we are not meant to subscribe to Talbert's attitudes about blood; we are meant to see them for what they are—various forms of insanity.

Gender, Coercion, Collaboration, and Racialized Criminality

Whereas the opening scene dramatizes how the blood politics of identity and authenticity short-circuit intergenerational relations, the second scene speaks to issues of legal jurisdiction, racialized criminality, and intragenerational gender relations two decades into the poststatehood era. Set in 1927, the scene opens with Bee Newcomb negotiating with a Rogers County sheriff about a previous agreement to elicit a murder confession from an unidentified man. As in the previous scene, Riggs reminds us through stage directions that this, too, is a scene of U.S. settler-colonial violence. As the lights come up, *"Two tiny cells separated by only bars, and with a wall in back, appear from the darkness, under the sloping metal roof of the Rogers County Jail. From behind, Claremore Mound looms in the darkness, dim and silent, dwarfing the scene."*[60] Whereas questions of legal and political jurisdiction inform every aspect of Oskison's frontier romance and Eaton's history, those contested histories have already been settled in this scene. Twenty years after statehood, the jail is no longer in the Cooweescoowee district of the Cherokee Nation but in Rogers County in the young settler state of Oklahoma. Combined with dark noiresque stage lighting and the relentless downpour of rain, the "dim and silent, dwarfing" apparition of Claremore Mound again marks this history. This time, however, it haunts the racialized and gendered dynamics of coercion, collaboration, and criminality that underwrite the scene.

The opening exchange between Bee and the sheriff illustrates these tensions.[61] The stage lights come up on their conversation in medias res as Bee expresses discomfort over her participation in the sting and her concern for the man implicated in the state's allegations:

> BEE: (*Shortly.*) I don't like it.
> SHERIFF: Now looky here, you said you'd go ahead and—
> BEE: I don't like it I said.

SHERIFF: (*Protesting.*) We got it all planned. It's got to be someone he knows. You cain't go and back out on me—

BEE: Who the hell says I cain't?

SHERIFF: (*Sharply.*) Say, I give you ten dollars and the promise of fifteen more, and I be goddamned if you're gonna back out on me! Now cut it out and git in that cell! (*He makes a move as if to force her. Without a word, she hands out a ten-dollar bill. He looks at it, astonished. He waves it away.*)

BEE: Take it.

SHERIFF: (*Changing his tactics.*) Aw listen, Bee. A good gal like you ort to—Say look, all you got to do is git him to talk. *He'll* talk. It won't hurt *you* none if he *tells* on hisself.

BEE: (*Quietly.*) Whut'll it do to him, though?

SHERIFF: What?

BEE: Whut'll it do to *him*?

SHERIFF: (*With relish.*) Hang him, by God, if we're lucky! Hang the hound dog!

BEE: (*Wryly.*) That'll be nice. They's nuthin' like hangin' a man to make you feel good.[62]

Despite her suspicions, Bee convinces herself to participate based on a personal dislike for the alleged perpetrator. Her rationale fails to alleviate her anxiety, however, and she self-medicates with two huge swallows of whiskey. As she pockets the flask and steps into the cell, Bee *"straightens up, and looks at [the sheriff] with a curious and acid stare, her brows narrowed."* She asks, "Say, how did I get to be on your side anyway?" When the sheriff reminds her of their monetary agreement, Bee takes her position in the cell while the sheriff, unbeknownst to her, installs a recording device in the adjacent cell. Before he leaves, Bee again interrogates him about the circumstances of the crime, questioning specifically the sheriff's insistence on murder, to which he replies—absent any hard evidence—"*Course* he killed her" and quickly exits the stage.[63] The trap set, Bee awaits the arrival of the alleged assailant whom we soon find out is fellow Cherokee Art Osburn.

There is a lot going on in these early pages that needs unpacking. Perhaps most significant are the intersectional dynamics of gender, sex, race, nation, and criminality at work here. On one level, Bee's characterization as a hypersexualized, mixed-race Indigenous woman recalls the disabling ambivalence embedded in Rayna Green's formulation of the "Pocahontas Perplex."[64] In this narrative framework, Indigenous women are forced into a reductive binary between the virtuous virginal princess whose love for white men and endorsement of settler culture implicitly legitimizes its presence in the Americas and the sexually promiscuous and socially deviant squaw whose refusal to abide by those norms reduces her to an object of male settler sexual desire, assault, and death. Caught in the "dysfunctional" ambivalence of such a paradox, the Indian woman is left with "little room to move . . . and by both race and sex stands damned."[65] Green's emphasis on dysfunction, ambivalence, and restricted mobility captures many of the complicated components of Bee's character. Her value to the state rests exclusively in her role as a collaborator with and informant for Oklahoma legal authority. In this, Bee is positioned as a Pocahontas figure who will exploit her relationship to a Cherokee man (and, by extension, to the entire community) in the service of the state. As a sexually active, mixed-race Cherokee woman who consistently challenges the sheriff's methods and refuses to accept his bribe, however, Bee can never fully occupy that position. Her reverse interrogation of the sheriff's motives, suspicion of state allegations of murder, and concern for Art's well-being over the swift exercise of retributive justice all work to cast doubt on the sheriff's claims to authority and the legitimacy of his methods. Combined with her repeated attempts to extricate herself from the arrangement and the various tactics the sheriff uses to compel her compliance—bribery, coercion, alcohol, psychological manipulation—this exchange reads more like a sexual assault than a negotiation about law and order. Indeed, as Luana Ross and Sarah Deer have explored, such dynamics are deeply embedded U.S. settler law and its disruption of Indigenous social, cultural, legal, and political institutions.[66] The fact that the scene takes place within the contexts of the death/murder of another Cherokee woman and the entrapment and eventual execution of a Cherokee man illustrates the institutional vulnerabilities produced for Indians in a post-statehood legal and political climate. Damned by race, sex, *and nation*, Bee is left little choice but to participate in the sheriff's sting.

Similar dynamics inform Art's character. As a mixed-race man with an unpredictable temper and a proclivity for violence, Art is also situated within a representational and legal history that positions Indigenous manhood on a spectrum between romantic nobility/heroism and savage violence/

criminality.[67] Best illustrated in Twain's Injun Joe, dime-store westerns, and cinematic frontier narratives, the savage's delight in violence, propensity for bloodlust, and inevitable descent into racially motivated vengeance positions him as an "unregenerate outlaw" or biological criminal.[68] On the surface, Art seems like such a figure. In the opening scene he responds to a verbal altercation with Viney Jones by slapping her face, and he becomes increasingly aggressive with Old Man Talbert as he berates Art and his friends. In scene 4 we see Art as a young boy whose already-racist imagination and paranoid fear of blackness produce a horrific imagining of interracial violence. In scene 2, under consideration here, Art *"strikes into the cell quickly,"* his eyes *"burn[ing] with a fierce and wild venomous glow,"* and *"like a caged panther [he] snarls at the Guard."*[69] As Bee makes her presence known and labels Art a murderer, he explodes again, *"fiercely, crazily, grabbing the bars between them."* Though initially denying any wrongdoing, Art eventually confesses to the murder, describing in gruesome detail how he repeatedly struck his wife with an axe while her daughter looked on.[70] Upon realizing Bee's complicity in the sting, Art descends into another act of misogynist violence, grabbing Bee through the bars and grasping her throat: "I'll kill you, I'll choke you till yer eyes come out of her head! You've killed me—you hear?—you've murdered me the way I murdered her! Anh! Before I die—they'll be another dead un! What's another'n! What difference does it make now?"[71] Before he is able to kill her, Art is dragged away, kicking and screaming, to his death, while Bee remains on the floor, having collapsed but still alive.

While images of mixed-blood violence and criminality inform Art's character, Riggs complicates any easy association between the two by providing insight into the fragility, vulnerability, and complicated circumstances of his situation. Over and over Riggs draws on the language of exhaustion, desperation, and trauma to depict Art's physical and psychological state. Upon recognizing a potentially friendly (or at least not overtly hostile) face in Bee, Art's *"legs give way under him,"* and he *"sinks to his stool, his arms sliding down wearily between the bars."*[72] When Bee suggests that Art brought his circumstances upon himself, he *"wearily"* accedes, and when she continues to press for details, Art *"helplessly, fiercely"* begs her to stop interrogating him. As Bee strategically relents, Art, with *"desperation and fear in his voice,"* wonders aloud, "How did I get here? What am I doin' here? . . . What's the matter with me? . . . What are they tryin' to do to me, what're they tryin'—!" In order to calm him down,

Bee engages him in conversation about their past and the people they used to know. In the course of the conversation, Bee reveals the troubling dynamics of Art's relationship with the older woman: "Shore treated you nice, too, didn't she? Appreciated you. Yeah! Onct last winter I seen her come in the picture show and climb all over everybody and drag you outside a-cussin' the livin' daylights out of you—and you never said *Boo.* (*Harshly.*) How much money'd she 'low you fer yer excitin' comp'ny, eh? Musta been a plenty to pay fer whut you tuck off of her!"[73] Though Art maintains his innocence after this exchange, Bee presses again, and he finally cracks and admits to murdering his wife in an act of rage motivated not by financial interests but by a long-standing personal hatred: "Don't you know what it is to hate? . . . You've saw her. I hated her. I wanted to kill her. I *always* wanted to kill her! . . . Not fer her money, though, don't you think that! I wouldn't do that. I hated her, that's why, hated *her*, hated everybody—!"[74]

As the stage descriptions and this exchange with Bee suggest, Art's outward manifestations of hypermasculine violence—whether directed at Viney, Old Man Talbert, his wife, Bee, state officials, or an imagined black threat—mask an interior vulnerability, organized by fear, which can only be expressed in violence and rage. Unlike the unmotivated racial violence that defines the mixed-blooded biological criminal of the settler imaginary, however, Art's violence is always motivated and directed at specific individuals. His assault on Viney occurs in the context of her relentless bullying of one of Art's close friends. When confronted with the possibility of violence that Talbert represents, Art threatens to reciprocate in order to defend himself and his companions. The later scene of imagined violence against blackness is similarly motivated by the antiblack racism that Art has already internalized as a young boy. Here, the murder of his wife is related to the troubling sexual and economic dynamics of their relationship, which produce powerful enough feelings of entrapment, exploitation, and hatred that Art sees no way out but self-destructive violence. His attempted strangulation of Bee is similarly motivated by dynamics of betrayal, confinement, and the looming reality of his own execution. In each case, Art acts in self-defense or in response to specific individuals perpetrating specific acts of injustice and oppression, however real or imagined. None of these excuse his actions; what he does is deplorable, and Riggs treats it as such. But as a character, Art is neither a villain nor an abject criminal. Rather, Riggs presents him as a broken man, one of "the dark ones, the unprivileged ones, the ones with the most desolate fields, the most dismal skies," of whom Riggs speaks in his essays. Art is governed by ideologies of toxic masculinity, antiblack racism, mixed-blood degradation, intracommunity violence, and coercive state power, which inform every aspect of his life and relationships with others in ways that he, like Talbert, is never fully able to comprehend. While declaiming Art's actions and refusing to redeem his character, Riggs provides a context for Art's dysfunctional, pent-up rage that exceeds the racialized and gendered ways he is understood and positioned by the state as a biological criminal.

In fact, it is precisely the coercive, mediating presence of the state and its habit of racializing and gendering Cherokee subjects in ways that prohibit productive relations between characters that Riggs targets for critique in this scene. As Harry Brown notes, mixed-blood criminality, which is reserved almost exclusively for Indian men but is also applied here to Bee as a sexualized social pariah, stands in direct opposition to the presumably rational, deliberative, and just mandates of white settler law and its commitments to procedural transparency, public argument, and due process.[75] The image of the poststatehood legal order that Riggs presents is anything but. As is evident in the opening exchange between Bee and the sheriff, the state possesses no hard evidence of Art's guilt, and the accusations of murder conflict with newspaper accounts of the incident as an accidental drowning. Absent material evidence to elicit a conviction, the sheriff is forced to resort to underhanded and likely illegal tactics to extract the confession necessary to make his circumstantial case stick. His exploitation of Bee's circumstances and the various tactics he uses to force her participation also position him as a misogynistic, oppressive, and morally bankrupt figure. Where physical assault is implied in Bee's case, it is a material reality for Art. He enters the jail *"shaken and troubled, . . . his hair in his eyes,"* and eventually he reveals that the authorities "beat the hell out of me."[76] This act of physical violence, absent any evidence of guilt, against an Indian man whose own confession remains ambiguous—Art provides two entirely different accounts of events that thoroughly contradict one another—complicates the presumed contrast between racialized criminality and the civilized workings of the rule of white settler law. As the scene plays out, it becomes glaringly apparent that Art's fate was sealed before he ever arrived at the jail. By hook or by crook, the sheriff was going to get his confession and hang his man. One wonders how many more Indians like Art and Bee suffered similar fates. That

Riggs returns to these dynamics in the final scene of the play—set on the verge of allotment and statehood—suggests a troubling answer to such questions.

Just as Talbert's investment in romantic discourses of Cherokee warrior nobility and cultural authenticity prevents him from finding common cause with younger generations of Cherokee youths, state-mediated discourses of mixed-blood deviance and criminality similarly close down moments of recognition and solidarity that open between Bee and Art. Though she is pressured into participating in the sting, Bee's concern for Art's well-being, her suspicion of the sheriff's motives, and her consistent challenge to the legitimacy of the entire situation clearly situate her as a reluctant informant. Bee states that she has no love for Art, yet she repeatedly softens her attack when confronted with the reality of his vulnerability. When Art collapses to the floor and admits to the beating he received from the deputies, Bee *"rises and for a moment makes as if to go toward him. Her impulse dies. She stares at him cooly."*[77] Later, when Art questions how he arrived at his present circumstances and becomes increasingly agitated, Bee admonishes him to "Shut up!" and calm down before *"remembering her mission"* and continuing with the deception.[78] As Art eventually confesses to the murder and identifies his motivations not as financial gain but as an overriding hate for his wife and the entire world, Bee interjects that she, too, shares that hatred—"Hate! Everybody! Me, too! . . . That's the way I feel—All the men I'd kill! I can see how you felt!"—and she vows never to give up Art's confession. She recognizes for the first time, however, that there is a recording device in the cell, and she realizes that she, too, has been deceived, used not as a witness with the power to confirm or deny Art's guilt but as an instrument to elicit a recorded confession that can be used with or without her corroboration or consent. As Art realizes his entrapment, Bee has *"a horrible realization of something further in her"* and repeatedly calls out to Art in what appears to be both a warning and an apology.[79] When Art is removed from the scene, Bee collapses on the floor, admonishing the guard quietly, "Leave me here. Slam the bolts to! What's the dif? I'm dead. Bury me."[80] As the scene ends, Art is on his way to certain execution, and Bee resigns herself to a life of prostitution and internalized self-loathing, a future that Riggs depicts in no uncertain terms as its own kind of death.

While the scene is devastating in the futures that it imagines for its Cherokee protagonists, it is important to note that in neither case does Riggs ascribe their circumstances exclusively in terms of blood. Bee never once mentions blood, and Art remains entirely vague about the origins of his anger and rage. Rather, what Riggs emphasizes throughout is the coercive nature of the state's power over Cherokee lives, a power dynamic that he drives home in a final exchange between Bee and the sheriff. As Art is dragged away in what can only be seen as a state-sanctioned lynching of a Cherokee man absent any opportunity for defense, the sheriff offers Bee the twenty-five-dollar fee they had agreed on earlier:

> BEE: What is it?
> SHERIFF: It's your'n, what I owe you. You shore earned it. Take it [the money].
> BEE: (*Wryly.*) Why not? (*She takes it, puts it in her stocking.*)
> SHERIFF: (*Delightedly.*) I shore am powerful indebted to you! He'll hang now! We got it all down—his own words. Why, his life ain't worth a damn! We'll rope that neck of his'n and jerk him so high he'll think a buzzard's got him. I shore do thank you!
> BEE: (*Harshly.*) You're welcome. It's a pleasure! Don't git too clost to a rope yerself, Mr. Sheriff! It'd jerk that head of yours plumb off! Yer wife ud have a hard time with no one to call her 'Honey'—somebody swell like you. (*Turning away, in disgust.*) Anh, Christ!
> SHERIFF: (*Nonplussed.*) 'F I can ever help you, in any way—The county shore owes you a lot.
> BEE: The county owes me plenty.[81]

Again emphasizing the gender dynamics of the exchange via Bee's perplexing position as settler collaborator/race traitor, Riggs frames their partnership in the sexualized language of prostitution. In this case, however, it is not the sexualized body of the Native woman that possesses exchange value, but the life of a Native man, valued at no more than twenty-five dollars, if that. What is truly valued here is Bee's collaboration in and legitimation of the legal elimination of that life, a dynamic she is all too aware of.

Her thinly veiled indictment of the criminality of the entire affair evident in this passage signifies on two levels. First, it situates practices of racial profiling and institutional racism as murderous tactics of repressive state violence against Indian people in a poststatehood legal and political environment. Positioned not as citizens of the Cherokee Nation but as racial and gendered subjects of the state of Oklahoma, Bee's and Art's lives—and by extension all

Indian lives—hold value only to the degree that they legitimize the coercive authority of the state. Second, the parallel she draws between the racialized dysfunction of Indian domestic violence and the sheriff's own domestic relationship implicates poststatehood settler life more broadly in that violence. Having attained a confession and gotten his man, the sheriff can return home to his own family, confident that justice was served and that peace was restored to the community. In this passage, however, Bee refuses to distinguish between the individual act of violence that Art is accused of and the systemic racial violence that invests the sheriff with the power to coerce a Cherokee woman and to entrap and execute a Cherokee man. By reframing poststatehood justice as racial violence, Bee recasts the sheriff not as a heroic figure of law and order but as a state-sanctioned murderer in his own right. In doing so she also reframes the safety, security, and respectability of settler domestic life as predicated fundamentally on state violence against Indian people. In this context, the overwhelming debt Bee speaks of refers not simply to her monetary exchange with the sheriff or even the metaphorical debt of gratitude owed her by the state, but rather the wake of exploitation, coercion, and anti-Indian violence that statehood and settler law wrought on Cherokee communities.

When situated more broadly in Cherokee history, such dynamics resonate powerfully with other conflicts resulting from settler-colonial interventions into Cherokee lives and relations. One example is the social and political factionalism and internecine violence fostered by the machinations of federal officials that emerged during the Removal crisis as chronicled by Eaton. Another is the tension between those arguing for Cherokee sovereignty and advocates of allotment and statehood in the late nineteenth century, which is documented in Oskison's romances and within Bronson's own family (discussed later). Because of the gender dynamics of this scene, however, the late eighteenth-century conflict between Nanye'hi (Nancy Ward) and her maternal relative Tsiyu Gansini (Dragging Canoe) is perhaps most resonant, speaking as it does to interpretive questions around gender, patriotism, and Cherokee national politics. Beholden to different social responsibilities and clan affiliations, these two figures often found themselves on opposing sides of internal debates over how best to deal with the violence and dispossession that increasingly came to define life on the Cherokee-Anglo frontier. Where early historians described Tsiyu Gansini's militant resistance as a function of a villainous Indian bloodlust, later writers have recuperated him as an anticolonial patriot and defender of Cherokee sovereignty. Similarly, where many early commentators interpreted Nanye'hi's advocacy of diplomacy and peace as an endorsement of civilization and the colonial project, others have positioned her as a traitor to her family, culture, and nation. As with the debates over the motivations and consequences of Removal, neither paradigm gets at the truth. If read within Cherokee cultural and social contexts, it might be more accurate to say, as Robert Conley and Daniel Justice argue, that both were operating according to their political, familial, and gendered obligations in the face of impossible circumstances and amid massive social changes produced by colonial violence and the increasingly disruptive influence of the U.S. settler state.[82]

Though what happens between Bee and Art in this scene is no longer a matter of Cherokee *national* politics, their interactions here dramatize ongoing gendered relations of coercion, betrayal, and retribution—mediated and amplified by the state—which continue to haunt Cherokee communities one hundred years after Removal. Hardly a consequence of essentialized mixed-blood deviance and criminality, Riggs, like Eaton and Oskison before him, locates the origins of intragenerational violence at least partially in the coercive power of the settler-colonial state—in this case, post-allotment Oklahoma—over Cherokee lives.

Blood, Culture, Class, and the Erosion of Matrilineal Kinship

If the first two scenes dramatize how blood discourse disrupts inter- and intragenerational Cherokee relations, the third scene, entitled "The Liniment Room," explores the collapse of familial relations within what Beth Piatote calls the "intimate domestic" of poststatehood Cherokee life.[83] Set in 1931, the scene focuses on a long-standing conflict between Viney Jones and Sarah Pickard, mixed-race Cherokee sisters whose lives have taken drastically different turns in the postallotment era and who possess conflicting relationships to Cherokee heritage, culture, identity, and place. Viney leads a privileged life of conspicuous consumption and material comfort as part of an acculturated economic and social elite in the nearby boomtown of Quapaw. In contrast, Sarah; her daughter, Masie; and Masie's husband, Roll, are barely able to make ends meet, having already mortgaged and lost their allotments in the wake of the economic depression. Conflict erupts when Viney shows up unexpectedly after a ten-year absence and begins to condescend to Sarah regarding her life and circumstances. In response, Sarah chastises Viney for her materialist lifestyle and for forgetting the Cherokee values of simplicity, humility, and fidelity to kin that their mother taught them. Having little use for such sentiments, Viney indicts Sarah for holding on to retrograde "Indian" values and for failing to progress in the modern world. As the scene ends, Viney and Sarah's relationship is irreparably damaged, and the Pickards still face the immediate crises of crushing poverty and dispossession.

As in previous scenes, momentary opportunities for mutual recognition and intimacy are confounded by racialized discourses, which, in this case, conflate blood with culture and class. In this schematic, Viney is the quintessential self-loathing, self-hating, thoroughly assimilated Indian woman who, having married up, has little use for anything Indian. In this sense, she is precisely the degenerate mixed-blood that Talbert rails against. Though Riggs provides little in the way of backstory, we get some sense of the tensions that divide the sisters via Viney's interactions with the other characters in the opening scene. She bullies Hutch Moree for his stutter, personal hygiene, and working-class background; berates Art for his broodiness and for his family's negative social reputation; and casts aspersions on Bee for not abiding by conventional gendered norms of sexual respectability.[84] In one of her most vicious attacks, Viney shames Gar for his familial ties to the Cherokee desperado Edgar Spench and denigrates his expulsion from college as a "Heap big Injun athulete."[85] She also makes fun of Gar for his interest in and sensitivity for Cherokee history and culture, which for Viney hold value only as historical anecdotes or cultural curiosities.

While on the surface such behaviors seem motivated by a kind of self-satisfied bourgeois condescension, they are, for Viney, also tied to essentialized understandings of Indian blood set against racialized and gendered markers of middle-class white respectability and poststatehood modernity. Against such prospects, Viney has at the time of this scene completely acculturated into white Oklahoma social and economic norms. The wife of white businessman and mayor of Quapaw, Jack Klepper, she enters, *"unmistakably complacent, righteous, and patronizing,"* and is *"well dressed in small town-town taste,"* sporting a fur coat.[86] When asked of her family, Viney reminds Sarah of Jack's election to mayor, informs her that her daughter attends a "fine" boarding school in a nearby town, and brags about their new home, which she says most people refer to as "the Mansion." At the same time, she comments on the meager state of Sarah's circumstances, disapproves of Masie's husband's occupation as a teamster and of her early marriage at seventeen, and chastises Sarah, *"in her old didactic manner,"* for not purchasing the necessary medicine to treat her rheumatism, which "costs only fifty cents a bottle."[87] If Talbert represents an attempt to recover a romantic warrior nobility and a racialized authenticity in the poststatehood era, Viney occupies the other side of the spectrum, electing for a full absorption (to use Riggs's word) into white Oklahoma individualism and consumerism.

Viney's "possessive investments in whiteness," to borrow from George Lipsitz and Aileen Moreton-Robinson, stand in stark contrast to Sarah and Masie's immediate circumstances.[88] As the lights come up on the scene, Riggs describes the *"shack"* as *"a sordid, miserable, chill-looking room, . . . sparsely furnished"* with only an oil stove, chairs, and Sarah's mother's *"wheezing"* organ.[89] Whereas Viney's life is defined by material comfort and good health, Sarah lives in cold, Spartan conditions and suffers with persistent arthritis, which she cannot afford to remedy. Though only seventeen, Masie, *"pathetically thin and white, with stringy hair,"* is also marked by Depression-era poverty and postallotment dispossession, a reality that she understands to be fundamentally unjust. Despite her husband's strong work ethic and the mortgages on each of the family's three allotments, Masie laments the fact that they "ain't got enough money to do anything about" Sarah's health and "cain't even keep her warm enough! . . . It ain't fair, it ain't fair!"[90] When Sarah tries to provide perspective by pointing out that others are worse off, Masie refuses to be comforted, recalling a time in the not so distant past when "we used to own our own farm and here we air like this—"[91] Whereas Viney ascribes Sarah's circumstances to her outmoded commitments to Indian values and as a function of Indian blood, Masie locates their situation in the early moments of the scene explicitly in the economic and political processes by which more than 90 percent of Cherokee allotments were lost over a roughly thirty-year period between 1898 and 1934.[92] As with the critique of state-sanctioned violence, entrapment, and murder evident in scene 2, Riggs alludes here to alternative contexts—allotment, statehood, and economic depression—to explain the divergent circumstances in which the two sisters find themselves.

As Womack and Justice have pointed out, the class tensions that organize conflicts between the sisters are more than simple disagreements over economics and material comfort. They are also inextricably tied to competing attitudes toward Cherokee ancestry and culture, which are framed through the discourse of Cherokee blood politics.[93] This is perhaps nowhere more apparent than in a tense dialogue that occurs in the final pages of the scene. When questioned about her onetime attraction to Hutch Moree, Viney responds "(*Viciously.*) I don't know and I don't care. It was Hutch that came close to ruining my whole life. That dumb Indian, that's all he was! You never could tell about him, couldn't get on to what he was up to! (*Thoughtfully, half to herself.*) He didn't have any *change* in him, he was stuck someway. He was broody and sullen, he could'nt seem to get hold of himself, like a lot of part Indians around here."[94] When reminded by Sarah that Viney is "more Cherokee than Hutch," Viney responds, "I'm thankful it doesn't show." This provokes one of the more painful exchanges between the sisters, one that ultimately leads to their permanent estrangement:

> SARAH: (*Strangely.*) Every word you say shows. Everything you say shames you. You try too hard to deny what you are. It tells on you. (*Harshly.*) You say Hutch didn't have any *change* in him. They's nuthin' else in you but change. You've turned your back on what you ought to a-been proud of.
>
> VINEY: (*Angrily.*) Being a part Indian? What would it get me? Do you think I want to be ignorant and hungry and crazy in my head half the time like a lot of 'em around here? Do you think I want to be looked down on because I can't do anything, can't get along like other people? Do you think I want to make the kind of mess of my life *you* have—and live in a filthy hole like this the rest of my days—?"
>
> SARAH: You won't have to. The hole you live in is filthier, and it suits you down to the ground. . . . Listen to me. You're not my sister. Your blood ain't mine and never was! Change, change till doomsday—one thing'll stay! Your heart's as black as ever and hard as flint. Be mean and cunning and full of hate, like the Indian. Be greedy and selfish the way the white man is. None of what's good—let the good things be! You're past 'em! Use the most shameful things you got in you to get ahead. *You'll get ahead, all right!*[95]

At this point Sarah launches into a pair of conflicting visions, one predicting Viney's decay and death after taking "a path you ain't meant to," the next, framed through the teachings of their mother, depicting a world of familial cooperation, security, humility, and abundance.[96] As Sarah collapses under the weight of these contradictory futures and her own perceived failure, Viney momentarily attempts to comfort her. However, Sarah indicts Viney as a failure as well, which provokes Viney to reaffirm her commitments to "money and a good home" and "living right."[97]

Both Sarah and Viney understand blood in terms that reflect allotment-era federal policies equating blood quantum with Indigenous cultural and national identity. For Sarah, Cherokee blood is a source of ethnic pride that connects her deeply to her mother, to their family allotment, and to Cherokee culture more broadly. For Viney, it stands as a racialized signifier of poverty, destitution, and ignorance existing in an intractable opposition to the material comfort, individual wealth, and bourgeois respectability she desires. What Sarah reads as a failure to abide by the Cherokee values and lifeways their mother taught is understood by Viney as the very evidence of her successful navigation of poststatehood Oklahoma modernity. As Womack argues, such tensions position culture explicitly against change, and in doing so foreclose possibilities for a reconciliation between the two.[98] Pushing Womack's observations further, Justice captures the damned-if-you-do-damned-if-you-don't dynamics of the sisters' racial conundrum: "Access to resources—alternately, the land and the culture—is indistinguishable from the characters' knowledge of themselves and their heritage. This knowledge is in turn dependent in the play upon the characters' degree of biological Indian ancestry, marked as 'blood' in the play and in U.S. Indian policy. The more Cherokee blood they possess, the more connected they are to both their culture and the land around them; it's an innate link between the self, the soil, and the community."[99] In such a paradigm, "Riggs's romantic nostalgia allows only for a redemptive self-sacrifice outside of the cruel realities of this world, not a healing change in circumstance in *this* life."[100]

Despite a couple of qualifications, this seems an accurate schematic for the play as a whole. However, what is interesting about this scene is that Viney and Sarah possess equal blood quanta but radically different connections to land and culture and thus to "the self, the soil, and the community." In much the same way that Riggs refuses any easy association between full-bloodedness and cultural authenticity in the figure of Talbert, or between mixed-blood deviance and criminality with Bee and Art, his attention in this scene to relations of family and place disrupt exclusive alignments between blood, culture, and identity.

While Sarah is willing to tolerate the poverty of her circumstances by recalling her mother's values of family and humility, it is the loss of the allotment to the bank and her and Masie's necessary reliance on male wage labor that prevent her from providing for her family in the way her mother imagined. Her failure, then, is due less to a loss of cultural connection, as with Talbert's, than to her alienation from the very place—her mother's allotment—that makes those cultural connections and familial responsibilities possible in the first place. Viney's failure might be read in similar terms. Her attitudes and behaviors are condemned not simply for their superficiality and mean-spiritedness but also for how they interrupt her responsibilities and obligations to her sister and her extended kin. Within the individualist framework of the patriarchal nuclear family, Viney's only obligations are to the wealth, security, and material comfort of herself and her immediate family.

Forced to choose between culture and modernity, poverty and affluence, a grounded sense of place and economic and social mobility, neither sister can accommodate the life the other has chosen. As Justice notes, they constitute seemingly irreconcilable responses to postallotment Cherokee life, which put them at odds with each other and ultimately eviscerate any relationship whatsoever. Considering the centrality of matrilineality to Cherokee cultural and political identity, such disidentifications signal profound, and in this scene irrevocable, disruptions to traditional notions of identity, community, and belonging, which are rooted in affirmative relationships between women.[101] As Rose Stremlau and Beth Piatote have documented, allotment sought not only to eliminate Indigenous lands and governments but also to transform the cultural fabric of Indigenous kinship and family relations.[102] Within a Cherokee context, this meant disrupting the expansive relations through which many Cherokees continued to collectively organize social and economic life well into the allotment era. Though their families were no longer exclusively matrilineal, women remained central to these relationships not only in terms of political and cultural ancestry but also as the conveyors of cultural knowledge and values. "Cherokees were a people of mothers and, perhaps even more so, of grandmothers," Stremlau writes, "because a person's physical connection to his or her nation derived from the oldest living female ancestor. But grandmothers served more than a symbolic role. They were vitally important to the day-to-day well-being of the descendants because they did much of the work associated with mothering by attending to the care, education, and loving of the young, thus freeing young, able-bodied women for more arduous work. A less tangible role was perhaps their most important—they passed on their knowledge and interpretation of the Cherokee worldview."[103] If Viney and Sarah's relationship is any indication, such dynamics have pretty clearly been disrupted thirty years into allotment. Without their mother to adjudicate differences and hold them accountable to one another and to the values of simplicity, humility, and gratitude for which she stood, they have little access to the intergenerational support necessary to maintain those relations. The division of collectively held Cherokee national lands into individual allotments, the subsequent alienation of that land from Cherokees like Sarah, and the increasing movements from figures like Viney away from their tribal-national home further disrupted the collective mechanisms that held Cherokee families and communities together. The fact that Viney and Sarah have no substantive relationships with their maternal nieces and nephews amplifies the tragedy of the scene by implicating their individual conflict in a cascading series of intergenerational disruptions to kinship and family relations.

Read in this context, as Viney storms out the door for the last time and as the lights fade to black, what lies broken is not just a Cherokee family but what should have been the life-sustaining relationship between Cherokee sisters and the intergenerational responsibilities and obligations of daughters to their mother and of aunts to their nieces and nephews. While I agree with Weaver, Womack, and Justice that the play documents with brutal honesty the multiple ways that allotment and statehood combined with racialized discourses of blood to disrupt Cherokee lives and communities, I believe that Riggs is most concerned in this scene with how such things affected matrilineal Cherokee relations in particular. What drives the sisters increasingly apart is not simply their conflicting ideas of blood, culture, class, and identity but the historical events and sociopolitical dynamics that produced those conflicts in the first place. That Riggs dramatizes the dissolution of a matrilineal family does not in any way suggest to me that he endorses that vision or that he subscribes to either Sarah's or Viney's attitudes and beliefs. Rather, he constructs the intimate space of "The Liniment Room" as a kind of laboratory in which to explore the aftermath of allotment and contemplate its devastating effects on matrilineal relations and Cherokee families more broadly. In doing so, the scene affirms Beth Piatote's observation that the assault on the "tribal national" did not end with the dissolution of the Cherokee state and the allotment of tribal lands. It continued through the ongoing attack on the cultural integrity and the kinship structure of the "tribal domestic," which was most immediately and tragically experienced within Cherokee families themselves.[104]

Blackness, Belonging, and Historical Accountability

If the opening scene of *The Cherokee Night* dramatizes the extent to which a particularly exclusionary articulation of blood purity divides generations of Cherokees, scene 4, "Where the Nigger Was Found," implicates the Cherokee Nation in larger imperialist discourses of intra- and interracial violence. Strategically situated in the middle of the play and set in 1906, the year of the final allotment of Cherokee lands and the closing of the Dawes rolls, Riggs presents Hutch Moree, Art, and Gar as prepubescent boys—*"ten or twelve years old"*—attempting to find evidence of the site where, as local gossip holds, a black man was brutally murdered, presumably by another black man, over a drunken game of cards.[105] As in the first scene, Riggs uses his characters' dialogue and actions to examine competing visions about what constitute notions of family, culture, race, and nation. Unique to this scene, however, is the introduction of blackness into the discussion, a significant addition, considering that Afro-Cherokee citizens and other black residents were actively petitioning the Cherokee and federal governments to deliver on their rights as Cherokee citizens during the 1930s. The stage directions describing the boys' racially charged state of mind is significant: *"Stalking carefully through the woods and into the bright circle of sun, three boys, about ten or twelve years old, come into sight. They are bent and tense, far apart, watchful—as if they expected to come upon some astonishing and fearful thing."*[106] What they fear, it soon becomes apparent, is blackness itself, whether in the form of whispered suggestions of black kinship or the threat of direct interaction with black male bodies.

Central to the scene are a struggle over narrative authority and the relationship of blackness to Cherokee history. As the scene progresses, more of the story about the murder is revealed; however, nothing about the story that the boys cobble together is verifiable much less authoritative. They each receive a thread of it from a different source, the character and content of which is questionable, if not entirely fabricated, and none of which appears to corroborate the others in any meaningful way. Art rejects Hutch's claim to authority based on Hutch's fraternal relationship to his source, reminding him that he heard the story not from his older brother but from Art. Hutch similarly dismisses Art's authority, calling into question the moral character of his informant, Tom Bussey, a fifteen-year-old vagrant who runs with a local gang whose members are best known as community pranksters and minor thieves. At an impasse, both boys remove to their respective corners, each unwilling to cede control of the narrative to the other. In these opening lines of dialogue, Riggs highlights the extent to which each argument is shaped by the boys' competing understandings of authority and belonging refracted through blood discourse. Whereas Hutch and Art appeal to essentialist ties of blood kinship or unquestioned deference to seniority in order to legitimize their narratives, Gar appeals to a distinctly antiessentialist sense of family and community. When challenged, Gar authenticates his narrative, which he received from his Anglo guardian, Mr. Ferber, by deferring to the reliability of his "pappy."[107] Both Art and Hutch immediately dismiss Gar's account, not because they question Mr. Ferber's reputation or credibility, but because he ostensibly has no jurisdiction in the matter as he is neither blood kin nor a Cherokee citizen. Hutch comments, "A guardeen ain't a pappy. . . . He *ain't* blood kin. He's a Dutchman. A furriner like him!" presumably referring to the black man in question.[108] Hutch's conflation of blood, kinship, and belonging aligns with what Circe Sturm and Eva Garroutte identify as a significant ideological signifier of belonging in Cherokee communities.[109] Such statements of political jurisdiction in what was still, in 1906, a sovereign Cherokee Nation affirm kinship as a persistent signifier of belonging despite the impending dissolution of the Nation's political and territorial autonomy.

The boys' statements are also troublingly laced with nationalist racial prejudices that continually frustrate the development of positive intra- and interracial/tribal relationships throughout the play. Just as he claims Old Man Talbert in the first scene, Gar ignores blood as a legitimate identifier of family, culture, or community and claims his Pappy as his own based on Mr. Ferber's kindness, generosity, mentorship, and support: "Mr. Ferber is same as my blood kin," Gar asserts, "good as my Pappy was—(*Thoughtfully.*)—better'n my pappy. (*Inside, to himself, turning, facing front.*) He wants me to be smart."[110] For Gar, Mr. Ferber's authority lies in his genuine desire to see Gar live a full and happy life, despite the painful hand he has been dealt as an orphan and ward of the Nation.[111] Considering the pervasive exploitation and graft that accompanied the practice of guardianship in the decades following allotment,

Gar's endorsement of Mr. Ferber's moral character also carries significant political weight. Much like Oskison's endorsement of the Keene and Dawes families as Cherokee nationalist patriots based on their commitment to Cherokee common property law and legal authority, it is Mr. Ferber's personal commitment to Gar's well-being, rather than blood ties or political status, that defines Gar's reciprocal commitment to his Pappy. In contrast to Talbert's racialized vision of Cherokee identity, Gar's more culturally and historically nuanced reckoning of kinship and belonging emphasizes action and mutual commitment rather than identity and ontology, reflecting an ethic that Jace Weaver terms "communitism."[112] While such passages position Gar as the only character in the play who approaches even a quasi-critical attitude toward issues of race, culture, community, and nation, even he is not immune from racist discourses of black othering. Having established for himself what constitute legitimate boundaries of authority and belonging, Gar holds his ground, quietly reasserting that the "nigger was kilt here. Mr. Ferber told me. (*He turns his back on them both, solid and final.*)"[113] Gar's easy use of racial epithets makes visible the contradictions inherent to racialized conceptualizations of belonging. Gar objectifies and dehumanizes black bodies while simultaneously struggling to legitimize antiessentialist ideals of Cherokee identity and belonging. His casual and seemingly unconscious use of such slurs problematically aligns him with Old Man Talbert's racist and classist comparisons of Cherokee youths with "white trash and black niggers" from scene 1.[114] Just as racialized discourses of authenticity prevent Talbert from seeing his role in the generational conflict that he laments, Gar's deference to racial epithets implicates him in the same madness that consumes Talbert. His near murder at the hands of religious zealots, for whom he becomes a similarly racialized scapegoat in scene 5 (1913), and his psychological breakdown and retreat into himself alluded to in a scene two years later, attest to the destructive self-loathing and internalized trauma that such contradictions engender.

The paranoid fear inspired by the prospect of encountering black otherness is intensified as the boys surrender their evidentiary arguments to their racially charged overactive imaginations. From questionable footsteps to an empty tin can containing traces of whiskey, to a playing card with a bent edge, everything suddenly confirms the frightening presence of the dead black man. As they speculate about the place where he lies, the boys are spooked by a bird flushed from the surrounding cover. Hutch sees a crow, Gar a hawk, and Art a buzzard. A bird that feeds on carrion, a buzzard, would signify that death was close by; however, the bird turns out to be a chicken hawk, a revelation that sends Hutch into a *"crazy, almost hysterical triumph."*[115] Hutch's intense relief at not having to confront the reality of blackness is short lived as Art begins speculating on the possibility of encountering not the dead black victim, but his living black murderer:

> ART: (*Absorbed.*) What if he'd come back?
>
> HUTCH: Who?
>
> ART: The nigger that done the killin.' (*He looks round tensely.*) What if he'd be hidin'—here in the bresh some'eres—lookin' at us—right now! What if he'd grab us?
>
> HUTCH: Art!
>
> ART: He *might.* He might kill us!
>
> HUTCH: (*Quickly.*) No, now Art! A man seen him up by Quapaw. The Sheriff's went up there to hunt fer him. Anyway—he'd be skeered to come here—whur—whur that—(*He looks at the heaped leaves.*)
>
> ART: No, he wouldn't. It wouldn't skeer him. Niggers is funny. They got a funny way. When the niggers was run out of Claremore, Pap said a funny thing. When a nigger would get shot, he wouldn't know it. He'd keep on runnin'.
>
> HUTCH: Couldn't he feel it?
>
> ART: (*With curious tensity, crossing way down left on speech.*) I'd a-shot him till he felt it. They was one all covered 'th blood run plumb to Inola. When he got there, he fell over dead.[116]

The imagined possibility of encountering black otherness transforms the murdered black man from a nonthreatening, racialized curiosity into the living threat of black violence symbolized in the murderer who is assumed by the boys to be black and who may or may not still be at large.

The very presence of blackness itself, and the anxiety it produces, becomes the fulcrum around which these competing narratives of Cherokee belonging begin to turn. In this, the boys' paranoid imaginings reflect what Toni Morrison argues is a common motif in Euro-American imaginations of blackness, which functions at once as the brute uncivilized antithesis against which civilized white male superiority is positioned and as a means of constructing whiteness as an unmarked and thus impenetrable category. Speaking of the character Jim in Twain's *Huckleberry Finn,* Morrison writes, "It is not what Jim seems that warrants inquiry, but what Mark Twain, Huck, and especially Tom need from him that should solicit our attention. . . . [This is] the parasitical nature of white freedom."[117] Morrison's use of Twain's classic novel is useful here in that both red and black male others are positioned in the text for similar purposes—to provide an outlet for the redemption of white masculinity. When applied to relationships between Indian and black characters, however, Morrison's frame becomes more complicated. The authors of this tale of threatening black masculinity are not privileged white men but mixed-blooded Cherokee boys who have been marginalized by the racialized power structures of both white and Cherokee societies which they in turn draw upon to marginalize blacks.[118]

The boys' fears and anxieties over blackness are rooted in larger debates over the contentious place of blackness in Cherokee society that date from at least the early nineteenth century. In fact, debates over slavery, the citizenship status of freedmen, and the residency of free blacks were thoroughly shot through with anxieties over miscegenation, national racial identity, and the balance of political power. Racialized as legal others in the Cherokee Constitution of 1827, Afro-Cherokees were denied the rights to citizenship, property ownership, education, intermarriage, and at various moments, legal residence in the Nation. Though the Treaty of 1866 with the federal government following the U.S. Civil War acknowledged that all freedmen and Afro-Cherokees would "enjoy all of the rights and privileges of Native Cherokees," the extent and reach of those rights—particularly as they related to property ownership, allotment, per capita payments from the sale of national lands, and other institutional benefits of citizenship—remained in question. While scholars disagree about the motivations and intentions of such laws, all agree that the qualified adoption of Western ideas and political structures radically shifted definitions of place and belonging from a flexible system of matrilineal clan relations to an increasingly racialized and hierarchical legal code that naturalized racial difference via the language of citizenship.[119] To this point, Circe Sturm writes, "At the center of the story of Cherokee identity and experience is an absence, an exclusion, a silence where the Cherokee freedmen might have been."[120] Consequently, many view the processes by which blackness came to be legally and culturally defined in opposition to Cherokee national identity as a consequence of the process of nationalization itself.[121] Read in this context, the silences and ruptures embedded in the boys' competing arguments over narrative authority parallel the historical silences fostered by racialized legal codes that positioned blackness in strict opposition to Cherokee and U.S. identity.

At issue are not simply historical and narrative injustices perpetrated by one people against another, however. As Tiya Miles argues, larger traumatic implications inhere in the silencing of unspeakable pasts: "For the void that remains when we refuse to speak of the past is in fact a presence, a presence both haunting and destructive."[122] The ease with which ten- or twelve-year-old boys perpetuate histories of violence by participating in racist discourses is evidence enough of the "haunting and destructive" influence that such discourses exert on the most vulnerable in society. Perhaps even more troubling, however, is the boys' failure to recognize their own subjugation to the values and assumptions of racial difference. Their internalization of antiblack racism, rooted in a complex history of Cherokee-black relations, prevents them from seeing themselves as part of the narrative of racial violence that they are attempting to reconstruct. Neither are they capable of fully understanding the blackness that they feel increasingly compelled to escape. Art's reference to the violent expulsion of blacks, many of whom were likely Afro-descendant Cherokees, from towns in the Cherokee Nation and elsewhere in Indian Territory—interpreted in heroic terms just as Talbert interpreted the valor of the Cherokee-Osage conflict—is the imagined, romanticized trace of a real history of Cherokee national violence against black bodies.[123]

Indeed, what was only the trace of the absent presence of blackness in the boys' imaginative reconstruction of events becomes, in the final image of the scene, the haunting, destructive presence to which Miles alludes. It is here that Riggs levies one of the play's strongest critiques against blood discourse. As the imaginative intensity of the scene progresses toward the kind of panic and hysteria that often lead to racial violence, anxiety over potentially finding the *dead* black man is transformed into a paranoid fear of coming face to face with a *real-life* black male body. In his attempt to control this fear by violently rejecting it, Art launches into one of the most virulently racist tirades in the text:

> 'F *I* found a nigger, I'd hack him!
> 'F *I* found a nigger, I'd hack him!
> 'F *I* found a nigger, I'd hack him! Hack him![124]

The other two boys then join in the chant, and they begin dancing and whooping in "Indian" fashion to the subtle beat of a drum that has emerged from

Claremore Mound in the distance. One of the boys suddenly stops, drops his tin can, bends down, and begins *"feverishly tearing leaves apart with his hands."* As he rises, he turns his hands over to reveal the "palms . . . streaked with blood . . . (*In ecstasy and horror*)." Art screams out, "Got blood on my hands!" and the boys rush off in terror. As they exit, the drum stops and the theater is bathed in silence. As if emerging from the land itself, *"a giant NEGRO, naked to the waist, lifts himself into the sun from behind the thick underbrush."* He stares at the fleeing boys, stretches, and then extends his hands from his waist and returns with a couple of large, overripe blackberries. The scene goes dark. As the lights come up, Claremore Mound is featured prominently in the distance: *"An Indian, slim, aristocratic, minute in the distance, stands up against the sky. A drum is beating—harsh and troubled. It is like a fevered and aching disquiet at the pit of the world."*[125]

While in many ways the murder serves as pretext for Riggs to engage complex questions of Cherokee legitimacy, recognition, and belonging, one cannot ignore the symbolic juxtaposition of Claremore Mound with the visible and apparently menacing presence of the black male body. If the first serves as a constant reminder of Indian-on-Indian violence resulting in the consolidation of Cherokee political power in the region—itself a consequence of federal policies of dispossession and relocation—the latter points to the history of antiblack racism, slavery, and social marginalization of black peoples in the Cherokee Nation from the early 1820s through the present. As in the first scene, these intersecting histories of violence acutely operate on everyone involved at this prominent site of settler-colonial violence. This scene depicts three boys imagining and inventing history as they go—on one hand, a history of blackness informed by the haunting presence of Claremore Mound, and on the other, a history of Indianness informed by the haunting reality of red-over-black slavery.[126] If nations are consolidated through narratives that render difference absent and silence dissenting experiences, then Riggs's juxtaposition of black bodies with Claremore Mound must be seen as a dramatic attempt to render visible experiences and events that Cherokee and U.S. nationalist histories seek to obscure, if not erase entirely.[127]

The subversive power of the scene is, arguably, the refusal of the black male body to comply with these narratives. By staging such acts and events and making them visibly present on stage, Riggs holds Cherokees accountable for the racial violence—both internal and external—upon which Cherokee national identity in the Southeast and, later, in Indian Territory was at least partially built. That such hatred, fear, and racist invective spills from the mouths not of mad Indian elders but of *ten-year-old boys* stands as a powerful statement, not of things "carried in the blood" but of attitudes learned and passed down. The scene thus indicts the insidious power of racist discourses to influence even the most vulnerable in society as well as the failure of that society to disrupt cycles of violence and trauma rooted in complex, overlapping histories of prejudice, bigotry, and violence. Though the boys flee the scene in terror from what they think is the blood of the murdered black man on *their* hands, the real blood is arguably on the hands of those Cherokees who advocated the adoption of black slavery and elders like Talbert for failing to prevent young boys from becoming men like them. One is not born with racism, the scene suggests. One learns it, and it is learned early.

Surrogate Families, Resurgent Nations

Scenes 5 and 6, which are not examined here, dramatize the traumatic and self-destructive effects on personal and political relationships when ahistorical notions of blood, culture, and race stand in for the material and historical events that are responsible for bringing characters to a given time and place. In the absence of historical explanations for the dissolution of the Nation, Gar's inability to locate himself in productive and healthy ways within Cherokee community leads to his trauma at the hands of the religious fanatics (scene 5), resulting in his withdrawal from college and his eventual psychological retreat into himself. In similar terms, without a concrete understanding of the historical significance of Claremore Mound in Cherokee and Osage histories, Hutch Moree is unable to discern the source of his debilitating deferral to his domineering older brother's anti-Osage Cherokee chauvinism or to understand his Osage fiancée's own nationalist class prejudice against the "uselessness" of Cherokee blood (scene 6). Combined with the complicated dynamics at work in the scenes analyzed above, these scenes suggest that a character's ignorance of and inability to fully claim their history not only frustrate opportunities for mutual recognition; they are, ultimately, *always* destructive and inherently inimical to the overall search in the play for affirmative models of Cherokee relationships outside racialized discourses of blood.

Considering the almost total breakdown of Cherokee social structures dramatized elsewhere in the play, the various acts of recognition and solidarity that occur in scene 7 come as somewhat of a shock. As in previous scenes, Riggs presents Cherokees related to one another through bonds of race, culture, kinship, and national filiation who are thrown together in a situation of conflict. Also like previous scenes, blood discourse structures and informs every aspect of these relationships. The scene opens with a Cherokee elder John Gray-Wolf educating his grandson in family history and oral traditions. This act of passing down intergenerational knowledge is particularly significant in light of the grandson's mother's conspicuous absence and his father's recent murder by territorial lawmen under questionable circumstances. They are interrupted when a mixed-blooded Cherokee outlaw named Edgar Spench bursts into the cabin seeking refuge from these same territorial authorities who have charged him with murder. In the moral argument that ensues—which reveals details of Spench's murder of a respected store clerk and his paternal relationship to Gar and Bee—Spench attributes his lawlessness and criminal behavior to his possession of "too much Indian blood," echoing similar sentiments through which Art Osburn understands his own criminality and propensity for violence in scene 2. The traditionalist elder Gray-Wolf counters that Spench's problem is that he does not possess *enough* Indian blood, recalling the language of mixed-blood degeneracy propounded by Talbert in scene 1 and embodied by Viney in scene 3. In both arguments, blood stands as an absolute, mutually exclusive signifier of moral worth. Conditioned by previous action, audiences and readers expect discussion and dialogue to break down at precisely this point. The play fails to deliver on this expectation, however, opening up moments of recognition in which seemingly antagonistic Cherokee characters come to some understanding of themselves and their relationships to one another outside of the racialized determinism and irresolvable contradictions of blood discourse.

This recognition occurs as Spench, in pain, whispers, "The blood . . . The blood . . . *Stop the blood.*"[128] Though Spench is speaking about both the lifeblood running out of his body and the racial force in the blood he sees as part of his violent nature, Gray-Wolf recognizes something else—perhaps kinship, perhaps a historical connection to Indian blood that was spilled in Northeastern Oklahoma and across the United States, perhaps the pain and weight of a history of violence, dislocation, and struggle. At this moment, Gray-Wolf dispenses with his moral diatribe against Spench's character and simply attempts to care for him, repeatedly admonishing him to remain still and encouraging him to "Fight to live!" in spite of Spench's overwhelming desire to die.[129] As Anglo territorial authorities descend on Gray-Wolf's cabin to bring Spench to justice, erroneously claiming legal jurisdiction in matters between Indians, Spench indicates his weariness of the fight, draws his gun, and is killed, his value for the authorities determined only by the reward offered for his capture. In response to Gray-Wolf's accusations, "You can't do that, can't do it! In cold blood!" Sheriff Tinsley informs him of the changing situation in the territory: "Let this be a lesson and a warnin'. Teach your grandson. Tell everybody what it means to oppose the law. You Indians must think you own things out here. This is God's country out here—and God's a white man. Don't forget that."[130] As Spench's wife, child, and pregnant mistress arrive at the cabin, Gray-Wolf admonishes the authorities to "Leave us, he's *our* dead," and the play comes to a somber end.[131]

I would like to tease out the significance of these final acts of recognition and push back against the tragic tone that is evident even in the stage directions. Unlike Talbert's rejection of Cherokee youths as a hopelessly corrupted and lost generation, Gray-Wolf claims Spench as Cherokee despite the seemingly objective reality of his propensity for violence. Whereas Viney rejects both Hutch and her sister by evoking racialized notions of class privilege, Gray-Wolf ignores the racial, cultural, and even moral differences that separate him from Spench. Rather than collaborate with territorial authorities to apprehend Spench and bring him to justice, as Bee does with Art in scene 2, Gray-Wolf provides shelter and care to someone who by the absolute standards of settler law in no way deserves sympathy. Tinsley's racist tirade against Indian sovereignty in a year—1895—in which Indian Territory was still a political geography of tribal nations further confirms, in its own Cherokee way, Gray-Wolf's opposition to territorial law as just.[132] Confronted with the very real threat to Cherokee national sovereignty that is embodied by the incursion of agents of the settler state into the intimate domestic space of his home, Gray-Wolf claims a murderous outlaw with whom he shares little more than a political identity as a Cherokee citizen and a common experience under the racist anti-Indian ideologies of Manifest Destiny. In this important moment of political awakening, Gray-Wolf seems to identify a parallel between Spench's death at the hands of legal authorities and the impending legal violation of Cherokee sovereignty by the federal government, dynamics which resonate with Art's situation in scene 2. Considering the massive post–Civil War effort to bring Indian Territory into the United States territorial system, Gray-Wolf's verbal and physical claiming of Spench and his refusal to recognize the posse's authority on Cherokee national lands represent both an affirmation of Cherokee sovereignty and a historically grounded, experientially localized conceptualization of Cherokee peoplehood.

Another significant moment of recognition that escapes the legal and moral restrictions of blood discourse emerges with the arrival of Spench's legitimate wife, Marthy Breeden, and his pregnant mistress, Florey Newcomb, shortly after Tinsley's authorities have fatally wounded Spench. As they look upon his broken body, Marthy, described in the text as a *"gaunt dark woman"* possessing a *"rich warm, earthy and compassionate power,"* contemplates his troubled life:

> They got you. We always knew they would, didn't we? . . . What you done was what they call wrong. You couldn't help it, I know that. You tried to do right. It was too much. You was hounded day and night, inside and outside. By day, men. At night, your thoughts. Now it's over. Sleep. Rest now. (*She shifts the child in her arms, looks down at it.*) But here's your son. In him your trouble. It goes on. In him. It ain't finished. (*She turns, calls to a young woman, who is weeping quietly. FLOREY comes over to her.*) Florey. Here's Florey Newcomb, bearin' your child. You're at rest. Sleep. Your disgrace, your wickedness, your pain and trouble live on a while longer. In her child, in my child. In all people born now, about to be born. (*Her face becomes luminous, as her mind gropes toward an impersonal truth.*) Someday, the agony will end. Yours has. Ours will. Maybe not in the night of death, the cold dark night, without stars. Maybe in the sun. It's got to! It's what we live for.[133]

As I read this passage, Marthy performs two remarkable acts. First, she calls out to Florey and recognizes her not as a harlot or home wrecker, as the social and gendered norms of conventional Christian monogamy might demand, but rather as a kindred soul who is grieving over the loss of the man they both deeply loved and who is thus deserving of her sympathy and respect. This act of solidarity between women contrasts the erosion of matrilineal relationships that is illustrated in the third scene. Whereas scene 3 seems to close the door on such relationships, the final scene reopens that possibility. Circumventing conventional social mores and settler-legal understandings of family, legitimacy, and community, Marthy's claiming of Florey and her unborn child as kin carves out a legitimate space for them within their immediate community in much the same way that Talbert's earlier acts of kindness to Gar legitimized his place in community despite Gar's position as the orphan child of a murderous outlaw.

In addition to privileging female lived experience over legal abstractions of legitimacy and belonging, Marthy's comments also suggest a more complicated understanding of blood, grounded less in biology than in a shared social location and experience. While this passage echoes the familiar fatalistic despondence of blood discourse, her words take on an ironic meaning when read in the context of similar statements from previous scenes. Absent from her account, for instance, is the racialized moral absolutism that is evident in both Gray-Wolf's early didacticism and Tinsley's narrative of Anglo triumphalism. Marthy's location of Spench's crimes as explicitly within a contested moral universe—"What *you* done was what *they* call wrong"—pierces into the moral relativism and cultural chauvinism through which outlaws like Spench (or Art) are positioned as scapegoats in arguments over racial/cultural supremacy, whether by white racists or fellow Cherokees. Such a distinction suggests that it is not literally Spench's mixed blood that determines his behavior and violent end but the way in which blood itself is constructed, understood, and experienced within racialized colonialist discourses that conflate race, nation, morality, and progress. Marthy's seemingly despondent vision that her son and Florey's unborn child might suffer similarly violent lives reads less as a statement of determinism than as a critique of the violence and trauma attending social conflicts born of race-based thinking. From this more ironic perspective, the disgrace, wickedness, pain, and trouble that defined Spench's life reach well beyond Gray-Wolf's cabin, or even Indian Territory, to "all people born now, about to be born." Whether in Talbert's romantic ideas of cultural purity, Viney's racialized class prejudice, Art's adolescent paranoia of black alterity, or Sheriff Tinsley's white supremacism, the schizophrenic madness that consumes Spench is here shared by all those whose lives it touches. Collapsed and embodied in the needless death of a Cherokee man, the agony of blood and the question of how to stop it are not Indian problems but crises experienced and responsibilities shared by every character in the play.

Marthy's wish that "the agony will end" reflects an optimism that discourses of cultural purity and racial determinism explicitly foreclose. One cannot, after all, change essential characteristics. If Spench's children share his blood and if it is his blood that determines his fate, then his children are by definition condemned to similarly violent ends. They have no choice in the matter. Marthy does not subscribe to this determinism. Countering Florey's nihilistic lament that "it goes on, it goes on!" Marthy replies, "In our children, yes. In our children's children, maybe no."[134] Though she acknowledges that their children might well be subject to the violence that defined their father's life—a very real prospect with the implementation of the Curtis Act just three years hence and Oklahoma statehood on the horizon—Marthy also imagines a possibility that Spench could not see and that Tinsley's narrative of racial triumphalism explicitly denies: the end of blood. Marthy's carefully optimistic vision of futurity in the final scene of the play thus stands in stark contrast to the opening scene in which Talbert rejects the very generation she refers to. Together with Gray-Wolf's claiming of Spench as "our dead," Marthy's sympathy toward Florey and her measured optimism model radically different ideas of identity, community, and belonging than are present in any of the preceding scenes.

To argue that Riggs subverts some of the divisive elements at work earlier in the play is far different from arguing that the play is entirely subversive or that it successfully puts forward a healthy idea of Cherokee communities, Cherokee nationhood, or Indian sovereignty. At the end of the day, Spench dies, both Florey and Marthy acknowledge that something of his restlessness lives on in their children, and Gray-Wolf remains in *"despair"* and mournful *"for his own life, for the life of his son, for his grandson, for* SPENCH, *for the* WOMEN, *for a whole race gone down into darkness."*[135] If, however, as I argue, the action of the play hinges on the capacity of characters to penetrate the seemingly irresolvable determinism of blood discourse and to claim one another as Cherokee, and if Gray-Wolf's and Marthy's actions in the final scene suggest that such opportunities are not inevitably overdetermined by history or blood, then we have to admit that Riggs leaves open the potential for different choices to result in vastly different ends. Indeed, in this final scene neither pseudoscientific nor legalistic notions of blood organize personal and political relationships. Rather, it is the recognition, however brief, of shared histories and experiences of violence, resistance, and continuance as Cherokees that join together this multigenerational surrogate national family as the final curtain falls.

Disrupting Time, Rewriting Nation

What then are we to make of the relationship between the more optimistic tone of the final scene—the earliest in historical time—and the pessimistic sense of doom that permeates the rest of a play? Are we meant to understand the play, as Weaver and Justice suggest, as a relatively conventional, if nostalgic, statement on the tragic passing of Indian communities in the wake of allotment, statehood, and progress? If so, why would Riggs—a man who was so self-conscious about the relationship between theatrical form and content and who had a faith in the revelatory power of politically committed theater to transform social conditions—tell a conventional narrative that was familiar to anyone versed in the ideology of Manifest Destiny? And why go out of his way to disrupt the progressive teleology on which such narratives depend? What are we to make of the relationship between Riggs's formal disruption of linear time throughout the play and his narrative disruption of the devastating effects of blood discourse in the final scene? Can we simply write it off as aesthetic experimentation, or is Riggs making a much more incisive political commentary about Cherokee relationships and Cherokee communities?

To answer these questions, let us imagine what kind of narrative emerges if the more affirmative and flexible models of belonging and community presented in the final scene become the barometers through which Cherokee relationships are structured rather than essentialist racialized discourses of blood that pull them apart at every turn. What would happen, for instance, if Talbert, unencumbered by romantic illusions of cultural purity, were able to recognize Gar's overtures of kinship and to redirect his knowledge into more productive acts of intergenerational healing and community affirmation? With more secure cultural and community moorings, Gar might very well have grown into a strong spiritual leader and visionary for his people. Consider also the productive lives that Hutch and Art might have lived divorced from the paranoia and fear of racial prejudice and intratribal chauvinism or the reaffirmation of matrilineal relationships that Viney and Sarah might have achieved absent the internalized self-loathing of racialized cultural and class antagonisms. Pushing further, one might even speculate on the kind of father that Edgar Spench could have been had he not been forced to negotiate racialized social and legal structures that denied him a legitimate place as a fully self-possessed Cherokee man.

In saving the most affirmative model of Cherokee relationships for the final scene, and setting the action of the scene as the earliest in chronological time, I believe that Riggs invites just such an imaginative rewriting of the play with Gray-Wolf's and Marthy's affirmations of recognition and belonging as the rule rather than the exception. If we perform this imaginative rescripting of the scenes in chronological time based on this model, we are suddenly confronted with a radically different play that categorically rejects the teleological determinism of narratives of Native absence in favor of the possibility that history can indeed be rewritten through present action. Thus, what appears at first to be a familiar narrative of Indian cultural dissolution in the face of cosmic forces beyond any of the characters' control becomes in the final scene at least the potential for a reaffirmation and restoration of community *in spite of* the dark age that allotment, tribal dissolution, and Oklahoma statehood would bring to the Cherokee Nation and Indian Territory in the first decades of the twentieth century.

It seems likely that had Riggs intended to simply perpetuate a conventional tragic narrative of Native absence, he would have told a chronological story, since such narratives assume the inexorable and final disappearance of Native peoples, communities, and nations, regardless of what Native peoples actually do, feel, or say. Such narratives deny Native agency by erasing the imperial histories of violence that force Native peoples into impossible situations and in doing so foreclose the possibility of alternative choices, possibilities, and endings. By refusing the linearity of settler-national time, and by situating the only scene in which productive acts of claiming both kin and jurisdiction occur at the end of the play but in the chronological beginning of the narrative, Riggs opens the possibility that choices for action and relationships exist on a daily basis *in this life*. Informed by history and armed with a critical awareness of the genocidal impulses of blood politics, the play powerfully suggests that while the past is often prologue to the future, it need not determine it. For, the community that remains at the end of the play represents the very thing that settler-colonialism seeks ultimately to destroy: Indigenous nations by way of Indigenous families.

Rather than read this final scene as a tragic confirmation of Cherokee social death in the onslaught of civilization and progress or as the inevitable dissolution of Cherokee sovereignty attending allotment and statehood, *The Cherokee Night* might more productively be read as a strong critique of blood discourse and a renewal of Cherokee families reconstituted anew out of the ruins of settler violence. Read through Riggs's own theory on the transformative potential of socially conscious experimental theater, *The Cherokee Night* presents a responsive, historically informed, and experience-based model of intimate and expanded kinship upon which might be based more affirmative understandings of Cherokee national identity as a confederation of families. If this is so, perhaps the play can be read as Riggs's extended answer to Art's rhetorical question from scene 2: "How did I get here? What am I doin' here?"[136] In its attempt to answer this question in all its complexity, the play models a kinder, more life-affirming, more historically accountable model of kinship, nationhood, and belonging than what allotment and statehood wrought on Cherokee peoples and communities.

FOUR

Cherokee Trans/National Stateswomanship in the Nonfiction Writings of Ruth Muskrat Bronson

An entire body of knowledge can be dismissed because it was not written, while material written by obviously biased men is readily accepted as reality. . . . No wonder our written history speaks so often of war but rarely records descriptions of our songs, dances, and simple joys of living. The voices of our grandmothers are silenced by most of the written history of our people. How I long to hear their voices!

Wilma Mankiller, Mankiller

The stories in this chapter are about movements: the processes of maturing, growing, learning, leaving home, and returning home. We all tell these types of stories. We separate from our homelands, our communities, our kin and friends, and, of course, from our best selves. And we return home, reunite with each other, and reestablish connections with our communities and homeland. We learn something about the world, about diversity, and about each other in the process. These stories are important to us. We know neither our departures nor our returns are assured.

Christopher B. Teuton, Cherokee Stories of the Turtle Island Liars Club

We must determine what the future of our race is going to be. You and I must decide right now, today, whether we want it to live on, worthy of the great traditions of the past. Or whether we are willing to see it fall deeper and deeper into decay. By the lives we each determine to live, and by our power to make such a determination into reality, we can show our choice. There is no other convincing answer.

Ruth Muskrat Bronson, "Address on the North American Indian"

In her 1993 autobiography, *Mankiller: A Chief and Her People*, the late former principal chief of the Cherokee Nation opens her book by taking to task the historical record on Cherokee people for racial and gender bias and for the erasure of Cherokee women from history. Such practices, Mankiller argues, present a decidedly one-sided and reductive narrative of Cherokee history focused on conflict, loss, and dislocation—those pesky tropes of the dark age—at the expense of "our songs, dances, and simple joys of living"—dynamics that Mankiller explicitly associates with Cherokee women. Motivated by her direct experiences of relocation from the Cherokee Nation to San Francisco in the 1950s and the activism and community development she participated in throughout the Bay Area, Mankiller's return to Adair County and her two decades of service as a staunch advocate of Cherokee sovereignty went a long way in publicly restoring Cherokee women within Cherokee intellectual, political, and cultural life. Her celebrity and the friendships she formed with figures such as Gloria Steinem, Angela Davis, and others also brought international attention to the Cherokee Nation and to Indian issues more broadly. Whether gathering women from across Indian Country into intimate conversations about family and community, contributing to edited collections by contemporary women of color, or standing in solidarity alongside feminist allies, Mankiller modeled an understanding of Cherokee nationhood that is anchored at once to the people, places, histories, and relations of her birth and to the political, diplomatic, and personal relationships she cultivated abroad.[1]

In this, Makiller's life and work importantly reflect what Joseph Bauerkemper and Heidi Kiiwetinepinesiik Stark define as an Indigenous trans/national politics that captures "how the legacies of Indigenous diplomacies—along with an affirmative, yet still incisive emphasis on Indigenous nationhood . . . intentionally and self-consciously underscore the sophisticated boundaries that differentiate Indigenous nations as discrete polities while also emphasizing the transnational flows of intellectual, cultural, economic, social, and political traditions between and across these boundaries."[2] Understanding Indigenous nationhood in both tribally specific and extratribal, relational terms, Indigenous transnationalism "describes the linkages, conversations, cross-references, and movement of ideas, practices, and obligations between indigenous nations," producing a model of diplomacy predicated on "the recognition of national autonomies and the establishment of collective responsibilities."[3] Such moves—whether understood in regional, intertribal, relational, or trans/national terms—are thus not about leveling tribal-national difference and distinction into transnational sameness. Rather, as Tol Foster writes, they seek to recover and (re)situate Indigenous understandings of identity, community, and nationhood as being "shaped not only by a nuanced and realist understanding of one's own group, but of the many relations it has with groups outside of it."[4] Part and parcel of this resituation is coming to more productive terms with "the intensely relational nature of sovereignty" and with the various visions of tribal nationhood produced by those relations.[5] As a literary-critical framework, Indigenous trans/nationalism affirms the central importance of tribally specific methodologies and the multiple sovereignties that they support while also accounting for how exchanges, relationships, responsibilities, and experiences that move back and forth across tribal-national borders inform, and at times transform, tribal-national lives. As a central figure in the revitalization and strengthening of Cherokee self-governance *and* as an outspoken advocate of gender equality, feminist political ideals, and Indigenous sovereignty more broadly, Mankiller rightly holds a prominent place in the trans/national political and intellectual histories of the Cherokee Nation, Indian Country, and twentieth-century human rights.

As she would be the first to admit, however, Mankiller was but one among many Cherokee women who were centrally committed—in both public and private affairs—to the continuance and security of their families, communities, and nations. Cherokee oral traditions, from Selu's self-sacrificing gifts of corn and community to Cherokee people to the menstruating women who rescue the community from violence and destruction at the hands of Stone Man, are filled with narratives that celebrate Cherokee women's centrality to the maintenance of healthy and productive Cherokee communities.[6] Such values can be seen in historic times in the various ways that Cherokee women negotiated social change, influenced national policy, and participated in the intellectual life of the Nation despite being excluded from public political participation in the constitution of 1827.[7] Some women, such as Nanye'hi, and Cherokee women's councils actively mediated political relationships between their communities and U.S. treaty negotiators, advocated for continued Cherokee autonomy, and repeatedly admonished their male relatives against further land cessions as a kinship responsibility to their mothers, aunties, sisters, nieces, daughters, and wives.[8] Others drew on educational opportunities afforded by Christian missions and the Cherokee national government to carve

Ruth Muskrat Bronson, Cherokee educator, essayist, activist, and organizer. Illustration by Roy Boney.

out self-determined lives as diplomats, entrepreneurs, teachers, writers, artists, and entertainers. Work by Catharine Brown, Narcissa Owens, and the "Rosebuds" of the Cherokee Female Seminary reflect the delicate negotiations of gender, class, race, and nation that characterized Cherokee life during the early national period.[9] Three women who attended the Female Seminary—Rachel Caroline Eaton, Lucy Lowrey Hoyt Keys, and Mabel Washbourne Anderson—travelled extensively and authored significant interventions into popular and academic histories on Cherokee peoples, while Anderson and Ora Eddleman Reed also published fiction, poetry, and life writing in Indian Territory magazines and newspapers.[10] The lives and letters of these socially mobile public women render visible and make audible the absences and silences of Cherokee women to which Mankiller refers and for which she stands so powerfully as a contemporary symbol and reminder. They also suggest an explicitly gendered tradition of Cherokee trans/national states(wo)manship in which performing one's cultural and political identity outside her national home and cultivating relationships across lines of difference constitute fundamental components of building sovereignty and self-determination within.

Ruth Muskrat Bronson was such a woman, and her life and work parallel Mankiller's in important ways. She was educated in local schools, possessed a strong connection to her childhood home, and had a special relationship to her father's Cherokee family. In much the same way that the relocation of Mankiller's family from her childhood home in Adair County to San Francisco in the 1950s laid the foundation for her later work as a community organizer, political activist, and public official, the dissolution of the Cherokee Nation in 1907 forever affected how Bronson viewed the world and the place of Indians in it. Once politicized, Bronson dedicated the better part of her adult life to increasing educational opportunities for Indian students, establishing leadership and professional training programs for Indian graduates, and marshaling support and much-needed resources for community development projects and trust protections for Indian communities. As with Mankiller, who formed alliances with feminists and other women of color, Bronson cultivated and maintained extensive relationships with Indians and non-Indians alike. Tempered always by her dedication to the needs and interests of the Indian communities she served, the life that emerges is one of sacrifice and service that impacted the lives of hundreds, if not thousands, of Indian people.

Despite this remarkable history, Bronson remains virtually unknown among Cherokee people and is remembered only in passing in larger histories of Indian political activism in the twentieth century. When she is mentioned, it is usually in reference to her tenure as a teacher at Haskell Institute alongside Ella Deloria, her work as a founding member and early leader of the National Congress of American Indians (NCAI), or her only book-length text, *Indians are People, Too,* published in 1944.[11] To be sure, such work has contributed important insights into Bronson's life and work, elucidating how her emerging racial identity as an Indian woman informed her lifelong commitment to educational and leadership development for Indian youth. These works also explore her critical understanding of the ways in which Native peoples were negatively positioned in U.S. racial and political structures, which necessitated not only broad-scale Indian solidarity but also pragmatic alliances with BIA bureaucrats and non-Indian advocacy organizations that many Indians understandably held with suspicion if not open hostility. For some, her willingness to cultivate such relationships signals an accommodationist politics, which later Red Power activists would ultimately reject on the road to sovereignty and self-determination.[12] Reading Bronson exclusively in terms of mediation and accommodation, however, captures only one historically situated element of her politics and restricts consideration of her work to a roughly twenty-five-year period in a political and professional life that spanned more than fifty-nine years, traversing some of the most complicated and contentious moments in American Indian history. Doing so ignores the political implications of a life's work of Cherokee trans/national service to Indian communities and the ways in which those experiences informed how she came to understand contemporary Indigenous nationhood and the resurgent politics of sovereignty and self-determination in the twentieth century.

In this chapter I examine some of Bronson's lesser-studied nonfiction writings across a roughly forty-year period, situating each explicitly within the personal and political context in which it was produced. Drawing on speeches, editorials, letters, and congressional testimonies regarding everything from education policy and leadership development to economic empowerment and trust responsibilities, I track a gradual shift in Bronson's politics: from a bootstrap commitment to individual self-reliance and Christian ethics to a structural critique of federal Indian policy before finally transitioning into an explicit politics of sovereignty and self-determination. As I demonstrate throughout, these shifts were tied inextricably to her experiences and to the relationships she developed outside her tribal-national home. Whether wrestling with issues of student retention and success at Haskell Institute, coming to terms with the disruptive effects that federal policies had wrought on Indian families, or fighting for Native Alaska land rights and protections of federal trust responsibilities, Bronson's movements within and among diverse Indian and non-Indian groups encouraged her to develop a more nuanced understanding of the complex forces that impacted the health, security, and prosperity of Indian communities during the first half of the twentieth century.

By historicizing and tracking these shifts through the mode of intellectual biography with close attention to key texts, I resituate what many have read as a concessionary politics of accommodation in her work into a relational ethic of Indigenous trans/national stateswomanship that was born of, informed by, and responsive to the families, communities, and geographies in which she moved. Though at times fraught with the discursive and ideological baggage of her time, Bronson, like Mankiller, never quit trying to understand how best to put her resources to work for the students, families, communities, and organizations that she loved. As both women's lives remind us, Cherokee women have always been at the center of such projects.

Family, Place, Nation, and the Politics of Education

Ruth Muskrat was born in 1897 in northeastern corner of the Delaware district at Cowskin Prairie just outside Grove in the Cherokee Nation to Cherokee citizen James Muskrat and Ida Kelly, a noncitizen English-Irish immigrant from Missouri. James's mother, Martha Fields, was the granddaughter of Richard Fields, an early advocate of removal west and an Old Settler who led an unsuccessful expedition to Mexico to secure Cherokee lands in Texas away from white encroachment. James's father, Jacob Muskrat, immigrated to Indian Territory during the Removal in the winter of 1838–39. Both families settled in the Delaware district in the northeastern corner of the Cherokee Nation where Martha and James met and were married.

A conservative traditionalist and a member of Redbird Smith's Keetoowah Society, James was a committed Cherokee nationalist. As momentum for allotment culminated in the Curtis Act of 1898, which effectively extended federal control over tribal governance in Indian Territory, James became convinced that allotment, though unconscionable, was inevitable. He reluctantly encouraged his family and others to accept the terms of the Curtis Act and cooperate with the Dawes Commission, for which he served as interpreter. As with the Creek writer Alexander Posey and countless others, this work put James at odds with resistant traditionalist organizations across Indian Territory that militantly opposed the dissolution of tribal governments and the allotment of the tribal estate, including James's own relatives in the Keetoowah Society.[13] Despite such tensions, James continued to advocate for cooperation and successfully registered his family and others. According to Bronson, her father welcomed adaptation to modernity as a strategy to promote Indian self-reliance, and he worked hard to productively accommodate white cultural, economic, and political practices into his own lifeways. Though James farmed his allotment until his death in 1944, Ruth and some of her siblings leveraged their allotments and used the proceeds to fund their continuing formal educations within Cherokee Country and abroad.

Education played a central role not only in Bronson's personal life but also in her long-term philosophy of Indian self-determination, one rooted in an extended commitment to formal education across the Cherokee Nation. From the first mission schools established at Spring Place, Hiwasee Town, and Chickamauga in the early nineteenth century to the national school system authorized by the 1839 constitution in Indian Territory, the Cherokee Nation had long lent qualified support to formal education as a means of defending the Nation against assaults on its sovereignty and equipping its young people with the knowledge and resources necessary to prosper in a modernizing political economy.[14] Precisely how the Nation should meet these goals was another matter, however, and debates raged over the means and ends of the educational system itself.[15] Those in the outlying rural, Cherokee-speaking communities lamented the lack of bilingual instruction, questioned the quality of teachers emerging from the seminaries, and demanded more local control over culturally specific curriculum and hiring decisions. Others criticized the emerging race and class stratification cultivated by the three-tiered educational system of rural common schools, urban seminaries, and segregated black and non-Indian subscription schools. Still more questioned the privileging of Western cultural practices that were fostered at the seminaries and the efficacy of a liberal arts curriculum for an economy that was still largely driven by agriculture. Educated in Cherokee common and primary schools, one of which was operated on her father's farm, Bronson likely absorbed at an early age many of the arguments over the goals and purposes of education for Cherokee and other Indian students.[16]

Such experiences would travel with her throughout her early life as she—like Eaton, Oskison, Riggs, and countless Cherokees before and after—left her home community to pursue educational opportunities elsewhere. In 1912 Bronson followed her sister to the Oklahoma Institute of Technology located just north of Oklahoma City in Tonkawa.[17] After graduating in 1916, Bronson spent the next year and a half in teacher training, first at the Henry Kendall Academy in Tulsa and then at Northeastern State Normal School in Tahlequah (formerly the Cherokee Female Seminary). After gaining her certificate, she taught in Oklahoma public schools from 1917 to 1919. That September she enrolled at the University of Oklahoma, overlapping with Riggs for a year, where she majored in English and maintained strong professional and social lives as a member of Theta Sigma Phi, the American Journalists Association, the Student Christian Fellowship League, and the Delaware County Club. Her funds were exhausted by the winter of 1920, so Bronson left OU and took a position with the Young Women's Christian Association (YWCA) as recreational coordinator on the Mescalero Apache reservation where she developed programing to assist Apache girls returning from residential schools to readjust to reservation life. Her time at Mescalero exposed her for the first time to the abject poverty and sociocultural challenges of the reservation, introduced her to the diversity of Indian thought and experience outside of Oklahoma, and served as the first of many tribal trans/national experiences across Indian Country that would powerfully affect how she understood the challenges facing Native peoples.

An essay documenting Bronson's time at Mescalero won her the attention of executives in the YWCA who awarded her a three-year scholarship to the University of Kansas. Accompanied by her sister Jewell, she enrolled in the school of journalism in the fall of 1921. The essay also drew the attention of the World's Student Christian Federation, which extended Muskrat an invitation to its annual international gathering of more than two hundred thousand students from fifty-nine countries, which was held in Beijing, China, in April 1922.[18] Traveling as a guest of the national board of the YWCA, Muskrat represented American Indians as one of nineteen U.S. delegates in attendance. Along the way she delivered lectures in Norman, Denver, Colorado Springs, San Francisco, Hawai'i, Manchuria, Japan, Korea, and Hong Kong. From these experiences generally and from her identification as a Cherokee with Koreans who were then under Japanese colonial rule, Muskrat began to develop a race consciousness as both a Cherokee and an Indian woman.[19]

Upon her return stateside in fall 1923, Bronson enrolled at Mount Holyoke in South Hadley, Massachusetts, on a full scholarship with advanced standing, where she majored in English and minored in economics and sociology. As the first American Indian student to ever attend the college—an interesting fact considering that the Cherokee female seminary based its curriculum on and recruited teachers from Mount Holyoke—she would later recall feeling less like a First American or U.S. citizen and more like a foreign national, which in a very real sense she was. Like Elias Boudinot and John Ridge before her, Bronson quickly came to understand how ignorant most Americans were about American Indian history and about the contradiction between the progressive assimilationist rhetoric of racial inclusivity and the structures and practices of racial othering. Recalling arguments by nineteenth- and early twentieth-century Native writers, anti-Removal Cherokee nationalists, and Indian GIs returning from World War I, Bronson believed colonialism and racism to be antithetical to Christian moral values and democratic principles.[20] She thus began cultivating the egalitarian language of Christian brotherhood as an ethical counterweight to white supremacy and as a discursive strategy to argue for increased educational access for Indian students and broader institutional and policy reforms.[21] Momentum toward such reforms in the 1920s and '30s would provide the political will, economic resources, and bureaucratic support necessary to gain traction toward some of the programs that Bronson hoped to develop.

The Council of One Hundred and Early Indian Policy Reform

As the 1920s got under way, it was becoming obvious to both proponents and opponents of assimilation not only that Indian peoples had refused to vanish, but that they were actively working to reconstitute their communities and nations.[22] The devastating effects of allotment and assimilationist policies on Indian communities; the widespread presence of prejudice, graft, and misconduct of the agency system; and the seemingly unlimited power of the Office of Indian Affairs began drawing intense criticism from Indians and progressive reformists alike. A series of assaults on Indian trust protections and widespread corruption in the Harding administration throughout the next decade ran afoul of the Supreme Court and galvanized a coalition of pro-Indian interests including the All Pueblo Council, the Society of American Indians, the Indian Rights Association, the American Indian Defense League, and a variety of influential non-Indian artists and intellectuals.[23] Warren Harding's appointment of Albert Fall, a former New Mexico senator and staunch opponent of Indian rights, as secretary of the interior and Fall's forced resignation following the Teapot Dome scandal consolidated opposition.[24] In order to repair the reputation of his administration and the Department of Interior, Harding appointed Postmaster General Hubert Work as Fall's replacement.[25]

Hoping to address current crises and anticipate potentially explosive federal Indian policy issues, Work convened the Council of One Hundred in 1923 to identify specific problems and discuss targeted reforms. Comprised largely of leading non-Indian experts on federal Indian policy, the council also included a significant number of influential nationally known Indian figures including many Red Progressive members of the Society of American Indians (SAI) such as Henry Roe Cloud (Winnebago), Reverend Sherman Coolidge (Arapaho), Dr. Charles Eastman (Dakota), Thomas Sloan (Omaha), and Arthur C. Parker (Seneca). The council, chaired by Parker, passed a series of resolutions supporting increased funding for Indian education and vocational training, improved health and sanitation programs, a quick and equitable resolution to Pueblo land claims, and the opening of the federal court of claims to tribal peoples.[26] Due to her influential connections at the YWCA and the notoriety she drew from her participation at the World's Student Christian Federation conference the previous year, Bronson was asked to participate at the gathering and to contribute a paper concerning Indian education reform.

On the second day of the conference, Bronson delivered a speech entitled "Indian Leadership, Past and Present," which focused on the needs of American Indian students and leadership development among a new generation of Indian youths.[27] Donning intertribal buckskin regalia that had been gifted to her by Apache and Comanche women and was designed to emphasize a shared Indian racial identity over tribal affiliations, she pushed for more college scholarships and access to other educational opportunities for Indian students. She then presented newly inaugurated President Calvin Coolidge with a copy of G. E. E. Lundquist's recent study of contemporary conditions in Indian Country, *The Red Man in the United States.* Adorned in a buckskin cover that was decorated with Cheyenne beadwork, written by a non-Indian of the interchurch movement, and published by the Rockefeller-supported Institute of Social and Religious Research, the book as an artifact reflects the pragmatic coalitional politics of the gathering itself.

Like most "pro-Indian" treatises of the period, the text is ambivalent with respect to the ends of policy reform. In its assumption of assimilation as the primary goal of reform and its reliance on Christian intervention as the most effective means of addressing material and political issues, *Red Man* reinforces some of the institutional prejudices that Indians and secular progressivist reformists were working hard to displace. In other ways, however, the text makes significant interventions. Its emphasis on contemporary challenges and devastating inequities facing reservation communities moves away from social evolutionist assumptions of Indian deficiency that defined federal policy discussions. Its survey of Indian communities and its mandate that Indians themselves play a significant role in solving the problems it documents—if only as an adjunct to federal and religious programs—also set it apart from the blatant paternalism of policy makers, bureaucrats, and many "Friends of the Indian" reform groups. As she presented the text to Coolidge, Bronson emphasized these latter points in order to frame Indian policy reform for the new president.

Gifting the text "in behalf of the many Indian students of America," Bronson asserts that the book "gives, for the first time, a comprehensive account of the social, economic, and religious conditions among my people as they are today" and "bears the best we have to offer—the story of our struggles and our tragedies, of our victories and our developments."[28] Emphasizing productive alliances between non-Indian allies and contemporary Native people, Bronson argues that the book demonstrates both "the story of the old type of Indian, greeting with the hand of friendship the founders of this great nation, and the story of the new Indian emerging from his semi-barbaric state, tilling the soil, and building for citizenship under the guidance of school."[29] Though such statements reflect the same reliance on developmentalist discourses of savagery and civilization with which Eaton negotiated, like Eaton, Bronson mobilizes them less to confirm narratives of vanishing and disappearance than to celebrate Indigenous cultural adaptation and the place of Indians as agents in modernity. To this point, Bronson draws attention to what she wryly refers to as "the so-called Indian problem" and reasonably asks, "May not we, who are Indian students of this generation, who must face the burdens of that problem, say what it means to us?"[30] In answer to her question, she offers a narrative of Indian statesmanship, diplomacy, patriotism, intellectual innovation, and agency.

In "Indian Leadership" Bronson lays claim to primacy of place and moral right by recalling the spirit of hospitality and friendship with which leaders like Powhatan and Massasoit welcomed "strange people to the shores of [their] country and called them brother."[31] Echoing William Apess's "Eulogy on King Philip," which had been delivered ninety years earlier at the height of the Removal debates that would forcibly relocate her father's family to Indian Territory, Bronson recalls figures like Philip, Chief Joseph, and Tecumseh as accomplished military thinkers and patriots. Others such as Cornstalk, Red Jacket, and Sequoyah, Bronson continues, drew on their Indian "energy," "ambition," and "keen penetration of vision" to emerge as statesmen and intellectuals capable of guiding their people along "new paths" in a new age.[32] Hardly relics of the historical past, Bronson argues that the same innovative energy and "potential for greatness" that these leaders possessed still exists in a new generation of Native leaders who are ready and willing to embrace U.S. citizenship and the challenges and promises of modernity. "Our old life has gone," she says. "A new trail must be found, for the old one is not good to travel farther. We are glad to have it so."[33]

Reflecting similar biases against cultural traditions that were shared by Cherokee progressives from Elias Boudinot and John Ridge to her own contemporaries Oskison and Eaton, Bronson too easily concedes acculturation and U.S. citizenship as necessary components of this new trail: "We want to understand and to accept the civilization of the white man; we want to become citizens of the United States and to share in the building of this great nation that we love."[34] Bronson contends, however, that such changes need not entail abject assimilation as a precondition for implementation. Reflecting a commitment to pluralism that she would hold throughout her life, Bronson argues that the most successful programs will allow Indian peoples "to preserve the best that is in our own civilization" so that they might "make our own unique contribution to the civilizations of the world."[35] Believing strongly in the power of education to better the lives of Indian communities and rejecting tragic narratives of Indigenous death outright, Bronson observes that the only thing preventing "this vigorous and by no means dying race" from success is inadequate access to educational and professional opportunities by which to "guide their people along new and untried paths" and to ensure "economic independence" in a modern world.[36] Like the political, military, and intellectual leaders of the past whom Bronson celebrates, this generation of Native peoples would also draw on all available opportunities, including those "which have been afforded us by the interest of the white man," to lead their communities into modernity.[37] With more schools, better infrastructure, and greater "encouragement and help from our White Brothers," she states, "the trail ahead for the Indian looks clear and bright with promise."[38]

As with other Indian writers and activists of the late nineteenth and early twentieth centuries, Bronson mobilizes progressive rhetorics of self-reliance and institutional and economic reform to "speak back to civilization" with a critical voice, challenging its advocates—President Coolidge, Secretary Work, and other white progressives in attendance—to live up to the ideals of self-reliance, self-improvement, and uplift that they espouse.[39] As Fredrick Hoxie and others have argued, Indian intellectuals "presented themselves not as disinterested scholars but rather as advocates of Indian culture who believed that their Indigenous heritage was equivalent to modern 'civilization' and that they would be considered fellow human beings rather than members of a 'savage' race."[40] Bronson's emphasis, for instance, on contemporary material conditions, as opposed to innate Indian racial and cultural deficiencies, implicitly challenges conventional representations of Native peoples that are rooted in ahistorical, social evolutionist assumptions of Indian disappearance. Her valorization of Indian military leaders as intelligent, innovative, and patriotic defenders of their homes and families rather than as anachronistic impediments to U.S. development and expansion similarly undermines the savage/civilized binary upon which much federal Indian policy and reform turned. The narrative of historical adaptation and innovation across Indian history similarly emphasizes survival and continuity over narratives of stasis, degradation, declension, and extinction. Rather, in Bronson's speech, Indians have done what all peoples have done in the face of change—innovate, adapt, and move forward. For this to occur, it follows that Native peoples must have a seat at the table and a forum in which to voice their needs, concerns, experiences, and aspirations. What the commission represented, and what Bronson chose to drive home, was a return to more equitable Indian-U.S. relations based on reciprocity and respect.

These narrative revisions of popular Indian history allow Bronson to reframe "the Indian problem" away from highly partisan and irresolvable questions of Indian racial and cultural fitness to more actionable, structural questions of institutional access, opportunity, and economic independence. Despite such rhetorical inversions and subversions, Bronson's pronouncements of the extinction of the "old life" and her expressions of "gratitude for the opportunities for education and culture which have been afforded us by the interest of the white man" elide the history of colonial violence, dispossession, and genocidal government policies that were largely responsible for the "social economic, and religious conditions" to which she refers. Similarly, the educational and cultural opportunities ostensibly granted Native peoples "by the interest of the white man" were in actuality hard-fought treaty provisions negotiated in exchange for Native land cessions and promises of peace, a distinction that would become central to her later critiques of termination. There also exists in Bronson's speech a propensity to speak on behalf of all Native people—what Elizabeth Cook-Lynn identifies as the self-appointed role of spokesperson—particularly in their presumed desire "to accept the civilization of the white man" and "to become citizens of the United States."[41] As scholars have demonstrated, such assumptions were contentiously debated in the Cherokee Nation and throughout Indian Country from the late nineteenth and into the twentieth centuries.[42] One might read such passages as evidence of the degree to which some Indian people, particularly those like Bronson, who were of mixed-race descent with Eastern educations and Christian affiliations, had internalized evolutionary discourses of human development and narratives of Anglo racial triumphalism.[43]

This would be a reductive reading of the rhetorical work that Bronson's speech performs, however. Juxtaposed with passages that bemoan the passing of the "old life" and an embrace of assimilation are assertions that Native peoples constitute "by no means [a] dying race of people," that even if the "old life has gone," there nonetheless exists an "awakened spiritual vigor" in Native communities anchored to a steadfast desire to "preserve the best that is in our own civilization" in order to make a "unique contribution" to the future.[44] Further, by recovering Native political, military, and intellectual leaders of the past and connecting them to the struggles of contemporary Native youths, Bronson constructs what Robert Warrior terms an "intellectual trade route" across Native history as a tool to respond to the challenges facing contemporary Indian peoples.[45] Though she recognizes that such challenges are vastly different from those of previous generations—yet perhaps more urgent—Bronson nonetheless locates them within a wider historical network of mutually influential relationships, or what Devon Mihesuah terms the "common context of colonization."[46] Carefully couched in rhetorics of accommodation, then, is the language of survivance evidenced in a steadfast assertion of a Native voice and a demand for a Native presence in the future she envisions.

The account of both Native presences and futures in her speech to the council exceeds savage/civilized, assimilationist/traditionalist dichotomies by staking out a place for Native peoples to speak and act for themselves as both Indian and modern. Viewing education as the engine necessary to realize such futures, Bronson dedicated the next two decades of her life to creating opportunities for Native students and reforming the educational system in service of this vision. Like Luther Standing Bear, Zitkála-Šá, and her contemporary D'Arcy

McNickle, as Bronson moved further into the machine of Indian bureaucracy, her confidence in ideologies of individual self-reliance would slowly give way to a more comprehensive understanding of the institutional hurdles and structural issues that impacted Indian opportunities for success.

From Bootstrap Ethics and Self-Reliance to Institutional Critique

Two years after the Council of One Hundred, Bronson graduated from Mount Holyoke College and boarded a train for Tahlequah to assume a summer position as special instructor and dean of women at Northeastern State Teachers College. A year later, at the age of twenty-eight, she accepted a position in the education division of the Office of Indian Affairs, where she could focus her attention specifically on Indian students.[47] Her first assignment was as an eighth grade teacher at Haskell Institute in Lawrence, Kansas, where she served for three years alongside Dakota anthropologist, novelist, and educator Ella Deloria and Ho-Chunk school administrator Henry Roe Cloud. While there, Bronson attempted to break down some of the educational barriers that Native students faced, expose students to the advantages and possibilities that education had afforded her, and encourage Indian young women specifically to pursue higher education in service of their communities.[48] A New Year's address given at Haskell on January 1, 1927 (later published in the February 1927 issue of the *American Indian*), provides one clear example of Bronson's early thinking and reveals the limitations of liberal rhetorics of self-reliance and racial uplift for addressing structural impediments facing Native students.

Invoking romantic images of Indian nobility, Bronson calls on Haskell students to remember the "heritage of courage and fearlessness" of Indian leaders of the past such as King Philip and Sequoyah who, faced with unimaginable challenges and against great odds, addressed "the crises of their time and rose nobly to meet them."[49] Paralleling the urgency with which African and Mexican American intellectuals of the period understood their own circumstances, Bronson asserts that the stakes are nothing less than the survival and security of Indian people: "We are the hope of the Indian race! And on the shoulders of this generation of Indian youth does rest the responsibility and the glory of our race. . . . I have believed for a long while that the Indian race is now at the greatest crisis in all of history! I believe we must literally live or die on the merit of the present generation."[50] Compounding this responsibility, Bronson emphasizes the hypervisibility of Haskell students, noting that all Indian peoples will be judged by the successes or failures of a select few: "Because we are a small group *in the midst of an alien civilization,* the focus of all eyes are centered upon us. Every success we make, every failure is conspicuous. Because we are such a small group no Indian boy or girl has a right to be a failure, for by failing we not only pull ourselves down but we pull down our whole race."[51] Consistent with her belief that Indian education was only useful to the extent that Indian students used it in service to their communities, Bronson admonishes the students not to turn away in fear from the enormity of this responsibility but to embrace it as their raison d'être: "The realization of this great responsibility ought to overshadow every action of our lives. It ought to color every waking thought we have or every action we take with the fire of its challenge."[52] She implores them to take advantage of the "vital, rich opportunities" at Haskell and to remain strong in their convictions even in the face of criticism and opposition.[53] Claiming that the "rich treasures of an education" are available to any "Indian boy or girl who wants it bad enough," Bronson further chains the prospect of Indian survival to individual achievement. "A great race," she continues, "must be made up of great individuals. And if we would be a great race we must put our minds to the difficult task of living greatly."[54] To put it bluntly, failure is not an option for to fail would be to sentence Indian families and communities to the ashbin of history.

At this point, Bronson goes on a lengthy and problematic indictment of what she viewed at the time as the propensity of Indian students to engage in frivolous activities and lean too heavily on disempowering narratives of victimization. Rather than investing time in popular romances, sensationalist fiction, and other "lesser things," Bronson charges students to engage with "good literature," to produce great art, and to cultivate their own "spiritual development," which she believed to be one of the Indians' "greatest contributions to mankind."[55] To make such a choice, she insists, requires students to recognize that time is precious, that resources are limited, that average is unacceptable, and that to blame the past for current conditions is to avoid responsibility for changing the present: "As a race, we think too much about the past, and we dwell too long on what someone has done to us. We do not think enough about what we are doing to ourselves and for ourselves."[56] Though she insists, "It is time now that we begin to stand on our own feet," Bronson believes that Indian students too easily become frustrated, distracted, and disinterested in their studies. Consequently, they either fail to achieve their full measure of potential or drop out as "Quitters!" at the first sign of difficulty, unable to "finish what had been begun."[57] Encouraging students to recover "the patience and courage that is necessary to give us the power to see a thing through," Bronson says, "we must *determine* what the future of our race is going to be. You and I must decide right now, today, whether we want it to live on, worthy of the great traditions of the past. Or whether we are willing to see it fall deeper and deeper into decay. *By the lives we each determine to live,* and by our *power to make such a determination into reality,* we can show our choice. There is no other convincing answer."[58] She concludes, "Your choice must be of your own, . . . and it is a deliberate choice" either for or against the futures of all Indian people.[59]

From a reductive understanding of retention issues as a function of courage and commitment to a framing of her own experiences of choice, mobility, access, and opportunity as representative of all Native students, Bronson's speech reflects a limited understanding of the multiple causes that might explain the success of one student and the failure of another as well as the very real significance of what she terms "lesser things."[60] Some students went "AWOL," as Bronson put it, as legitimate acts of defiance against regimented curricular and cultural discipline. Others made the conscious choice to drop out in order to provide for their families or to fulfill significant cultural responsibilities and kinship obligations.[61] Similarly, tribally and regionally centered social groups, overnight off-campus stomp dances, and nighttime pranks against facilities and personnel allowed students to bring a bit of home to their campus lives; reaffirm tribal identities, kinship relations, and cultural practices; and claim agency over lives and conditions that were not entirely of their own making.[62] By framing such activities either as frivolous distractions from the real work of academic training or as failures of individual will, Bronson not only reaffirms the atomizing mission of boarding school curricula, she also ignores the abject failure of such policies to usher Indian communities into an age of prosperity and self-reliance, ignoring the very real critiques of bureaucratic surveillance and resistances to structural power in which the students were engaging.

Bronson's confidence in the liberal politics of self-reliance might be explained as a consequence of youthful naïveté. Holding her own experience as representative for all Indian students suggests a young Cherokee woman not yet attuned to the structural inequities that condition Indian policy and impact Indian lives. While undoubtedly naïve and underdeveloped, her confidence in liberal individualism and her deployment of the bootstrap ethics of hard work and dogged determination are also indicative of the Red Progressive reformist politics of the day.[63] Whether advocating the abolition of the BIA and the extension of U.S. citizenship to all Indians or seeking to better mobilize much-needed services and protections provided by existing institutions, most Indian reformers of the period believed that increased individual self-determination coupled with strategic relationships with non-Indian allies was the only way Native peoples might collectively recover from the fallout of the policies of the previous three decades. They thus recognized the benefits that English literacy and formal education afforded their communities, particularly as they prepared their students for lives in an industrial world. At the same time, they remained highly critical of the community and cultural dislocations fostered by an overly zealous and blatantly anti-Indian system. The question for Indians like Bronson—and here she parallels similar debates from decades earlier in the Cherokee Nation—was not whether Indian children should receive formal education, but how the system might be reformed to better serve Indian interests so that they might enter the U.S. mainstream in their own time and at least partially on their own terms.[64]

Thus, while the rhetorical means by which she delivers her message appear naïve and unsympathetic, the speech as a whole suggests a commitment to the idea that Indian people, as First Americans, deserved the same rights, protections, and opportunities that settlers and arrivants enjoyed, and it looks to citizenship and education as crucial mechanisms through which to achieve those goals.[65] As with her presentation to Coolidge, this speech also evidences the gravity of the material and economic circumstances facing Native peoples and a strong commitment to boldly address those challenges. The stakes, as she understood them, were nothing short of survival. Though no doubt trying to convey this immediacy and to encourage Indian students not simply to acknowledge the stakes but to embrace them, in defining success strictly as a function of hard work, determination, and stick-to-itiveness, Bronson lays the enormous responsibility of collective self-determination entirely on their young shoulders. At the time of this speech, she had not yet come to understand how the language and assumptions of liberal self-reliance reduce complicated social and political issues to matters of individual responsibility and depoliticizes what has always been, for Native peoples, expressly political issues of land tenure, sovereignty, and self-determination. Her continued tenure at the BIA would go a long way in providing her such an understanding.

In 1927, at the age of thirty, Bronson exchanged her teaching position for a post as registrar and supervisor of Haskell's Outing Program for young women.[66] With the installation of the Hoover administration and a shift in BIA leadership in 1930, she accepted a position as guidance and placement officer for the Office of Education in which she administered federal loan and scholarship funds and located employment and higher education opportunities for boarding school graduates.[67] During this time Lewis Meriam charged her with conducting a survey on the state of Indian education in both government and mission schools across the United States.[68] Completed in 1932, the report documented academic, economic, and social conditions at various schools; surveyed student successes and failures; revealed woefully low academic standards; and exposed widespread bias among teachers against Indian fitness for nonvocational curricula and the possibility for academic achievement. Bronson parlayed the attention that the report attracted into broad recommendations for reforms of the loan and scholarship program.[69]

A paper presented before the Committee on the American Indian at the National Conference on Social Work in 1931 outlines Bronson's rationale for such reforms and points to a shift in her thinking concerning the direction and intent of federal policy. Titled "The Indians' Attitude toward Cooperation," it levies a general critique of federal policies of wardship, restriction, and segregation and specifically argues for the incorporation of Native students into state educational systems coupled with a gradual phasing-out of the federally operated boarding school apparatus.[70] The cooperation evoked in the title refers to jurisdictional questions between Indian communities and state and federal governments that emerged after the passage of the Indian Citizenship Act seven years earlier. Of particular concern for states was whether and to what extent they would assume from the federal government primary legal authority over Indian life and land as well as administrative responsibilities for health care, public education, and other treaty-based services that were formerly managed through the BIA.[71] The continued restricted trust status of Indian individuals and allotments, unsettled tribal claims against the federal government regarding the management of tribal estates, and the bureaucratic authority that the BIA exerted over virtually every aspect of Indian lives complicated any neat resolution to such questions.

Unlike the implicit criticism of federal policy evident in Bronson's address to Coolidge, "The Indians' Attitude toward Cooperation" explicitly indicts wardship and segregation as "a deeply humiliating experience" that reaches across generations, ultimately impeding contemporary Indian people from fully enjoying the rights, privileges, and presumed benefits of their recently acquired citizenship.[72] For Indians from her grandmother's generation, Bronson argues, the restrictions and limitations of wardship serve as a consistent reminder of the pain and loss engendered by allotment and statehood. Nearer in experience to the Trail of Tears than to the presumed benefits of civilization and U.S. citizenship, many Indians from this generation understandably view states less as potential partners for community empowerment and more as sources of Indian exploitation. Similarly, while those of her father's generation desire economic independence and political participation consistent with "the standards of living of the white people," they have had limited and often exploitative experiences with non-Indian communities, business practices, political systems, and social norms. Though they are more open to cooperation than previous generations, many in her father's generation find that segregation and wardship have left them adrift without a coherent social philosophy or vocational infrastructure to replace the old ways and customs to which they have often turned for security.[73] Ostensibly distanced from their grandparents' historical memory of brutality and armed with more education, training, and geographic mobility than their parents, this new generation of Indian graduates seems most equipped to succeed in an industrial and increasingly urban economy. Nevertheless, Bronson observes, they are still hampered by the effects of segregation. They often arrive in the city alone, without a strong support system, and lack access to continuing education, job training, adequate health care, and other social services. Because they have been educated separate from white students in boarding and mission schools, they share their parents' and grandparents' skepticism of white motivations. Consequently, they often enter the job market at the lowest levels and, unable to form productive relationships with non-Indian superiors and colleagues, stall out, eking out meager lives until they ultimately "become overwhelmed by increasing burdens and responsibilities" and return home.[74]

Though the picture Bronson paints of Indian futures is bleak, she is careful to frame her descriptions as composite experiences rather than universal types that define every Indian community. For every despondent elder there is an optimist; for every adrift father a loving parent; and for every frustrated boarding school graduate a lawyer, doctor, teacher, or entrepreneur. Such successes, however, are more to the credit of resolute individuals and resilient communities than government policies, which encourage dependence, frustrate individual ambition, and engender suspicion among "our young people."[75] In a departure from the bootstrap rhetoric of the Haskell address four years earlier, Bronson here lays the blame for poverty, economic dependence, and social dysfunction at the feet of federal policy. Lest her audience subscribe to the popular notion that such issues are particular to Native communities, Bronson reminds them, "There is nothing especially Indian in most of our problems. . . . They are just human problems that all groups everywhere have to face."[76] What has given such issues a particularly Indian flavor is the "sheer stupidity" of segregation policies that prevent Indian peoples from entering into the social, political, and economic structures of the United States as equals to their non-Indian counterparts.[77]

At this point, Bronson targets the very structural issues that were absent from the Haskell address: federal paternalism and systematic efforts to undermine Indian kinship and family structures through state-sponsored, forced educational programs. "Social workers have known for a long time that the conservation of the family is the basis of sound community life and progress," she writes. "Yet in Indian education, up until the present [Hoover] administration, the whole tendency has been directed toward destroying Indian family life and tearing down Indian family responsibility. . . . It has taken many costly years to prove the fallacy of such a program. Nobody knows how much this very thing can be held to be responsible for the present degeneration of many Indian families."[78] Recalling strong critiques of boarding school practices from Luther Standing Bear, Zitkála-Šá, and others, and anticipating contemporary conversations about the intergenerational effects of residential school experiences, Bronson broadly indicts Indian education for impeding the social and structural integration of Indian peoples as citizens into the United States. More specifically, and importantly, she specifically targets its efforts—*as a matter of policy*—to fundamentally undermine the fabric of the Native family, depriving parents and children "of their greatest means of growth and development."[79] Rather than acting as a partner and adjunct to early familial socialization, boarding schools assumed primary social and educational responsibilities that they neither understood nor were fully equipped to deliver. Declaiming both paternalism and wardship as failures, Bronson argues that the restoration of proper Indian family relationships and the success of individual students ultimately depend on equal treatment and equal access to educational, vocational, and other opportunities. "Our great objective for the Indian," she argues, "must be exactly the same as it is in all social work for all other groups—to make him self-sustaining and independent, emotionally, economically, and socially. All our future policy must be shaped and controlled by this objective."[80]

With respect to Indian education, Bronson advocates the movement of Indian students from federally operated segregated boarding schools into state public schools. Allowing Indian children to attend schools locally, she reasons, would allow them to maintain significant cultural and familial relationships and thus would go a long way toward restoring healthy communities. Equal access to public education would also provide Indians students with the education, exposure, and familiarity with non-Indian communities and institutions that would allow them to succeed personally, academically, and professionally alongside non-Indian colleagues and competitors. For Bronson, failure to act would mean nothing less than the continued social marginalization and economic deprivation of Native communities: "So long as our schools are segregated, so long as we feel that we do not need to keep in line with the state courses of study, so long as our laws are not the same as those of our white neighbors across the road, so long as our health standards and health advantages are not the same, so long as there are other special privileges given or denied us, then just so long will Indian progress be retarded, and just so long will there be an Indian problem to be solved."[81] Despite the immediacy of the stakes—or perhaps because of them—Bronson cautions patience, noting that such reforms cannot be rushed into, but must proceed gradually and with careful thought toward allowing those affected to make the transition in as reasonable and efficient a manner possible. "We must not forget," she reminds her audience, "that it has taken five hundred years to destroy American Indian home life. We cannot restore it by an official order to abolish a government boarding school. There must be patient years of skilful [*sic*] work to rehabilitate what we in our stupidity have so ruthlessly torn down."[82] With cooperation between state and federal agencies, reeducation in Indian communities, and extensive efforts to stamp out "serious and harmful prejudice against the Indian" in public schools, Bronson contends that reform efforts can work to cultivate "mutual understanding and appreciation" between Indians and their non-Indian neighbors and to serve as a model for further cooperation and reform.[83]

Compared to her earlier writings, "The Indians' Attitude toward Cooperation" demonstrates clear shifts in Bronson's thinking and approach concerning Indian education as well as larger relationships between policy, community development, and individual achievement. Most obvious is Bronson's refusal to speak authoritatively about or for all Indian peoples. She opens her paper, in fact, by cautioning her audience to "guard against every general statement about Indians" and admits that even her own identity as a Cherokee woman provides her no "open sesame into the thinking and the philosophy of Indian peoples. . . . I can only tell you what I know some Indians to be thinking and can only speak with authority about what I think myself."[84] While she openly admits that personal experience remains central to how she thinks about pressing concerns, she no longer presents her individual experiences as representative or universally achievable for all. This move suggests a more mature understanding of the potential dangers of speaking in broad strokes about Indian life outside of Indian Country, an understanding undoubtedly influenced by her four-year tenure negotiating the frustrating, inefficient, and at times impenetrable workings of federal bureaucracy.

Gone also is the do-it-yourself language of individual responsibility, replaced instead with a more historically and institutionally informed understanding of the myriad ways in which policy and paternalism conspire to impede Indian self-determination. Though Bronson regrets what she views as a "philosophy of defeat" that seems to structure her grandmother's generation, she also realizes that such responses have deep historical roots in traumatic experience.[85] Denationalized by the federal government, dispossessed by racist policies and prejudicial courts, and alienated from traditional relationships and cultural practices, her grandmother "clings to the old ways and cherishes the old customs" not out of some stubborn resistance to modernity, but because the promises of civilization and citizenship have failed her so completely.[86] Likewise, while Bronson laments the pull that tradition exerts on those of her father's generation, it is neither "the old ways" nor laziness nor a failure of will that keeps them from succeeding as farmers, entrepreneurs, or businessmen but policies of economic segregation that prevent them from entering U.S. social structures on equal footing with their non-Indian competitors. And it is not a lack of intelligence, ambition, or effort that leads Indian graduates from the cities back to the reservation in despair but bankrupt educational philosophies and the absence of sufficient economic and structural support to allow them to succeed.

Though Bronson's confidence in individual ambition and personal responsibility remains, and though she clearly holds tradition and modernity in an uncomfortable opposition, she no longer views the challenges facing Indian peoples strictly as a function of individual effort and persistence. Indeed, her appeal to the universal human character of the issues facing Indian communities rejects race as a factor entirely and redirects the conversation toward redress of systemic inequities, institutional prejudices, and structural challenges that impeded Indian self-determination. As an employee of the BIA and a former educator at Haskell, Bronson's repudiation of existing educational philosophies, the boarding school model, and the principles of wardship upon which postallotment policies were based also stands in stark contrast to both the confidence in federal policy reform that she projected in the Coolidge speech and the presumed advantages of boarding school education that she valorized in the Haskell address. If her plan to gradually dismantle the infrastructures of wardship as a mechanism to return more direct control over Native lives to Native people can be seen as a model for future reforms, what Bronson envisioned was a complete overhaul of federal Indian policy. Echoing similar efforts by Native women such as Angel De Cora and Laura Cornelius Kellogg, Bronson demands a shift in the BIA's mission from administration to education and from the micromanagement of Indian lives to the structural empowerment of Indian communities.[87]

While she was still years away from openly advocating a return to the trust relationship between Indian peoples and the federal government and denouncing any attempt to undermine the unique political status of Indian nations, Bronson had already come to believe that any real solutions to the challenges facing Indian peoples were going to come from Indians themselves rather than from legislative chambers, court benches, or offices of "Friends of the Indian" organizations. Her continued work with the BIA under the impending New Deal reforms of the Collier administration and amid increasingly intense calls for termination following the Second World War would sharpen the stakes of both her work and her politics.

Tongass, Termination, and the Move to Sovereignty and Self-Determination

Four years into Bronson's appointment as Indian education guidance and placement officer, Congress passed the Indian Reorganization Act (IRA) of 1934. The brainchild of newly appointed BIA director John Collier, the IRA officially repudiated the policies of allotment and assimilation in favor of a corporate-inspired form of Indian "home rule." It stopped the allotment and liquidation of the tribal estate and provided for the reconsolidation of tribal lands; acknowledged the importance of group life for healthy communities; and revalorized Indian cultural beliefs and practices as fundamental components of policy reform and tribal self-determination. To foster economic independence, the IRA established tribally controlled charters for economic enterprise, provided for independent contracts with state and municipal agencies, and set up a revolving credit fund to provide capital for investment. It also advocated hiring preferences for Indians in the bureau, increased funding for educational and professional training, and shifted financial and political support away from boarding schools and toward government-operated Indian day schools. In its most significant and long-lasting reform, the IRA provided the theoretical framework to shift conceptualizations of Indian self-determination from a state-centered philosophy of delegated power to a human rights philosophy of inherent power.[88]

While the IRA failed to achieve universal support among tribal communities for a variety of reasons, not least of which was the insistence on BIA and Department of Interior oversight, a majority of Indian communities voted to reorganize under its measures.[89] As a consequence of its educational component, the Indian Scholarship and Loan Program that Bronson directed saw its appropriations increase twentyfold to $250,000, though only $150,000 was actually distributed. The growth of the program spurred the bureau to provide Bronson with a permanent assistant and stenographer and relocated her offices to Washington, D.C., in 1935. As the bureau's sole guidance and placement officer, over the next eight years Bronson worked to promote higher education across Indian Country, extending the loan program to as many qualified students as possible, advancing culturally sensitive reforms in education philosophy and curriculum development, and tracking the progress and employment opportunities for Indian graduates. Though requiring extensive personal and professional travel, her work paid huge dividends; on the eve of the U.S. entry into World War II in 1941, Bronson reported that more than six hundred Native students had received support from the loan program during her tenure.

The following year, however, her offices were relocated to Chicago in order to make room for war-related agencies in D.C. The move proved too challenging on her family life, and Bronson submitted her resignation to the BIA effective November 1943, though she remained contracted as a consultant to the Office of Education for the next two years. In 1944 she joined the board of directors of the Indian Rights Association and authored a volume on Indian history and contemporary issues targeting high school–age church groups sponsored by the Protestant Missionary Education Movement in New York City and published by the publishing arm of the National Council of Churches, the Friendship Press. Titled *Indians Are People, Too,* the text, as Chadwick Allen argues, targets white progressive Christians and mobilizes the discourses of civic, political, and Christian equality in order to argue for the unprejudiced inclusion of American Indians as fully integrated, full-participant citizens in U.S. society.[90] As its publication outlet, title, and rhetorical intentions suggest, the book sought to introduce *contemporary* Indian issues to a wide audience and to mediate understandings of Indian racial, cultural, and political difference in an accommodationist language that would be legible to its progressive Christian readership.

In many ways, the text synthesizes Bronson's work up to this point. It unequivocally claims Indigenous primacy on the continent, indicts federal paternalism over and surveillance of Native lives (especially regarding reservations and boarding schools), advocates reforms geared around individual and community self-determination, and situates Native peoples as contemporary agents in their own lives and in the United States at large.[91] As with her other work, *Indians Are People, Too* evidences an understanding of the long-term histories that impact contemporary Indian lives and that should inform any efforts at policy reform. In an early passage, which concludes the book's opening historical context, Bronson writes:

> But deeds of such magnitude [past wrongs] cannot be over and done with. They do not stand alone in a period of time. Their tentacles reach out to

> oncoming generations and touch the lives of people who live centuries after the deeds themselves are only echoes in history. I am an Indian, living in the present *now*, but I carry the burden and the responsibility of those distant years. So do you, whether you are Indian or white. The Indian cannot be understood separated from his past, for what has happened to him over the centuries has had its large share in molding the character that is his today. That past shadows every act and thought of his life; it circumscribes his dreams; and, to a large degree, it limits his future. Thus, for the Indian, the past is living history. Only one who understands the forces compelling Indian and white relationships during those early years can comprehend the dilemma of the living Indian in our present time. As for America, it is well that she should remember those dark years lest she allow herself to be lulled once more into forgetfulness of the rights of her people.[92]

Bronson proceeds for the rest of the book to initiate white Christian readers into these histories of violence, dispossession, and marginalization as the basis of her critiques of that history and of policy reform efforts that might legitimately address its legacies. While she would continue to engage in such projects throughout her life, Bronson was increasingly forced by her position as founding member and executive secretary of the National Congress of American Indians (NCAI) and by the organization's efforts to protect the trust relationship with the federal government to couple arguments for civic and political equality with protections for Indian treaty rights and vociferous opposition to divestment and termination policies that threatened them.[93]

By the time Bronson was forty-seven, she had assumed responsibility for virtually all of the NCAI's administrative duties. In addition to managing the organization's Legislative News Service and its Legal Aid and Service Bureau as well as editing its monthly membership letter, the *Bulletin*, she acted as host and lobbyist for tribal delegations visiting the Capitol on business. She also took the lead on NCAI efforts to assist Tlingit and Haida peoples of Alaska in their opposition to industrial development in the Tongass National Forest and efforts by statehood advocates to quickly settle Indian legal claims and extinguish aboriginal title in the territory. Created in 1909, the Tongass National Forest encompassed more than sixteen million acres of Native Alaskan lands, the claims to which remained undefined in both the Alaska Purchase of 1867 and the territorial Organic Act of 1884. From 1909 through 1934 Native Alaskans continually brought suit against the United States for infringing on their land rights. In somewhat of a compromise, provisions in the IRA and the Alaska Reorganization Act (1936) granted the secretary of the interior authority to create reservations from Tongass lands, and hearings were scheduled to determine the extent and legitimacy of aboriginal land claims. Under pressure from paper and pulp interests, however, the claims went unheard, and little progress toward establishing protected reserves occurred. These same interests coalesced in support of the Tongass Timber Act a decade later, which granted the secretaries of agriculture and the interior the authority to lease Native lands and to conduct business without Native consent; profits would be deposited into escrow accounts until legal title to the land was determined. As Thomas Cowger notes, the bill essentially "allowed Congress the authority to extinguish Native title" unilaterally, setting a dangerous precedent for more wide-reaching legislation that was enacted over the next two years.[94]

It was in this context that Bronson delivered the keynote address at the sixty-fourth annual convention of the Indian Rights Association on January 23, 1947, which was later published in the January–April edition of the *Indian Truth.* Titled "Shall We Repeat Indian History in Alaska?," it levies scathing indictments of collusion between the Alaskan territorial government, the BIA, and the fishing and timber industries, and makes a strong emotional appeal to her Indian Rights Association audience to strongly oppose the act that was then under consideration. The stakes, as Bronson understood them, were grave: "If I were to choose one word to portray the spirit of the Indians of southeast Alaska that word would have to be 'despair.' The Indians know they are standing with their backs to a wall, fighting a situation which they see clearly has a single, inevitable ending if help does not come to them soon. That ending is poverty—a property-less, marginal existence on the fringes of dependency so long as they survive as a race."[95] Despised by industrial and territorial interests because of their unique legal status and their claims to resource-rich homelands, Native Alaskans "are being pushed ruthlessly and inexorably lower and lower in the economic scale, not because they are less able, but because they are defenseless under discriminatory laws and practices."[96] In public, Bronson notes, Native Alaskans are popularly disparaged as racially inferior, hopelessly backward impediments to progress and are dismissed as a vanishing race. In private they are ignored and betrayed by the institutions assigned to protect them. Unable to afford independent legal counsel, they are forced to accept representation by BIA lawyers whose primary allegiances rest not with their Native clients but with a federal government and Department of Interior, which are beholden to the very economic and political interests dispossessing them in the first place. Connecting the graft, exploitation, and attempted dispossession of Indigenous lands by timber companies and political insiders to the nineteenth-century dispossession of her own people's resource-rich Indian lands in the Southeast, Bronson characterizes the Tlingit and Haida struggle as the twentieth-century equivalent of a removal crisis. Invoking Helen Hunt Jackson's 1881 exposé of the graft, corruption, and hypocrisy at the center of federal Indian policies, Bronson asks, "Will the decent people of the United States stand idle while another century of dishonor occurs in Alaska?"[97]

Having posed the question, Bronson introduces her audience to the peoples for whom she advocates, emphasizing their own Native industry and capacity to productively adapt non-Indian social, political, and economic practices to their own advantage. Claiming southeastern Alaska as their home from time immemorial, the Tlingit and Haida, as Bronson presents them, are hardly the anachronistic savages or romantic primitives of imperial travel narratives, world's fair exhibitions, Jack London short stories, and imperialist documentaries, but are rather "a fiercely proud and highly competent people."[98] In addition to their unparalleled industry as fishermen, sailors, and craftsmen, many also excel in school and go on to become doctors, lawyers, entrepreneurs, and politicians. In fact, Bronson argues that long-held cultural traditions of trade, negotiation, and competition make southeastern Native Alaskans more adept to succeed and thrive in white society than whites themselves. Further, their adaptation of non-Native organizational structures such as labor unions and strong social organizations such as the Alaska Native Brotherhood and Sisterhood have emerged as political players in territorial politics and as strident protectors of Native Alaskan rights and claims. Expanding on her arguments from "Indian Cooperation," Bronson claims that, given half a chance, Tlingit and Haida peoples "can make their own way and become a solid asset to any country" in addition to their own communities.[99]

Unfortunately for Native Alaskans, all things are not equal and they at present "do not have that half chance."[100] In addition to having business and political interests aligned against them, Tlingit and Haida communities are also subject to intense institutional racism that permeates every aspect of territorial social and political life. Facing widespread discrimination and exclusion, which Bronson explicitly parallels to the Jim Crow South, Native Alaskans face a situation that is "in many respects no better than that of the Negro in the United States."[101] For Bronson, this is most tragically expressed by the pervasive anti-Indian racism of the territorial educational system. Plagued by prejudicial teachers and administrators, anti-Indian curriculum, and scant support from territorial legislators, both government and territorial schools undermine Native Alaskan self-confidence, self-respect, and self-worth, and fail entirely to deliver the tools necessary for students to succeed as fully participating citizens. As a result, many Native Alaskan youth were rejecting their heritage and attempting to pass as whites. "As I got deeper into the Alaska situation," Bronson recalls, "I came to understand this attempted repudiation was in reality a blind effort to escape from an intolerable position."[102]

This position, inculcated through the territorial school system, is compounded by the blatant anti-Indian attitudes of territorial officials toward Native peoples and governmental practices that strip Native Alaskans of resources and opportunities necessary to provide for themselves, their families, and their communities. Despite the fact that Native Alaskans pay taxes equal to their non-Indian neighbors, Bronson documents how territorial officials continue to relegate the responsibility for Alaska Native education to the federal government. Conversely, federal agencies such as the Fish and Wildlife Service and Forest Service consistently privilege industrial fishing, timber, and trapping interests over those of Native Alaskan communities and often fail to enforce regulations and protections that are already in place. Additionally, the Department of Interior and the BIA, under a new administration, suspended hearings to determine the extent of Native Alaskan claims by right of aboriginal occupation, claims that were fundamental to the restoration of adequate land bases from which they derived a sustainable standard of living.

Together with industry-produced propaganda that pit Indian rights as antithetical to territorial interests, such measures all but guarantee the failure of "any move to accord justice to the Indians."[103] Bronson thus recommends a pragmatic, four-point plan that includes the solicitation of financial assistance to help secure independent legal representation and fund court costs; oversight over relationships between the Forest Service, Interior Department, and BIA with big timber and other industries; legislative vigilance and opposition to any measures seeking to reduce Native land holdings; and public pressure by allied non-Indian organizations to reopen hearings and adjudicate Native Alaskan land claims. "Here is a right before us [the Indian Rights Association] that is immediate and urgent," Bronson concludes. "To help in the winning of it will justify all the years of our existence as an organization to protect the rights of a defenseless minority, and it will help to keep our national honor clean. We cannot ignore this responsibility."[104] Only through public opposition to negative measures and open advocacy for Native land claims can organizations like the NCAI and IRA fulfill their missions to protect and empower Native communities.

Harsher in tone and more critical of BIA corruption and institutional racism than her previous writing, "Shall We Repeat Indian History in Alaska?" is Bronson's most comprehensive and critical treatment of federal Indian policy and its effects on Native peoples. Similar to her earlier arguments, Bronson's speech establishes the historical and legal primacy of aboriginal claims to the region and undermines arguments against trust relationships and protections for Native communities as nothing more than rationales for racial discrimination and economic opportunism. She also mobilizes the language of civic and political equality alongside historical parallels to nineteenth-century removals to bolster a moral argument against government corruption, industrial exploitation, and racial prejudice. As in "Cooperation," discourses of Christian charity and moral equity that had defined her early thinking through *Indians Are People, Too* are conspicuously absent, reflecting perhaps a developing commitment to structural and political reform in what was quickly becoming an openly hostile political climate. Bronson thus continues to move away from the abstract pan-Indian generalizations that dominated her early writings and toward more pragmatic and nonsectarian questions of policy, activism, and advocacy as they affect specific tribal communities.

While the immediacy of the speech captures the intensifying stakes in increasingly anti-Indian circumstances, it also reflects Bronson's extensive travels across Native Alaska in which she spent countless hours interviewing Tlingit and Haida community members, listening to and documenting personal stories, and coordinating legal strategies and media campaigns to support the effort. In much the same way that Bronson's personal experiences and relationships affected how she thought about the connection between policy and healthy Indian communities, her extensive firsthand experiences over eight weeks in southeastern Alaska seem to have had a similar effect. Just as social segregation and economic marginalization became facts of life for her grandmother, father, and former students, poverty and dependence were quickly becoming the norm for Tlingit and Haida peoples. However, rather than signaling some racially determined incompatibility with modernity—a longstanding discourse applied specifically to Native Alaskans from at least the 1870s as Shari Huhndorf has extensively documented—Bronson locates such problems in the comprehensive failures of political and social structures. What social dysfunction or economic degradation exists, Bronson demonstrates, has less to do with the historically resilient and highly adaptable Native Alaskans than with systematic land dispossession, government privilege of industrial interests over Indigenous occupancy rights, inequitable legal treatment, and prejudicial educational systems. As in "Cooperation," Bronson continues to move the discussion of the economic, social, and political issues facing Native Alaskan communities further toward explicit critiques of institutional inequity, racial prejudice, structural discrimination, and the moral failure of government agencies to protect the vulnerable against powerful interests intent on securing Tlingit and Haida lands and resources.

Bronson no longer presumes that the integration of Native peoples into U.S. social and economic orders as individual citizens will be easy and problem free. Whereas she previously emphasized caution with respect to global policy reforms of wardship, she now advocates continued, if not intensified, structural protections for Native Alaskans. Perhaps as a consequence of the real threats to their survival and way of life, and as a reflection of the NCAI's commitment to collective tribal rights and trust protections, Bronson here assumes the survival of Tlingit and Haida communities "as a race" as a starting point for any discussion of reform and political action. In a departure from her earlier work, she seeks Indian community survivals and futures as the explicit ends of policy decisions rather than seeing them as evidence of a specific policy's failure. Indian survivals become in this essay viable and worthwhile goals not only of policy but of political activism and advocacy of allied non-Indian groups as well. Considering that absolute assimilation had long been the goal of such organizations and that most still presumed it to be a worthwhile endeavor, Bronson's defense of Indian survivals as both Indians and U.S. citizens delivered to this particular audience constitutes a significant challenge to such positions. The central issue, in this context, becomes not how best to ease Native Alaskans' transition into the Alaskan territorial structure but how best to protect their Indigenous claims to land, resource management, and community self-determination as fundamental components of that transition. Without such protections—all of which are consequences of human action and, as Bronson suggests, the moral imperative of any democratic society—poverty, dependency, and despair are all but inevitable. In the aftermath of the Second World War and the emergence of international human rights discourse, Bronson rightly situates the Tongass crisis as not simply an Indian problem but a fundamental human rights issue. Indeed, by 1947 Bronson had come to understand that individual success and community health were inextricably linked to the continued protections embedded in the trust status and that no real form of self-determination could exist without those protections.

Despite numerous trips to Alaska and massive publicity and lobbying campaigns across Indian Country and the United States, the Tongass Bill became law in August 1947.[105] As many feared, this victory of settler economic and political interests over tribal claims set off a conservative fury bent on dissolving the trust relationship and finally getting the federal government "out of the Indian business." Fueled by a postwar shift in liberalism from cultural pluralism to minority assimilation and a backlash against government expenditures and bureaucratic excess, a consortium of conservative social and political interests began calling for the "emancipation" and "liberation" of Native peoples from government control. The Zimmerman Report of 1947 proposed a three-tiered system to determine which tribal nations were deemed best prepared to enter mainstream society, set out a calendar for termination, and recommended a program to prepare other tribal communities for the same. Intensified efforts culminated in a series of laws passed in 1953, which were highlighted by the now-infamous HCR 108 and PL 280—termination legislation designed explicitly to end the trust relationship with Native peoples, abolish the BIA, and extend state jurisdiction over Indian individuals and lands.[106] Though often framed in the discourses of liberation and cooperation, the unilateral and coercive measures contained in HCR 108 and PL 280 reveal that any semblance of partnership was a ruse.[107] According to NCAI leadership, forced termination "would end federal services without insuring they would be provided by the states; cut off tribal funds, liquidate tribal property; abolish federal protection of Indian land and potentially lead to loss of Indian trust property."[108] Their fears proved to be correct as twelve termination bills affecting tribal nations in New York, California, Florida, and Texas as well as individual tribal communities in other parts of the country were introduced and debated in Congress the next year.[109] Over the next twenty years, more than 1.3 million acres of the Indian estate were lost and an estimated 13,263 Indians from more than sixty-one tribal nations, bands, and communities were terminated.[110]

As termination policies gained momentum on Capitol Hill, Bronson, the NCAI, and a wide array of Native and non-Native advocacy groups publicly opposed any measure that advocated withdrawal, emancipation, or termination without tribal consent and vigilantly challenged any effort to evacuate the tribal estate, abdicate the trust relationship with the federal government, or deny tribal treaty rights. Bronson's experiences advocating for Tlingit and Haida land rights in Alaska afforded her keen insight into the continued significance of tribal sovereignty and trust protections for the health and security of Indigenous communities. Whereas she had once presumed that Native assimilation into American society was the best course of action, she now cultivated a developing commitment to the maintenance of tribal autonomy. This move is evident in an editorial penned in 1955, which intensely criticizes the policies of termination and relocation endorsed by the 83rd Congress.[111]

More confrontational even than her critique of the prejudicial and exploitative conditions in Alaska, this document reveals Bronson's use of a rhetorical ploy that is evident in her earliest writings: appealing to the common sense of average Americans as a veiled means of indicting them for their uninformed ignorance and moral apathy regarding federal Indian policy.[112] Bronson notes that "average Americans" possess two qualities that influence how they think and act toward Native peoples: "sympathy with the underdog" in general and a "romantic sentiment for the American Indian" more specifically. The latter, she argues, is rooted in a "vague sense of guilt for the actions of his forebears in ousting the original inhabitants of the rich land they adopted and for the long and shameful history of broken treaties with these dispossessed," leading *most* Americans into the respectable "tendency toward impulsive action based on a desire to make amends."[113] However, action based on "superficial or inaccurate" misinformation of conditions in Native America or of the aspirations and goals of Native peoples themselves leads to destructive measures like termination and relocation, both of which "jeopardize the Indian's very existence and unquestionably would lead to his eventual—literal—extinction."[114] In a relatively deft rhetorical move, Bronson compliments the well-intentioned desire of Americans to root for the underdog against corporate and government authority in order to disarm her non-Indian audience before challenging sympathetic and unsympathetic readers alike to identify which side of the moral fence they reside on with respect to Indian peoples.

Intensifying this moral play and recalling her framing of the theft of Native Alaskan lands as another removal crisis in the contemporary moment, Bronson's equating of policy decisions with the "eventual—literal—extinction" of Native peoples leverages recent memories of the Nazi holocaust in order to implicate termination legislation in a similar genocide of Native peoples in a post–World War II United States. To bolster this parallel Bronson issues a litany of logical arguments that point at once to the hypocrisy of the rhetoric of benevolence inherent in termination discourse as well as its incompatibility with both American idealism and international treaty law.

She first points out that trusteeship is not a function of federal largesse, but rather is the result of Native cessions of land outlined in peace treaties between sovereign nations. Understanding the "special privileges" that Indians seemingly enjoy as the consequence of treaty deliberations, Bronson informs her readers that "the Indians agreed to end their fighting and cede lands and specific services which the Indians could not provide for themselves and which are provided by the States and local communities for non-Indian citizens."[115] Though undermined by allotment policies, this treaty/trust relationship was reaffirmed, Bronson notes, by the Indian Reorganization Act of 1934: "Consolidating numerous individual treaties that had been effected with Indian tribes over the years, the Indians were granted by this Act the right to exist as distinct communities, with their own properties, culture, and religion, and the promise of certain services to be furnished by the Federal Government."[116] Rejecting arguments that the trust relationship between Indian nations and the federal government frustrates Indian self-determination and economic independence—a position that Bronson and many other Indian intellectuals had argued earlier in the century—she points to the special "status" and "preferential treatment" given to other demographic groups and economic interests expressly for the purposes of empowering them politically and economically. "It is hard to see how benefits make a 'second class' citizen out of an Indian, especially when preferential treatment seems not to jeopardize the status of veterans, farmers, subsidized airlines and steamship companies, manufacturers protected by tariffs, or the businessman with rapid tax write-offs."[117] Recalling the wit and biting criticism of William Apess and anticipating the satirical rhetorical voices of Vine Deloria Jr. and Thomas King decades later, Bronson wryly notes, "It would seem to be our established political philosophy that the economic well-being of particular groups is a legitimate concern of the Federal government—all this aside from the fact that, in the case of the Indians, it is a matter of solemn treaty."[118] She then reframes current efforts moving toward termination not as emancipation from federal paternalism but as a complete abrogation of the terms of agreement between Native peoples and the federal government per the Indian Reorganization Act of 1934. By putting an end to this relationship and the resources it provides tribal peoples, Bronson contends that termination policy would actually undermine efforts to address many of the material, economic, and social circumstances affecting their communities.[119]

Having exposed the motivations behind termination as a not-so-veiled recycling of allotment and assimilation rhetoric from sixty years earlier, Bronson's most powerful critique occurs in her final comments concerning what we would today recognize as principles of free, prior, and informed consent and a commitment to tribal-national cultural integrity and political autonomy. Noting the "haste" with which Congress was pushing through termination legislation with little, if any, concern for "the conditions of individual tribes," Bronson is more importantly angered over the coercive nature of such measures. Paralleling Eaton's similar indictment of the duplicity and coercion that underwrote many Cherokee treaties from the nineteenth century, Bronson writes, "And most of all we are deeply concerned that termination is being decided upon *without the consent*, nay, over the protests, of the Indians concerned. Too often when Indian consent is given it has been obtained by unfair pressures amounting to nothing less than administrative blackmail, as in the case of two tribes which accepted termination bills because they were denied their own funds until they consented. This seems to them a shocking violation of faith."[120] Against such tactics Bronson counsels patience, deliberation, and fact-based studies geared not toward how to most quickly and efficiently end the trust relationship but rather how to substantively and legitimately "attack . . . at the root" the real issues facing many tribal communities: "ill health, lack of educational opportunities, widespread poverty." As in the shift from individual self-reliance to structural critique outlined above, the stakes for Bronson are not simply about alleviating these common human problems, but doing so for the express purpose of keeping tribal communities whole according to their own self-determined aspirations. "Maintenance of the tribal integrity," she writes, "must be assured in any program looking toward [the Indians'] future healthy integration into the American way of life," which is all predicated on the consent of Indian people themselves.[121]

The distinction that she makes here between assimilation and integration is central in understanding the arc of Bronson's work, activism, and politics. If assimilation can be broadly defined as the complete absorption of one group into the dominant cultural, political, and economic lifeways of another, nowhere—and this cannot be stressed enough—nowhere does Bronson argue that the prosperity and survivance of Native peoples is predicated on the political detribalization and cultural absorption of Native communities. While various degrees of acculturation—generally in the context of religion, education, political empowerment, and economic opportunity—may strengthen the abilities of Native communities to address contemporary issues, the central problems facing Native peoples, as Bronson came to understand them, were not cultural in nature but structural and political. Paralleling D'Arcy McNickle's movement from the language of cultural assimilation to that of structural integration—and recalling similar arguments made by nineteenth-century Cherokee statesmen from John Ross, Elias Boudinot, and John Ridge in the Removal era to William Potter Ross, William Penn Adair, William Penn Boudinot, and Dewitt Clinton Duncan during allotment—Bronson argues here for the maintenance of tribal distinctiveness and autonomy.[122] Her insistence on the "maintenance of tribal integrity" is up for neither debate nor accommodation. Rather, this singular goal, and only this singular goal, she argues, should be the basis of any program or legislative policy designed with at least the stated intention of bettering Indian communities.

In this critique, Bronson's thirty-year shift from a politics of individual self-reliance to one of collective and community self-determination—anchored first and foremost to the political autonomy of Native peoples that is embedded in the trust relationship—has come full course. Rather than accommodating Indian people to the social, political, cultural, and economic structures of the settler state, her later work demands that the United States honor the legal and political nation-to-nation relationships upon which any claims to settler sovereignty are based. It is precisely in such language that organizations such as the National Indian Youth Council, the Indians of All Tribes, and the American Indian Movement would anchor their direct-action politics and demands for Indian self-determination in a new decade. Though often lost in official histories of the Red Power era and the American Indian literary renaissance, work from those movements owed more than a small debt to figures like Bronson who had remained diplomatically and politically engaged throughout the previous four decades.

Grassroots Organization, Community Development, and the Intellectual Politics of Diplomacy

Tiring of the internal strife, posturing, and politicking that had begun to define Indian politics, Bronson attended her last NCAI conference in Omaha in September 1954.[123] Though she remained peripherally involved in the organization, she resigned finally from all positions in 1956 at the age of fifty-nine. She left D.C. entirely the next year in order to assume a position as health education specialist for the newly created Indian Health Service in San Carlos, Arizona. Over the next five years Bronson worked with the tribal council and community members to modernize tribal health practices that respected and complemented traditional forms of healing. Her work also involved forming a community advisory committee for Indian Health Service employees residing on the reservation, bringing sanitary plumbing to thirty-five Apache homes, and fostering social and political organization and community solidarity among San Carlos Apache women.

In 1964 Bronson once again retired from government service and relocated with her husband to Tucson, Arizona, but went to work almost immediately as a field representative for Save the Children's American Indian Program. Building on the grassroots community-centered strategies developed at San Carlos, she organized a series of Indian community committees that would define needs, propose programs, solicit financial assistance, and oversee the distribution of community development funds, which became the national model for all of Save the Children's interactions with Indian communities.[124] Such work at the Tohono O'odham reservation south of Tucson allowed the community to construct and repair pasture fences, restore water wells, establish summer ranching education and training programs for teenage boys, and construct a modern community meeting house. Though non-Indian observers often criticized the committees and education programs as slow and inefficient, Bronson consistently defended them as crucial components for Indian community and economic development.

Though she drastically reduced her workload following the death of her husband in 1966, Bronson continued to encourage Indian grassroots activism and opposed federal paternalism in any form as inimical to Indian self-sufficiency and self-determination. The organization that she had helped to found and keep afloat in its tenuous early years recognized her long service on behalf of Indian communities by awarding her the NCAI Citation of Merit at its twenty-fifth anniversary convention in 1969. In 1970, at the age of seventy-two, Bronson attended her last national conference on Indian affairs. Though her activism was severely restricted by a stroke that she suffered two years later, Bronson would keep Indian issues and affairs close to her heart until her death on June 12, 1982, at the age of eighty-four.

In light of this remarkable history, one wonders how a woman like Bronson could have so completely fallen out of twentieth-century Cherokee and American Indian intellectual and political histories. One explanation is undoubtedly linked to issues of accessibility: most of her work is contained in archives, on hard-to-find microfiche sources, or in nonlending special collections scattered throughout the country, making research difficult and expensive due to travel costs. Another explanation might be the centrality of Indian men and the marginalization, if not erasure, of Indian women in nineteenth- and early twentieth-century Indian intellectual, literary, and political histories to which Mankiller refers in the passage opening this chapter. Taken together, we might simply say that the massive recovery efforts that have reintroduced work by Samson Occom, Joseph Johnson, William Apess, John Joseph Mathews, and Todd Downing as well as Pauline Johnson, Alice Callahan, Mourning Dove, Ella Deloria, and others from this still-understudied period have yet to catch up to Bronson. The story I have related here, I hope, will encourage such efforts to bring her work to a wider audience and to invigorate critical interest in this significant figure in both Cherokee history and Indian political activism.

I also believe, however, that the story of Bronson's marginalization signals a more acute problem in Native Studies that continues to impede how we understand writers, texts, and politics from the first half of the twentieth century. Put simply, a field defined by post–Red Power militancy and a nationalist politics of sovereignty and self-determination is hesitant to recover, much less engage, writers and texts that fail to conform to those parameters. However, as Joshua Nelson has recently suggested, it is precisely because of their failure to neatly fit into the models by which we structure and understand the field that we should study them.[125] Doing so not only enriches our understanding of the enormous diversity of thought, opinion, and strategy evident across this period, it also challenges us to more precisely define the stakes, methods, and approaches that we deploy in response to our own circumstances and investments. Figures like Bronson, whose lives and work traverse some of the most contentious moments in twentieth-century Indian history not only complicate the conventional periodicities by which we structure and understand the field (allotment/assimilation, New Deal/accommodation, termination/resistance, self-determination/sovereignty). They also suggest much more continuity across twentieth-century Indian history—both in terms of personalities and philosophies—than has previously been acknowledged.

While Bronson never dispensed with her faith in hard work, determination, self-reliance, and Christian humanist ethics, her diplomatic experience as an official in the BIA and the political battles she fought while at the NCAI forced her to develop a more nuanced understanding of the complex forces that impact the health, security, and prosperity of Indian communities. As this chapter demonstrates, such experiences led her on a decades-long intellectual journey toward a collective politics of self-determination that is capable of accommodating acculturation while maintaining trust protections and self-government for Native peoples. When read within the larger context of American Indian political activism, Bronson's later work reveals not an outdated and outmoded politics that younger militant nationalists necessarily had to break with but the emergence of the very consciousness that they would draw on in years to come. By considering what Indian writers like Bronson had to say about themselves and other Indians as well as white America, we can better appreciate not just how previous generations wrote or spoke back to the non-Indian world but also how they wrote, spoke, organized, lobbied, protested, fought, sang, and danced to and for one another within and across tribal differences. Effecting this critical shift will enrich future recovery projects and critical dialogues, not only by gifting writers like Bronson with the comprehensive and nuanced treatments they deserve, but also by fostering a respectful critical space in which to honestly consider how such work might inform issues facing tribal nations today.

To this point, as a Cherokee scholar I am compelled by Bronson both as a person and as an activist-intellectual. In a climate where we often hear that

Native scholars should put their money—and their bodies—where their mouths are, Bronson did just that for more than fifty years of her life. As with the works of Oskison, Eaton, Riggs, and others from this period, her work does not always sound like we would like it to, and many of the political positions and critical solutions she puts forward will strike contemporary readers as naïve and shortsighted. But she never quit trying to understand her times and how best to put her own individual strengths and resources to work for the Indian students, organizations, and communities she loved. If that meant striking strategic accommodations with federal policy makers, intervening in curriculum development and educational reform, or seeking financial and political support from non-Indian allies, she was willing to do so provided that such choices worked for rather than against Indian people. She cultivated lifelong relationships with non-Indian religious and political organizations capable of influencing Indian affairs, and she insisted always that they consult with Indian communities and develop political platforms geared toward the goals, needs, and desires of those communities. And while willing to play the role of mediator, educator, and spokesperson, Bronson was also capable of levying scathing indictments against hypocrisy, racism, prejudice, and institutional oppression. Though she preferred the white path of peace, respect, negotiation, and accommodation, Bronson proved time and again that she was more than willing to travel the red path of resistance when circumstances demanded it.[126] Accommodation, then, was less a defined political position than a diplomatic strategy predicated on respect, reciprocity, and long-term relationships with Indian communities.

In these and other ways, Bronson is not so different from that Cherokee girl from Adair County with the funny name who, decades later, would travel from her Cherokee home, across the continent, and into political consciousness before returning to a life of service to her people. Though the arc of Bronson's life increasingly took her away from the landscapes and scenes of her youth, like Mankiller she carried her home, history, and fierce pride of nation with her wherever she traveled. That her work was largely targeted at Indian communities outside of the Cherokee Nation should be no surprise to those familiar with Cherokee history. As Joshua Nelson and others have amply demonstrated, diplomacy and tribal-international cultural and political exchange are as deeply embedded in Cherokee traditions as nationalist defenses of borders and boundaries are. In fact, diplomacy is a crucial means by which national communities substantiate claims to political and cultural autonomy and gain recognition within intertribal and international communities. Though marginalized from conventional political histories that situate Cherokee men at the center of such discussions, Cherokee women such as Bronson and Mankiller have always occupied a crucial place as social, cultural, and intellectual mediators, diplomats, and where necessary, critical opponents. Though working within radically different historical circumstances—Bronson's defined by tribal dissolution and termination, Mankiller's by tribal reorganization and self-determination—their efforts to not only build the nation from within but also cultivate relations across difference might legitimately be read within a long gendered tradition of diplomacy and stateswomanship through which Cherokee women continue to hold our families, communities, and nations together.

Looking back on the tenuous early years of the NCAI, former president John Ranier noted that Ruth Muskrat Bronson "was like Washington and Jefferson for us."[127] When read within the narrative of Cherokee diplomacy and stateswomanship that I have suggested here, we might say that Mankiller was like Ruth Muskrat Bronson for us. That Bronson achieved such a reputation working in an era absent a recognized Cherokee government makes her life and accomplishments all the more remarkable and worthy of our attention. To echo Mankiller, we should all long to hear her voice!

Afterword

John Milton Oskison's last published fictional work, *Brothers Three* (1938), chronicles one Cherokee family's struggles, successes, failures, and attempts at redemption on their small farm in the northeast corner of the Cherokee Nation. Unlike his other novels, which are set exclusively in a pre–Oklahoma statehood past, *Brothers Three* follows its Cherokee family from the marriage of Francis Odell and Janet Keith (Cherokee) and the establishment of their farm in 1873 through the financial collapse of the Great Depression. As with *Black Jack Davy*, the novel is firmly situated in recognizable Cherokee geographies and rooted in Cherokee social and political history. A recent arrival to Indian Territory from California, Odell secures, through his marriage to a Cherokee citizen, a lease to land from Janet's father on which they establish the Under-Ridge farm just east of the Verdigris River. As with the Dawes and Keene families, Odell freely accepts tribal jurisdiction and his place as an intermarried noncitizen and flatly resists agitation for territorialization and statehood. His boys are raised on the farm, are educated in Cherokee public schools, participate in local politics, and as citizens receive allotments carved from the Under-Ridge lands. With the exception of Henry, the Odell sons all marry and raise families within driving distance of one another and spend the balance of their lives on or near their allotment land. In this respect, *Brothers Three* is an intensely local narrative of family struggle, survival, and persistence across some of the most chaotic and unstable periods of Cherokee history.

Extending past allotment and statehood well into the twentieth century, the novel also situates the Odell family within the larger currents that transformed

Indian Territory from an isolated geography of Indian republics into an industrialized U.S. state that is increasingly enmeshed in larger national and international affairs. In addition to their negotiations with noncitizen intruders, railroad and industrial interests, and allotment and territorialization agitators, the Odells also contend with agricultural reform groups such as the Grange and the Farmers' Alliance and express concern over how labor movements and the fallout from the Haymarket Riots will affect commodity markets in the North. National economic crises in 1893, 1914, and 1929 similarly threaten the security of the Under-Ridge farm, and the latter forces the Odells to sell vast portions of their interests in order to salvage the family estate. Personal investments by each of the Odell sons in land speculation, banking and mining interests, and commodities and stock trading also threaten, but ultimately fail, to bring down the farm. Whereas descriptions of Klan violence in 1914 situate the text within a context of racial conflict that swept through the South in the 1910s and '20s, Henry's service as one of an unprecedented number of American Indians who fought in World War I demonstrates the increasing impact of international relations on Indian families.

Though it expands the reach of Cherokee history both in terms of historical time and historical context, the narrative arc and central message of the story return to the local as the novel refracts such transformations through the lives of the Odell family members and their relationships to the farm and their land. As with many Cherokees from Oskison's generation, each son possesses a different relationship to the land. Though remaining on the farm well into his late twenties, the eldest son, Timothy, eventually relocates his family to the budding railroad town of Redbud—a stand-in for boomtowns such as Vinita and Claremore—where he opens a neighborhood dry goods store and becomes a land speculator and major shareholder in the local bank. An extremely competitive child of modern agricultural practice, the middle son, Roger, systematically transforms the farm from an intimate family affair into a large industrial producer, extending its economic interests into commodity cattle and mineral speculation. Made restless by his experiences at Stanford and later in the First World War, Henry, the youngest, is drawn to the bright lights and glamor of New York City, becoming a relatively successful writer, socialite, and for a time, stock market investor, a trajectory that parallels much of Oskison's own life.

While their initial successes suggest a largely positive accommodation with modernity, the narrative quickly adopts a cautious attitude; the farther removed their lives are from the farm, the more unstable their lives become. After the railroad goes bust, Redbud dries up, rendering Timothy's investments worthless. Having lost the store, his bank, and his roadster convertible—the material symbol of his wealth and masculinity, a device which is also leveraged for similar purposes in John Joseph Mathews's *Sundown*—Timothy begrudgingly returns to the farm and to his estranged wife, May. Meanwhile, Roger's aggressive expansion and leveraging of the farm's assets brings the Under-Ridge estate to the verge of bankruptcy, and the constant stress and anxiety of his business dealings leave him incapacitated by a stroke that eventually takes his life. Henry, the figure most representative of the promises of geographic, social, and economic mobility, moves from one superficial relationship to another and is consumed by anxious conflict between his ties to home and the allure of city life, which he is never fully able to reconcile. His one attempt to put his education and worldly experience to work for the farm results in economic catastrophe as he watches his monumental returns in the stock market vanish overnight.

Despite these seemingly despondent events, the central message of *Brothers Three* is optimistic. Through ethics of hard work, honest dealing, and modest ambition that she gained from Francis Odell, Timothy's wife, May, recovers the original lands of the Under-Ridge farm and reconciles with her husband. Roger, too, lives out the rest of his life on the family estate and, though silenced by stroke, is able to pass his experiences down to his sons and nephews. Henry also comes home, and it is in his return that the text makes its clearest statement on the relationship between family, home, place, and belonging. Looking out over a fallow field with his nephews, Henry finally realizes what it is about the farm that insistently calls him home:

> Yes [I always come back]. And so will anybody else that belongs to the family as long as the Farm's vital. Buddie and C. F. know it is. Bud and I grew out of its soil. . . . It all comes to this. . . . The Farm's a living organism. It's on starvation rations just now, but we've got to do better by it. It's nourished by the lives that are fed into it. If they're clean and sane and competent, like Pa's and Ma's were, the Farm will flourish. . . . The Farm as we look down on it from here is worth giving ourselves to; it's real and solid still—beautiful![1]

As he stands next to his dead brother's sons and looks out on the farm his mother and father built, Henry sees not fences, barns, cattle, and cotton but the histories and relationships that are forged and continually renewed through the collective labor required to keep the farm healthy and productive. Speaking of the cedar posts put down by their father, Henry notes, "It's cedar, and good for forty-five years more. See, that's what I mean. Pa put down posts that outlasted him, and will outlast us. Someday, of course, they'll decay, but the Farm's owners—your kids and mine perhaps—will have plenty of time to renew them. If Pa's successors build as solidly as he did—why, there's permanence!"[2] As a "living organism," the real strength of the farm lies neither in the composition nor the construction of materials but in the relationships that the farm makes possible. It is this kinship-oriented, labor-intensive, communitist ethic of family and place—"real and solid" and "beautiful"—that calls Henry home and that, ultimately, "is worth giving ourselves to." It is precisely this ethic that sustains the Odell family across historical circumstances, economic crises, political upheaval, dislocation, and personal tragedy. And it will be the foundations of this ethic and the landed relationships to family and place—"put down" by their mother and father, sustained by those like May whom they brought into the family through marriage and kinship, and reset/restored by the brothers upon their various returns—that they will pass down to future generations. The novel ends not with an appeal to wealth, social mobility, material comfort, or other markers of political and economic success, but with an affirmation of a communitist ethic of kinship, place, and the grounded labor required not simply to form relationships but to perpetually cultivate, renew, and restore them.[3]

This ethic also sustains nations. As the survival of Cherokee communities and the contemporary presence of the Cherokee Nation suggest, while the Cherokee national government might well have gone into a period of dormancy following allotment and Oklahoma statehood during the early twentieth century, Cherokee nationhood persisted as Cherokees continued to stoke the fire by cultivating and renewing relationships in a variety of ways. Rural Cherokees adapted kinship practices and innovative community development programs in the early twentieth century to sustain families throughout allotment and to strengthen community self-reliance. Relationships were also cultivated and renewed through religious and spiritual practice. While members of the Nighthawk Keetoowahs perpetuated ceremonial and spiritual life at traditional stomp grounds, Cherokee Christian denominations and the Native American Church offered alternative sites for religious worship, fellowship, and social gathering. Those away at boarding schools, college, and the military similarly organized associations with explicit ties to their home communities as did a host of Cherokees who were forced by economic circumstances to relocate west. By the 1920s and '30s, Cherokee political reorganization, community development, and language revitalization under the Cherokee Executive Council and the Keetoowah Society began to take shape locally, while a host of Cherokees continued to organize under national organizations like the SAI and the NCAI. As scholars are only beginning to discover, what were once presumed to be the cultural and political dark ages of Cherokee history are revealing themselves to be a much more active—if not activist—period of Cherokee cultural and political resurgence.

As I have demonstrated throughout, Oskison, Eaton, Riggs, and Bronson were deeply embedded in this milieu, both in their historical relationships to Cherokee families and communities and in the intellectual and political projects they pursued. Part of a geographically and economically mobile class of Cherokees, they, like other Indians from similar backgrounds, put their knowledge and experiences of Cherokee life to work with their education and professional training to speak back to the dominant culture and to carve out a more productive space for Cherokee peoples.

Trained in literary and historical traditions, Eaton and Oskison mobilize nineteenth-century Cherokee legal and political history to advance stories of Cherokee sovereignty and national survival within popular and academic genres that explicitly work against such narratives. Where these narratives recover the political and legal components of Cherokee nationhood, Riggs's drama reminds us that Cherokee identity and belonging are also negotiated in intensely personal and highly localized ways that exceed political questions of sovereignty and citizenship. In the absence of legal definitions of community and belonging and a functioning state to adjudicate those claims, Cherokees in Riggs's narrative are left to navigate the cultural and experiential fallout of race discourse that touches every aspect of Cherokee life. Combining training in literature, education, and social work, Bronson's activism, diplomacy, and Indigenous transnational stateswomanship reminds us that nationhood depends also on forging alliances outside of the national community as much as it does on cultivating relationships within it. Her geographic movement from the tribal-national to the settler-national and back again, as well as her political movement toward a nation-centered politics of self-determination, also highlights the significance that trans-Indigenous personal relationships to community have for political activism and intellectual work. Together, this body of writing captures much of the diversity and historical complexity of the Cherokee national experience and evidences one arena among many in which ostensibly denationalized Cherokee citizens were working not simply to preserve Cherokee nationhood but to actively stoke it into a new generation.

As Frederick Hoxie writes, due to the generally hostile political and social climates in which they wrote, such negotiations were almost always vexed with compromise and contradiction. Both Eaton's and Oskison's texts reflect such tensions. While their appropriations of the frontier romance and the Indian biography into nineteenth-century Cherokee national contexts subvert both genres' explicit colonialist intentions, the implication of Cherokee legal history within the gendered and racialized histories of settler-state nationalism consigns female, black, and conservative Cherokees to the narrative margins. The maturation of Bronson's politics suggests a similar struggle to mobilize discourses of Christian charity, reformist benevolence, and self-reliance that had often been levied against Native people in service of Indian-centered policy reform. Her gradual movement toward a protoseparatist, oppositional politics of self-determination suggests her inability to fully reconcile the two. And while Riggs undoubtedly intended his modernist drama to be a social critique of racialized thinking and blood politics, his largely non-Indian audiences often found both his formal experimentation and his subject matter difficult to comprehend. Recognizing such limitations in no way dismisses the monumental task these authors were undertaking but rather honors the fact of the effort itself and all that they were able to achieve.

After all, they chose to act. They chose to write. They chose to speak. The words of Henry Odell again come to mind:

> Aside from my writing, who am I, and of what importance to anybody? If there's substance to Henry Odell, it's expressed in his writing. He thinks it's important. He does it honestly, with all the talent he has. Compared to other writers, he may not be significant, but what he does is his own; and he thinks it's grand.[4]

> What's an education for if not to enable one to relate the past to the present, and forecast the future?[5]

Spoken by a character whose life and experience most closely align with the writers studied here, Henry attempts to make sense of the farm's rapid deterioration and to identify his responsibility in its decline. His words express anxieties concerning the relevance of intellectual work to contemporary life and the responsibility of putting one's talents to work for the interests of family and community. Such concerns highlight three assumptions that drive this study: (1) Cherokee writing from this period is important because it evidences the continuing presence of Cherokee nationhood and an active national imaginary in a time when both were popularly assumed to be either defunct or dead; (2) intellectual work from previous generations deserves our attention, sympathy, and respectful consideration not only for what it has to say about the past but also how it might speak to our contemporary moment; and (3) contemporary critical work that critically engages history in order to imagine and bring into being more productive futures can be a powerful resource for informing crucial debates about identity, family, community, belonging, and nation facing our communities today.

Bronson's and Eaton's lives and work, for instance, recover Cherokee female leadership and intellectual traditions that, while perhaps valorized at the local level, are often elided in discussions of Cherokee intellectual and political histories. Resituating them alongside Nanye'hi and Mankiller restores Cherokee women to their rightful place in our national story—something that Eaton herself was unable to do—and enriches our understandings of both the breadth and depth of early twentieth-century Cherokee intellectual production. Riggs and Oskison also have important things to say with respect to contemporary questions of citizenship and belonging. Riggs's critique of the self-destructive imperative embedded in ahistorical discourses of blood can and should be used as a critical lens through which to critique how the racialized, "non-Indian" rhetoric directed at Cherokee freedmen descendants coming from both the Cherokee government and local communities erases the complex, complicated, and often violent interracial history of Cherokee-black relations. Likewise, Oskison's inscription of a politically strong, explicitly multicultural Cherokee state rooted in a concept of citizenship based on political commitment, relationality, and reciprocal sacrifice similarly counters contemporary reckonings of citizenship and belonging that are based on rigid qualifications of direct, lineal descent tied to government rolls and federal blood quantum cards. Read together, they pose serious challenges to contemporary political and legal efforts that claim racism as an act of sovereignty or marshal prejudice in the name of self-determination. Considering the social condemnation and legal attacks to Cherokee sovereignty that such moves provoked within Indian Country and across the United States, Bronson's life's work on behalf of other Indian communities emphasizes the continuing necessity of intertribal diplomacy, extratribal alliance, and broad-based coalition building in efforts to protect, strengthen, and expand Cherokee sovereignty and self-determination.

If intellectual sovereignty is the process by which Native peoples negotiate what it means to be Indian in a given historical moment and in doing so find out "what possibilities traditions open up for finding a way to relate to the world of which we are a part," we have to read Cherokee writers from this period as attempting to imagine and write their way into such possibilities from the complicated realities of their own times.[6] As significant as these writers are to both Cherokee and American Indian literary and intellectual histories, it is important to note that their work represents only a fraction of a much more diverse, expansive, and understudied body of Cherokee writing from this period. From the historical sketches, commentaries, and creative writings of Mabel Washbourne Anderson and Ora Eddleman Reed to the legal decisions, political writings, and correspondences of political figures such as J. B. Milam and N. B. Johnson, to further study of popular figures such as Henry Starr and Will Rogers, to all of those waiting to be rediscovered and brought back into the conversation, we have only begun to scratch the surface of what is out there. Put simply, there is plenty of good work the remains to be done.

Reclaiming this work from the dark ages of poststatehood ambivalence and loss is about much more than recovering a long-neglected archive of Cherokee literary, intellectual, and political thought, however. More importantly, it is about putting that archive to work in contemporary debates over history, identity, family, community, and belonging—that is, nationhood—even if we ultimately fail to subscribe to the visions or buy into the conclusions that emerge from it. For, what writing from this period most importantly reminds us is that nationhood persists not only through the political and administrative mechanisms of the Cherokee state but through the lives we live, the stories we tell, and the relationships we maintain with one another, with other Indian peoples, and with the non-Indian world. The Cherokee Nation that many of us now enjoy exists in no small part because Cherokees like those studied here—as well as countless others who will never find their way into the history books—refused to let it pass quietly away. For that they deserve our attention, honor, admiration, and respect not only for how they responded to their own circumstances but also for what their lives and work might teach us about—to paraphrase one of Riggs's characters—who we are, how we got here, what we're doing here, and where we're going. Living through a period of profound uncertainty and change, these writers remind us that there may be no more-important questions to ask—and to continue asking over and over again—in order to continue stoking the fires of Cherokee nationhood in our own moment and for generations to come.

Notes

Preface

1. Due to health concerns, Chief Mankiller was unable to attend the symposium.
2. For a similar formulation, see Teuton, *Cherokee Stories*, 84–89.
3. Royce, *The Cherokee Nation*, 129–371; T. Wilkins, *Cherokee Tragedy*; Woodward, *The Cherokees*; Ehle, *Trail of Tears*; McLoughlin, *Cherokee Renascence*; Oliphant, *Peace and War*; Perdue and Green, *Cherokee Removal*; Perdue and Green, *The Cherokee Nation*.
4. Confer, *The Cherokee Nation*; McLoughlin, *After the Trail of Tears*. Work in Cherokee-Black Studies is also crucial in understanding the racial politics of Cherokee nationhood during this time. Cf. Halliburton, *Red over Black*; Perdue, *Slavery*; Minges, *Slavery in the Cherokee Nation*; Miles, *Ties That Bind*; Miles, *The House on Diamond Hill*; Yarbrough, *Race and the Cherokee Nation*; Naylor, *African Cherokees in Indian Territory*.
5. Wardell, *A Political History*; Denson, *Demanding the Cherokee Nation*; Stremlau, *Sustaining the Cherokee Family*; Parins, *Literacy and Intellectual Life*.
6. Mankiller and Wallis, *Mankiller*; Sturm, *Blood Politics*; Sturm, *Becoming Indian*; Wahrhaftig, "In the Aftermath of Civilization."
7. Published works include Carroll, *Roots of Our Renewal*, 78–98; Cushman, *The Cherokee Syllabary*, 138–78; Justice, *Our Fire Survives the Storm*, chap. 3; Conley, *The Cherokee Nation*, chaps. 24–26; R. Strickland and W. Strickland, "Beyond the Trail of Tears." Unpublished dissertations include Hochtritt, "Rural Cherokees, Chickasaws, Choctaws"; Wynn, "The Embodiment of Citizenship."
8. Cf. Justice, *Our Fire Survives the Storm*; Stremlau, *Sustaining the Cherokee Family*; Parins, *Literacy and Intellectual Life*; Nelson, *Progressive Traditions*. See also Carney, *Eastern Band Cherokee Women*.
9. For framings of the period as an ambivalent, uneasy "endurance," see Justice, *Our Fire Survives the Storm*. For examples of continuity structured through elision, see Carney, *Eastern Band Cherokee Women*; Nelson, *Progressive Traditions*; Parins, *Literacy and Intellectual Life*.

10. Craig Womack notes a similar pattern at work in historical texts on Creek literature. Womack, *Red on Red*, 28.
11. Meredith, *Bartley Milam*, iii–iv.
12. Many Cherokees fled Indian Territory, north to Kansas and south to Texas, to avoid the catastrophic devastation and internal factionalism that were visited on the territory during the Civil War. See McLoughlin, *After the Trail of Tears*; Confer, *The Cherokee Nation*; Dale and Litton, *Cherokee Cavaliers*.
13. According to Howard Meredith, Milam sought to unite competing Cherokee factions under a locally organized political structure; led efforts to resist tribal reorganization under the corporate model and BIA oversight of the Oklahoma Indian Welfare Act; worked to purchase and place Cherokee lands back into federal trust; and developed plans for the Cherokee Historical Society and Cherokee Heritage Center in Park Hill on the site of the former female seminary. Meredith, *Bartley Milam*. See also Mankiller and Wallis, *Mankiller*, 177–78; Sturm, *Blood Politics*, 90–91; Conley, *The Cherokee Nation*, 205–14; Carroll, *Roots of Our Renewal*, 90–91, 95.
14. See Conley, *The Cherokee Nation*, 205–14; Carroll, *Roots of Our Renewal*, 90–91, 95.
15. Historians, ethnographers, and bureaucrats include historians Grant Foreman, Howard Meredith, and Muriel Wright; Salish and Kootenai scholar and activist D'Arcy McNickle; Cherokee ethnologists Jack Kilpatrick and Anna Kilpatrick; officials with the National Congress of American Indians; and administrators at Chilocco, Haskell, and other federally operated boarding schools.
16. Cherokee writings include Catherine Brown's memoir, papers by John Ross and Elias Boudinot, two biographies and a novel by John Oskison, a biographical history of John Ross by Rachel Caroline Eaton, Cherokee and English editions of the Gospel of John, and sympathetic firsthand accounts of nineteenth-century Cherokee life and Removal by John Howard Payne and Henry Timberlake. Other holdings include poetry by Creek writer Alexander Posey, naturalist histories by Osage writer John Joseph Mathews (such as *Wah-Kon-Tah: The Osage and the White Man's Road* and *Talking to the Moon*), a popular tourist's guide to Oklahoma that was coedited by John Oskison and Angie Debo, and multiple volumes by Oklahoma historians including Angie Debo, Grant Foreman, Muriel Wright, and E. Everett Dale.
17. Reformists include Helen Hunt Jackson, Elaine Goodall Eastman, Francis Leupp, John Collier, and Oliver LaFarge. Milam's academic holdings count George Bancroft, Francis Parkman, and Walter Prescott Webb; G. E. E. Lindquist and Arthur Schlesinger; Henry Rowe Schoolcraft, Lewis Henry Morgan, James Mooney, Ruth Underhill, and Frances Densmore; and Paul Radin and J. Frank Dobie as influences.
18. Among such materials are catalogs from the Newberry Library at the University of Chicago, the Museum of the American Indian in New York, the Gilcrease Museum of Western History in Tulsa, and the Etowah papers at Phillips Academy. Multiple sources relating to the histories of Mexico and Texas also evidence Milam's interest in Cherokees' relationships with their neighbors to the south, especially having to

do with Cherokee emigrations to Texas in the 1810s, after the Removal, and during the Civil War; Cherokee plans for emigration to Mexico in the late nineteenth century as a strategic response to allotment; and Sequoyah's legendary mission to locate Cherokee relatives in Mexico earlier in the century.

19. For a tribally specific reading of Rogers's life and work, see Ware, *The Cherokee Kid.*
20. Cf. J. Kilpatrick and A. Kilpatrick, *Friends of Thunder*, 123; Justice, *Our Fire Survives the Storm*, 119–32; Ware, *The Cherokee Kid*, 132–44.
21. As Ware shows, the silent film *Two Wagons, Both Covered* (1924) frames nefarious banking practices leading to white dispossession as being akin to the federal duplicity and dispossession of Indians during the previous century.
22. See Justice, *Our Fire Survives the Storm*, 119–32; Ware, *The Cherokee Kid*, 132–44. For a regionalist take on Rogers's work and an incisive reading of his complicated racial politics, see Foster, "Of One Blood," 265–302.

Introduction

1. Cf. Wilkins and Stark, *American Indian Politics*, 33–38, 47. See also D. Wilkins, *American Indian Sovereignty*, 4, 29; Deloria and Wilkins, *Tribes, Treaties, and Constitutional Tribulations*, 7, 13–20, 70; Deloria and Lytle, *American Indians, American Justice*, 3.
2. Cf. Holm, Pearson, and Chavis. "Peoplehood," 7–24; Justice, *Our Fire Survives the Storm*; Corntassel, "Who Is Indigenous?," 75–100.
3. Cf. Womack, *Red on Red*; Konkle, *Writing Indian Nations*; Lyons, "Rhetorical Sovereignty," 447–68; Lyons, *X-Marks.*
4. Cf. Alfred, *Peace, Power, Righteousness*; Alfred, *Wasáse*; Coulthard, *Red Skin, White Masks.*
5. Cook-Lynn, *Why I Can't Read Wallace Stegner*, 31, 89, 91.
6. Womack, *Red on Red*, 26, 14.
7. Justice, *Our Fire Survives the Storm*, 206; Brooks, "The Constitution," 57–59.
8. Doerfler, *Those Who Belong*, ix, x.
9. Weaver, *That the People Might Live*, 42.
10. Lyons, *X-Marks*; Konkle, *Writing Indian Nations*; Andersen, "Indigenous Nationhood," 180–98.
11. Deloria and Lytle, *American Indians, American Justice*, 8; Lyons, "Rhetorical Sovereignty," 454–55. See also Alfred, *Peace, Power, Righteousness.*
12. Cook-Lynn, *Why I Can't Read Wallace Stegner*, 89–91; Justice, *Our Fire Survives the Storm*, 24, 215.
13. Brooks, in Weaver, Womack, and Warrior, *American Indian Literary Nationalism*, 229; Brooks, *The Common Pot*, xxii.
14. Carroll, *Roots of Our Renewal*, 81.
15. Lyons, *X-Marks*, 132–60.

16. Weaver, "More Light Than Heat," 249.
17. Cf. Konkle, *Writing Indian Nations*; Lyons, "Rhetorical Sovereignty"; Bruyneel, *The Third Space of Sovereignty*; Rifkin, *Manifesting America*; Rifkin, "Making Peoples into Populations," 149–87; Byrd, *The Transit of Empire*; Moreton-Robinson, *The White Possessive.*
18. Burton, *Indian Territory*, 142; Prucha, *The Great White Father*, 255–56. For an examination of the various strategies that Cherokees and other Five Tribes nations deployed to resist territorialization, see Denson, *Demanding the Cherokee Nation.*
19. Bruyneel, *The Third Space of Sovereignty*, 27–64.
20. Debo, *And Still the Waters Run*, 91.
21. Conley, *The Cherokee Nation*, 204.
22. Mankiller and Wallis, *Mankiller*, 62–74; Conley, *The Cherokee Nation*, 208. See also Smithers, *Cherokee Diaspora.*
23. Teuton, *Cherokee Stories*, 85.
24. Wright, "Rachel Caroline Eaton," 509–10.
25. Harvey, "Cherokee and American," 116–96.
26. Weaver, foreword to *The Cherokee Night and Other Plays*, ix–xv.
27. P. Deloria, *Indians in Unexpected Places.*
28. For different versions and discussions of Cherokee migration narratives, see Mooney, *History, Myths, and Sacred Formulas*, 428–29; Meredith, *The Cherokee Vision of Elohi*; Conley, *The Cherokee Nation*, 5–6; Justice, *Our Fire Survives the Storm*, 49–52; Teuton, *Cherokee Stories*, 56–59.
29. For the most recent critical treatment of Rogers's life and work, see Ware, *The Cherokee Kid.*
30. Teuton, *Cherokee Stories*, 83.
31. Stremlau, *Sustaining the Cherokee Family.*
32. Nelson, *Progressive Traditions.* See also Conley, *The Cherokee Nation*, 196–202; Mankiller and Wallis, *Mankiller*, 169–71.
33. Cushman, *The Cherokee Syllabary*, 165–72.
34. Carroll, *Roots of Our Renewal*, 78–98.
35. Mankiller and Wallis, *Mankiller*, 176–80; Conley, *The Cherokee Nation*, 203–12; Sturm, *Blood Politics*, 90–94. Though in one sense the Cherokee Executive Council was a "legal fiction" made necessary by the establishment of the Indian Claims Commission in 1948, and significant tensions remained with local communities and with the Oklahoma Indian Welfare Act–incorporated United Keetoowah Band, it nonetheless represented the first steps in the return to Cherokee constitutional self-governance by the early 1970s.
36. Justice, *Our Fire Survives the Storm*; Parins, *Literacy and Intellectual Life*; Ware, *The Cherokee Kid*; Smithers, *Cherokee Diaspora.*
37. Mankiller and Wallis, *Mankiller*, 167.
38. Green, "The Pocahontas Perplex," 698–714; P. Allen, *The Sacred Hoop*, 222–24. For an early critique that anticipates contemporary work concerning the representation of Indigenous women, see Johnson, "A Strong Race Opinion." For further studies

on how Indigenous female images were used in the service of colonialism and revolution, see Jaimes and Halsey, "American Indian Women"; P. Deloria, *Playing Indian*, chap. 1. See also Rhea, *A Field of Their Own.*

39. Theda Perdue's *Cherokee Women* ends in 1835 with the lead-up to Removal, while Carolyn Johnston's *Cherokee Women in Crisis* and Karen Kilcup's edited volume *A Cherokee Woman's America* both culminate with the impending devastation of Oklahoma statehood. Cherokee women are entirely absent from Denson's study, only tangentially mentioned in Parins's recent work on Cherokee literary and intellectual life, and rarely appear as anything other than peripheral figures in conventional political or social histories.
40. Perdue, *Cherokee Women*; Johnston, *Cherokee Women in Crisis.*
41. Carney, *Eastern Band Cherokee Women*, 4.
42. Parker, *Changing Is Not Vanishing*; Kilcup, *Native American Women's Writing*; Parins, *Literacy and Intellectual Life.*
43. Hill, *Weaving New Worlds.*
44. Shoemaker, *Negotiators of Change.*
45. Cf. P. Allen, *The Sacred Hoop*, 263–64; Mihesuah, *Indigenous American Women*; Huhndorf, introduction to *Mapping the Americas*; Suzack and Huhndorf, introduction to *Indigenous Women and Feminism*; Arvin, Tuck, and Morrill, "Decolonizing Feminism."
46. Cf. Justice, *Our Fire Survives the Storm*, xv–xvi, 20; Nelson, *Progressive Traditions*, 120–23, 165–200; Stremlau, *Sustaining the Cherokee Family*, 109, 148; Parins, *Literacy and Intellectual Life*, 190–217.
47. Cf. Stremlau, *Sustaining the Cherokee Family*, 19, 39. See also Julia Coates, "'This Sovereignty Thing,'" 124–50.
48. Womack, *Red on Red*, 235.
49. Goeman, *Mark My Words*, 125.
50. Womack, "The Integrity of American Indian Claims," 127, 169.
51. Foster, "Of One Blood," 270, 272.
52. Brooks, *The Common Pot*, 244.
53. Doerfler, *Those Who Belong*, xxxi, xxxiii; Lyons, *X-Marks*, xii.
54. Bauerkemper and Stark, "The Trans/National Terrain," 3–5.
55. Ibid., 11–12.
56. Foster, "'Of One Blood,'" 278.
57. Bauerkemper, "Indigenous Trans/Nationalism," 400.
58. Weaver, *That the People Might Live*, ix, 41; Warrior, *The People and the Word*, xix; Justice, "Indigenous Writing," 291–307.
59. Weaver, *That the People Might Live*, xii.
60. Weaver, *The Red Atlantic*; Parker, *The Invention of Native American Literature*, viii; Cox, *The Red Land to the South*, 23–25; Teuton, *Deep Waters*, 1–52; Brooks, "The Constitution," 48–76.
61. In *The Search for an American Indian Identity*, Hazel W. Hertzberg views SAI politics as the search for a new form of collective identity that would allow Native

peoples to enter modernity as both Indian and American. Robert Warrior defines their broadly "integrationist" project as an attempt to "[put] the best face on the violent realities" of allotment and assimilation. Warrior, *Tribal Secrets*, 14. Lucy Maddox locates the SAI's focus primarily on "pan-Indian issues . . . arising from the wardship status of Indians." Maddox, *Citizen Indians*, 6–7.

62. For treatments of writing from this period as decidedly nonnational, see Larson, *American Indian Fiction*, 10–11, 37, 169; P. Allen, *The Sacred Hoop*; Owens, *Other Destinies*, 24–25, 40–89.
63. Warrior, *Tribal Secrets*; Cook-Lynn, *Why I Can't Read Wallace Stegner*; Weaver, *That the People Might Live*; Womack, *Red on Red*; Weaver et al., *American Indian Literary Nationalism*; Brooks, *The Common Pot*. See also Konkle, *Writing Indian Nations*.
64. Cox, *The Red Land to the South*, 8–9. Cf. Warrior, *Tribal Secrets*, 5–14; Weaver, *That the People Might Live*, 86–120; Womack, *Red on Red*, 6; Justice, *Our Fire Survives the Storm*, 16; Sean Teuton, *Red Land, Red Power*, 165–67.
65. Justice, *Our Fire Survives the Storm*.
66. Hoxie, *Talking Back to Civilization*; C. Allen, *Blood Narrative*; Powell, "Rhetorics of Survivance," 386–434; Maddox, *Citizen Indians*.
67. Holm, *The Great Confusion*, 58, 64; Cornell, *The Return of the Native*, 115–18. See also Hertzberg, *The Search for an American Indian Identity*; Warrior, *Tribal Secrets*; Maddox, *Citizen Indians*; Martínez, *The American Indian Intellectual Tradition*; and Hoxie, *Talking Back to Civilization*. Despite these larger goals, the SAI eventually dissolved in 1922 because of significant tensions over non-Indian membership, the organization's relationship with the Office of Indian Affairs, its support for universal U.S. citizenship, its opposition to peyote, and its inability to meet the specific demands of tribal communities.
68. Lyons, "Rhetorical Sovereignty," 458.
69. Here I borrow Maureen Konkle's reading of William Apess's production of counterhistory and political presence by interpellating "Euroamerican history *through* Native experience." Konkle, *Writing Indian Nations*, 105 (emphasis added). For Native intellectual engagements with and translations of dominant discourses, see also Turner, *This Is Not a Peace Pipe*.
70. P. Deloria, *Indians in Unexpected Places*; Troutman, *Indian Blues*; Ware, *The Cherokee Kid*; Bold, "'Aboriginally Yours.'"
71. Huhndorf, *Mapping the Americas*; Cox, *Red Land to the South*; Piatote, *Domestic Subjects*; Piatote and Allen, *The Society of American Indians*.
72. Martínez, *The American Indian Intellectual Tradition*; Cobb, *Say We Are Nations*. See also Cobb and Fowler, *Beyond Red Power*.
73. Lyons understands an "X-mark" to be an Indigenous accession to modernity under conditions of coercion but with the hope that something new and even good might result. Lyons, *X-Marks*, 40, 70, 169.
74. Konkle, *Writing Indian Nations*, 105.

Chapter 1

For the Cherokee Constitution, see Cherokee Nation, *Constitution and Laws of the Cherokee Nation*. All subsequent references to Cherokee constitutions and Cherokee laws are from this series, hereafter cited as *LCN* followed by date and page number.

1. Rennard Strickland writes, "The Cherokee legal system did not spring forth as a mature instrument. The historical development of Cherokee law ways illustrates the process of gradual evolution building upon existing social institutions. That the Cherokees pursued slow and systematic adaptation is . . . a tribute to the wisdom of tribal leadership. For, in this way, the early and less sophisticated procedures of the tribal regulators and light-horsemen built a firm foundation for the more complex written constitution and tribal courts." R. Strickland, *Fire and the Spirits*, 72.
2. In her essay on Indigenous constitutional traditions, Lisa Brooks notes, "Constitutional literature often emerges during a period of transition, during which 'the people' are undergoing a significant transformation, when there is a pressing need for consolidation and unification, and a strong desire for the articulation and formation of principles that can chart the course of the emerging or changing nation." Brooks, "The Constitution," 55. For an in-depth study of how Cherokees mobilized discourses of nationhood, constitutionalism, and civilization throughout the nineteenth century to maintain political autonomy, see Denson, *Demanding the Cherokee Nation*, 28–51. For nineteenth-century assaults on Indian sovereignty in Indian Territory, see Debo, *And Still the Waters Run*; Carter, *The Dawes Commission*.
3. Tribal dissolution was accomplished legally through unilateral federal legislation, beginning with the General Allotment Act of 1887, the Curtis Act of 1898, the Burke Act of 1906, and the Oklahoma Act of Union in 1907. While the Cherokee Nation did not reorganize under the Oklahoma Indian Welfare Act of 1936, the United Keetoowah Band did in 1950. The Eastern Band of the Cherokee Nation continues to operate under its 1889 North Carolina state charter and never officially reorganized under the Indian Reorganization Act of 1934.
4. Other important revisions include clearly identifying citizenship criteria (art. 4) and refiguring the Judicial Appeals Tribunal as the Cherokee Supreme Court (art. 8). For the most recent version of the constitution, see www.cherokee.org/Portals/0/Documents/2011/4/308011999-2003-CN-CONSTITUTION.pdf.
5. I do not mean to suggest here that the Nation is the horizon of experience and identity for all Cherokee people. In fact, for some, filiation to a family or clan and affiliation with specific civil and spiritual communities constitute primary sources of community and individual identity. See Sturm, *Blood Politics*, 108–200; Stremlau, *Sustaining the Cherokee Family*.
6. Oskison's elder brother, William, was born in 1872, while his younger brother, Richard, arrived two years after John's birth, in 1876. He had another half-brother born to John Oskison and his second wife after Rachel died and a half-sister by Rachel from a previous marriage.

7. California has always held an interesting place in Cherokee history. Such experience would be captured by Cherokee journalist and novelist John Rollin Ridge in his own journeys through the region in the 1850s and '60s. They would also be explored in essays by John Oskison Jr. and his contemporary Mabel Washbourne Anderson later in the century.
8. In his autobiography Oskison writes of his trip to the Chicago World's Fair with Rogers and other classmates. Whereas Oskison recounts "riding the rails" to the fair, Rogers remembers accompanying his father on a business trip. An inscription to Will Rogers from Oskison's 1935 novel *Brothers Three* reads, "For Will Rogers—in memory of our school days together at Willie Halsell, and of a period in the old Indian Territory that we both knew and, I hope, loved. Cordially—*as one Cherokee to another*—yours" (emphasis added). Looking back at his time at Willie Halsell, Rogers remarked of Oskison with characteristic humor, "I believe that John Oskison was the only one we really got educated, but they taught a lot of 'em to go out and lead fine useful lives to their communities." Rogers, *The Papers of Will Rogers*, 1:109. For a tribally specific study of Will Rogers's life and work, see Ware, *The Cherokee Kid*.
9. Throughout his decade-long association with the group, Oskison served as assistant editor of its quarterly magazine and as executive secretary.
10. Hertzberg, *The Search*, 189.
11. *Wild Harvest: A Novel of Transition Days in Oklahoma* (1925), *Black Jack Davy* (1926), *A Texas Titan: The Story of Sam Houston* (1929), *Brothers Three* (1935), *Tecumseh and His Times: The Story of a Great Indian* (1938), *Oklahoma: A Guide to the Sooner State* (1941). A collection of traditional stories, which Oskison compiled from notes collected during an extensive trip throughout the Southwest and across Indian Territory in 1914, was later published by Jack Gregory and Rennard Strickland under the title *American Indian Spirit Tales* (1974). According to archival information obtained from the J. B. Milam Papers at the University of Tulsa's McFarlin Library, Oskison penned two other novels, *Vision Victorious* (1931) and *The Lone Rider* (1933), both of which apparently went unpublished. As of this printing, I have been unable to gain any further information about these manuscripts.
12. Though living for most of his adult life in New York City, Oskison maintained strong connections to Oklahoma and his Cherokee relations. He remained close to his mother's Cherokee-speaking family through a maternal aunt, Betsy, and two cousins, Liza and Jennie, who appear as characters in the short story "The Problem of Old Harjo." Additionally Oskison served on civic committees for the Vinita Pioneer Days Festival and for Willie Halsell College, and he consulted on six murals memorializing Cherokee history that were installed at the Vinita post office in 1941.
13. Lionel Larré recently published Oskison's unfinished memoir and a collection of his short fiction and political editorials and is set to publish the biography of John Ross, both with University of Nebraska Press. Oskison, *Tales of the Old Indian Territory*.

14. L. Anderson, "Obituary."
15. Holm, *The Great Confusion.*
16. Larson, *American Indian Fiction*, 36, 51, 63.
17. A. Strickland, "John Milton Oskison," 126; Widget, *Native American Literature*, 66, 73–74; Oaks, "The First Generation," 57–65; Peyer, *The Tutor'd Mind*, 278–95; Whitson, "John Milton Oskison," 178–79.
18. P. Allen, *The Sacred Hoop*, 76–77; Ruoff, "Pre-1968 Fiction," 161–73; Ruoff, "Native American Writing," 152; Ruoff, *American Indian Literatures*, 71.
19. Warrior, *Tribal Secrets*, 21; Womack, *Red on Red*, 306.
20. Weaver, foreword to *The Singing Bird*, xi, xii. See also Whitson, "*Wild Harvest*," 249–50.
21. Nelson, "Keeping Oklahoma Indian Territory," 638.
22. Ronnow, "John Milton Oskison," 83.
23. Mullikin and Powell, introduction to Oskison, *The Singing Bird*, xxi.
24. Justice, *Our Fire Survives the Storm*, 108–19.
25. Cox, "Learn to Talk Yaqui,'" 400–421; Nelson, "Keeping Oklahoma Indian Territory"; Hudson, "Domesticated Species," 80–108; Hunnef, "Outlaws and Nation-Making."
26. Littlefield and Parins, "Short Fiction Writers," 23–38. For the most thorough treatment of these dynamics, see Justice, *Our Fire Survives the Storm*; Nelson, "Keeping Oklahoma Indian Territory."
27. Womack, *Red on Red*, 40, 49.
28. Warrior, *People and the Word*, 51.
29. Ibid., 53.
30. Brooks, "The Constitution," 53, 50.
31. Lyons, *X-Marks*, 188; Doerfler, *Those Who Belong*, ix, x; Stark, "Marked by Fire," 125.
32. Brennan, "The National Longing for Form," 49.
33. Renan, "What Is a Nation?," 11.
34. Bruyneel, "The Trouble with Amnesia"; Bruyneel, "Codename Geronimo," 349–64.
35. For studies on the American historical romance, see Bell, *Hawthorne and the Historical Romance*; Henderson, *Versions of the Past*; Dekker, *The American Historical Romance*; S. Frye, *Historiography and Narrative Design*; Hughes, *The Historical Romance.*
36. Henderson, *Versions of the Past*, 9; S. Frye, *Historiography and Narrative Design*, 8.
37. Here I draw on the work of Edward Said and Stuart Hall concerning the processes by which discourse and ideology frame common-sense understandings of the world. See Hall, "Culture, the Media"; Said, introduction to *Orientalism.*
38. Critical work on the relationship between space, epistemology, and narrative are crucial to my understanding of the cultural work that frontier romances perform to consolidate settler-state hegemony in U.S. popular culture and to the significance

of Oskison's intervention in the genre. Cf. Certeau, *The Practice of Everyday Life*; Trouillot, *Global Transformations*, 117–140; Soja, *Postmodern Geographies*. Within Native American and Indigenous Studies, see Rifkin, *Manifesting America*; Goeman, *Mark My Words*.

39. Cf. Berkhofer, *The White Man's Indian*; Pearce, *Savagism and Civilization*; H. Smith, *Virgin Land*; Drinnon, *Facing West*; Huhndorf, *Going Native*.
40. In his foundational study on the topic, Henry Nash Smith illustrates how in the early literature of the colonies, the American West is depicted as a moral and materially threatening "Devil's Den" of sin and depravity. H. Smith, *Virgin Land*, 4. Partially due to anxieties that savage environments would encourage cultural regression and partially due to the practical realities of British colonial interest, settlement of the interior—and thus its imaginative construction as a desirable location—was virtually ignored. With American independence, however, the wilderness was gradually transformed into the western frontier, an idealized imagined space of freedom, liberty, and plenty—what Smith refers to as the myth of the garden—where opportunity abounds and social hierarchies are abolished (at least for whites) for those enterprising pioneers willing to take up the Puritan-cum-bootstrap ethic.
41. Ibid., 130.
42. Lawlor, *Recalling the Wild*, 2; Slotkin, *Regeneration through Violence*.
43. LeMenager, *Manifest and Other Destinies*, 4.
44. Cf. Bruyneel, *The Third Space*; Rifkin, *Manifesting America*; Goeman, *Mark My Words*.
45. Konkle, *Writing Indian Nations*, 6.
46. Hughes, *The Historical Romance*, 6.
47. Cox, *Muting White Noise*, 208, 249.
48. See also Lawlor, *Recalling the Wild*, 131; S. Frye, *Historiography and Narrative Design*, 8.
49. LeMenager, *Manifest and Other Destinies*, 4, 5.
50. Ibid., 5–6.
51. Oskison, *Black Jack Davy*, 1.
52. Cox, "Tribal Nations," 359–60.
53. Littlefield and Parins, "Short Fiction Writers," 36.
54. See R. Strickland, *Fire and the Spirits*, 51. McLoughlin draws similar conclusions, noting, "Nationalism among the Cherokees, as well as the demand for sovereignty (self-government under their own laws and chiefs and with communal ownership of land guaranteed by the federal government), was in part an effort to use the European concept of nationhood to defend their freedom and their land base." McLoughlin, *After the Trail of Tears*, 6.
55. The 1827 constitution refers to previous treaties with the United States that define the boundaries of the Nation in the east, including cessions by western emigrants that were concluded in 1817 and 1819. As a post-Removal document, the 1839 constitution refers to the Treaty of 1833 with the Western Cherokees, which clearly

defines the land holdings of the Nation in northeast Indian Territory, the Cherokee Strip, the Cherokee Outlet, and "neutral lands" in Kansas, which were exchanged for Cherokee lands in Arkansas. The strip and neutral lands were subsequently ceded in the Treaty of 1866, and the boundaries of the Nation outlined in the 1839 constitution were amended accordingly. Interestingly, the 1839 constitution omits the language of sovereignty and jurisdiction, perhaps because intrusion by whites was at this time less intensive than it had been in Georgia or than it would become in subsequent decades.

56. *LCN*, 1839, secs. 1, 2, 118–19.
57. *LCN*, 1839, 119. This section of the constitution of 1839 is virtually identical to the 1827 document.
58. McLoughlin, *Cherokee Renascence*, 163.
59. For an in-depth study of how Cherokees mobilized such arguments and strategies throughout the nineteenth century, see Denson, *Demanding the Cherokee Nation*, 28–51.
60. R. Strickland, *Fire and the Spirits*, 52.
61. Oskison, *Black Jack Davy*, 12–13.
62. Ibid., 12.
63. *LCN*, 1868, 148–49.
64. *LCN*, 1881, chap. 12, art. 14, 272–74.
65. *LCN*, 1892, chap. 12, art. 15, 326–29.
66. While permit workers who were employed legally in the Nation in no way enjoyed political rights as citizens, they were afforded civil protections under the Cherokee constitution, as is evidenced by numerous court cases in which permit employees stood as both defendants and plaintiffs.
67. Oskison, *Black Jack Davy*, 3–4.
68. Ibid., 4.
69. Ibid., 5.
70. Ibid., 14.
71. Ibid., 24–25.
72. Ibid., 19.
73. Ibid., 86.
74. Ibid., 98.
75. Ibid., 61–62.
76. Cox, "Tribal Nations," 360.
77. Debo, *And Still the Waters Run*, 91.
78. Oskison, *Black Jack Davy*, 70.
79. Ibid., 91.
80. Located in Fort Smith, Arkansas, Parker's court was established by an act of Congress in 1871 and held absolute jurisdiction over all crimes in Indian Territory except those between citizens of Indian nations. Subsequent acts passed in 1885, 1887, and 1888 all but eviscerated the rights and capacities of Indian nations to arrest,

prosecute, and punish their own citizens for crimes committed between Indians. As Wardell notes, such acts were geared as much at creating offices to meet the needs of political nepotism and protecting business interests as they were at dissolving tribal governments and dealing finally with the "Indian problem." Though he was referred to as the "hanging judge" for his execution of eighty-eight men during his twenty-five-year tenure, Parker often spoke on behalf of Indian nations in the Territory and solicited their input before rendering decisions regarding the trust relationship with the United States. Wardell, *Political History*, 308–9.

81. Oskison, *Black Jack Davy*, 17–18.
82. For instance, articles 2 and 3 of the Treaty of Devil's Corner between Cherokees and the governments of Georgia and South Carolina, which was concluded in May 1777, established the boundaries between Cherokee and state lands and prohibited incursions by one party into the territories of another. Treaties between Cherokee communities bordering North Carolina and Virginia similarly drew definitive boundary lines and provided for the removal and punishment of U.S. squatters on Cherokee lands, stipulating that "no white man on any pretence whatsoever, shall build, plant, improve, settle, hunt, or drive stock below said Boundary line on pain of being drove off by the Indians, and further punished according to Law." See Deloria and DeMallie, *Documents of American Indian Diplomacy*, 70–73.
83. Oskison, *Black Jack Davy*, 79.
84. Consistent with its articulation throughout the Cherokee legal code, the use of "white" in this discussion should be read as a signifier of race, national affiliation, and power. Early provisions codifying intermarriage between "white men and Cherokee women" and "white women and Cherokee men" (*LCN*, 1852, 10, 57) were later amended explicitly to address intermarriage with non-white, noncitizen "foreigners" as well as noncitizen Indians (*LCN*, 1892, 329, 334). It should also be noted that four resolutions were passed between 1820 and 1824 legally excluding black slaves and free blacks from citizenship and legal protections, defining free blacks as intruders, condemning intermarriage between slaves and Cherokees or whites, and forbidding blacks from owning or inheriting property (*LCN*, 1852, 24–25, 37–39). Such provisions, incorporated into the constitutions of 1827 and 1839 (art. 3, sec. 5) and strengthened in subsequent acts relating to citizenship, intermarriage, and education, were excised in article 9 of the Treaty of 1866, the provisions of which were incorporated as amendments to the constitution later that year (*LCN*, 1892, 33–34, 35).
85. *LCN*, 1852, 10–11.
86. Ibid., 57. For the sociopolitical impacts of nationhood and the constitution on Cherokee women, see McLoughlin, *Renascence*, 326–49; Perdue, *Slavery*, 50–52; Perdue, *Cherokee Women*, 115–58; Johnston, *Cherokee Women in Crisis*, 11–55.
87. *LCN*, 1892, 370–73. As an adopted citizen by marriage, Oskison's own father fell into this category, though his three sons by Rachel enjoyed the privileges of citizenship.

88. *LCN*, 1881, 276–77. Among other provisions, in its assignation of federal rights of removal for U.S. intruders from Indian Country, the Trade and Intercourse Act of 1834 represented a significant incursion into Indian political autonomy.
89. McLoughlin, *After the Trail of Tears*, 67.
90. Oskison, *Black Jack Davy*, 167.
91. For instance, a resolution from September 24, 1839, restricts the erection of improvements by a citizen within a half mile of another citizen's improvements without their consent. *LCN*, 1852, 29.
92. H. Smith, *Virgin Land*, 61–62.
93. Ibid., 62.
94. Cox, *Muting White Noise*, 203–50; Lyons, *X-Marks*, 148–50.
95. Denson identifies the ironic redirection of dominant Anglo discourses as a central Cherokee rhetorical strategy throughout the nineteenth century, one which Oskison is clearly participating in here. See Denson, *Demanding the Cherokee Nation*, 28–51.
96. Lawlor, *Recalling the Wild*, 24.
97. Cox, *Muting White Noise*, 206, 207.
98. Ibid., 13.
99. Cox, "'Learn to Talk Yaqui'"; Conley, *Cherokee Thoughts*, 49–65; Hunnef "Dangerously Free." Together Conley's and Hunnef's accounts provide the most rigorous study of the parallels between Warrior's character and Christie's life.
100. "Indian Outlawry; Recent Battle with Outlaws Recalls Memory of Territory Desperadoes; Record of Crimes Committed," *Daily Oklahoman*, March 18, 1906.
101. Conley, *Cherokee Thoughts*, 49–65. See also Hunnef, "Dangerously Free," 3.
102. Conley, *Cherokee Thoughts*, 62.
103. Ibid., 65.
104. Oskison, *Black Jack Davy*, 68–70, 88–93.
105. Ibid., 112–25.
106. Ibid., 305.
107. Ibid., 170.
108. Ibid., 171.
109. Ibid., 271–72.
110. Hunnef, "Dangerously Free," 185–89.
111. Ibid., 188.
112. My conflation of an individual citizen-protagonist with the Nation as a whole should be read within the generic conventions of the romance, where the hero generally stands in as an allegorical figure for the national community and its people. In reality, of course, no such absolute correspondence exists. Indeed, part of the work of national narratives is to institutionalize such narrative relationships by erasing the differences and complexities that frustrate at every turn efforts to collapse the moral hero and the national community.

113. Oskison, *Black Jack Davy*, 272.
114. In an essay examining the parallels between Indian Territory and Indigenous Mexico in the works of Oskison and Will Rogers, James Cox notes that reading *Wild Harvest* and *Black Jack Davy* as companion novels complicates any easy reading of Oskison as either assimilationist or resistant. Rather, across his entire corpus his politics remain "unpredictable and inconsistent." My attention to the Cherokee geographies in Oskison's texts is greatly indebted to our conversations about these and other texts of the period. Cox, "'Learn to Talk Yaqui,'" 408.
115. For various models of belonging in Indian Country, see Lyons, *X-Marks*, 170–89; Justice, "Go Away Water," 150–55; Holm et al., "Peoplehood"; Alfred, *Peace, Power, Righteousness*, 85–88; Garroutte, *Real Indians*, 118–34.
116. McLoughlin, *After the Trail of Tears*, 59 (emphasis added).
117. Justice, *Our Fire Survives the Storm*, 118.
118. Oskison, *Black Jack Davy*, 312. Larson early identified Oskison's ironic use of the signifier "Dawes" described here. Larson, *American Indian Fiction*, 49. However, the generational typology into which he positions Oskison as an abject "assimilationist" prevents him from reading it as anything more than narrative play rather than exploring the potentially radical narrative and political implications of this choice.
119. Bhabha, *Nation and Narration*," 297.
120. Ibid., 300.
121. Lyons locates the nation as a distinctly modern form of political identification that is centered less on ties to an ethnic community and more on a political commitment to the sovereignty and autonomy of the Cherokee nation-state. Though Cherokee citizenship moved in this direction throughout the nineteenth century, which is evidenced in numerous resolutions to extend citizenship to non-Cherokees *outside the convention of marriage*, kinship and familial descent still remained deeply embedded as a major bedrock of Cherokee political belonging. An argument might forcefully be made that contemporary citizenship requirements based on lineal descent from early twentieth-century government rolls retain at least the traces of that commitment to kinship, though tying political legitimacy to a single document affords much less flexibility than more "modern" naturalization procedures, contemporary theories of peoplehood, or earlier clan systems did. For a concise and provocative discussion of nationhood and citizenship as it pertains to Indian Country, see Lyons, *X-Marks*, chaps. 3–4.
122. For the implications of Cherokee constitutionalism for slaves and free blacks in the Nation from the national period through statehood, see Perdue, *Slavery*, 50–118; Sturm, *Blood Politics*, 52–81; Miles, *Ties That Bind*, 100–203; Naylor, *African Cherokees*, 25–50, 155–78.

Chapter 2

1. O'Brien, *Firsting and Lasting*, xi–xxiii; P. Deloria, "Historiography," 6–24; Huhndorf, *Going Native*; Blackhawk, *Violence over the Land*. See also L. Smith, *Decolonizing Methodologies*, 29.
2. Holm et al., "Peoplehood," 14; Corntassel, "Who Is Indigenous?," 7, 24, 27, 214, 215–16; Carroll, *Roots of Our Renewal*, 40, 46, 81.
3. Fixico, introduction to *Rethinking American Indian History*, 8; A. Ortiz, "Indian/White Relations," 14–15; Tuhiwai-Smith, *Decolonizing Methodologies*, 26; Alfred, "Sovereignty," 469.
4. L. Smith, *Decolonizing Methodologies*, 28, 34. See also Mankiller, introduction to *Reflections on American Indian History*, xiii–xix; A. Ortiz, "Indian/White Relations," 3–10; Trask, *From a Native Daughter*, 120–21; Edmunds, "National Expansion," 159–77; Lowery, "Telling Our Own Stories," 518.
5. Born from an anxiety not dissimilar to that expressed by Eaton almost a century ago, the Cherokee Nation formed the Sequoyah Historical Commission in 2007 to ensure that the Indian history of the state of Oklahoma would not be minimized in official preparations for the centennial celebrations taking place later that year. Its original mandate was to bring prominent Indigenous scholars and local authorities together to discuss that history and its relationship to contemporary issues facing Native peoples across the state. Over the next few years, the commission broadened its focus, bringing scholars working in a variety of disciplines together with an array of artists, activists, elders, oral historians, technologists, entrepreneurs, and Indian government employees from tribal nations across the country. Though the focus of the symposium remained historicist and local through its final gathering in 2012, its expanded mandate captured the range of work taking place across Indian Country and reaffirmed the vital relationships between tribal communities, Indian governments, and community-centered, politically committed intellectual work.
6. For the film, see https://youtu.be/S8ooheHXQF8.
7. For the most comprehensive treatment of Eaton's background and her position as a historian, see Rhea, *A Field of Their Own*, 150–62.
8. *The History of Rogers County, Oklahoma*, vol. 1.
9. For the most comprehensive treatment of these families as told through correspondence and letters, see Dale and Litton, *Cherokee Cavaliers*.
10. *The History of Rogers County, Oklahoma*, vol. 1.
11. Mihesuah, *Cultivating the Rosebuds*, 57, 61.
12. Skelton, "A History."
13. Fry, *Cherokee Female Seminary Years*, 75, 100, 121–22.
14. Mihesuah, *Cultivating the Rosebuds*, 61.
15. For a comprehensive discussion of the publication history of Eaton's master thesis, 1914 manuscript (examined here), 1919 PhD dissertation, 1921 revised publication,

and revised 1935 manuscript, see Rhea, *A Field of their Own*, 158–61. See also note 95 below.

16. Mihesuah, "Rachel Caroline Eaton," 99.
17. Mihesuah, *Cultivating the Rosebuds*, 104; Sanders, *Who's Who among Oklahoma Indians*, 18; Berry, "Rachel Caroline Eaton."
18. Foreman, "Aunt Eliza of Tahlequah," 53.
19. *Chronicles of Oklahoma*, editorial, 8; *Pocahontas Spirit*, 17.
20. *As I Recollect*, 169.
21. Ibid.
22. Wright, "Rachel Caroline Eaton," 509.
23. Cf. Thomas L. McKenney and James Hall, *History of the Indian Tribes of North America, with Biographical Sketches and Anecdotes of the Principal Chiefs* (1836–44); Henry Rowe Schoolcraft, *The American Indians: Their History, Condition and Prospects: From Notes and Manuscripts* (1851); George Bancroft, *History of the United States, from the Discovery of the American Continent* (1854–78); Francis Parkman, *The Oregon Trail* (1849); Francis Parkman, *The Conspiracy of Pontiac and the Indian War after the Conquest of Canada* (1851); Lewis Henry Morgan, *The League of the Ho-de-no-sau-nee or Iroquois* (1851); Lewis Henry Morgan, *Ancient Society* (1877). For a discussion of these writings in the contexts of American romanticism and the development of ethnology, anthropology, and other social sciences, see Berkhofer, *The White Man's Indian*, 44–96. I discuss Eaton's sources in the next section of this chapter.
24. Hoxie, *Final Promise*, 21–23.
25. Rhea, *A Field of Their Own*, 4–7.
26. Hoxie, *Final Promise*, 18.
27. Perdue, *Cherokee Women*; Perdue, "Women, Men, and American Indian Policy," 90–114; R. Strickland, *Fire and the Spirits*; Denson, *Demanding the Cherokee Nation*; Nelson, *Progressive Traditions*; Parins, *Literacy and Intellectual Life*. See also Cushman, *The Cherokee Syllabary*; Carroll, *Roots of Our Renewal*.
28. Cf. Bruyneel, *The Third Space of Sovereignty*, 27–64; Konkle, *Writing Indian Nations*, 42–96. For an outline of specific rhetorical strategies, see Denson, *Demanding the Cherokee Nation*, 28–51. Individual chapters examine in greater detail how Cherokees deployed such strategies in response to specific historical challenges.
29. *American State Papers*, 1:40–44.
30. Kilcup, "Nancy Ward and Early Cherokee Women," 26–30. See also Moulder, "'They Ought to Mind What a Woman Says.'"
31. Perdue, *Cherokee Editor*; Nelson, *Progressive Traditions*, 165–200.
32. For these writings, see Kilcup, *Native American Women's Writing*.
33. Cf. Denson, *Demanding the Cherokee Nation*; Parins, *Literacy and Intellectual Life*.
34. Justice, *Our Fire Survives the Storm*. See also Ware, *The Cherokee Kid*.
35. See also Bruyneel, *The Third Space of Sovereignty*, 27–64.

36. Denson, *Demanding the Cherokee Nation*, 5.
37. M. Powell, "Rhetorics of Survivance."
38. Even texts that are relatively sympathetic to assimilation, such as Alice Callahan's *Wynema: A Child of the Forest* (1891) and Charles Eastman's *From the Deep Woods to Civilization* (1916), are unable to contain outrage, disgust, and disappointment at catastrophic failures of American idealism that are evident in events like the massacre at Wounded Knee.
39. Cf. Hoxie, *Talking Back to Civilization*, 1–28; Maddox, *Citizen Indians*, 13–14; Holm, *The Great Confusion*, 52–53, 58.
40. Foreword in Eaton, *John Ross and the Cherokee Indians*.
41. Ibid.
42. Ibid.
43. Ibid.
44. Ibid.
45. Cox, "'Learn to Talk Yaqui,'" 400–421; Cox, "Tribal Nations," 356–72.
46. Eaton, *John Ross and the Cherokee Indians*.
47. Ibid., 34.
48. Ibid., 35.
49. Ibid., 11.
50. Ibid.
51. Nelson, *Progressive Traditions*, 4–6, 233n4.
52. Eaton, *John Ross and the Cherokee Indians*, 18–19.
53. Ibid., 19.
54. Lyons, *X-Marks*, 1–3, 13, 40, 70. See also Lyons, "Rhetorical Sovereignty," 462.
55. Konkle, *Writing Indian Nations*, 6.
56. Pearce, *Savagism and Civilization*; Berkhofer, *The White Man's Indian*; Vizenor, *Manifest Manners*; Vizenor, *Fugitive Poses*.
57. Simpson, *Mohawk Interruptus*, 94–97.
58. Nelson, *Progressive Traditions*, xii, 4–6.
59. Byrd, *The Transit of Empire*; Moreton-Robinson, *The White Possessive*.
60. Eaton, *John Ross and the Cherokee Indians*, 38.
61. Ibid., 13.
62. Ibid., 135.
63. Ibid., 12, 15.
64. Ibid., 15.
65. For a more complete analysis of the legal gymnastics and implications of these decisions, see Norgren, *The Cherokee Cases*.
66. Eaton, *John Ross and the Cherokee Indians*, 38.
67. Ibid., 69.
68. Ibid., 70.
69. Ibid., 27.
70. Ibid., 61.

71. Ibid.
72. Ibid., 70.
73. Ibid.
74. Ibid.
75. Ibid.
76. Cf. Wilkins and Lomawaima, *Uneven Ground*; Deloria and Wilkins, *Tribes, Treaties and Constitutional Tribulations*; Williams, *The American Indian.* See also Bruyneel, *The Third Space of Sovereignty*; Rifkin, *Manifesting America.*
77. Rhea, *A Field of Their Own*, xiii, xiv.
78. Eaton, *John Ross and the Cherokee Indians*, 99.
79. Ibid., 120.
80. Ibid., 28. Eaton here echoes similar critique levied by William Apess in "Indian Nullification" (1835) and "Eulogy on King Philip" (1836). Apess, *On Our Own Ground*, 163–276.
81. Eaton, *John Ross and the Cherokee Indians.*
82. Ibid., 110.
83. Ibid., 27, 104.
84. Ibid., 64.
85. Ibid.
86. Ibid., 66.
87. Ibid., 79.
88. Ibid.
89. Ibid., 80.
90. Ibid.
91. Ibid., 79.
92. Ibid., 112.
93. Ibid., 112–13, 114.
94. Ibid., 117.
95. See Rhea, *A Field of their Own*, 158–61. According to Rhea, Eaton submitted the revised 1935 manuscript to University of Oklahoma Press in June of that year hoping for a quick reply about its placement in the Civilization of the American Indian Series. However, due to the sudden illness of the acquisitions editor and subsequent competing submissions of Cherokee histories, her manuscript languished for months. In February 1936 Eaton was informed that the press had opted to publish one of the other submissions. The editor noted that while external reviewers thought the scholarship was sound and were confident that it would be a popular selection, it was ultimately deemed not as "definitive" as the other one. Adding insult to injury, another reviewer highlighted that Eaton "occasionally revealed a bias" that was "too-partisan, pro-Cherokee" (159–60). The other manuscript that was selected was University of Oklahoma historian Morris Wardell's *Political History of the Cherokee Nation.* As Rhea writes, Wardell had previously reviewed another biographical history of John Ross by another Cherokee writer, John Milton Oskison, which was

similarly critiqued for bias and for being written from "a Cherokee point of view." While it is unknown whether or not Wardell also reviewed Eaton's manuscript—the reviewers remain anonymous—Rhea notes that the institutional, "sexual, racial, and cultural biases" that led to Eaton's and Oskison's rejections are clear (160–61).

96. Eaton, *John Ross and the Cherokee Indians*, 104.
97. Ibid.
98. Ibid., 116.
99. Ibid., 190, 196–97.
100. Ibid., 154, 176.
101. On the "vanishing American," see Dippie, *The Vanishing American*. On "settler moves to innocence," see Tuck and Yang, "Decolonization Is Not a Metaphor."
102. Justice, *Our Fire Survives the Storm*, 171.
103. Eaton, *John Ross and the Cherokee Indians*, 125.
104. Here I draw on on Renato Rosaldo's foundational concept of imperialist nostalgia. Rosaldo, "Imperialist Nostalgia."
105. Eaton, *John Ross and the Cherokee Indians*, 125.
106. When Henry Dawes, the architect of allotment, visited the Nation in the late nineteenth century, he observed, "There was not a family in that whole nation that had not a home of its own. There was not a pauper in that nation, and the nation did not owe a dollar." The problem, as Dawes infamously understood it, lay in common land tenure. Absent individual allotments of land to cultivate and improve, Indians would never develop the intense self-interest, competitiveness, and enterprise that would allow them to fully progress as modern citizens. Debo, *And Still the Waters Run*, 21–22.
107. For the historical relationship between empathy and human rights discourse, see Hunt, *Inventing Human Rights*.
108. Eaton, *John Ross and the Cherokee Indians*, 135.
109. Cf. Denson, *Demanding the Cherokee Nation*; Maddox, *Citizen Indians*; Martínez, *The American Indian Intellectual Tradition*, 99–113.
110. I draw here on Edward Said's characterization of the relationship between colonial intellectual production and representation as one that institutionalizes and normalizes racialized epistemological categories in order to consolidate and reproduce inequitable power relations through the construction of "an interreferential mass of textual authority" about colonial others. Said, *Orientalism*, 20. See also L. Smith, *Decolonizing Methodologies*.
111. Conventional primary sources include *American State Papers, Indian Affairs*, vols. 1–2; *Annals of Congress*; multiple issues of *Congressional Documents*; the *Congressional Globe*; Indian Office Manuscript Records, 1913; Supreme Court reports; Niles's *Weekly Register*; James D. Richardson, *The Compilation of the Messages and Papers of the Presidents*. Popular secondary sources include Thomas L. McKenney and James Hall, *History of the Indian Tribes of North America*; George Bancroft, *History of the United States*; Samuel G. Drake, *Biography and History of the American*

Indians in North America; Samuel G. Drake, *Early History of Georgia*; Horace Greeley, *The American Conflict*; Wilson Lumpkin, *The Removal of the Cherokee Indians from Georgia*; Annie Heloise Abel, *The History of Events Resulting in Indian Consolidation West of the Mississippi*.

112. Justice, *Our Fire Survives the Storm*, 20.
113. Scholars have noted how Adair's widely erroneous misrepresentations of Indigenous cultural practices within Judeo-Christian frameworks, his mapping of Native geopolitical spaces, and his endorsement of colonization and early articulations of the civilization program ultimately serve colonialist ends by encouraging a view of Indigenous peoples as the exotic antitheses of the enlightened, modern, technologically adept, fully actualized Christian citizen-subject and by setting Indigenous places and peoples on the periphery of European colonial space from which conquest, settlement, and civilization—and thus history itself—proceed from east to west. Adair, *The History of the American Indians*.
114. Bartram, *Travels and Other Writings*. Though "not for levelling [*sic*] things down to the simplicity of Indians," Bartram believes that Euro-Americans might "possibly better our condition in civil society, by paying some more respect to and impartially examining the system of legislation, religion, morality, and economy of these despised, persecuted *wild people*" (550). Thus, while civilization remains the stick by which Bartram measures Native societies, he does not presume that any one religious, political, or cultural community possesses an exclusive claim to it. Consequently, his defense of Native peoples reads much like a point-by-point refutation of the rhetorics of savagery that are firmly located within the Noble Savage tradition of Rousseau, Montaigne, and Chateaubriand.
115. Eaton describes the nine-volume collection of writings as "containing the Cherokee official records before 1838; letters of missionaries on the condition of the Indians before 1830 and during Removal; letters of Cherokee children in the Mission Schools to philanthropic people in the north; traditions and myths as related to John Howard Payne by prominent members of the tribe in 1836." Eaton, *John Ross and the Cherokee Indians*, 211.
116. Royce, *The Cherokee Nation of Indians*. The purpose of Royce's assignment from then director of the Bureau of Ethnology John Wesley Powell was to document how the Cherokees' contact with civilization positively influenced their development out of Indian savagery and into civilized, Anglo-Saxon enlightenment. In its extensive documentation of the legal history between the Cherokee Nation and the U.S. government, as well as its strong criticism of U.S. graft, duplicity, and self-interested aggression, Royce's text undermines Powell's mandate by unequivocally establishing Cherokee claims to both nationhood and modernity and by advocating for the continued national status of the Cherokee Nation. Royce's commitment to the savage/civilized binary and his exclusivist associations of nationhood with civilization, modernity, and international law—rather than with the Cherokees' centuries-long occupation of their southeastern homelands—forces his narrative

into a series of contradictions, however. Not least of which is the text's reinforcement of a narrative of domestication of both Native lands and peoples under U.S. legal and political jurisdiction and the ascription of violence and corruption as a consequence of the "tide of civilization" and the "struggle against fate" (214, 373–74).

117. Mooney. *History, Myths and Sacred Formulas.*
118. Eaton, *John Ross and the Cherokee Indians*, 211.
119. Parins, *Literacy and Intellectual Life*, xiv.
120. Quoted in Rhea, *A Field of Their Own*, 157.
121. Both Mooney's and Starr's histories rely heavily on Cherokee informants as well, though via different methodologies and to vastly different ends. Whereas Mooney's is a narrative of Cherokee rupture, acculturation, and loss of authenticity, Starr's is a story of adaptation, continuity, and continuance. Starr, *History of the Cherokee Indians.* For an analysis of the "Chickamauga consciousness" of Starr's text, see Justice, *Our Fire Survives the Storm*, 132–43.
122. Eaton, preface to *John Ross and the Cherokee Indians.*
123. Cf. Perdue, *Cherokee Women*; Johnston, *Cherokee Women in Crisis.*
124. Carney, *Eastern Band Cherokee Women*, 4.
125. For the story of Selu, the First Woman and bringer of life, community, and corn to Cherokee people, see Mooney, *History, Myths, and Sacred Formulas*, 242–49, 323–24; J. Kilpatrick and A. Kilpatrick, *Friends of the Thunder*, 129–34; Perdue, *Cherokee Women*, 13–40; Stremlau, *Sustaining the Cherokee Family*, 21–22, 242–43.
126. Eaton, *John Ross and the Cherokee Indians*, 3–4.
127. Ibid., 24.
128. Fixico, introduction to *Rethinking American Indian History*, 8.
129. *Wado* to James Cox for making this point explicit.
130. P. Deloria, "Historiography," 8.
131. Bruyneel, *Third Space of Sovereignty*; Rifkin, *Manifesting America*; Rifkin, "Making Peoples into Populations"; Goeman, *Mark My Words.*
132. Klein, *Frontiers of Historical Imagination*, 7.
133. Cox, *Muting White Noise*, 208.
134. Klein, *Frontiers of Historical Imagination*, ix. Here I draw on Audra Simpson's notions of ethnographic refusal, but in a narrative and ideological context, as well as Glen Coulthard's understanding of the politics of "turning away" from a settler politics of recognition. While Eaton's necessary engagement with discourses of civilization and progress necessarily prohibit her from the kinds of categorical refusals and turnings away theorized by Simpson and Coulthard, her text nonetheless anticipates these moves in a context where outright refusals and turnings away were not widely possible. Simpson, *Mohawk Interruptus*; Coulthard, *Red Skin, White Masks.*
135. Carroll, *Roots of Our Renewal*, 16.
136. Bruyneel, *The Third Space of Sovereignty*, xvii.
137. Krupat, *For Those Who Come After*, 48–49.
138. *Wado* to James Cox, who clarified this point in a previous version of the text.

139. Alfred, "Sovereignty," 460, 469.
140. Royce, *The Cherokee Nation of Indians*, 348.
141. Cf. Nelson, *Progressive Traditions*; Stremlau, *Sustaining the Cherokee Family*; Carroll, *Roots of Our Renewal*; Coates, "'This Sovereignty Thing.'" See also Parins, *Literacy and Intellectual Life*, esp. chap. 8.
142. See Nelson's analysis of the conflicts between John Ross and Elias Boudinot from *Progressive Traditions*, chaps. 4–5.
143. Eaton, *John Ross and the Cherokee Indians*, 32.
144. Ibid., 74–75.
145. For tragic renderings of Treaty Party, see T. Wilkins, *Cherokee Tragedy*.
146. Eaton, *John Ross and the Cherokee Indians*, 133.
147. Mooney, *History, Myths, and Sacred Formulas*, 114. Thomas Carlyle is widely acknowledged as one of the nineteenth century's greatest proponents of this historiographic approach. Herbert Spencer's contention that circumstances produce historical figures constitutes a philosophical counterargument. American pragmatist William James offers an attempted synthesis of both positions, arguing that great men and their environments mutually constitute each other. Eaton would have likely been educated in precisely these debates, and her story of John Ross's emergence and election by a people in crisis suggests more of a Jamesian reconciliation between Carlyle's emphasis on human agency and personality and Spencer's privileging of social Darwinism. Carlyle, *On Heroes, Hero-Worship*; Spencer, *The Study of Sociology*; James, *Great Men and Their Environment*.
148. Konkle, *Writing Indian Nations*, 1–33.
149. Mooney, *History, Myths, and Sacred Formulas*, 146 (emphasis added).
150. Ibid., 146, 147.
151. Eaton, *John Ross and the Cherokee Indians*, 22, 57.
152. Ibid., 38.
153. Ibid., preface.
154. Eaton's shift here prefigures Lyons's formulation of the "X-mark," Nelson's notion of "progressive traditions," Carroll's understanding of "Cherokee state transformation," David Carlson's recent positioning of sovereignty as a discursive and legal "middle ground" between Native American and U.S. settler claims to legal and political authority, and a host of other articulations of adaptation, syncretism, and indigenizing European genres, forms, institutions, and modes of self-representation and self-governance discussed throughout this project. Lyons, *X-Marks*, 70; Nelson *Progressive Traditions*, xiii; Carroll, *Roots of Our Renewal*, 17–23, 96, 113; Carlson, *Imagining Sovereignty*.
155. Cox, *Muting White Noise*, 206, 249.
156. Eaton, *John Ross and the Cherokee Indians*, 207.
157. Ibid.
158. Ibid., 208.
159. Ibid.
160. Ibid., 209.

161. Sayre, "Autobiography," 150.
162. Fixico, "American Indian History," 553; Fixico, introduction to *Rethinking American Indian History*, 8; A. Ortiz, "Indian/White Relations," 1–16; Axtell, "The Ethnohistory of Native America," 14; Hagan, "The New Indian History"; L. Smith, *Decolonizing Methodologies*, 28. For critiques of how colonialist time reaffirms state sovereignty, see Bruyneel, *The Third Space of Sovereignty*, 6–8; Bauerkemper, "Narrating Nationhood," 28, 50; P. Deloria, "Historiography," 8–20; Edmunds, "National Expansion," 159–77.
163. Alfred, "Sovereignty," 469; Simpson, *Mohawk Interruptus*, 10–11. For how national histories and narratives attempt to deny plurality, reduce difference, and silence dissent, see R. Young, *White Mythologies*, 1–3, 35; Bhabha, *Nation and Narration*, 1–4, 292–301; Bruyneel, *The Third Space of Sovereignty*, 5–8. For more on multiple, nested, and transnational sovereignties, see Weaver, "Splitting the Earth," 46–50, 74; Bauerkemper and Stark, "The Trans/National Terrain," 9, 14; Bauerkemper, "Indigenous Trans/Nationalism," 396–41; Wilkins and Stark, *American Indian Politics*, 233.
164. P. Deloria, "Historiography," 19; Mihesuah, "Should American Indian History," 144. Mihesuah's catalog of concerns includes legal issues such as treaty rights, territorial jurisdiction, and resource management; acute health issues such as diabetes, obesity, and access to healthy foods; and social problems such as alcoholism, substance abuse, and violence against women and children.
165. Fixico, introduction to *Rethinking American Indian History*, 8.
166. David Edmunds writes that "the Indian" played a significant role in the intellectual and political construction of a distinctly American national identity, particularly for a young republican nation struggling to find its place in the community of nations: "Not only did their 'republican virtue' separate them from European corruption, but their achievements assured them that they no longer were 'primitives' like the Indians. The Indians symbolized a wilderness that was being transformed and conquered, and the tribespeople's demise was indicative of the 'grand dame of progress' sweeping westward across the United States." Edmunds, "National Expansion," 174. For colonial ambivalence, see Bhabha, *Nation and Narration*.
167. Sayre, "Autobiography," 150.
168. Eaton, *John Ross and the Cherokee Indians*, 5.
169. Ibid., 56.
170. Ibid., 124.
171. Ibid., 19.
172. Perdue, "Writing the Ethnohistory."
173. For a recent analysis of these dynamics, see Nelson, *Progressive Traditions*, chaps. 3–5.
174. Eaton, *John Ross and the Cherokee Indians*, 20, 120, 171–72.
175. Ibid., 178.
176. Mihesuah, "Should American Indian History," 154.

Chapter 3

1. Numerous scholars have traced such currents as being a function of complex and rapid social transformations resulting from colonial conflict, interracial marriage, federal policies of assimilation, the development of racialized capitalist plantation economies, and nationalization. For studies that emphasize political and economic factors, see Wardell, *Political History of the Cherokee Nation*; McLoughlin, *Cherokee Renascence*; McLoughlin, *After the Trail of Tears.* For studies that focus specifically on slavery and its effects on Cherokee cultural and political identity, see Halliburton, *Red over Black*; Littlefield, *The Cherokee Freedmen*; Perdue, *Slavery*; Minges, *Slavery in the Cherokee Nation.* For an emphasis on Afro-Cherokee experiences and the legal pressures that racialized ideologies exert upon questions of Indian national identity, citizenship, and sovereignty, see Miles, *Ties That Bind*; Naylor, *African Cherokees in Indian Territory.* For more general discussions of race and the Cherokee Nation, see Zissu, *Blood Matters*; Yarbrough, *Race and the Cherokee Nation.* Circe Sturm's *Blood Politics* remains the most comprehensive study of this history as it relates to local experience in the Cherokee Nation. See also Sturm, "Race, Sovereignty, and Civil Rights."
2. Riggs, *The Cherokee Night*, 125.
3. Little Thunder, "Mixedbloods and Bloodlust in *Cherokee Night*."
4. Womack, *Red on Red*, 271–303.
5. Darby, "Introduction"; Driskill, "Han'ts"; Stanlake, *Native American Drama*, 39–106.
6. Weaver, *That the People Might Live*, 95–103. Weaver tempers this sense of hopelessness and loss in his 2004 introduction to the play in Riggs, *The Cherokee Night*, noting the "underlying themes of preserving one's passing culture instead of running from it and of intercultural respect and understanding." Nonetheless, he reads an early statement from scene 1, "Night Has Come to Our People," as a declaration of fact rather than one of contingency, as the recognition of the arrival at an endgame rather than one move in a much longer strategic battle, which is a problematic conclusion that I deal with in detail below.
7. Weaver, *That the People Might Live*, 103.
8. Justice, *Our Fire Survives the Storm*, 94–108.
9. Ibid., 102.
10. Cox, *The Red Land*, 65–105.
11. Ibid., 104–5.
12. Darby initiated the conversation about the subversion of linear time in the structure of the play as an explicit challenge to dominant nineteenth-century realist conventions, the assumed "authority of mimesis to constitute truth," and American theater's decidedly uncritical "positivist vision" of the American Dream. Darby, "Broadway (Un)Bound," 9, 10. Darby also argues that Riggs's use of "ritual time" also imbues the play with a distinctly Cherokee form of spiritual resistance rooted in the principles of opposition, balance, and reciprocity. Though Darby's analysis is pro-

vocative, I here wish to redirect the focus, not identifying what is distinctly Native or Cherokee about the structure of the play, but rather examining how the thoroughly modernist (rather than traditional) disruption of linear time functions to continually reorient how we are to read the final action of the play.

13. In her critical introduction to the memoirs of nineteenth-century Cherokee musician, teacher, artist, and socialite Narcissa Owen, Karen Kilcup, following Elizabeth Cook-Lynn, makes a powerful argument that locating Native writers in both tribally specific and broader intellectual and political contexts enriches our understandings of tribal specificity by illuminating the relationship between "a writer's negotiations with Euroamerican culture and her commitment to Native communities." Kilcup, introduction to *A Cherokee Woman's America*, 3, 4.
14. *Green Grow the Lilacs* had its Broadway debut at the Theatre Guild on January 26, 1931. *The Cherokee Night* debuted at Hedgerow Theatre on June 18, 1932, "to overflow crowds."
15. Riggs's film scripts include MGM's *Laughing Boy* (1930), an adaptation of Oliver LaFarge's popular novel of the same name; Cecile B. DeMille's Paramount production, *The Plainsman* (1935); and Selznick International's *The Garden of Allah* (1936), starring Marlene Dietrich and directed by Moscow Art Theatre alum and American Laboratory Theatre cofounder Richard Boleslawski.
16. Nine years later (1950), a young Anthony Quinn would star in the leading role as "Texas" in a revised short Broadway run of *Borned in Texas*.
17. Weaver, foreword to *The Cherokee Night*, ix–xv.
18. Walker, *Expressionism and Modernism*, 6, 113.
19. Wentz, "The Hedgerow Theatre," 47–52.
20. Riggs inscribed the 1930 edition of *The Iron Dish*, "For Alice Corbin—Affection—Lynn—Santa Fe—Sept. 13, 1931." A few months later Riggs sent Henderson a 1928 first edition of *Sump'n Like Wings and A Lantern to See By* in which he wrote, "For Alice Corbin—who has both—Wings and a lantern.—Lynn Christmas, 1931." A 1931 second printing of *Green Grow the Lilacs* contains the inscription, "For Alice Corbin—who knows a thing or two about cowboys herself—With warm regards—Lynn. Santa Fe—June 4, 1931." In 1940 Riggs gave Henderson the 1936 publication of *Russet Mantle and The Cherokee Night*, writing, "For Alice—After these years!—Affectionately, Lynn La Jolla—May 14, 1940." To Johnson, Riggs sent copies of *Big Lake: A Tragedy in Two Parts* (1928) and a copy of the final play he wrote, *Toward the Western Sky: A Music Play* (1951). In the former, Riggs jokes, "For Spud—Who didn't have to, but would have played part of a horse in this one, if he'd been called on. Heartily, Lynn. New York. Oct. 27, 1927." In the latter, only three years before Riggs's death, he thanks Johnson for his friendship and consistent correspondence: "For Spud—And thanks, my friend, for your nice wire, Ever,—Lynn, Shelter Island, New York." See the Alice Corbin Henderson and Spud Johnson Collections, Harry Ransom Center, University of Texas at Austin.
21. Levine, *Left-Wing Dramatic Theory*, 47–50.

22. Braunlich, *Haunted by Home*, 123–24.
23. Levine, *Left-Wing Dramatic Theory*, 112.
24. Gainor, *Susan Glaspell in Context*, 10–12.
25. Levine, *Left-Wing Dramatic Theory*, 84.
26. Quoted in Braunlich, *Haunted by Home* (emphasis added), 82.
27. Riggs, "Poetry—and Poetry in the Theatre," 7.
28. Braunlich, *Haunted by Home*, 135.
29. Ibid., 109.
30. Riggs, "When People Say 'Folk-Drama,'" 39–41.
31. Ibid., 12.
32. Quoted in Braunlich, *Haunted by Home*, 151 (emphases added).
33. Riggs, "Some Notes on the Theatre," 7.
34. Ibid., 4 (emphasis added).
35. Ibid., 6 (emphasis added).
36. Riggs's concern with Indigenous social justice is most forcefully articulated in his play *A Year of Pilar* (1938), which chronicles the travails of an exiled hacendado family negotiating the massive land reforms of Cardenas-era Mexico. Initially exiled in New York, the Cuerpo family eventually returns to their hacienda in the Yucatán only to have it taken over in the end by Indigenous *peones*, one of whom is Don Cuerpo's illegitimate son by an Indigenous woman. In a powerfully symbolic finale, Riggs ties the sacrificial rape of the title character by Indigenous *peones* to the racialized, sexualized violence and exploitation of Indigenous peoples on which the family's wealth and status depend, a scene which eerily anticipates the rhetoric of reciprocal violence articulated by African decolonization critics two decades later. While the critique in *The Cherokee Night* is predominantly internally directed at Cherokee peoples, the overall recognition of the violence and trauma attending colonialism is everywhere evident in both plays. For a provocative discussion of the revolutionary politics in Riggs's dramas of Mexico, see Cox, *Red Land to the South*, 65–106.
37. Letter to Paul Green, Paul Green Papers, Southern Historical Collection, Manuscripts Department, Wilson Library, University of North Carolina at Chapel Hill. *Wado* to James Cox for sharing this document with me.
38. Ibid., 5.
39. Ibid., 3–4.
40. Ibid., 4, 5.
41. Ibid., 12.
42. Braunlich, *Haunted by Home*, 153–56.
43. See Womack's discussion of Riggs's dramatic theory of Oklahoma in *Red on Red*, 273–82.
44. Weaver, introduction to *The Cherokee Night*, 103.
45. Cox, *Muting White Noise*, 206–8, 243.
46. Riggs, *The Cherokee Night*, 122, 124, 125.

47. Ibid., 124.
48. Ibid.
49. Ibid., 125 (emphasis added).
50. Ibid., 126.
51. For more detailed accounts of Osage-Cherokee relations, see Rollings, *The Osage*, 233–39; Baird, *The Osage People*, 29–46; Burns, *A History of the Osage People*, 154–95.
52. Mathews, *The Osages*, 408–76.
53. Riggs, *The Cherokee Night*, 127.
54. Though Little Thunder rightly observes the failure in this scene to use the ominous presence of Claremore Mound as a vehicle through which to accurately and honestly depict the brutality of the Cherokee massacre of Osage women, children, and elderly, her indictment of Riggs as lazily falling back on stereotypical and racist notions of bloodlust is misplaced. Little Thunder, "Mixedbloods and Bloodlust," 361. It is not Riggs who rejects the kids but Talbert, and it is his absurd, convoluted, and racist logic that Riggs explicitly frames as a kind of insanity.
55. Some of these include Tecumseh and Tenskatawa's efforts to unite Native peoples against U.S. aggression in 1811 and the widespread practice of Wovoka's Ghost Dance religion, which ultimately led to the U.S. massacre of Lakota peoples at Wounded Knee eighty years later.
56. McLoughlin, *Cherokee Renaissance*, 168–85.
57. Ibid., 181.
58. I am here invoking N. Scott Momaday's definition of Indigenous peoplehood as a people's "good idea of themselves." Momaday, *The Way to Rainy Mountain*, xx.
59. Riggs, *The Cherokee Night*, 125.
60. Ibid., 131. Unless otherwise noted, italics signify either stage directions or emphasis of dialogue as written in the play.
61. Ibid.
62. Ibid., 131–32.
63. Ibid., 132.
64. Green, "The Pocahontas Perplex."
65. Ibid., 714.
66. Cf. Ross, *Inventing the Savage*; Deer, *The Beginning and Ending*; Stremlau, *Sustaining the Cherokee Family*.
67. Brown, *Injun Joe's Ghost*, 20.
68. Ibid., 120.
69. Riggs, *The Cherokee Night*, 135.
70. Ibid., 139.
71. Ibid., 140.
72. Ibid., 135.
73. Ibid., 138.
74. Ibid., 139.

75. Brown, *Injun Joe's Ghost*, 20, 89.
76. Riggs, *The Cherokee Night*, 136.
77. Ibid.
78. Ibid., 137.
79. Ibid., 140.
80. Ibid., 141.
81. Ibid., 141–42.
82. Conley, *The Cherokee Nation*, 68–70; Conley, *Cherokee Thoughts*, 158–60; Justice, *Our Fire Survives the Storm*, 34–42.
83. Piatote, *Domestic Subjects*, 2–4. Piatote usefully distinguishes between three primary geopolitical spaces in settler-colonial relations: the settler national domestic, the tribal national domestic, and the intimate domestic.
84. Riggs, *The Cherokee Night*, 112–13, 114, 116–17.
85. Ibid., 120.
86. Ibid., 147.
87. Ibid., 148.
88. Lipsitz, *The Possessive Investment in Whiteness*; Moreton-Robinson, *The White Possessive*.
89. Riggs, *The Cherokee Night*, 144.
90. Ibid., 145.
91. Ibid.
92. See Debo, *And Still the Waters Run*.
93. Womack, *Red on Red*, 293–94; Justice, *Our Fire Survives the Storm*, 99–100.
94. Riggs, *The Cherokee Night*, 151.
95. Ibid.
96. Ibid., 152–53.
97. Ibid., 154.
98. Womack, *Red on Red*, 294.
99. Justice, *Our Fire Survives the Storm*, 100.
100. Ibid., 102.
101. Cf. Perdue, *Cherokee Women*.
102. Stremlau, *Sustaining the Cherokee Family*, 69–104; Piatote, *Domestic Subjects*, 1–10, 173.
103. Stremlau, *Sustaining the Cherokee Family*, 47.
104. Piatote, *Domestic Subjects*, 173.
105. Riggs, *The Cherokee Night*, 156.
106. Ibid.
107. Ibid., 158.
108. Ibid.
109. Sturm writes, "To most contemporary Cherokees, blood has become a potent hegemonic construct, a symbolic medium uniting all Cherokees to one another. Cherokee blood, in part, defines 'Cherokeeness' and anyone without Cherokee blood

would automatically fall outside the boundaries of the Cherokee community." Sturm, *Blood Politics*, 179. Cherokee scholar Eva Marie Garroutte similarly examines the at times serviceable, at times problematic role that biology and blood play in articulating and negotiating Native identity. She writes that while blood stands as a relatively stable bureaucratic marker of political identity, which invests a "stronger claim on identity" in racially identifiable Indian people, others reject it as a colonialist imposition whose goal is statistical extermination; as a rationale for racist federal policies and often-violent cultural policing within Native communities in the name of purity; or as a restricting paradigm in debates over the sovereign right of tribal nations to self-definition. Garroutte, *Real Indians*, 51–52, 60.

110. Riggs, *The Cherokee Night*, 158.
111. In his critique of the debates over William Apess's Indianness and questions over his rightful place in a Native intellectual tradition, Robert Warrior argues that "rather than waste our time debating whether or not Apess was 'Indian' enough to be considered a major figure in Native intellectualism," contemporary Native scholars should look at their own work, lives, and experiences to see whether they measure up to what intellectuals such as Apess were "able to accomplish in such little time and with such little resources and privileges." Warrior, *The People and the Word*, 47. With the exception of Gar's racist relationship to blackness discussed below, his idea of peoplehood expressed throughout the play seems to align with Warrior's critique here.
112. "Communitism" is a term coined by Jace Weaver that combines "community" and "activism" to describe an ethic of "proactive commitment to . . . [and] valorization of Native community and values . . . including what I term the 'wider community' of Creation itself," which he argues animates much Native American writing. Weaver, *That the People Might Live*, xxi, 45.
113. Riggs, *The Cherokee Night*, 158.
114. Ibid., 125.
115. Ibid., 160.
116. Ibid., 161.
117. Morrison, *Playing in the Dark*, 57.
118. Ibid.
119. Sturm, *Blood Politics*; Naylor, *African Cherokees*; Denson, *Demanding the Cherokee Nation.*
120. Sturm, *Blood Politics*, 161.
121. See note 1 above.
122. Miles, *Ties That Bind*, xvi.
123. Sturm, *Blood Politics.* For references to such violence in the Cherokee and Creek Nations, see Ellsworth, *Death in a Promised Land*; May, *African Americans and Native Americans.*
124. Riggs, *The Cherokee Night*, 164.
125. Ibid., 164–65 (emphasis added).

126. I take this description from Rudi Halliburton Jr.'s 1977 monograph *Red over Black: Black Slavery among the Cherokee Indians.* The title reflects the inequitable power relations between Cherokees and their black slaves but also the manner in which that power was consolidated through Cherokee legislation and law over a period of almost eighty years, from the early 1820s through the late 1890s. The title also indicates the degree to which such laws obfuscated—or covered over—complicated interracial political and kinship relations between Cherokees and blacks from before Removal through allotment.
127. Cf. Renan, "What Is a Nation?," 11, 19; Brennan, "The National Longing for Form," 44.
128. Riggs, *The Cherokee Night,* 206–7 (emphasis added).
129. Ibid., 209.
130. Ibid.
131. Ibid., 211.
132. Denson makes an important distinction between U.S. territories and Indian Territory. As Denson reads the treaties responsible for allocating parts of the Arkansas Territory as Indian Territory, the Indian Territory was fully and wholly independent of the judicial and military authority of the United States. Hence, the United States made massive efforts after the Civil War to absorb it into the Union by incorporating it into the territorial system, thereby extending U.S. jurisdiction over Indian nations. Denson, *Demanding the Cherokee Nation.*
133. Riggs, *The Cherokee Night,* 210.
134. Ibid.
135. Ibid., 211.
136. Ibid., 136.

Chapter 4

1. Cf. Harjo and Bird, *Reinventing the Enemy's Language*; Mankiller et al., *The Reader's Companion to U.S. Women's History*; Labaton and Martin, *The Fire This Time*; Mankiller, *Every Day Is a Good Day*; Hurtado, *Reflections on American Indian History.*
2. Bauerkemper and Stark, "The Trans/National Terrain," 3, 5. See also Bauerkemper, "Indigenous Trans/Nationalism," 395–408; Womack, "The Integrity of American Indian Claims," 111, 169; Womack, *Red on Red,* 7, 19, 235; Lyons, "Rhetorical Sovereignty," 457; Huhndorf, *Mapping the Americas,* 2. For an Indigenous critique of mainstream transnationalism, see Warrior, "Native American Scholarship," 119–30. For examples of a diversity of critical transnational approaches as applied to Native Studies, see Huhndorf, *Mapping the Americas*; Goeman, *Mark My Words*; Byrd, *The Transit of Empire*; Guidotti-Hernández, *Unspeakable Violence*; Cox, *The Red Land to the South*; C. Allen, *TransIndigenous.*
3. Bauerkemper and Stark, "The Trans/National Terrain," 8, 12.

4. Foster, "Of One Blood, 278.
5. Bauerkemper, "Indigenous Trans/Nationalism," 400.
6. For Selu, see Mooney, *History, Myths, and Sacred Formulas*, 242–49, 323–24; J. Kilpatrick and A. Kilpatrick, *Friends of the Thunder*, 129–34; Perdue, *Cherokee Women*, 13–40; Stremlau, *Sustaining the Cherokee Family*, 21–22, 242–43. For narratives of Stone Man, see Mooney 319–20; J. Kilpatrick and A. Kilpatrick, *Friends of the Thunder*, 59–61; Justice, *The Way of Thorn and Thunder*.
7. Cf. Shoemaker, *Negotiators of Change*; Kidwell, "Indian Women as Cultural Mediators," 97–107.
8. Perdue, *Cherokee Women*; Perdue, "Men, Women and American Indian Policy;" Kilcup, "Nancy Ward and Early Cherokee Women"; Moulder, "'They Ought to Mind What a Woman Says.'"
9. Nelson, *Progressive Traditions*, 82–109; Mihesuah, *Cultivating the Rosebuds*; Kilcup, *Native American Women's Writing*, 401–13; Cherokee entries from Parker, *Changing Is Not Vanishing*.
10. Kilcup, *Cherokee Women's Writing*, 71–108, 248–58, 350–98; Parins, *Literacy and Intellectual Life*, 240–44.
11. Harvey, "Cherokee and American"; Gere, "Indian Heart/White Man's Head," 38–65; Cowger, *The National Congress of American Indians*; C. Allen, *Blood Narrative*, esp. 76–78. Harvey's study remains the most comprehensive biographical source on Bronson's life and work and is invaluable for its documentation of the numerous archives in which her editorials and professional and personal correspondences are located.
12. C. Allen, *Blood Narrative*, 76–78.
13. These organizations included the Keetoowah Society, the Mvskogee/Creek "Crazy Snakes" led by Chitto Harjo, and the intertribal Four Mothers Society. See Thomas, "The Origin and Development"; Starr, *History of the Cherokee Indians*, 479–87; Holm, *Great Confusion in Indian Affairs*, 32–33. For Posey's conflicts with the Snakes, see Sivils, introduction to *Lost Creeks*, 1–98.
14. In 1845 it authorized the construction of what would become a vast compulsory education system comprising more than 150 common schools that provided basic primary education and vocational training to rural Cherokee students. Two years later the council made provisions for the Cherokee male and female seminaries, or high schools, modeled on the liberal arts curricula of eastern schools like Mount Holyoke. Additionally, the Nation operated a segregated, coeducational seminary for black citizens just north of the capital of Tahlequah and continued to support mission and subscription schools for an increasingly growing noncitizen resident population. For general histories of the seminaries, see Skelton, "A History of the Educational System"; Fry, *Cherokee Female Seminary Years*; Mihesuah, *Cultivating the Rosebuds*; Szasz, "Through a Wide-Angle Lens," 187–201.
15. Mihesuah, *Cultivating the Rosebuds*, 3, 84, 102–3; Szasz, *Education and the American Indian*, 191–92, 211; Parins, *Literacy and Intellectual Life*, 68–101.

16. Though the Curtis Act of 1898 severely eroded Cherokee political authority, the national council continued to manage internal national affairs until the Oklahoma Act of Union in 1907.
17. As a preparatory school for the University of Oklahoma, the Oklahoma Institute of Technology's curriculum, anchored to the study of music, European languages, business, literature, military science, and the performing arts, paralleled that of OU. OIT was accredited by the North Central Association of Colleges and Universities in 1948 and in 1965 was renamed Northern Oklahoma College. "History of NOC," Northern Oklahoma College, www.noc.edu/history-of-noc.
18. This was the youth and student arm of the global ecumenical movement focused on improving interracial understanding, promoting world peace, and advocating for social justice through cross-denominational Christian outreach.
19. Harvey, "Cherokee and American," 16, 22, 33–34.
20. Denson, *Demanding the Cherokee Nation*, esp. chaps. 3, 6–7; Parins, *Literacy and Intellectual Life*, esp. chaps. 7–9; McLoughlin, *After the Trail of Tears*, 255–367.
21. Aligned with its rhetorical assaults on civilized discourse, Native writing also has a long history critiquing the gulf between Christian values and political practice, from Samson Occom, William Apess, and Sarah Winnemucca to Charles Eastman, Oskison, Zitkála-Šá, John Joseph Mathews, D'Arcy McNickle, and others. As Denson notes, Cherokees also effectively mobilized this strategy throughout the Removal crisis of the 1820s and '30s, and both Harvey and Allen identify it as one of Bronson's central rhetorical moves. See Denson, *Demanding the Cherokee Nation*, 10–51; Harvey, "Ruth Muskrat Bronson," 45; C. Allen, *Blood Narrative*, 83.
22. Holm, *Great Confusion in Indian Affairs*, xiii–xv.
23. Some measures included efforts to tax Indian allotments in Oklahoma (1912), to extinguish Pueblo title to land in New Mexico (1913), and to criminalize peyote use in reservation spiritual communities (1914, 1918). Supreme Court decisions incorporating Pueblo Spanish land grants into federal trust and upholding the trust relationship prevented states from unilaterally evacuating Indian land titles and from taxing allotments. Despite widespread opposition from progressivist "Friends of the Indian" and Christian temperance organizations, the SAI and other allies defeated efforts to criminalize the use of peyote in Native spiritual practices on the basis of constitutional protections for religious freedom. See Deloria and Lytle, *Nations Within*, 32–39.
24. Holm, *Great Confusion in Indian Affairs*, 15, 53.
25. Ibid., 40–42.
26. Ibid., 42–43.
27. According to documentation, the speech has no official title, although Harvey notes that it was modeled on a chapter from Lindquist's book entitled "Indian Leadership, Past and Present." The *Mount Holyoke Alumni Quarterly* reported on the speech a year later in an article entitled, "Ruth's Speech to President Coolidge, December 13, 1923." For the purposes of identification, I have adopted Lindquist's title for Bronson's speech.

28. Bronson, "Ruth's Speech," 1.
29. Ibid.
30. Ibid.
31. Ibid.
32. Ibid., 2.
33. Ibid.
34. Ibid., 3.
35. Ibid., 2.
36. Ibid., 2, 3.
37. Ibid., 3.
38. Ibid., 3.
39. I take this phrase from Hoxie, *Talking Back to Civilization.* See also Hertzberg, *The Search for an American Indian Identity*, 22; Maddox, *Citizen Indians*, 3, 13–14; Holm, *Great Confusion in Indian Affairs*, 52–53, 58; Martínez, *The American Indian Intellectual Tradition*, 99; Denson, *Demanding the Cherokee Nation*, 10–51.
40. Hoxie, *Talking Back to Civilization*, 15.
41. Cook-Lynn, "You May Consider Speaking," 58.
42. While some, such as the Society of American Indians, viewed citizenship as providing much-needed constitutional protections for Indian individuals, others viewed it as yet another federally imposed infringement on the trust relationship of Native nations. See Hertzberg, *The Search for an American Indian Identity*; Hoxie, *Talking Back to Civilization*; Bruyneel, *The Third Space of Sovereignty.*
43. For studies that examine the intersection of American nationalist identity and discourses/images of American Indians, see Pearce, *Savagism and Civilization*; Berkhofer, *The White Man's Indian*; P. Deloria, *Playing Indian*; Huhndorf, *Going Native.*
44. Bronson, "Ruth's Speech," 2, 3.
45. Warrior, *The People and the Word*, 181–85.
46. Mihesuah, *Indigenous American Women*, xvi.
47. Though it was originally the Cherokee Female Seminary, Northeastern State Teacher's College (now Northeastern State University) was incorporated into the Oklahoma state college system in 1909 and opened to all citizens of the state. By the time of Bronson's arrival, then, she was likely serving both Indian and non-Indian students.
48. Harvey, "Ruth Muskrat Bronson," 69. To this point, Muskrat used funds from a postgraduate scholarship awarded by Mount Holyoke to send a Laguna Pueblo Haskell student, Verna Nori, to Mount Holyoke. Upon her graduation in 1932, Nori worked as administrator of a government day school in Santo Domingo Pueblo until her early death in 1939. Later that year Muskrat gained permission from the Laguna Pueblo tribal council to adopt Nori's infant daughter, Dolores. Perhaps inspired by Nori's success, and in honor of the memory of her friend, Muskrat set up a personal loan account for Indian students, administered through the YWCA, which comprised honorariums she received as well as any donations she was able to acquire.
49. Bronson, "Miss Muskrat's Address," 2.

50. Ibid.
51. Ibid., 3 (emphasis added).
52. Ibid., 2.
53. Ibid., 3.
54. Ibid.
55. Ibid.
56. Ibid.
57. Ibid.
58. Ibid., 15 (emphasis added).
59. Ibid.
60. By the late 1920s most boarding schools in the United States actively encouraged Indian cultural and artistic production, removed Indigenous language restrictions, and increasingly incorporated elements of Indian culture and history into the curriculum. See Lomawaima, *They Called It Prairie Light*, 99–122; Adams, "Beyond Bleakness," 35–57.
61. Adams, "Beyond Bleakness," 35–57.
62. Lomawaima, *They Called It Prairie Light*, 98–99; Adams, "Beyond Bleakness," 56–7.
63. For an explanation of this progressive antagonism to tribalism, see Cornell, *The Return of the Native*, 115–16; Hertzberg, *The Search for an American Indian Identity*. For a refutation of this position, see McNickle, *Native American Tribalism*.
64. Hoxie, *Talking Back to Civilization*, 39.
65. I here employ the terms "Native," "settler," and "arrivant" per Jodi Byrd's formulation in *The Transit of Empire*.
66. Harvey, "Ruth Muskrat Bronson," 69–71. Conceived primarily as a means to keep students isolated from their home communities and prepare them for domestic work, the program had come under heavy criticism following the release of the Meriam Report in February 1928. Muskrat attempted to reform the program by carefully screening and selecting Outing sponsors and explicitly seeking opportunities outside of domestic labor. Despite her efforts, most student participants of the Outing Program ended up working as domestic servants in and around Kansas City, a pattern which caused Muskrat great consternation.
67. Ibid., 77–82. Charles Rhoads and Henry Scattergood were appointed by Hoover as commissioner and assistant commissioner of Indian affairs respectively. Both Quakers with strong records as humanitarians, they immediately began instituting reforms to the BIA, most directed at educational reform. Under their administration, appropriations for the American Indian Higher Education Fund increased dramatically, boarding school curriculum shifted its emphasis from vocational to professional and higher academic focuses, and the Outing Program was reformed and brought under the Guidance and Placement Division. They came under attack by figures such as John Collier of the American Indian Defense Association for not acting swiftly and comprehensively enough. In 1933 Collier would take over as BIA commissioner.

68. Meriam also commissioned reports from other Indian activists; most notable is Zitkála-Šá's report, "Oklahoma's Poor-Rich Indians."
69. Harvey, "Ruth Muskrat Bronson," 88–94. Bronson's comprehensive policy called for enacting procedures to more quickly and efficiently facilitate disbursements; removing agency superintendents from the process entirely; developing a culturally sensitive curriculum and greater academic standards; increasing educational opportunities for Indian students; instituting economic protections for loan recipients; and establishing mentor programs designed to help students adjust to life away from their communities and cope with anti-Indian racism from the public sector.
70. Bronson, "The Indian Attitude toward Cooperation," 32–40.
71. While the Citizenship Act brought such issues back into the spotlight, they actually had their origins in the allotment policies of the previous three decades. Formerly considered domestic dependent *nations* with a unique trust relationship to the United States, allotment dissolved tribal governments and legal institutions, terminated the collective ownership of the tribal estate, and opened up excess lands to non-Indian settlement. Citizens of Indian nations were theoretically to be transformed into citizens of the United States and of the respective states in which their former estates rested.
72. Bronson, "The Indians' Attitude toward Cooperation," 33.
73. Ibid., 34.
74. Ibid., 35.
75. Ibid., 36.
76. Ibid.
77. Ibid.
78. Ibid.
79. Ibid., 37. In this, Bronson also anticipates academic critiques of the boarding school apparatus that were later levied by Lomawaima, Stremlau, Piatote, and others.
80. Ibid.
81. Ibid., 38.
82. Ibid.
83. Ibid., 39.
84. Ibid., 32.
85. Ibid., 33.
86. Ibid.
87. Cf. Kellogg, "Industrial Organization for the Indian," 156–65; Kellogg, "The Lolomi Program of Self Governance," 66–80. For more on Angel De Cora's role in reforming American Indian art education at Carlisle, see Holm, *Great Confusion in Indian Affairs*, 85–110.
88. Deloria and Lytle, *The Nations Within*, 188.
89. Ninety-three tribal governments reorganized under the provisions of the IRA between 1935 and 1945. The Oklahoma Indian Welfare Act of 1936 extended the IRA to Oklahoma tribes, which had been previously excluded from its measures.

While the Cherokee Nation refused to reorganize under this measure, the United Keetoowah Band of Cherokee Indians did.

90. C. Allen, *Blood Narrative*, 81–83. Bronson, *Indians Are People, Too.*
91. Bronson, *Indians Are People, Too.* For Indians as original sovereigns in the hemisphere, see pp. 3, 13. For strong critiques of paternalism, surveillance, wardship, reservations, and boarding schools, see pp. 1–30, 47, 48. For statements on self-determination and policy reform, see pp. 80, 83, 85. The entire book makes an extended argument for Indians as contemporary, self-determining agents.
92. Ibid., 34.
93. Cowger, *The National Congress of American Indians*, 9–10.
94. Ibid., 59. A series of proposed bills over the next two years sought to exempt commercial salmon traps and canning interests from reforms (S1446); rescind authority to establish reservations from the secretary of the interior (S162); settle Indian land claims by denying treaty, civil, and legal rights to Alaska Natives (HR7002); and transfer jurisdiction over Alaskan Native peoples from the federal to the territorial government (S2037). While the first three bills were either defeated or rescinded, the latter bill proved more difficult to oppose and led to more broadly construed legislation designed to abolish the Indian Claims Commission, the only extracongressional means for Indian communities to redress grievances against the federal government (S1737); extend state jurisdiction over all Indian peoples regardless of their consent (HR4725); and emancipate competent Indians from federal wardship (HR1113).
95. Bronson, "Shall We Repeat Indian History," 1.
96. Ibid., 2.
97. Ibid.
98. Ibid. For more on this history, see Huhndorf, *Going Native*, 19–128; Huhndorf, *Mapping the Americas*, 25–70.
99. Bronson, "Shall We Repeat Indian History," 4.
100. Ibid.
101. Ibid.
102. Ibid.
103. Ibid., 7.
104. Ibid., 9.
105. Cowger, *The National Congress of American Indians*, 62. With the assistance of the NCAI, the Alaska Native Brotherhood and Sisterhood, the Indian Rights Association and the Confederated Association of Women's Clubs, Tlingit and Haida communities immediately filed suit with the Indian Claims Commission while Muskrat began yet another large-scale public relations and lobbying campaign on their behalf. Though Secretary of the Interior Krug authorized the Hydaburg, Barrow, and Shungnak reservations in 1949, Native land claims to Tongass lands would not be settled until the Alaska Native Claims Settlement Act of 1971. In exchange for rescinding all future claims and forfeiting reserve lands, the ANCSA recognized Native title to forty million acres, provided compensation upwards of one billion dol-

lars, and authorized the creation of twelve regional economic boards and numerous village corporations.

106. House Concurrent Resolution 108 identified tribes that were to be removed from federal trust and states that were to assume services and responsibilities. Public Law 280 extended state civil and criminal jurisdiction over selected Indian reservations in California, Minnesota, Nebraska, Oregon, and Wisconsin with the implication that other states could do the same should they choose to amend their constitutions. Together the bills committed the federal government to coercive, compulsory termination. See Deloria and Lytle, *Nations Within*, 192–93; Cowger, *The National Congress of American Indians*, 112–13; Fixico, *Termination and Relocation*, 112; Philp, *Termination Revisited.*

107. Cowger, *The National Congress of American Indians*, 99–125. As with questions over allotment and citizenship generations earlier, opinion in Indian Country varied widely about the proposed measures. On one hand, most Indians believed that excessive bureaucratic controls hampered economic development in reservation communities, restricted self-determination, and encouraged institutional discrimination against Native peoples. Recalling Bronson's speech at the National Conference on Social Work, they also felt that states might more efficiently and responsively administer social services like health care and public education. On the other hand, many Indians feared that the absence of trust protections would result in the further erosion of the tribal estate, loss of social programs like housing and welfare, and retreat from gains made through the IRA. While some communities resisted termination outright, others subscribed to its basic tenets provided that Indians retained rights of consultation and free, prior, and informed consent and that measures would be implemented to ensure the health and security of Native communities throughout the transition.

108. Ibid., 112.

109. Those initially targeted included the Flatheads of Montana, Klamaths of Oregon, Menominees of Wisconsin, Potawatomis of Kansas, and Chippewas of North Dakota.

110. Cowger, *The National Congress of American Indians*, 100; Fixico, *Termination and Relocation*, 180–81.

111. Proposing and passing more federal Indian legislation than any other congressional body in U.S. history, the 83rd Congress introduced 288 resolutions in its first two years alone, of which forty-six were passed into law. Bronson's letter is anthologized as "Ruth Muskrat Bronson (Cherokee) Criticizes the Proposed Termination of Federal Trusteeship, 1955," in *Major Problems in American Indian History.*

112. Bronson, "Ruth Muskrat Bronson," 454–57.

113. Ibid., 454–55.

114. Ibid., 455.

115. Ibid.

116. Ibid.

117. Ibid.
118. Ibid. Cf. "The Eulogy on King Philip," in Apess, *On Our Own Ground*; V. Deloria, *Custer Died for Your Sins*; King, *The Truth about Stories*; King, *The Inconvenient Indian*.
119. Bronson, "Ruth Muskrat Bronson," 455–56. In addition to political autonomy, tribal constitutional law, and resource protection/development, Bronson also lists education and health and welfare services.
120. Ibid., 456.
121. Ibid.
122. As with Bronson, McNickle's gradual shift from evolutionist-inspired rhetorics of cultural adaptation to structure-based rhetorics of "functional integration" align with his movement away from the BIA and into Indian political activism as well as his mentorship of what would become the National Indian Youth Council. For the former, see McNickle, *They Came Here First*. For the latter, see McNickle, *Native American Tribalism*. For the most comprehensive treatments of nineteenth-century Cherokee political rhetorics, see Parins, *Literacy and Intellectual Life*, esp. chaps. 6–9; Denson, *Demanding the Cherokee Nation*; Nelson, *Progressive Traditions*, chaps. 4–5.
123. Harvey, "Ruth Muskrat Bronson," 186.
124. Ibid., 236.
125. Nelson, "Keeping Oklahoma Indian Territory," 638–54.
126. For Cherokee rhetorics of the "white" or "beloved" path, see Churchill, "Walking the 'White Path'"; Justice, *Our Fire Survives the Storm*.
127. Cowger, *The National Congress of American Indians*, 37.

Afterword

1. Oskison, *The Brothers Three*, 448.
2. Ibid., 157.
3. On "communitism," see note 112 in chapter 3; Weaver, *That the People Might Live*, xxi, 45.
4. Oskison, *The Brothers Three*, 370.
5. Ibid., 345.
6. Warrior, *Tribal Secrets*, 106.

Bibliography

Acoose, Janice. "Honoring Ni-Wahkomakanak." In Acoose et al., *Reasoning Together,* 216–33.

Acoose, Janice, Lisa Brooks, Tol Foster, LeAnne Howe, Daniel Heath Justice, Phillip Carroll Morgan, Kimberly Roppolo, Cheryl Suzack, Christopher B. Teuton, Sean Teuton, Robert Warrior, and Craig S. Womack, eds. *Reasoning Together: The Native Critics Collective.* Norman: University of Oklahoma Press, 2008.

Adair, James. *The History of the American Indians.* Edited by Kathryn E. Holland Braund. Tuscaloosa: University of Alabama Press, 2005.

Adams, David Wallace. "Beyond Bleakness: The Brighter Side of Indian Boarding Schools, 1870–1940." In Trafzer et al., *Boarding School Blues,* 35–64.

———. *Education for Extinction: American Indians and the Boarding School Experience, 1875–1928.* Lawrence: University Press of Kansas, 1995.

Allen, Chadwick. *Blood Narrative: Indigenous Identity in American Indian and Maori Literary and Activist Texts.* Durham, N.C.: Duke University Press, 2002.

———. *Transindigenous: Methodologies for Global Native Literary Studies.* Minneapolis: University of Minnesota Press, 2012.

Allen, Paula Gunn. *The Sacred Hoop: Recovering the Feminine in American Indian Traditions.* Boston: Beacon, 1986.

———. *Spider Woman's Granddaughters: Traditional Tales and Contemporary Writing by Native American Women.* New York: Faucett Columbine, 1989.

———. *Studies in American Indian Literatures: Critical Essays and Course Designs.* New York: Modern Language Association, 1983.

Alfred, Taiaiake. *Peace, Power, Righteousness: An Indigenous Manifesto.* Oxford: Oxford University Press, 1993.

———. "Sovereignty." In *A Companion to American Indian History,* edited by Philip J. Deloria and Neal Salisbury, 460–74. London: Blackwell, 2002.

———. *Wasáse: Indigenous Pathways to Action and Freedom.* Peterborough, Ontario: Broadview, 2005.

American State Papers: Documents, Legislative and Executive, of the Congress of the United States. Indian Affairs. 2 vols. Washington, D.C.: Gales and Seaton, 1832.

Andersen, Chris. "Indigenous Nationhood." In *Native Studies Keywords,* edited by Stephanie Nohelani Teves, Michelle Raheja, and Andrea Smith, 180–98. Tucson: University of Arizona Press, 2015.

Anderson, Benedict. *Imagined Communities: Reflections on the Origins and Spread of Nationalism.* New York: Verso, 2006.

Anderson, LaVere. "Obituary: John Milton Oskison." Western History Collection, University of Oklahoma, John Milton Oskison Collection, box D-8, folder 1.

Anghie, Antony. *Imperialism, Sovereignty, and the Making of International Law.* Cambridge: Cambridge University Press, 2005.

Apess, William. *On Our Own Ground: The Complete Writings of William Apess, A Pequot.* Edited by Barry O'Connell. Amherst: University of Massachusetts Press, 1992.

As I Recollect. Claremore: Indian Women's Pocahontas Club, 1949.

Axtell, James. "The Ethnohistory of Native America." In Fixico, *Rethinking American Indian History,* 11–28.

Baird, W. David. *The Osage People.* Phoenix: Indian Tribal Series, 1972.

Bartram, William. *Travels and Other Writings.* New York: Literary Classics of the United States, 1996.

Bataille, Gretchen M. "American Indian Novels." *Rocky Mountain Review* 47, nos. 1/2 (1993): 61–66.

Bauerkemper, Joseph. "Indigenous Trans/Nationalism and the Ethics of Theory in Native Literary Studies." In *Oxford Handbook of Indigenous Literature,* edited by James H. Cox and Daniel Heath Justice, 395–408. Oxford: Oxford University Press, 2014.

———. "Narrating Nationhood: Indian Time and Ideologies of Progress." *Studies in American Indian Literatures* 19, no. 4 (Winter 2007): 27–53.

Bauerkemper, Joseph, and Heidi Kiiwetinepinesiik Stark. "The Trans/National Terrain of Anishinaabe Law and Diplomacy." *Journal of Transnational American Studies* 4, no. 1 (2012).

Berry, Christina. "Rachel Caroline Eaton: Cherokee Woman, Historian, and Educator." All Things Cherokee, www.AllThingsCherokee.com/rachel-caroline-eaton/. January 2, 2001.

Bhabha, Homi K. *Nation and Narration.* London: Routledge, 1995.

Bell, Michael Davitt. *Hawthorne and the Historical Romance of New England.* Princeton, N.J.: Princeton University Press, 1971.

Berkhofer, Robert F., Jr. *The White Man's Indian: Images of the American Indian from Columbus to the Present.* New York: Vintage, 1978.

Blackhawk, Ned. *Violence over the Land: Indians and Empires in the Early American West.* Cambridge, Mass.: Harvard University Press, 2008.

Bold, Christine. "'Aboriginally Yours': Vaudeville Performers, Transnational Circuits, Research Challenges." Paper presented at the Western Literature Association Conference, Victoria, BC, October 2014.

Borowitz, Albert. "'Poor Jud is Daid': Violence and Lawlessness in the Plays of Lynn Riggs." *Legal Studies Forum* 27 (2003): 157–84.

Braunlich, Phyllis Cole. "*The Cherokee Night* of R. Lynn Riggs." *Midwest Quarterly* 30 (Autumn 1988): 45–59.

———. *Haunted by Home: The Life and Letters of Lynn Riggs.* Norman: University of Oklahoma Press, 1988.

———. "The Oklahoma Plays of R. Lynn Riggs." *World Literature Today* 64 (Summer 1990): 390–94.

Brennan, Timothy. "The National Longing for Form." In Bhabha, *Nation and Narration,* 44–70.

Bronson, Ruth Muskrat. "The Callin' of the Farm." *The Crimson Rambler: Official Student Organ of the OIT* 9, no. 3 (November 1914).

———. "The Indian Attitude toward Cooperation." *Cooperation in Indian Administration. Federal, State, County, and Local: Four Papers Presented before the Committee on the American Indian of the National Conference of Social Work,* Minneapolis: June 1931, 32–40.

———. *Indians Are People, Too.* New York: Friendship, 1944.

———. "The Killing of Gillstrape." *The Crimson Rambler: Official Student Organ of the OIT* 9, no. 4 (December 1914): 9–11.

———. "Miss Muskrat's Address on the North American Indian." *The American Indian* (1927): 2–3, 15.

———. "Much Work Needed." *Indian Truth* 37, no. 1 (1960): 1–5.

———. "Oklahoma as a Background for Literature." *The Crimson Rambler: Official Student Organ of the OIT* 10, no. 1 (September 1915): 13–16.

———. "Ruth Muskrat Bronson (Cherokee) Criticizes the Proposed Termination of Federal Trusteeship, 1955." In *Major Problems in American Indian History,* 3rd ed., edited by Albert L. Hurtado and Peter Iverson, 454–57. Belmont, Calif.: Wadsworth, 2014.

———. "Ruth's Speech to President Coolidge, December 13th, 1923." *Our Indian Student: Mount Holyoke Alumni Quarterly* (January 1924): 218–20.

———. "The Serpent," *Mount Holyoke Monthly* 33 (March 1925): 160–68.

———. "The Shady Deeps." *The Crimson Rambler: Official Student Organ of the OIT* 10, no. 2–3 (November 1915): 12.

———. "Shall We Repeat Indian History in Alaska? An Address." *Indian Truth* 24, no. 1 (1947): 1–9.

———. "The Wail of the Helpless." *The Crimson Rambler: Official Student Organ of the OIT* 10, nos. 2–3 (November 1915): 4.

Brooks, Lisa. *The Common Pot: The Recovery of Native Space in the Northeast.* Minneapolis: University of Minnesota Press, 2008.

———. "The Constitution of the White Earth Nation: A New Innovation in a Longstanding Indigenous Literary Tradition." *Studies in American Indian Literatures* 23, no. 4 (Winter 2011): 48–76.

Brown, Harry. *Injun Joe's Ghost: The Indian Mixed-Blood in American Writing.* Columbia: University of Missouri Press, 2004.

Bruyneel, Kevin. "Codename Geronimo: Settler Memory and the Production of American Statism." *Settler Colonial Studies* 6, no. 4 (2016): 349–64.

———. *The Third Space of Sovereignty: The Postcolonial Politics of U.S.-Indigenous Relations.* Minneapolis: University of Minnesota Press, 2007.

———. "The Trouble with Amnesia: Collective Memory and Colonial Injustice in the United States." In *Political Creativity: Reconfiguring Institutional Order and Change,* edited by Gerald Berk, Dennis C. Galvan, and Victoria Hattam, 236–57. Philadelphia: University of Pennsylvania Press, 2013.

Burton, Jeffrey. *Indian Territory and the United States, 1866–1906.* Norman: University of Oklahoma Press, 1995.

Burns, Louis. *A History of the Osage People.* Tuscaloosa: University of Alabama Press, 2004.

Byrd, Jodi A. *The Transit of Empire: Indigenous Critiques of Colonialism.* Minneapolis: University of Minnesota Press, 2011.

Carlson, David J. *Imagining Sovereignty: Self-Determination in American Indian Law and Literature.* Norman: University of Oklahoma Press, 2016.

Carlyle, Thomas. *On Heroes, Hero Worship, and the Heroic in History.* London: Fraser, 1841.

Carney, Virginia. *Eastern Band Cherokee Women: Cultural Persistence in Their Letters and Speeches.* Knoxville: University of Tennessee Press, 2005.

Carroll, Clint. *Roots of Our Renewal: Ethnobotany and Cherokee Environmental Governance.* Minneapolis: University of Minnesota Press, 2015.

Carter, Kent. *The Dawes Commission and the Allotment of the Five Civilized Tribes, 1893–1914.* Orem, Utah: Ancestry, 1999.

Certeau, Michel de. *The Practice of Everyday Life.* Berkeley: University of California Press, 2002.

Chaat Smith, Paul, and Robert Warrior. *Like a Hurricane: The Indian Movement from Alcatraz to Wounded Knee.* New York: New Press, 1997.

Cherokee Nation. *Constitution and Laws of the Cherokee Nation.* Tahlequah, Okla.: Cherokee Phoenix, 1852, 1868, 1875, 1881, 1892. Reprinted in *The Constitution and Laws of the American Indian Tribes,* vols. 5–10. Wilmington, Del.: Scholars Resources, 1973.

Chronicles of Oklahoma. Editorial. 10, no. 1 (March 1932): 5–9.

Churchill, Mary. "Walking the 'White Path': Toward a Cherokee-Centric Hermeneutic for Interpreting Cherokee Literature." PhD diss., University of California–Santa Barbara, 1997.

Coates, Julia. "'This Sovereignty Thing': Nationality, Blood, and the Cherokee Resurgence." In *Who Is an Indian? Race, Place, and the Politics of Indigeneity in the Americas,* edited by Maximilian C. Forte, 124–50. Toronto: University of Toronto Press, 2014.

Cobb, Daniel, ed. *Say We Are Nations: Documents of Politics and Protest in Indigenous America Since 1887.* Chapel Hill: University of North Carolina Press, 2015.

Cobb, Daniel, and Loretta Fowler. *Beyond Red Power: American Indian Politics and Activism since 1900.* Albuquerque: School for Advanced Research, 2007.

Confer, Clarissa W. *The Cherokee Nation in the Civil War.* Norman: University of Oklahoma Press, 2007.

Conley, Robert J. *The Cherokee Nation: A History.* Albuquerque: University of New Mexico Press, 2005.

———. *Cherokee Thoughts: Honest and Uncensored.* Norman: University of Oklahoma Press, 2008.

Cook-Lynn, Elizabeth. "American Indian Intellectualism and the New Indian Story." In Mihesuah, *Natives and Academics,* 111–38.

———. "American Indian Studies: An Overview. Keynote Address at the Native Studies Conference, Yale University, February 5, 1998." *Wicazo Sa Review* 14, no. 2 (Autumn 1999): 14–24.

———. "Literary and Political Questions of Transformation: American Indian Fictional Writers." *Wicazo Sa Review* (Spring 1995): 46–51.

———. "Should American Indian History Remain a Field of Study?" In *Indigenizing the Academy: Transforming Scholarship and Empowering Communities,* edited by Devon Mihesuah and Angela Cavender Wilson, 143–59. Lincoln: University of Nebraska Press, 2004.

———. "Who Stole Native American Studies?" *Wicazo Sa Review* 12, no. 1 (Spring 1997): 9–28.

———. *Why I Can't Read Wallace Stegner and Other Essays: A Tribal Voice.* Madison: University of Wisconsin Press, 1996.

———. "You May Consider Speaking about Your Art . . ." In *I Tell You Now: Autobiographical Essays by Native Americans,* edited by Arnold Krupat and Brian Swann, 55–63. Lincoln: University of Nebraska Press, 1987.

Cornell, Stephen. *The Return of the Native: American Indian Political Resurgence.* Oxford: Oxford University Press, 1988.

Corntassel, Jeff J. "Who Is Indigenous? 'Peoplehood' and Ethnonationalist Approaches to Rearticulating Indigenous Identity." *Nationalism and Ethnic Politics* 9, no. 1 (Spring 2003): 75–100.

Coulthard, Glen Sean. *Red Skin, White Masks: Rejecting the Colonial Politics of Recognition.* Minneapolis: University of Minnesota Press, 2014.

Cowger, Thomas. *The National Congress of American Indians: The Foundational Years, 1944–1963.* Lincoln: University of Nebraska Press, 1999.

Cox, James H. "'Learn to Talk Yaqui': Mexico and the Cherokee Literary Politics of John Milton Oskison and Will Rogers." *Western American Literature* 48, no. 4 (Winter 2014): 400–421.

———. *Muting White Noise: Native American and European American Novel Traditions.* Norman: University of Oklahoma Press, 2007.

———. *The Red Land to the South: American Indian Writers and Indigenous Mexico.* Minneapolis: University of Minnesota Press, 2012.

———. "Tribal Nations and the Other Territories of American Indian Literary History." In *A Companion to American Literary Studies,* edited by Robert S. Levine and Caroline F. Levander, 356–72. London: Blackwell, 2011.

Cushman, Ellen. *The Cherokee Syllabary: Writing the People's Perseverance.* Norman: University of Oklahoma Press, 2011.

Dale, Edward Everett, and Gaston Litton. *Cherokee Cavaliers: Forty Years of Cherokee History as Told in the Correspondence of the Ridge-Watie-Boudinot Family.* Norman: University of Oklahoma Press, 1995.

Darby, Jay T. "Broadway (Un)Bound: Lynn Riggs's *The Cherokee Night.*" *Baylor Journal of Theatre and Performance* 4, no. 1 (Spring 2007): 7–23.

———. "Introduction: A Talking Circle on Native Theater." In *American Indian Theater in Performance: A Reader,* edited by Hanay Geiogamah and Jay T. Darby, 1–6. Los Angeles: UCLA American Indian Studies Center, 2000.

Debo, Angie. *And Still the Waters Run: The Betrayal of the Five Civilized Tribes.* 1940. Princeton, N.J.: Princeton University Press, 1991.

Deer, Sarah. *The Beginning and Ending of Rape: Confronting Sexual Violence in Native America.* Minneapolis: University of Minnesota Press, 2015.

Dekker, George. *The American Historical Romance.* 1987. Cambridge, Mass.: Harvard University Press, 1990.

Deloria, Philip J. "Historiography." In *A Companion to American Indian History,* edited by Philip J. Deloria and Neal Salisbury, 6–24. London: Blackwell, 2002.

———. *Indians in Unexpected Places.* Lawrence: University Press of Kansas, 2004.

———. *Playing Indian.* New Haven, Conn.: Yale University Press, 1998.

Deloria, Vine, Jr. *Custer Died for Your Sins: An Indian Manifesto.* 1969. Norman: University of Oklahoma Press, 1988.

Deloria, Vine, Jr., and Raymond J. DeMallie. *Documents of American Indian Diplomacy: Treaties, Agreements, and Conventions, 1775–1979.* Norman: University of Oklahoma Press, 1999.

Deloria, Vine, Jr., and Clifford Lytle. *American Indians, American Justice.* Austin: University of Texas Press, 1997.

———. *The Nations Within: The Past and Future of American Indian Sovereignty.* Austin: University of Texas Press, 1998.

Deloria, Vine, Jr., and David E. Wilkins. *Tribes, Treaties and Constitutional Tribulations.* Austin: University of Texas Press, 2000.

Denson, Andrew. *Demanding the Cherokee Nation: Indian Autonomy and American Culture, 1830–1900.* Lincoln: University of Nebraska Press, 2004.

Dippie, Brian W. *The Vanishing American: White Attitudes and U.S. Indian Policy.* Lawrence: University Press of Kansas, 1991.

Doerfler, Jill. *Those Who Belong: Identity, Family, Blood, and Citizenship among the White Earth Anishinaabeg.* East Lansing: Michigan State University Press, 2015.

Drinnon, Richard. *Facing West: The Metaphysics of Indian-Hating and Empire Building.* 1980. Norman: University of Oklahoma Press, 1997.

Driskill, Qwo-Li. "Han'ts: The Booger Dance Rhetorics of Lynns Riggs's *The Cherokee Night.*" In *American Indian Performing Arts: Critical Redirections,* edited by Hanay Geiogamah and Jaye T. Darby, 179–96. Los Angeles: UCLA American Indian Studies Center, 2010.

Eaton, Rachel Caroline. "The Battle of Claremore Mound." *Chronicles of Oklahoma* 8, no. 4 (December 1930): 369–77.

———. *John Ross and the Cherokee Indians.* Menasha, Wisc.: George Banta, 1914.

Edmunds, R. David. "National Expansion from the Indian Perspective." In Hoxie and Iverson, *Indians in American History,* 159–77.

Ehle, John. *Trail of Tears: The Rise and Fall of the Cherokee Nation.* New York: Anchor Doubleday, 1988.

Ellsworth, Scott. *Death in a Promised Land: The Tulsa Race Riot of 1921.* Baton Rouge: Louisiana State University Press, 1982.

Fagan, Kristina. "Tewatatha:wi: Aboriginal Nationalism in Taiaiake Alfred's *Peace, Power, Righteousness: An Indigenous Manifesto.*" *American Indian Quarterly* 28, no. 1/2 (Winter/Spring 2004): 12–29.

Fixico, Donald. "American Indian History and Writing from Home: Constructing an Indian Perspective." *American Indian Quarterly* 33, no. 4 (September 2009): 553–60.

———, ed. *Rethinking American Indian History.* Albuquerque: University of New Mexico Press, 1997.

———. *Termination and Relocation: Federal Indian Policy, 1945–1960.* Albuquerque: University of New Mexico Press, 1990.

Foreman, Carolyn Thomas. "Aunt Eliza of Tahlequah." *Chronicles of Oklahoma* 9 (March 1931): 43–55.

Foster, Tol. "Of One Blood: An Argument for Relations and Regionality in Native American Literary Studies." In Acoose et al., *Reasoning Together,* 265–302.

Fry, Maggie Culver. *Cherokee Female Seminary Years.* Claremore: Rogers State College Press, 1988.

Frye, Northrup. *The Anatomy of Criticism: Four Essays.* 1957. Princeton, N.J.: Princeton University Press, 2000.

———. *The Secular Scripture: A Study of the Structure of Romance.* Cambridge, Mass.: Harvard University Press, 1978.

Frye, Steven. *Historiography and Narrative Design in the American Romance—A Study of Four Authors.* Studies in American Literature 44. Lewiston, N.Y.: Edwin Mellen, 2001.

Gainor, J. Ellen. *Susan Glaspell in Context: American Theater, Culture, and Politics, 1915–48.* Ann Arbor: University of Michigan Press, 2001.

Garroutte, Eva Marie. *Real Indians: Identity and the Survival of Native America.* Berkeley: University of California Press, 2003.

Gere, Anne Ruggles. "Indian Heart/White Man's Head: Native-American Teachers in Indian Schools, 1880–1930." *History of Education Quarterly* 45, no. 1 (2005): 38–65.

Goeman, Mishuana. *Mark My Words: Native Women Mapping Our Nations.* Minneapolis: University of Minnesota Press, 2013.

Green, Rayna. "The Pocahontas Perplex: The Image of Indian Women in American Culture." *Massachusetts Review* 16, no. 4 (Autumn 1975): 698–714.

Guidotti-Hernández, Nicole. *Unspeakable Violence: Remapping U.S. and Mexican National Imaginaries.* Raleigh, N.C.: Duke University Press, 2011.

Hagan, William T. "The New Indian History." In Fixico, *Rethinking American Indian History*, 29–42.

Hall, Stuart. "Culture, the Media and the Ideological Effect." In *Mass Communication and Society*, edited by M. Gurevitch and J. Woolacott, 315–48. London: Edward Arnold, 1977.

Halliburton, Rudi, Jr. *Red over Black: Slavery among the Cherokee Indians.* Westport, Conn.: Greenwood, 1977.

Harjo, Joy, and Gloria Bird, eds. *Reinventing the Enemy's Language: Contemporary Native Women's Writings of North America.* New York: Norton, 1997.

Harvey, Gretchen G. "Cherokee and American: Ruth Muskrat Bronson, 1897–1982." PhD diss., Arizona State University, 1996.

Hauptman, Laurence M. "Three Stories of War: History and Memory in an American Indian Community." In Hurtado, *Reflections on American Indian History*, 58–86.

Henderson, Harry B., III. *Versions of the Past: The Historical Imagination in American Fiction.* New York: Oxford University Press, 1974.

Hertzberg, Hazel W. *The Search for an American Indian Identity: Modern Pan-Indian Movements.* Syracuse, N.Y.: Syracuse University Press, 1971.

Hill, Sarah. *Weaving New Worlds: Southeastern Cherokee Women and Their Basketry.* Chapel Hill: University of North Carolina Press, 1997.

The History of Rogers County, Oklahoma. Vol. 1. Claremore, Okla.: Claremore College Foundation, 1979.

Hochtritt, James Gribble, Jr. "Rural Cherokees, Chickasaws, Choctaws, Creeks, and Seminoles in Oklahoma During the Great Depression." PhD diss., University of Oklahoma, 2001.

Hogan, Lawrence J. *The Osage Indian Murders: The True Story of a Multiple Murder Plot to Acquire the Estates of Wealthy Osage Tribal Members.* Frederick, Md.: AMLEX, 1998.

Holm, Tom. *The Great Confusion in Indian Affairs: Native Americans and Whites in the Progressive Era.* Austin: University of Texas Press, 2005.

———. "Sovereignty and Peoplehood." *Red Ink* 8, no. 2 (Spring 2000): 41–44.

Holm, Tom, J. Diane Pearson, and Ben Chavis. "Peoplehood: A Model for the Extension of Sovereignty in American Indian Studies." *Wicazo Sa Review* 18 (Spring 2003): 7–24.

Hoxie, Frederick E. "Exploring a Cultural Borderland: Native American Journeys of Discovery in the Early Twentieth Century." *Journal of American History* 79, no. 3 (December 1992): 969–95.

———. *A Final Promise: The Campaign to Assimilate the Indians, 1880–1920.* Lincoln: University of Nebraska Press, 2001.

———. *Talking Back to Civilization: Indian Voices from the Progressive Era.* New York: Bedford/St. Martin's, 2001.

Hoxie, Frederick E., and Peter Iverson, eds. *Indians in American History: An Introduction.* Chicago: Newberry Library, 1988.

Hudson, Brian K. "Domesticated Species in D'Arcy McNickle's *The Surrounded* and John M. Oskison's *Brothers Three.*" *Studies in American Indian Literatures* 28, no. 2 (Summer 2016): 80–108.

Hughes, Helen. *The Historical Romance.* London: Routledge, 1993.

Hunnef, Jenna. "Dangerously Free: Outlaws and Nation-Making in Literature of the Indian Territory." PhD diss., University of Toronto, 2016.

Hunt, Lynn. *Inventing Human Rights: A History.* New York: Norton, 2008.

Huhndorf, Shari M. *Going Native: Indians in the American Cultural Imagination.* Ithaca, N.Y.: Cornell University Press, 2001.

———. "Literature and the Politics of Native American Studies." *PMLA* 120, no. 5 (October 2005), 1618–27.

———. *Mapping the Americas: The Transnational Politics of Indigenous Culture.* Cornell, N.Y.: Cornell University Press, 2009.

Hurtado, Albert L., ed. *Reflections on American Indian History: Honoring the Past, Building the Future.* Norman: University of Oklahoma Press, 2008.

"Indian Outlawry; Recent Battle with Outlaws Recalls Memory of Territory Desperadoes; Record of Crimes Committed." *The Daily Oklahoman,* March 18, 1906.

Iverson, Peter. "Our Future Is Burning Bright: American Indian Histories as Continuing Stories." In Hurtado, *Reflections on American Indian History,* 87–112.

———. *When Indians Became Cowboys: Native Peoples and Cattle Ranching in the American West.* Norman: University of Oklahoma Press, 1997.

Jackson, Robert. *Sovereignty: Evolution of an Idea.* Cambridge: Polity Press, 2007.

Jaimes, M. Annette, and Theresa Halsey. "American Indian Women: At the Center of Indigenous Resistance in North America." In *The State of Native America: Genocide, Colonization, and Resistance,* edited by M. Annette Jaimes, 311–43. Boston: Beacon, 1992.

James, William. *Great Men and Their Environment.* Kila, Mont.: Kessinger, 2005.

Jameson, Frederick. *The Political Unconscious: Narrative as a Socially Symbolic Act.* Ithaca, N.Y.: Cornell University Press, 1981.

Johnson, E. Pauline. "A Strong Race Opinion: On the Indian Girl in Modern Fiction." Toronto: *Toronto Sunday Globe,* 1892.

Johnston, Carolyn Ross. *Cherokee Women in Crisis: Trail of Tears, Civil War, and Allotment, 1838–1907.* Tuscaloosa: University of Alabama Press, 2003.

Justice, Daniel Heath. "'Go Away Water!' Kinship Criticism and the Decolonization Imperative." In Acoose et al., *Reasoning Together,* 147–67.

———. "Indigenous Writing." In *The World of Indigenous North America,* edited by Robert Warrior, 291–307. London: Routledge, 2014.

———. *Our Fire Survives the Storm: A Cherokee Literary History.* Minneapolis: University of Minnesota Press, 2005.

———. *The Way of Thorn and Thunder: The Kynship Chronicles.* Albuquerque: University of New Mexico Press, 2011.

Kellogg, Laura Cornelius. "Industrial Organization for the Indian." In Martínez, *The American Indian Intellectual Tradition*, 156–65.

———. "The Lolomi Program of Self Governance." In Martínez, *The American Indian Intellectual Tradition*, 66–80.

Kidwell, Clara Sue. "Indian Women as Cultural Mediators." *Ethnohistory* 39, no. 2 (Spring 1992): 97–107.

Kilcup, Karen. Introduction to *A Cherokee Woman's America: Memoirs of Narcissa Owen, 1831–1907.* Gainesville: University of Florida Press, 2005.

———. "Nancy Ward and Early Cherokee Women." In Kilcup, *Native American Women's Writing, 1800–1924*, 27–30.

———, ed. *Native American Women's Writing, 1800–1924: An Anthology.* Oxford: Blackwell, 2000.

———. "Writing 'The Red Woman's America': An Introduction to Writing by Earlier Native American Women." In Kilcup, *Native American Women's Writing, 1800–1924*, 1–12.

Kilpatrick, Jack, and Anna Kilpatrick. *Friends of the Thunder: Folktales of the Oklahoma Cherokees.* Dallas: Southern Methodist University Press, 1964.

Klein, Kerwin Lee. *Frontiers of Historical Imagination: Narrating the European Conquest of Native America, 1890–1990.* Berkeley: University of California Press, 1997.

King, Thomas. *The Inconvenient Indian: A Curious Account of Native People in North America.* Minneapolis: University of Minnesota Press, 2013.

———. *The Truth about Stories: A Native Narrative.* Minneapolis: University of Minnesota Press, 2005.

Konkle, Maureen. *Writing Indian Nations: Native Intellectuals and the Politics of Historiography, 1827–1863.* Chapel Hill: University of North Carolina Press, 2004.

Krupat, Arnold. *For Those Who Come After: A Study of Native American Autobiography.* Berkeley: University of California Press, 1989.

———. *Red Matters: Native American Studies.* Philadelphia: University of Pennsylvania Press, 2002.

———. *The Turn to the Native: Studies in Criticism and Culture.* New York: Bison Books, 1998.

———. *The Voice in the Margin: Native American Literature and the Canon.* Berkeley: University of California Press, 1989.

Labaton, Vivien, and Dawn Lundy Martin, eds. *The Fire This Time: Young Activists and the New Feminism.* New York: Anchor, 2001.

Larson, Charles R. *American Indian Fiction.* Albuquerque: University of New Mexico Press, 1978.

Lawlor, Mary. *Recalling the Wild: Naturalism and the Closing of the American West.* New Brunswick, N.J.: Rutgers University Press, 2000.

LeMenager, Stephanie. *Manifest and Other Destinies: Territorial Fictions of the Nineteenth-Century United States.* Lincoln: University of Nebraska Press, 2004.

Levine, Ira A. *Left-Wing Dramatic Theory in the American Theatre.* Ann Arbor: UMI Research Press, University of Michigan, 1985.

Lincoln, Kenneth. *Native American Renaissance.* Berkeley: University of California Press, 1983.

Lipsitz, George. *The Possessive Investment in Whiteness: How White People Profit from Identity Politics.* Philadelphia: Temple University Press, 2006.

Littlefield, Daniel F. *The Cherokee Freedmen: From Emancipation to American Citizenship.* Bridgeport, Conn.: Greenwood, 1977.

Littlefield, Daniel F., and James Parins. "Short Fiction Writers of Indian Territory." *American Studies* 23, no. 1 (Spring 1982): 23–38.

Little Thunder, Juliette. "Mixedbloods and Bloodlust in *Cherokee Night.*" *Midwest Quarterly* 43, no. 4 (Summer 2002): 355–66.

Lomawaima, K. Tsianina. *They Called It Prairie Light: The Story of Chilocco Indian School.* Lincoln: University of Nebraska Press, 1994.

Lowery, Malinda Maynor. "Telling Our Own Stories: Lumbee History and the Federal Acknowledgement Process." *American Indian Quarterly* 33, no. 4 (Fall 2009): 499–522.

Lukács, George. *The Historical Novel.* 1955. Lincoln: University of Nebraska Press, 1983.

Lyons, Scott Richard. "Rhetorical Sovereignty: What Do American Indians Want from Writing?" *College Composition and Communication* 51, no. 3 (2000): 447–68.

———. *X-Marks: Native Signatures of Assent.* Minneapolis: University of Minnesota Press, 2010.

Maddox, Lucy. *Citizen Indians: Native American Intellectuals, Race, and Reform.* Ithaca, N.Y.: Cornell University Press, 2006.

Mankiller, Wilma. "Coda." In *The Fire This Time: Young Activists and the New Feminism,* edited by Vivian Labaton and Dawn Lundy Martin, 291–94. New York: Anchor, 2001.

———. *Every Day Is a Good Day: Reflections by Contemporary Indigenous Women.* Golden, Colo.: Fulcrum, 2001.

———. Foreword to *Selu: Seeking the Corn Mother's Wisdom,* by Marilou Awiakta. Golden, Colo.: Fulcrum, 1993.

———. Introduction to Hurtado, *Reflections on American Indian History,* xiii–xix.

Mankiller, Wilma, Gwendolyn Mink, Marysa Navarro, Barbara Smith, and Gloria Steinem, eds. *The Reader's Companion to U.S. Women's History.* New York: Houghton Mifflin, 1999.

Mankiller, Wilma, and Michael Wallis. *Mankiller: A Chief and Her People.* New York: St. Martin's, 1993.

Martínez, David, ed. *The American Indian Intellectual Tradition: An Anthology of Writings from 1772–1972.* Ithaca, N.Y.: Cornell University Press, 2010.

Mathews, John Joseph. *The Osages: Children of the Middle Waters.* Norman: University of Oklahoma Press, 1961.

May, Katja. *African Americans and Native Americans in the Cherokee and Creek Nations, 1830s–1920s: Collision and Collusion.* London: Routledge, 1996.

McLoughlin, William G. *After the Trail of Tears: The Cherokees' Struggle for Sovereignty, 1839–1880.* Chapel Hill: University of North Carolina Press, 1994.

———. *Cherokee Renascence in the New Republic.* Princeton, N.J.: Princeton University Press, 1986.

McNickle, D'Arcy. *Native American Tribalism: Indian Survivals and Renewals.* 1973. Oxford: Oxford University Press, 1993.

———. *They Came Here First: The Epic of the American Indian.* 1945. London: Octagon Books, 1975.

Memmi, Albert. *The Colonizer and the Colonized.* 1967. Boston: Beacon, 1991.

Meredith, Howard L. *Bartley Milam: Principle Chief of the Cherokee Nation.* Muskogee, Okla.: Indian University Press, 1985.

———. *The Cherokee Vision of Elohi.* Oklahoma City: Noski, 1997.

Mihesuah, Devon Abbot. *Cultivating the Rosebuds: The Education of Women at the Cherokee Female Seminary, 1851–1909.* Urbana-Champagne: University of Illinois Press, 1993.

———. *Indigenous American Women: Decolonization, Empowerment, Activism.* Lincoln: University of Nebraska Press, 2003.

———, ed. *Natives and Academics: Researching and Writing about American Indians.* Lincoln: University of Nebraska Press, 1998.

———. "Rachel Caroline Eaton." In *Native American Women: A Biographical Dictionary*, edited by Gretchem M. Bataille and Laurie Lisa, 99. New York: Taylor and Francis, 2001.

———. "Should American Indian History Remain a Field of Study?" In *Indigenizing the Academy: Transforming Scholarship and Empowering Communities*, edited by Devon Abbott Mihesuah and Angela Cavender Wilson, 143–60. Lincoln: University of Nebraska Press, 2004.

Miles, Tiya. *The House on Diamond Hill: A Cherokee Plantation Story.* Chapel Hill: University of North Carolina Press, 2010.

———. *Ties That Bind: The Story of an Afro-Cherokee Family in Slavery and Freedom.* Berkeley: University of California Press, 2005.

Minges, Patrick. *Slavery in the Cherokee Nation: The Keetoowah Society and the Defining of a People, 1855–1867.* Studies in African American History and Culture, edited by Graham Russell Hodges. London: Routledge, 2003.

Momaday, N. Scott. *The Way to Rainy Mountain.* New York: Ballantine, 1969.

Mooney, James. *History, Myths and Sacred Formulas of the Cherokees.* Asheville, N.C.: Bright Mountain Books, 1992.

Morrison, Toni. *Playing in the Dark: Whiteness and the Literary Imagination.* New York: Vintage, 1993.

Moreton-Robinson, Aileen. *The White Possessive: Property, Power, and Indigenous Sovereignty.* Minneapolis: University of Minnesota Press, 2015.

Moulder, M. Amanda. "Cherokee Practice, Missionary Intentions: Literacy Learning among Early Nineteenth-Century Cherokee Women." *College Composition and Communication* 63, no. 1. (September 2011): 75–97.

———. "'They Ought to Mind What a Woman Says': Early Cherokee Women's Rhetorical Traditions and Rhetorical Education." PhD diss., University of Texas, 2010.

Naylor, Celia E. *African Cherokees in Indian Territory: From Chattel to Citizens.* Chapel Hill: University of North Carolina Press, 2008.

Norgren, Jill. *The Cherokee Cases: The Confrontation of Law and Politics.* New York: McGraw-Hill, 1996.

Nelson, Joshua M. "Keeping Oklahoma Indian Territory: Alice Callahan and John Oskison (Indian Enough)." In *Oxford Handbook of Indigenous American Literature,* edited by James H. Cox and Daniel Heath Justice, 638–54. Oxford: Oxford University Press, 2014.

———. *Progressive Traditions: Identity in Cherokee Literature and Culture.* Norman: University of Oklahoma Press, 2014.

O'Brien, Jeanne M. *Firsting and Lasting: Writing Indians Out of Existence in New England.* Minneapolis: University of Minnesota Press, 2010.

O'Sullivan, John L. "Annexation." *The United States Magazine and Democratic Review* 17, no. 1 (July–August 1845): 5–10.

———. "The Great Nation of Futurity." *The United States Democratic Review* 6, no. 23 (November 1839): 426–30.

Oaks, Priscilla. "The First Generation of Native American Novelists." *MELUS* 5, no. 1 (Spring 1978): 57–65.

Oliphant, John. *Peace and War on the Anglo-Cherokee Frontier, 1756–63.* Baton Rouge: Louisiana State University Press, 2001.

Ortiz, Alfonso. "Indian/White Relations: A View from the Other Side of the 'Frontier.'" In Hoxie and Iverson, *Indians in American History,* 1–16.

Ortiz, Simon. "Foreword: Speaking-Writing Indigenous Literary Sovereignty." In Weaver, Womack, and Warrior, *American Indian Literary Nationalism,* vii–xxii.

———. "Towards a National Indian Literature: Cultural Authenticity in Nationalism." *MELUS* 8, no. 2 (Summer 1981): 7–12.

Oskison, John Milton. *Black Jack Davy.* New York: Appleton, 1926.

———. *Brothers Three.* New York: Macmillan, 1935.

———. *The Singing Bird: A Cherokee Novel.* Edited by Timothy B. Powell and Melinda Smith Mullikin. Norman: University of Oklahoma Press, 2006.

———. *A Tale of the Old I.T.* Unpublished manuscript. May 7, 1946. Western History Collection, University of Oklahoma.

———. *Tales of the Old Indian Territory and Essays on the Indian Condition.* Edited by Lionel Larré. Lincoln: University of Nebraska Press, 2012.

———. *Tecumseh and His Times.* New York: Putnam, 1938.

———. *A Texas Titan: The Story of Sam Houston.* Garden City, N.Y.: Doubleday, 1929.

———. *Unconquerable: The Story of John Ross, Chief of the Cherokees, 1828–1866.* Unpublished manuscript. 1936. McFarlin Library, University of Tulsa.

———. *Wild Harvest: A Novel of Transition Days in Oklahoma.* Chicago: White House Publishers, 1925.

Owens, Louis. *Mixedblood Messages: Literature, Film, Family, Place.* Norman: University of Oklahoma Press, 1998.

———. *Other Destinies: Understanding the American Indian Novel.* Norman: University of Oklahoma Press, 1992.

Ozieblo, Barbara. *The Provincetown Players: A Choice of Shorter Works.* Sheffield, UK: Sheffield Academic Press, 1994.

Parins, James. *Literacy and Intellectual Life in the Cherokee Nation, 1820–1906.* Norman: University of Oklahoma Press, 2014.

Parker, Robert Dale. *Changing Is Not Vanishing: A Collection of American Indian Poetry to 1930.* Philadelphia: University of Pennsylvania Press, 2012.

———. *The Invention of Native American Literature.* Ithaca, N.Y.: Cornell University Press, 2003.

Pease, Donald. "National Narratives, Postnational Narration." *Modern Fiction Studies* 43, no. 1 (1997): 1–23.

Pearce, Roy Harvey. *Savagism and Civilization: A Study of the Indian and the American Mind.* 1953. Berkeley: University of California Press, 1988.

Perdue, Theda. *Cherokee Editor: The Writings of Elias Boudinot.* Athens: University of Georgia Press, 1996.

———. *Cherokee Women: Gender and Cultural Change, 1700–1835.* Lincoln: University of Nebraska Press, 1998.

———. *Sifters: Native American Women's Lives.* New York: Oxford University Press, 2001.

———. *Slavery and the Evolution of Cherokee Society, 1540–1866.* Knoxville: University of Tennessee Press, 1979.

———. "Women, Men and American Indian Policy: The Cherokee Response to 'Civilization.'" In Shoemaker, *Negotiators of Change*, 90–114.

———. "Writing the Ethnohistory of Native Women." In Fixico, *Rethinking American Indian History*, 73–86.

Perdue, Theda, and Michael Green. *The Cherokee Nation and the Trail of Tears.* New York: Penguin, 2008.

———. *Cherokee Removal: A Brief History with Documents.* New York: Bedford/ St. Martin's, 2004.

Peyer, Bernd C. *The Singing Spirit.* Tucson: University of Arizona Press, 1989.

———. *The Tutor'd Mind: Indian Missionary Writers in Antebellum America.* Amherst: University of Massachusetts Press, 1997.

Philp, Kenneth R. *Termination Revisited: American Indians on the Trail to Self-Determination, 1933–1953.* Lincoln: University of Nebraska Press, 2002.

Piatote, Beth H. *Domestic Subjects.* New Haven, Conn.: Yale University Press, 2013.

Piatote, Beth H., and Chadwick Allen. *The Society of American Indians and Its Legacies.* *Studies in American Indian Literatures* 37, no. 3, and *American Indian Quarterly* 25, no. 2 (Summer 2013).

Pocahontas Spirit—the First 100 Years: A 100 Year History of the Indian Women's Pocahontas Club. Claremore, Okla.: Indian Women's Pocahontas Club, 1999.

Powell, Malea. "Rhetorics of Survivance: How American Indians Use Writing." *College Composition and Communication* 53, no. 3 (2002): 386–434.

Powell, Timothy B., and Melinda Smith Mulliken. Introduction to *The Singing Bird,* by John M. Oskison, xix–xlvii. Norman: University of Oklahoma Press, 2007.

Prucha, Francis Paul. *The Great White Father: The United States Government and the American Indians.* Abridged. Lincoln: University of Nebraska Press, 1986.

Pulitano, Elvira. *Toward a Native American Critical Theory.* Lincoln: University of Nebraska Press, 2003.

Renan, Ernst. "What Is a Nation?" In Bhabha, *Nation and Narration,* 8–22.

Reyhner, Jon Allen, and Jeanne M. Oyawin. *American Indian Education: A History.* Norman: University of Oklahoma Press, 2004.

Rhea, John. *A Field of Their Own: Women and American Indian History, 1830–1941.* Norman: University of Oklahoma Press, 2016.

Rifkin, Mark. "Making Peoples into Populations: The Racial Governance in Settler-Colonial Contexts." In *Theorizing Native Studies,* edited by Audra Simpson and Andrea Smith, 149–87. Durham, N.C.: Duke University Press, 2014.

———. *Manifesting America: The Imperial Construction of U.S. National Space.* Oxford: Oxford University Press, 2009.

Riggs, Lynn. *The Cherokee Night and Other Plays.* Edited by Jace Weaver. Norman: University of Oklahoma Press, 2003.

———. "Poetry—and Poetry in the Theatre." WSUI radio address, Iowa City, November 16, 1932. Box 23, folder 379, Beinecke Rare Books Library, Yale University.

———. "Some Notes on the Theatre." Address to San Diego Community Theatre, February 19, 1940. Box 23, folder 380, Beinecke Rare Books Library, Yale University.

———. "We Speak for Ourselves." *Theatre Arts* 27 (December 1943): 752–57.

———. "What Theatre Can Mean to All of Us." Speech to the Wednesday Luncheon Group, San Diego, March 27, 1940. Box 23, folder 382, Beinecke Rare Books Library, Yale University.

———. "When People Say 'Folk-Drama.'" *The Carolina Playbook: Toward a Native American Theatre* 4, no. 2 (June 1931): 39–41.

Rogers, Dorothy, and Therese B. Dykeman. "Introduction: Women in the American Philosophical Tradition 1800–1930." *Hypatia* 19, no. 2 (March 2004): viii–xxxiv.

Rogers, Will. *The Papers of Will Rogers.* Vol. 1, *The Early Years, November 1879–April 1904.* Edited by Arthur Frank Wertheim and Barbara Bair. Norman: University of Oklahoma Press, 1996.

Rollings, Willard H. *The Osage: An Ethnohistorical Study of Hegemony on the Prairie-Plains.* Columbia: University of Missouri Press, 1992.

Ronnow, Gretchen Lyn. "John Milton Oskison: Native American Modernist." PhD diss., University of Arizona, 1993.

Rosaldo, Renato. "Imperialist Nostalgia." *Representations* 26 (Spring 1989): 107–22.

Ross, Luana. *Inventing the Savage: The Social Construction of Native Criminality.* Austin: University of Texas Press, 1998.

Royce, Charles C. "The Cherokee Nation of Indians." In *Fifth Annual Report of the Bureau of Ethnology to the Secretary of the Smithsonian Institution, 1883–84,* 129–371. Washington D.C.: Government Printing Office, 1887.

Ruoff, A. Lavonne Brown. *American Indian Literatures.* New York: Modern Language Association, 1990.

———. "Native American Writing: Beginnings to 1967." In *Dictionary of Native American Literature,* edited by Andrew Widget, 145–54. New York: Routledge, 1996.

———. "Pre-1968 Fiction." In *Cambridge Companion to American Indian Literatures,* edited by Joy Porter and Kenneth Roemer, 161–73. Cambridge University Press, 2005.

Ruppert, James. *Mediation in Contemporary Native American Fiction.* Norman: University of Oklahoma Press, 1995.

Said, Edward. *Orientalism.* New York: Vintage, 1979.

Sanders, J. G. *Who's Who among Oklahoma Indians.* Oklahoma City: Trave, 1927.

Sayre, Robert F. "Autobiography and the Making of America." In *Autobiography: Essays Theoretical and Critical,* edited by James Olney. Princeton, N.J.: Princeton University Press, 1980.

Schoolcraft, Henry Rowe. *The American Indians: Their History, Condition and Prospects, from Original Notes and Manuscripts.* Buffalo, N.Y.: Derby, 1851.

Shoemaker, Nancy ed. *Negotiators of Change: Historical Perspectives on Native American Women.* New York: Routledge, 1995.

Simpson, Audra. *Mohawk Interruptus: Political Life across the Borders of Settler States.* Durham, N.C.: Duke University Press, 2014.

Sivils, Matthew Wynn. Introduction to *Lost Creeks: Collected Journals by Alexander Posey,* edited by Matthew Wynn Sivils, 1–95. Lincoln: University of Nebraska Press, 2009.

Skelton, Robert Howard. "A History of the Educational System of the Cherokee Nation." PhD diss., University of Arkansas, 1970.

Slotkin, Richard. *Regeneration through Violence: The Mythology of the American Frontier, 1600–1860.* 2nd ed. Norman: University of Oklahoma Press, 2000.

Smith, Henry Nash. *Virgin Land: The American West as Symbol and Myth.* 1957. Cambridge, Mass.: Harvard University Press, 2007.

Smith, Linda Tuhiwai. *Decolonizing Methodologies: Research and Indigenous Peoples.* London: Zed Books, 2002.

Smith, Wendy. *Real Life Drama: The Group Theatre and America, 1931–1940.* New York: Knopf, 1990.

Smithers, Gregory D. *Cherokee Diaspora: An Indigenous History of Migration, Resettlement, and Identity.* New Haven, Conn.: Yale University Press, 2015.

Soja, Edward. *Postmodern Geographies: The Reassertion of Space in Critical Social Theory.* 2nd ed. New York: Verso, 2011.

Spencer, Herbert. *The Study of Sociology.* New York: Appleton, 1901.

Stanlake, Christy. *Native American Drama: A Critical Perspective.* Cambridge: Cambridge University Press, 2009.

Stark, Heidi Kiiwetinepinesiik. "Marked by Fire: Anishinaabe Articulations of Nationhood in Treaty Making with the United States and Canada." *American Indian Quarterly* 36, no. 2 (Spring 2012): 119–49.

Starr, Emmet. *History of the Cherokee Indians and Their Legends and Folklore.* Oklahoma City: Warden, 1921.

Story of Craig County: Its People and Places. 2 vols. Vinita, Okla.: Craig County Heritage Association, 1991.

Stremlau, Rose. *Sustaining the Cherokee Family: Kinship and the Allotment of an Indigenous Nation.* Chapel Hill: University of North Carolina Press, 2011.

Strickland, Arney L. "John Milton Oskison: A Writer of the Transitional Period of the Oklahoma Indian Territory." *Southwestern American Literature* 2 (Winter 1972): 125–34.

Strickland, Rennard. *Fire and the Spirits: Cherokee Law from Clan to Court.* 1975. Norman: University of Oklahoma Press, 1982.

———. "In Search of Cherokee History." Foreword to *A Political History of the Cherokee Nation,* 2nd ed., by Morris L. Wardell. Norman: University of Oklahoma Press, 1977.

Strickland, Rennard, and Jack Gregory, eds. *American Indian Spirit Tales.* Muskogee, Okla.: Hoffman, 1974.

Strickland, Rennard, and William Strickland. "Beyond the Trail of Tears: One Hundred and Fifty Years of Cherokee Survival." In *Cherokee Removal: Before and After,* edited by William Anderson, 112–36. Norman: University of Oklahoma College of Law, 1991.

Sturm, Circe. *Becoming Indian: The Struggle over Cherokee Identity in the Twenty-First Century.* Santa Fe: School of Advanced Research, 2011.

———. *Blood Politics: Race, Culture, and Identity in the Cherokee Nation of Oklahoma.* Berkeley: University of California Press, 2002.

———. "Race, Sovereignty, and Civil Rights: Understanding the Cherokee Freedmen Controversy." *Cultural Anthropology* 29, no. 3 (2014): 575–98.

Suzack, Cheryl, and Shari M. Huhndorf. Introduction to *Indigenous Women and Feminism: Politics, Activism, Culture,* edited by Cheryl Suzack, Shari M. Huhndorf, Jeanne Perreault, and Jean Barman, 1–12. Vancouver: University of British Columbia Press, 2010.

Szasz, Margaret Connell. *Education and the American Indian: The Road to Self-Determination since 1928.* Albuquerque: University of New Mexico Press, 1999.

———. "Through a Wide-Angle Lens: Acquiring and Maintaining Power, Position, and Knowledge through Boarding Schools." In Trafzer et al., *Boarding School Blues,* 187–201.

Teuton, Christopher B. *Cherokee Stories of the Turtle Island Liars' Club.* Chapel Hill: University of North Carolina Press, 2013.

———. *Deep Waters: The Textual Continuum in American Indian Literature.* Lincoln: University of Nebraska Press, 2010.

———. "Theorizing American Indian Literature: Applying Oral Concepts to Written Traditions." In Acoose et al., *Reasoning Together*, 193–215.

Teuton, Sean Kicummah. *Red Land, Red Power: Grounding Knowledge in the American Indian Novel.* Raleigh-Durham, N.C.: Duke University Press, 2008.

Thomas, Robert. "The Origins and Development of the Redbird Smith Movement." MA thesis, University of Arizona, 1953.

Tompkins, Jane. *Sensational Designs: The Cultural Work of American Fiction, 1790–1860.* Oxford: Oxford University Press, 1986.

Trafzer, Clifford E., Jean A. Keller, and Lorene Sisquoc, eds. *Boarding School Blues: Revisiting American Indian Educational Experiences.* Lincoln: University of Nebraska Press, 2006.

Trask, Haunani-Kay. *From a Native Daughter: Colonialism and Sovereignty in Hawai'i.* Revised edition. Honolulu: University of Hawai'i Press, 1999.

Trouillot, Michel-Rolph. *Global Transformations: Anthropology and the Modern World.* New York: Palgrave Macmillan, 2003.

Troutman, John. *Indian Blues: American Indians and the Politics of Music, 1879–1934.* Norman: University of Oklahoma Press, 2004.

Tuck, Eve. "Suspending Damage: A Letter to Communities." *Harvard Education Review* 79, no. 3 (Fall 2009): 409–27.

Tuck, Eve, and K. Wayne Yang. "Decolonization Is Not a Metaphor." *Decolonization: Indigeneity, Education, and Society* 1, no. 1 (2012).

Turner, Dale. *This Is Not a Peace Pipe: Toward a Critical Indigenous Philosophy.* Toronto: University of Toronto Press, 2006.

Vizenor, Gerald. *Fugitive Poses: Native American Indian Scenes of Absence and Presence.* Lincoln: University of Nebraska Press, 1998.

———. *Manifest Manners: Narratives of Postindian Survivance.* Lincoln: University of Nebraska Press, 1999.

Wahrhaftig, Albert L. "In the Aftermath of Civilization: The Persistence of Cherokee Indians in Oklahoma," PhD diss., University of Chicago, 1975.

Wainscott, Ronald H. *The Emergence of the Modern American Theater, 1914–1929.* New Haven, Conn.: Yale University Press, 1997.

Walker, Julie A. *Expressionism and Modernism in the American Theatre: Bodies, Voices, Words.* Cambridge: Cambridge University Press, 2009.

Wardell, Morris L. *A Political History of the Cherokee Nation, 1838–1907.* Norman: University of Oklahoma Press, 1938.

Ware, Amy. *The Cherokee Kid: A Study of Tribal Influence on American Popular Culture.* Lawrence: University Press of Kansas, 2015.

Warrior, Robert. "Native American Critical Responses to Transnational Discourse." *PMLA* 122, no. 3 (2007): 807–8.

———. "Native American Scholarship and the Transnational Turn," *Cultural Studies Review* 15, no. 2 (September 2009): 119–30.

———. "Native Critics in the World: Edward Said and Nationalism." In Weaver, Womack, and Warrior, *American Indian Literary Nationalism*, 179–253.

———. *The People and the Word: Reading Native Non-Fiction.* Minneapolis: University of Minnesota Press, 2005.

———. *Tribal Secrets: Recovering American Indian Intellectual Traditions.* Minneapolis: University of Minnesota Press, 1994.

Weaver, Jace. Foreword to *The Cherokee Night and Other Plays,* by Lynn Riggs, ix–xv. Norman: University of Oklahoma Press, 2003.

———. Foreword to *The Singing Bird,* by John Milton Oskison, ix–xv. Norman: University of Oklahoma Press, 2006.

———. "Indigenousness and Indigeneity." In *A Companion to Postcolonial Studies,* edited by Henry Schwarz and Sangeeta Ray, 221–35. Oxford: Blackwell, 2000.

———. "More Light Than Heat: The Current State of Native American Studies." *American Indian Quarterly* 31, no. 2 (Spring 2007): 233–55.

———. *The Red Atlantic: American Indigenes and the Making of the Modern World, 1000–1927.* Chapel Hill: University of North Carolina Press, 2014.

———. "Splitting the Earth: First Utterances and Pluralist Separatisms." In Weaver, Womack, and Warrior, *American Indian Literary Nationalism,* 1–89.

———. *That the People Might Live: Native American Literatures and Native American Community.* Oxford: Oxford University Press, 1997.

Weaver, Jace, Craig S. Womack, and Robert Warrior, eds. *American Indian Literary Nationalism.* Albuquerque: University of New Mexico Press, 2006.

Wentz, John C. "The Hedgerow Theatre: An Historical Study." PhD diss., University of Pennsylvania, 1954.

Whitson, Kathy J. "John Milton Oskison." In *Native American Literatures: An Encyclopedia,* 178–79. Santa Barbara: ABC-CLIO, 1999.

———. "Wild Harvest." In *Native American Literatures: An Encyclopedia,* 248–250. Santa Barbara: ABC-CLIO, 1999.

Widget, Andrew. *Native American Literature.* Boston: Twain Publishers, 1985.

Wilkins, David E. *American Indian Sovereignty and the U.S. Supreme Court: The Masking of Justice.* Austin: University of Texas Press, 1999.

Wilkins, David E., and K. Tsianina Lomawaima. *Uneven Ground: American Indian Sovereignty and Federal Indian Law.* Norman: University of Oklahoma Press, 2002.

Wilkins, David E., and Heidi Kiiwetinepinesiik Stark. *American Indian Politics and the American Political System.* 3rd ed. New York: Rowman and Littlefield, 2011.

Wilkins, Thurman. *Cherokee Tragedy: The Ridge Family and the Decimation of a People.* 1938. 2nd ed. Norman: University of Oklahoma Press, 1989.

Williams, Robert A. *The American Indian in Western Legal Thought: The Discourses of Conquest.* Oxford: Oxford University Press, 1992.

Womack, Craig S. "The Integrity of American Indian Claims (Or, How I Learned to Stop Worrying and Love My Hybridity)." In Weaver, Womack, and Warrior, *American Indian Literary Nationalism,* 91–177.

———. *Red on Red: Native American Literary Separatism.* Minneapolis: University of Minnesota Press, 1999.

———. "Review: *The Cherokee Night and Other Plays.*" *Studies in American Indian Literatures* 17, no. 1 (Spring 2005): 114–21.

———. "A Single Decade: Book-Length Native Literary Criticism between 1986 and 1997." In Acoose et al., *Reasoning Together*, 3–104.

Woodward, Grace Steele. *The Cherokees.* 1963. Norman: University of Oklahoma Press, 1982.

Wright, Muriel H. "Rachel Caroline Eaton, 1869–1938." *Chronicles of Oklahoma* 16, no. 4 (December 1938): 509–10.

Wynn, Kerry K. "The Embodiment of Citizenship: Sovereignty and Colonialism in the Cherokee Nation, 1880–1920." PhD diss., University of Illinois–Urbana-Champagne, 2006.

Yarbrough, Faye A. *Race and the Cherokee Nation: Sovereignty in the Nineteenth Century.* Philadelphia: University of Pennsylvania Press, 2008.

Young, Katherine Evans. *Staged Encounters: Native American Performance between 1880 and 1920.* PhD diss., University of Texas–Austin, 2010.

Young, Robert J. C. *White Mythologies: Writing History and the West.* 2nd ed. London: Routledge, 2004.

Zissu, Erik March. *Blood Matters: The Five Civilized Tribes and the Search for Unity in the Early Twentieth Century.* PhD diss., University of Michigan, 1998.

Index

Page numbers in *italics* indicate illustrations.